T0328832

'I have been using this esteemed book for years for executive master's students in strategic public management. The second edition enriches the importance of "context" for understanding public organizations by new mini-cases and adds a very relevant chapter on collaborative governance, making the book even more topical.'
— **Nicolette van Gestel**, *Tilburg University, The Netherlands*

'The encyclopedic coverage of decades of research makes Ferlie and Ongaro's contribution an invaluable resource for scholars. The mini-cases, drawn from a variety of organizational and policy environments, enrich the book and bring the subject of strategic management to life.'
— **Jeffrey D. Straussman**, *University at Albany, USA*

'Ferlie and Ongaro are to be congratulated on producing this exemplary volume. It is set to become the standard reference point for students and researchers alike.'
— **Stephen P. Osborne**, *University of Edinburgh, UK*

Strategic Management in Public Services Organizations

Strategic Management in Public Services Organizations takes a comparative and international view on the appropriate use of strategic management models that are affecting the way public services organizations are managed.

In an era of New and post New Public Management reforms, public managers at all levels are expected to respond to these new approaches, which profoundly affect their work practices, skills, and knowledge bases. Choosing a promising strategic management model and implementing it in a way that works for the organization or inter-organizational network in question also depends on an understanding of local politico-administrative and cultural contexts: this book helps the readers identify how to successfully tailor strategic management approaches to their specific circumstances and needs. This second edition builds upon the successes of the well-received first edition. Thoroughly updated to help public managers meet the challenges of a new decade, it has a refreshed collection of mini-cases and now includes chapter summaries. It also includes a new chapter on collaborative strategy and co-creation, in response to the growth of interest in more open forms of public policymaking.

This is an advanced textbook aimed at the postgraduate level, particularly students on MPAs and MBAs with a public sector option or MScs in public policy and public management.

Ewan Ferlie is Professor of Public Services Management at King's College London, UK. He was also Hon Chair of the Society of Studies for Organizing in Health Care, a Learned Society. He has published widely in the field of public management change and reorganizing.

Edoardo Ongaro is Professor of Public Management at the Open University, UK. He is immediate past president of the European Group for Public Administration (EGPA – President 2013–2019) and an editor of *Public Policy and Administration*. He has published extensively in the field of comparative public management.

Strategic Management in Public Services Organizations

Concepts, Schools and Contemporary Issues

2nd edition

Ewan Ferlie and Edoardo Ongaro

LONDON AND NEW YORK

Cover image: Malin Englund

Second edition published 2022

by Routledge

4 Park Square, Milton Park, Abingdon, Oxon, OX14 4RN

and by Routledge

605 Third Avenue, New York, NY 10158

Routledge is an imprint of the Taylor & Francis Group, an informa business

First edition published by Routledge 2015

British Library Cataloguing-in-Publication Data
A catalogue record for this book is available from the British Library

Library of Congress Cataloging-in-Publication Data
Names: Ferlie, Ewan, 1956- author. | Ongaro, Edoardo, author.
Title: Strategic management in public services organizations : concepts, schools and contemporary issues / Ewan Ferlie and Edoardo Ongaro.
Description: 2nd edition. | New York, NY : Routledge, 2022. | Revised edition of the authors' Strategic management in public services organizations, 2015. | Includes bibliographical references and index.
Identifiers: LCCN 2021050877 | ISBN 9780367517151 (paperback) | ISBN 9780367517168 (hardback) | ISBN 9781003054917 (ebook)
Subjects: LCSH: Public administration. | Strategic planning. | Administrative agencies–Management.
Classification: LCC JF1351 .F457 2022 | DDC 352.3/4–dc23/eng/20211028
LC record available at https://lccn.loc.gov/2021050877

ISBN: 978-0-367-51716-8 (hbk)
ISBN: 978-0-367-51715-1 (pbk)
ISBN: 978-1-003-05491-7 (ebk)

DOI: 10.4324/9781003054917

Typeset in Baskerville
by Apex CoVantage, LLC

Contents

Acknowledgements

We would like to thank various people who have collaborated with us on turning the idea of this book into a reality. First of all, we would like to thank our distinguished list of international collaborators who have kindly written cases for us on the basis of their research for inclusion in the book: Elio Borgonovi (the Italian case, Chapter 2), John Bryson (theoretical box on strategizing, Chapter 3), Tom Christensen (the Chinese case, Chapter 7, and the Norwegian cases, co-authored with Per Laegreid, Chapter 7), Jean-Louis Denis and Johanne Preval (the case of Quebec, Canada, Chapter 3), Mauricio Dussauge-Laguna (the Mexican experience, Chapter 2) Robert Fouchet and Marius Bertolucci (the French case, Chapter 2), Hiroko Kudo (the Japanese case, Chapter 7), Per Laegreid (the Norwegian case), Jenny Lewis (the Australian case, Chapter 8), Raquel Gallego (the case of Catalonia, Spain, Chapter 10), Isabella Proeller (Germany and Switzerland, Chapter 7), Stephen Reid (Appendix to Chapter 1), Elisa Ricciuti (NGOs case, Chapter 5), Eva Sørensen and Jacob Torfing (the co-creation of practices box, Chapter 9), Jeffrey Straussman (the US case, Chapter 5), Turo Virtanen (the Finland case, Chapter 3), and Nicolette van Gestel (The Netherlands case, Chapter 3 – we are grateful to Nicolette also for her precious advice for writing this second edition in as much a student-friendly way as we possibly could, based on her extensive usage of the book for teaching over the years). The result of all their efforts has been that the book has acquired a much richer international flavour and has allowed the further exploration of a key idea of this book: that strategic management of public services organizations is deeply affected by their 'context' and contextual influences. We acknowledge their major contribution to the book.

Second, the writing of the brand new Chapter 4 has also been facilitated by the participation of the authors in the Collaborative Governance (COGOV) research project funded by the EU Horizon 2020 Research and Innovation Programme (grant agreement 770591).

Finally, we are indebted to many colleagues for invaluable exchanges of ideas and reflections that have helped shape this book, the roots of which go well back in time: naming each of them individually would make this section long indeed and more importantly would expose us to the almost certainty of missing some of them. We just want to acknowledge the great benefits we have received from having actively participated over some decades in the communities of scholars interested in public management, strategic management, public administration, and public policy. Whilst the errors are only ours, an important part of the credit for this book goes to those animating these thriving, lively communities. Over the years, the work of some senior colleagues proved especially influential on our thinking, and conversations with them and their advice helped inform some of the underlying ideas we have sought to develop in the book; we would thus like to mention them: Elio Borgonovi, Geert Bouckaert, Andrew Pettigrew, and the late Christopher Pollitt.

1 Introduction

Our core argument and overview

This book proposes an approach to the analysis of the adoption of models of strategic management for public services organizations which conceives of strategy as multifaceted, as a prism composed of different lenses each shedding light on one aspect of what strategy is for a public services organization. Our approach is much in line with that of Mintzberg et al. (2009), and indeed we consider our book to represent the equivalent for the public sector, and public services broadly intended, of the approach proposed by Mintzberg and colleagues for the 'private' sector and commercial organizations.

We also argue that the field of strategic management, although it has developed over the past decades mostly in relation to the study of private sector settings (see a new Appendix 1 which reports a bibliometric analysis of scholarly articles in strategic management respectively in the public and private sectors; also Bryson et al. 2010), has nowadays enhanced applicability to many contemporary public services organizations, specifically as certain models of strategic management underpinned by broader social sciences than industrial economics are amenable to being systematically applied to such settings.

We recognize that this is a contested view: political scientists might well stress the continuing distinctively democratic nature of public administration (De Leon 2005), still unlike that of private firms' approach to competitive strategy for profit maximization objectives, and where there is less concern for a public deliberative process (this view has famously been expressed in the statement that public and private management 'might be alike, but only in unimportant respects,' where market forces and legislative oversight are seen as representing two radically distinct governance structures, see Allison 1983). Public choice economists (Niskanen 1971, 1973), from another viewpoint, might argue that the main (even if implicit) goal of a public bureaucracy is to constantly grow its budget and jurisdiction, without any interest for wider strategic reflections about the overall direction or about the cost or quality of the services it provides for citizens (unlike high-quality firms which are customer-centric and who have learnt how constantly to innovate, Peters and Waterman 1982).

However, a number of public management authors (Andrews et al. 2006; Boyne 2006; Bryson 2018; Llewellyn and Tappin 2003; Lusk and Birks 2014; Moore 1995; Vining 2011) have called for the adoption of generic strategic management models in public services organizations, even if significantly adapted to the still distinctive context of the public sector and public services. Indeed, adaptation may be required not just generically when shifting from the private to the public sector as such, but more broadly to a plurality of geographical contexts, given the diversity of

DOI: 10.4324/9781003054917-1

politico-administrative and cultural contexts in which public services organizations operate in different jurisdictions internationally (see Chapter 7). These cultural and politico-administrative contexts frame the autonomy of public organizations as well as societal expectations towards them and the ways in which they are ultimately held accountable.

With these caveats in mind, we argue that contemporary public management can learn from the broad field of strategic management as it has developed, mostly for the private/commercial sector, over the past decades. This is indeed our core message and the theme of this book.

This introductory chapter suggests two underlying reasons for the enhanced significance of generic strategic management models for managing public services organizations in the contemporary world. The first lies within the academic domain, and it is the proliferation and broadening of schools of strategic management, in particular from social sciences other than orthodox industrial economics, that have produced strategic management models and theories which are amenable to be applied, properly adapted, to public services organizations. The second reason lies on the public policy side: the long-term transformative effects of public sector reform doctrines (notably the New Public Management, a set of doctrines which has had a highly contested yet significant impact in the field) and trajectories that have changed the landscape of the public sector and the public services in many jurisdictions across the world. In other words, both the conceptual context for the study of strategic management in public services organizations (the theories that can be employed to understand how strategy forms) and the factual context, the 'reality out there' where public services organizations operate (Virtanen 2013), may to a significant extent have changed, opening up the possibility to treat in a more systematic and encompassing way the contribution of strategic management to public management.

In outlining the contribution of strategic management to public management, what we propose in this book, which is probably differently from most other books written on the topic of the strategic management of public organizations, is an approach to conceiving of strategy as both *multifaceted* and *contextualized*. Multifaceted: we suggest conceiving of strategy as a prism, as a phenomenon which can more fully be appreciated by looking at it from a variety of angles, much in line with the argument made by Mintzberg et al. (2009) about the composite nature of strategy, yet this insight is developed in this book more specifically for public services organizations and their distinctive mandates, goals, and configuration. Contextualized: we suggest an understanding of strategy making in and by public services organizations as shaped in its very premises by the varied cultural, political-institutional and administrative contexts in which they operate, in line with key streams of scholarly approaches to public management (Painter and Peters 2010; Pollitt 2013; Pollitt and Bouckaert 2017).

In the remainder of this chapter, we elaborate on the two pillars of our core argument, namely the developments of scholarly work on strategic management and why this has brought about an enhanced applicability to public services organizations (section 1.1) and how narratives of public management reforms have created conditions facilitating the application of models of strategic management in the public sector (section 1.2). After having elaborated in more detail our core argument, we discuss the issue whether strategic management in public organizations should be considered as 'contingent' on the specifics of contemporary public administration, or whether it is an approach universally applicable, meaningful, and useful for running public sector organizations 'anytime and anywhere' (section 1.3). The concluding section of this introductory chapter provides a brief overview of the later chapters and the over-all structure of the book (section 1.4). The Appendix to this chapter (Appendix 1) provides a bibliometric analysis of scholarly publications about strategic management in, respectively, the field of generic management (the business-orientated literature) and the field of public administration and management. It appears there is a trend in more recent times for these two literatures to diverge: this is a dangerous trend, from our viewpoint, as strategic management can benefit a lot from cross-fertilization between the business sector and the sector of public services. The Appendix shows the manifold interconnections and bridges between these literatures: it is a purpose of this book to provide ideas and contents to further consolidate these valuable bridges.

1.1 The proliferation and broadening of schools of strategic management

Mintzberg et al. (2009) characterize no fewer than ten different schools of stra-tegic management in their overview of the field, many of which exhibit different basic assumptions and reflect distinct theoretical perspectives. These theoretical perspectives come from the social sciences (rather than the natural sciences or the humanities); so the field of strategic management can be seen as an applied and interdisciplinary social science (Schendel 1994), drawing on various basic social sci-ences, including economics, political science, organizational sociology, and social psychology, whilst more occasionally applying findings also from the humanities (e.g. anthropology for the cultural school of strategy). The academic field of strategic management (like neighbouring social science fields such as organizational studies) exhibits a historic proliferation of different models and approaches (Scherer 1998; Pettigrew et al. 2002). In the 1960s, the early strategic design and planning schools were dominant, if only because of the lack of developed alternatives; yet many newer schools have since developed.

How and why does this process of long-range proliferation occur? Strategic manage-ment has been a rapidly growing discipline since the 1980s, reflecting the expansion of business schools or schools of management in which it is housed and of its core ter-ritory of MBA programmes. Thus, it has been an attractive field to enter for authors and publishers. We suggest that new theories of strategic management appear and are championed by key authors keen to build their reputation and to reinterpret an important field. Reputation is more easily won by inventing a visible new theory than through the confirmation of existing theories. These accounts are published in newly established journals with different academic orientations, depending on their found-ers and editorial direction, with publishers keen to enter the expanding market.

Newer schools coexist alongside the older ones, rather than displacing them entirely, so that over time the field of strategic management becomes more pluralist and even fragmented. For example, social practice theory has fuelled a novel 'strategy as practice' stream which distinctively focuses on the analysis of micro-level strategic practices in use (Johnson et al. 2007); the new 'green management' approach associ-ated with the corporate social responsibility perspective brings in a concern with strat-egy making in the context of the long-term sustainability of resources; and so forth.

While early influential models of strategy have their roots in industrial economics (Porter 2004), with its typical focus on market structure, others come from other disciplines such as organizational sociology (Mintzberg 1983), social psychology and its stress on 'sense making' (Weick 1995, 2001), or social practice theory (Johnson et al. 2007), which do not display strong assumptions about competitive markets. Many recent theories come from disciplinary perspectives other than economics and often include behavioural perspectives. So, they may be easier to apply in public sector settings than orthodox economics-based models of strategy making centred on the operations of the markets.

We see increasing pluralism both in underlying theories of strategic management and in the use of associated methodologies (Scherer 1998), which vary from orthodox formal quantitative modelling to qualitative or mixed approaches including the use of organizational case studies. This methodological pluralism suggests different notions may emerge of what constitutes 'knowledge' about strategic management in the different schools, as we explore when we provide an overview and review of the various schools of strategy in Chapters 2 and 3. The anthropological perspective of the cultural school, for instance, takes a more qualitative view than the market-based analysis of the Porterian school. In other words, the disciplinary perspective utilized has implications for preferred methods and the constitution of what counts as evidence as well as for the use of a preferred theory.

1.2 Narratives of public management reform: getting beyond the traditional Weberian bureaucracy

We further argue that some models of strategy are more applicable to current public services organizations because of major changes which have occurred in the very configuration of the public sector. Changes which originated in shifts in the political economy have produced high level narratives of public policy change, which in turn have transformed traditional public sector organizational forms.

The Weberian public bureaucracy

The original and 'default' form of organizing in the (modern age) public sector is the classic Weberian public bureaucracy. Weber's sociological analysis of the upper German civil service in the late nineteenth century suggested a configuration of basic features (Weber 1946; Meier and Hill 2005) apparent within public bureaucracies, for example the expanding central ministries in Berlin after German unification in 1870. We outline these six core dimensions next, adding some contemporary examples:

(i)   Jurisdictions are fixed and official, ordered by rules, laws, and regulations (thus, the Ministry of Foreign Affairs has legitimate jurisdiction over policy regarding a nation state's relations with other nation states);
(ii) The principle of hierarchy is the main coordination mechanism, whereby structures in public bureaux are established with superior and subordinate relationships (so that there is a vertical chain of office holders with lower ranks reporting upwards);
(iii) The management of the office relies on the written file (so a bureaucracy records extensive information on cases and decisions for ease of reference and for future office holders);

(iv)   The occupation of offices is based on expertise and training (this meritocratic principle suggests that offices cannot be bought or bestowed through political patronage; rather access to office occurs via public competition composed of formal examinations);

(v)   Personnel are employed on a full-time basis and are compensated and can expect employment to be a lifelong career (as opposed to short-term appointments or 'portfolio' careers which mix posts in the public and private sectors); and

(vi)   The administration of the office follows general rules that are stable and can be learnt (as a body of knowledge or even codified into a body of administrative law).

This characterization appears to have wide face validity in describing the behaviour of many ministries in different countries and time periods. The advantages and disadvantages of the Weberian bureaucratic form have been much debated. On the basis of empirical work in two French public agencies, Crozier (reprinted 2003 with a good introduction by Friedberg) described some pathological manifestations of what were seen as 'vicious bureaucratic cycles':

(i)   The development of a vaster and vaster body of detailed, written, and impersonal rules and procedures specifying what is to be done in all conceivable circumstances;

(ii)   The centralization of decision making at the top, putting great distance between those who have to decide and those who have relevant information for these decisions;

(iii)   The creation of hierarchical strata insulated one from another and exerting great pressure for conformity on its members; avoidance of face-to-face relations and of interpersonal conflict; and

(iv)   The creation of parallel informal power relations around groups and individuals who can cope with uncertain contingencies that always arise; but this can create the demand for yet more rules, which brings back to point (i).

As Friedberg suggests, Crozier was not only an acute analyst of organizations but also a political reformer as he saw such high levels of bureaucratization as a mark of a stalled society. His work may have helped inspire the decentralization reforms of the 1980s by the Mitterrand governments in France.

Du Gay (2000), by contrast, defends the enduring virtues of the Weberian bureaucracy model, such as neutrality, a sense of due process, the treatment of equal cases equally, probity, and the placing of limitations around personalized and charismatic political rule which may be unstable, idiosyncratic, or even out of effective control. Allegations of so-called sofa government during the New Labour period in the UK suggested a small coterie of politicians and advisers were taking major decisions informally without listening seriously to civil service advice, without formal notes and records which had serious negative implications for the quality and later scrutiny of those decisions. Despite a growing discourse about 'post bureaucratic' forms of organization, including in public administration (Bogason 2005), Meier and Hill (2005) suggest that the Weberian form is highly resilient in practice and that the heralded transition to post bureaucratic forms may be illusory.

The implications of an embedded Weberian bureaucratic form for strategic management models are restrictive. Traditional bureaux such as central ministries continue largely unchanged in this view, with strong and direct political/ministerial oversight. They are likely to work to tightly defined mandates and jurisdictions. There are few links with private sector firms; rather public bureaux form a distinctive domain with a separate labour market and expectation of a stable and lifelong career for civil servants. Key tasks include the making of policy, supporting ministers in Parliament, and the handling of cases, but there is little awareness of 'strategy.' Strong vertical reporting lines limit operational autonomy lower down the line. A strong process (procedures) orientation and low tolerance for risk crowd out innovation and more entrepreneurial behaviours.

Under these circumstances, long-run strategic planning is likely to be the preferred mode of strategic management, perhaps undertaken rather modestly to guide long-term capital budget decisions (capital monies are here likely to come from the Ministry of Finance rather than from private sector sources of finance). Alternative and broader forms of strategic management are unlikely to be adopted as they do not fit with the underlying configuration of the public sector according to the Weberian model.

The rise of the New Public Management

A key question is therefore whether this classic Weberian bureaucratic form has changed or whether it is still resilient (Meier and Hill 2005). In this section, we outline and discuss the main features of the New Public Management (NPM) reform wave of the 1980s and 1990s and its endurance, while often coexisting with other administrative models, in a range of public sectors across the world. We argue that the NPM has reshaped many public agencies – particularly at the operational or service delivery level – to become more firm-like and that they now more often operate in 'market like' conditions, including quasi markets.

This shift is connected to the new political economy of the 1980s and the rise of the New Right in the intellectual domain. We see the NPM as having profound and enduring effects on the organization of public services rather than as being a superficial fad, at least in a cluster of 'high NPM impact' countries, notably including the UK (Hood 1995; Pollitt and Bouckaert 2017). We are also rather sceptical of claims, at least in the UK and other 'high on NPM' jurisdictions, about a more recent movement to a post NPM configuration (Benington and Moore 2011a), as NPM principles may now be embedded and resilient, even if dysfunctionally so, in these jurisdictions (Lodge and Gill 2011; Trenholm and Ferlie 2013). We accept, however, that post-NPM accounts may well be proper depictions in other European countries, and beyond (Chapter 7), as shown also by a number of the cases from many jurisdictions across the world which are reported throughout this book.

We here briefly paint the historical backcloth to the rise of the NPM. Between the 1930s and 1980s, a core tendency in many countries was the continuing growth of government, of public expenditure, and of public sector organizations, especially in such social policy fields as health, education, and social security. The growth of the welfare state was supported by electorally successful Democratic, Labour, and Democratic Socialist parties, securing political support from trade unionists and working-class voters who valued the social protection public services afforded, given vivid folk memories of the Great Depression of the 1930s and later the Second World War. The USA led the way with the New Deal of the 1930s under President F.D. Roosevelt which substantially increased the scope of federal government programmes. In the UK, strategic industries (such as coal and steel) were nationalized and a basic welfare state established after the election of a Labour government in 1945. Large public sectors emerged, often with strong trade unions (and poorly developed managerial cadres), and embedded public sector professions (doctors, nurses, teachers, lawyers, academics, etc.) in many advanced capitalist countries. In the 1960s and early 1970s, further significant growth took place in health, education, and social security spending: even in the USA (with its traditional dislike of 'big government'), the Great Society programmes of the 1960s introduced major social programmes such as Medicare and Medicaid. Public expenditure programmes expanded and were in turn subjected to more intense scrutiny by sceptics. The Nordic countries in Europe also built up well-developed welfare states in this period, reflecting their core values of social solidarity. Highly professionalized public sector organizations – such as hospitals and universities – expanded as major sites for social programmes, but with characteristically professionally dominated (doctors, academics), growth-oriented, incremental forms of strategic decision making (Mintzberg 1983, Chapter 10) and a weak corporate core.

By the mid-1970s, the high economic growth rates which had been a relatively painless way of financing expanding public services collapsed, given oil price shocks and then alarming and unexpected 'stagflation' (simultaneous increases in stagnation of the economy, unemployment, and inflation) appeared. Additionally, a lagged effect of the political 'events of 1968' and the radicalization of the student movement had been a 'long march' through public sector institutions by growing New Left forces. Growing industrial unrest was associated with a shop stewards movement, more spontaneous and unpredictable than the old national trade union hierarchies and particularly strong in the public sector. These developments began to stimulate critique from New Right writers. The growing 'New Class' (Kristol 1995) of left-wing professionals (community lawyers, public health doctors, public policy researchers) was seen by such New Right critics as capturing expanding welfare state bureaucracies for their own interests.

These conditions provided a potent brew for the political and intellectual rise of the New Right (Kristol 1995) and its critique of the old public sector from the late 1970s onwards. In the underpinning social structure, there was now a growth of a middle-class electorate and shrinking of the old working class, many of whom had become affluent workers and more volatile in their voting habits. There were increasing questions being asked in the political domain about the value for money, responsiveness, and indeed the sheer (un)governability of large public services organizations. Large and ambitious social programmes seemed to be producing unexpected and even perverse effects, such as generous welfare payments leading to the decline of traditional family structures (Kristol 1995).

In the intellectual domain, American public choice theorists (see Niskanen 1971, 1994) developed novel ideas about public bureaux under conditions of representative government, given the growing disappointment about their performance. Niskanen critiqued the 'bureau shaping' and bureau maximizing behaviours of public bureaucrats, using powerful and novel ideas drawn from organizational economics. In the absence of markets, prices, or choosing consumers, public bureaux would be likely to grow, he argued. A rational public bureaucrat would seek to grow the budget of his or her agency, as such growth is correlated with personal status and power. While control nominally lay with elected politicians, in practice, higher bureaucrats controlled key information (informal as well as formal) and it might well be rational for them to ensure the minimal visibility of information about performance and effort levels reported upwards. Politicians have weak oversight over public bureaux which in practice are controlled by their bureaucrats. Politicians are also governed by a re-election constraint, so it may well be rational for them to agree to expanded public expenditure in politically sensitive areas (e.g. new bridges in their constituencies, raising benefit levels for well organized and visible clienteles), whether they are cost effective or not. We add that over time, such localized but continuing growth in public expenditure levels results in a need to increase overall levels of taxation which eventually creates a national level 'taxpayers revolt,' as occurred in a number of countries in the 1980s.

These ideas critiqued the previous sociological characterization by Max Weber (1946) of the upper civil servant as motivated by a sense of vocation and acting as a defender of the public interest as naive. While bureaucrats cloaked themselves in the rhetoric of the 'public interest,' this could be a smokescreen for budget maximization. Niskanen saw the behaviour of bureaux from an economic 'supply side' perspective, emphasizing the incentives facing bureaucrats, which made certain behaviours appear rational. Niskanen also moved from analysis to prescription, and his public policy reform agenda (Niskanen 1971, conclusion) called for greater competition in the supply of public services, privatization and outsourcing, a realignment of the incentives facing public bureaucrats, and a reassertion of budgetary control in the hands of the US president, seen as more responsive to middle-range voters than other politicians. We discuss Niskanen's and more recent theorizations of bureau-shaping, notably Dunleavy's one, in Chapter 10 – where we attempt to appraise their explanatory power *vis á vis* strategic management models – yet the influence of Niskanen's original ideas on public sector reformers in the 1980s and beyond is undisputable.

In the UK, the 'winter of discontent' (1978–1979) with its successive public sector strikes dramatized these questions of an ungoverned and ungovernable public sector, answered politically by the election (1979) and then re-election of Mrs Thatcher (1983 and 1987) as a radical right leader and change agent. A break point emerged in the political economy of the public sector in various countries, such as the UK (under Thatcher governments) and the USA (under the Reagan administrations). As the Reaganite slogan put it, government was now the problem, rather than the solution. The previous pattern of long-term government growth now came under both ideological and political challenge. In the 1980s and 1990s, there were repeated politically sponsored attempts to 'reform' large public sectors as a political project. Policies typically sought to reduce the scope of government and increase markets or quasi markets, to reduce the power of public sector trade unions and professions in favour of a more assertive management, and to cut public expenditure and taxation levels.

The operational consequences of these meta level shifts to the New Right and the New Public Management will be considered in more detail in Chapter 7, along with implications for the adoption of strategic management models. Public bureaux changed significantly from the earlier Weberian form, and they became characterized by more operational autonomy, less direct political oversight, stronger management capacity, and more 'firm like' conditions. Hybrid forms which spanned the traditional boundary between the public and private sectors expanded. In these changed circumstances, private sector models of strategy might no longer be considered wholly inappropriate: indeed, they started to be seen as potentially useful.

Another important strand of theoretical work developed around the principal-agent theory (Fama 1980; Fama and Jensen 1983) concerned with the relations between principals (shareholders in private firms; elected politicians in the public sector) and their agents (senior managers in private firms, higher bureaucrats in government). Principal-agent theory has been influential in the financial services sector, supporting the awarding of long-term stock options to managerial agents to align their incentives with principals' (the shareholders). The theory's implications for the redesign of organizations have been well reviewed by Eisenhardt (1989). Agency problems arise when the interests or behaviours of the principals and agents may diverge (for example, in the orientation to take risk) and where the work of agents is not easily observed. A particular focus is how to design contracts so as to align the interests and behaviours of the principals and agents, seen within the perspective of organizational economics with its assumptions of self-interest and utility maximization. The handling and distribution of risk between the principal and agents is important here: while the principal may seek to transfer risk to agents in contracts, the agents may be risk averse (as the principals find it easier to diversify investments than the agents do to diversify employment).

There are many implications of principal-agent theory in the commercial sector. A long standing argument in relation to the modern corporation is that power has flowed from the shareholders to the senior executives (Berle and Means 1932): ownership has become divorced from control. Strong and outcome-based contracts may be one way of redressing this imbalance in governance, especially when reinforced by more transparent information systems so that any agent opportunism and 'shirking' become more visible. The possession of information becomes a key resource in governance. The measurement of organizational outcomes gains centrality, yet it may in practice be difficult, as complex outcomes will be difficult to measure in an uncontested manner. This perspective supports the strengthening of corporate governance systems, so that boards cease to play a decorative or symbolic role and begin to exercise substantial control over senior executives, using if needed their power to hire and fire chief executive officers (CEOs).

Agency theory has strong implications for public sector restructuring, and it provided additional intellectual impetus behind the NPM (Aucoin 1990). It would support, for instance a move from vertical hierarchy to systems organized around contracts, with strong incentives for senior managers, aligned with performance targets and transparent performance indicators. It would advocate better information systems within public bureaux so that more information on the performance of agents is made available to political principals (and also citizens). The Information and Communication Technologies (ICTs), which have emerged and rapidly developed since the 1980s and 1990s, are a new technological resource available to support these ambitions. Principal agent theory would further support changes in traditional public sector labour markets so that senior managers are brought in on well compensated but short-term and renewable contracts, dependent on principals' assessment of their performance. In Chapter 3, we explore in more detail how agency theory helped inform changes to corporate governance in public sector organizations in an attempt to align principals and agents.

Summing up, the narratives of the NPM contributed to reshaping the public sector in a number of jurisdictions across the world in ways that facilitate or even stimulate the adoption of strategic management models. The final results of NPM reforms have been intensely criticized, and it is highly contested whether NPM-ized public sectors are better performing or rather worse performing, with many observers contending that limited gains in dimensions of performance such as efficiency may have been more than offset by losses along other dimensions of performance, from effectiveness to due process. But for the purposes of the argument of this book, that is, that reforms of the public sector have created conditions facilitating a wider adoption of strategic management models, the observation that the NPM has had a transformative effect in reshaping the configuration of the public sector is an important starting point.

Alternative reform narratives

The NPM offers a strong example of macro-level changes in public policy which moved many public sector agencies closer to private sector patterns. There are, however, at least two other reform narratives beyond the NPM that we need to consider, as NPM reforms were strongly contested internationally, and countries such as France and Germany (and many others across the world) undertook different reform trajectories and remained 'low' NPM-based jurisdictions (Pollitt and Bouckaert 2017). First, we see the 'policy network' and governance strand, notably in the so-called New Public Governance (NPG) variant (Rhodes 1997, 2007; Newman 2001; Osborne 2010b). It is a post-NPM narrative which re-emphasizes principles of collaboration within the public sector rather than NPM-style competition or strong incentives and contracts. More sociological notions of high trust, reciprocity, and relational contracts replace in the NPG narrative concepts derived from organizational economics. The use of networks rather than hierarchy or markets as a governance mechanism is a core component of the NPG narrative, leading to practical reform doctrines such as the 'Joined Up Government.' The Evidence Based Policy movement also gained traction in the early 2000s. Both these post-NPM policy reforms were strongly supported by the New Labour governments in the UK (1997–2010), while also retaining some NPM elements such as performance measurement and management.

What are the implications of an NPG perspective for the adoption of strategic management models? Notions of collaborative (rather than competitive) forms of strategy become important in the NPG narrative (Vangen and Huxham 2010), given the emphasis on networks and partnerships. There is also a debate about the extent to which this narrative decentres the State (Rhodes 2007): should the State now be seen as just one of many actors in loose and pluralist policy arenas or does it retain a meta level steering capacity (Peters 2010), and if so, how does it seek to steer? More recently, there have been important attempts, especially on the scholarly side, to link the public governance narratives – from the 'original' NPG formulation to collaborative governance, co-production, co-creation – with certain approaches to strategic management (Ferlie 2021; Torfing et al. 2021; Ongaro et al. 2021), and we will provide an account of this (inchoate) forming of interconnections between these two fields of inquiry and practice in Chapter 4.

Second, the 'Neo Weberian State' narrative (Pollitt and Bouckaert 2017) posits a trajectory of 'Weber lite' in some countries where Weberian principles have historically been highly embedded (Rosser 2018), notably including Germany, but which are now experiencing some modernization without moving into the NPM cluster. While the central role of the constitutional State (or *Rechtsstaat)* here remains accepted, there are some significant changes around the edges. Ultimately, the Neo-Weberian model is predicated on integration and synthesis between Weberian and managerial elements leading to a distinctive trajectory of administrative reform (Byrkjeflot et al. 2018).

What might be the implications for strategic management? First, there is a concern here to promote a high-quality and user facing ethos and more responsive services, which may involve attempted organizational culture change. There is also an increased interest in high levels of performance by public services agencies. Finally, the knowledge bases of public bureaucrats broaden from their traditional core in administrative law to a greater interest in management-orientated forms of knowledge (including we suggest core topics of strategic management and the management of change). In short, the Neo-Weberian model of State seems to provide a favourable terrain for the selective adoption of models of strategic management, notably those not rooted in the non-market strategy literature and those we are not predicated on markets or quasi-markets being established. We explore these alternative narratives of public management reform further in Chapter 7, considering their implications for the adoption of strategic management models, and we introduce and discuss a number of cases of public agencies operating in Neo-Weberian contexts which have developed a strategic management approach (see Box 2.4 and Box 3.1).

Summing up, we argue that contemporary public services organizations have become more receptive to models of strategic management. This is first of all because of the proliferation in the scholarly literature and broadening of such models theoretically, which now provide a wider set of lenses through which to understand and practise 'strategy' in public services settings (as we explore further in the next chapters). Second, this is related to various narratives of public management reform, notably including but also going beyond the NPM, which have profoundly reconfigured the public sector in a number of jurisdictions and acted to move public services organizations beyond the classic Weberian bureaucratic agency towards hybrid or other organizational forms that are more amenable to adopting strategic management models.

1.3 Strategic management in the public sector: contingent or perennial?

Our argument may have left the reader with one more unanswered question: is strategic management useful and meaningful only in the 'current' public sector, because of specific and novel transformations introduced by macro-level changes in the public sector through the spate of NPM-inspired and other narratives of reform, or does it have some sort of 'general applicability,' albeit varied according to the varying configurations of the public sector in different jurisdictions and over time? In other words, is strategic management 'contingent' on the specifics of contemporary public administration which may vary by jurisdiction, or is it an approach universally applicable, meaningful, and useful for running public sector organizations 'anytime and anywhere'?

If we look at the scholarly debates in countries usually associated with a more limited impact of NPM, hence allegedly 'laggards' in adopting strategic management approaches, we can in fact detect a significant stream of literature that puts emphasis on a conception of the public sector as a system of interdependent but relatively autonomous organizations whose 'functioning' may benefit from the systematic adoption of a managerial approach, in which strategic management figures prominently (for essays in this stream in specific countries, in Italy, see Borgonovi 1984; in the German-speaking area, Schedler and Pröller 2007; in France, Bezes 2009). It may be noticed that the basic stance, to some extent inevitably ideological, of these authors (a group in which we may include Bryson 2018 as well as Bozeman and Straussman 1990) is the opposite of Llewellyn and Tappin's (2003), who conceive of strategic management as having been transplanted from the private sector into the previously 'wild,' uncultivated (to growing the plant of strategic management) territory of the public sector.

According to the first set of authors, instead, strategic management may have been 'discovered' and brought to the fore in more recent decades (so in this regard it is 'contingent'), but it also represents a constituent part, an essential and permanent ('perennial,' as we have qualified it) component of running public services organizations (or at least of running them where improving performance is a key concern). According to this perspective, specific models of strategic management have been imported from the private sector only recently because, first, it is only in more recent times that these models have been developed and theorized, and, second and crucially, it is recently that major transformations of the public sector has enhanced the autonomy of public services organizations and at the same time a strong demand for improved performance has been placed upon them (what we define as the strategic space of public services organizations, see Chapter 7), but strategic management as such is part and parcel of the way in which public organizations are managed, and it is in this sense a 'perennial component' of public management. (With a different terminology, the argument is made also by Carpenter in his comparative study of the differential developments of US agencies during the formation of the American administrative state: according to Carpenter, the ways in which the federal agencies were 'strategically' led represents the differentiating factor in their development and ultimate 'success' or failure, see Carpenter 2001).

We may sum up these considerations by considering that strategic management in public services organizations is contingent as regards the extent to which it is applicable (models of strategic management have nowadays enhanced applicability to many contemporary public sector organizations compared to what they had in the past because of transformations that occurred in the configuration of the public sector, as well as thanks to the advancements in the elaboration of models and theories of strategy). However, it is perennial if we consider that strategic management is part and parcel of managing public services organizations, or at least managing them where improving performance is a key goal, and in this sense, it may have been 're-discovered' in more recent decades, but it has always somehow 'been there' and practised by public decision makers.

1.4 Overview of the book

We now briefly provide signposts to the rest of the chapters of the book. Our discussion of the models of strategy is organized chronologically. In Chapter 2, we introduce and discuss the content of a number of major and distinct early schools of strategy (up to the 1980s), including the classic and rational analytic design and planning schools

(1960s) with a strong emphasis on the strategic plan as a tool. We then discuss in turn, the so-called positioning school (closely associated with the work of Michael Porter on competitive forces), the more emergent approach to strategy and the learning school (perspectives heavily associated with the work of Henry Mintzberg) which arose as a counterweight to formal long-term planning, and then the entrepreneurial school, which may have special relevance to not-for-profits and social enterprises with powerful founders, and finally, the more anthropological cultural school which emphasizes the underpinning role (positive or negative) of organizational culture as opposed to formal structure. For each of these schools, after a general presentation, we discuss possible application and adaptation for public services organizations.

Chapter 3 looks at the continuing recent proliferation of further schools of strategic management, since the 1980s starting with the important resource-based view (RBV) which examines the local core competences of the firm or organization as a key basis of its performance. The chapter then briefly introduces the process school of strategy (considered in more detail in Chapter 6) and then presents and examines the corporate governance perspective which has a particular interest in the oversight role of 'boards,' now evident in the public as in the private sector. It goes on to introduce network-based and collaborative models of strategy (considered in more depth in Chapter 4) and then reviews the increasingly important 'strategy as practice' school. Finally, it reviews the influential Public Value school which, notably, originated in the public sector rather than being 'imported' from the private sector. The picture painted is one of continuing proliferation of different schools without, however, older schools disappearing: indeed, the original strategic design and planning school remains important in many public agencies, if in an adapted form.

As already indicated, Chapter 4 is a new chapter prepared for the second edition of this book which examines in greater depth the rise of network-based and collaborative (rather than competitive) forms of strategy. Within the public sector, this school is associated with so-called Network Governance ideas which stress the importance of different agencies collaborating to address so-called wicked problems beyond the control of any one single agency. This strand of literature also raises the broader question of whether the nature of the state has changed fundamentally since the 1980s. The chapter also explores the possible role of novel forms of leadership in such settings, along with a recent move to 'downwards facing' forms of co-creation and co-production with users and citizens.

Chapter 5 considers the extent to which certain models of strategic management literature are (or are not) applicable in third-sector organizations and social enterprises, which have become increasingly important in the delivery of publicly funded services in what is now a more pluralist delivery system going well beyond the classic public sector. Some of these third-sector organizations have recently 'scaled up' and professionalized their management, perhaps associated with the greater adoption of strategic management models and techniques.

Chapter 6 examines the assumptions and the implications of the strategy as process school in more depth, as an approach that one of the authors of this book (Ewan Ferlie) has taken a special interest in within earlier work. This is a qualitative and case base approach which looks at how (public services) organizations evolve over time and also takes an interest in surrogate measures of their organizational performance.

Chapter 7 addresses the crucial issue of the influences of 'context' – the politico-administrative and cultural context in which strategic management organizations are embedded and operate – on strategic management. It introduces and discusses the reasons why strategic management cannot be interpreted as context-free, all alike, and applicable in the same way across countries, jurisdictions, and cultures. On the contrary, context does matter, and the chapter introduces and examines theories for analyzing contextual influences on strategic management. The chapter discusses theories for the analysis of contextual influences in relation to the notion of the 'strategic space' of a public services organization and the important issue of the autonomy of public organizations, and the societal expectations placed upon them.

Chapter 8 discusses the question of whether strategy makes a difference to the performance of public services: what is the impact of strategically managing a public services organization on its performance? The chapter discusses the widely held, yet far from unproblematic, idea that strategic management improves performance. In line with important research works, we argue that it does, but such a statement requires important qualifications, and the schools approach we develop throughout this book may represent an important way forward to furthering our understanding of the linkages between strategy and public sector performance.

The related issue of which 'best practices' may be extrapolated from cases of strategically managing one public services organization for application to other public services organizations, under different circumstances, is examined in Chapter 9. It discusses both the complicacies of assessing whether a practice is actually 'best in class' and the issue of how to detect it, on one hand, and the challenges of extrapolating a practice from one case to reproduce its effects elsewhere, on the other hand. A protocol for conducting the process of extrapolation of practices is suggested and illustrated. A more recent approach about co-creating practices to tackle extant problems by practitioners and academics/researchers working together is also proposed in this chapter.

The concluding Chapter 10 reflects on the very nature of strategic management in public services organizations as both 'science' and 'art and profession.' We argue throughout the chapter that strategic management contributes both to public administration as science and to public administration as art and profession. Our claim is that the strategic management of public services organizations has become a very significant component of both the social scientific knowledge of public administration (*to know* public organizations and public managers) and the art and profession of public administration (*to understand* public organizations and public managers, and how to actually run public services organizations and transmit the – often tacit – necessary knowledge across the generations). We conclude by noting that, as a growing field of research and practice, strategic management surely can further develop its contribution to both public administration as science and to the art and profession of the public administrator.

Throughout the text, we deliberately relate the immediate policy issues found in the public management literature to the different bodies of social science theory found in the range of key texts reviewed. Public management has sometimes been portrayed as an applied and a theoretical field (Vogel 2014), but we would disagree with this statement and further argue that many of the schools of strategy reviewed have distinctive theoretical underpinnings which need to be identified and discussed critically for their significance to be understood fully.

It is for this reason that we also comment on questions of research method used in underpinning studies as preferred methods may have important implications for what is claimed as valid 'knowledge.' Some authors prefer to use survey-based or modelling-based techniques; whilst others use more qualitative methods such as case studies or ethnography. These methodological differences relate back to core underlying academic disciplines, so that economics tends to use quantitative methods, while anthropology (important for example in the cultural school in strategic management) tends to use qualitative and ethnographic methods; the process school draws on a historical perspective within its longitudinal case studies; and so on. We see strategy as an applied social science, which rightfully raises issues of theory and method as well as of empirics and policy application. We discuss such issues throughout the book, and we further address certain foundational questions in the final chapter (10).

In the chapters, we draw extensively on our own prior research work as well as the work of others, trying to identify and summarize elaborated models and also present current case study examples (for which we are grateful to our distinguished list of international collaborators who have been so generous with their time and have worked hard to prepare a range of very rich cases for this book, mostly reported in dedicated boxes throughout the manuscript). We hope this approach will be helpful in creating a useful work of reference for the reader.

Appendix 1

A bibliometric analysis of scholarly publications on strategic management in the fields of business administration (generic management) and public administration and management

by Stephen Affleck Reid

This book's core argument, as outlined in this chapter, is that some generic strategic management models have enhanced applicability to public services organizations. In other words, there are relevant models in the generic strategic management literature which may have explanatory power and normative relevance for strategic management in the public sector. This appendix explores how intertwined or separated the academic discourses on strategic management are in the generic business administration and management literature and the public management literature, respectively.

Using bibliometric analysis, we seek to map two different academic fields of strategic management, the relatively large field of strategic management in business and management and the comparatively smaller strand of public administration literature which focuses on strategic management in the public sector. The analysis has been developed on publications up to the end of the year 2020 (the latest access to the databases detailed later occurred on 24 March 2021). The results of the analysis reveal how the relationship between these fields has developed over time, and it also points to the two strands of literature now being relatively separate, albeit maintaining some important connections. We may hypothesize that too wide a gulf between the two literatures may entail that significant developments in one field may be outright missed out by the other.

Over the recent years, there has been a sharp rise in the use of bibliometric methods to gain knowledge about specific fields of academic inquiry as well as individual journals or specific authors. Some recent examples in the field of public administration are Kumar et al. (2020), Chandra and Walker (2019), Nunes et al. (2020), and Ropret and Aristovnik (2019). In the Web of Science-categories of 'Business' and 'Administration' alone, 293 articles published only in the year 2020 used bibliometric analyses, which is almost a fivefold increase since 2015. A significant contribution to this rise in bibliometric methods is the increased accessibility of two resources. First, scientific journal databases like Scopus and Web of Science increasingly provide the opportunity to download rich bibliometric data files. Second, there has been a development and proliferation of computer programmes that allow researchers to perform various statistical analyses, including advanced network analysis.

This appendix utilizes bibliometric data from the Web of Science Core Collection database (WoS) and has prepared and analyzed these data by using BibExcel and VosViewer. The database allows separating references into different categories, like

'Business,' 'Management,' and 'Public Administration.' The WoS categories are constituted of thematic groupings of journals. The category 'Public Administration' clusters and gathers data from 49 relevant journals (Table A.7), whereas the categories of 'Business' and 'Management' collect data from 408 journals (Management: 227, Business: 261.78 of these journals are journals listed in both categories). Only one journal appeared in both the 'Management' category and 'Public Administration[1]').

There are various approaches to analyzing bibliometric data. Zupic and Čater (2015) describe citation, co-citation, bibliographic coupling, co-author analysis, and co-word analysis. Each of these approaches also has several options for use. *Bibliographic coupling* (Kessler 1963) can map the intellectual sources of new and emerging research fields, whereas *co-citation analysis* (McCain 1990) is well suited to map established research fields. These two approaches follow in a sense an opposite logic. Co-citation assumes relationships between documents when they are cited together. The more sources which cite them together, the stronger the assumed association. In contrast, bibliographic coupling assumes relationships between documents when they cite the same sources (Zupic and Čater 2015).

Citation analysis uses various techniques to estimate the influence of documents, authors, or journals. In this appendix, we employ citation analysis by asking how much the two fields in question cite each other. *Co-author analysis* bases its analysis on who collaborates in writing papers together – thus mapping social networks in a scientific field. Finally, co-word analysis (Callon et al. 1983) is the only bibliometric method that analyses a scientific field's semantic content. The words included for analysis can be article titles, keywords, abstracts, or entire article contents. When words coincide in the same articles, for example when articles contain both *strategic management* and *performance*, a conceptual bond is assumed between these concepts. Using this technique in a research field creates a conceptual map of interactions with stronger and weaker bonds between concepts. For all such methods, their pros and cons must be attentively pondered when using them. Co-word analysis provides a powerful tool for mapping semantic structures in a research field, thus offering a systematic, transparent, and reproducible supplement to the traditional narrative literature review. Also, using different bibliometric methods may contribute with substantial new knowledge about a narrow or broad, emergent or established research field that is not possible with classical review approaches alone. Limitations for all methods which should be noted are linked to the quality of the data produced by the database, for example when some (mostly older) journals do not offer keywords for articles or in some cases, the same author is listed with slightly different names. To counter the latter, a thorough process of data cleaning is required. Also, the reason an article is cited is not conveyed by bibliometric methods. Refutations also count as citations. However, one can question how much such citations skew bibliometric results (Zupic and Čater 2015).

In this appendix, we limited our focus to the search for the term 'strategic management.' This is a limitation of the scope of our data, as obviously a range of articles that are relevant to strategic management do not employ the expression 'strategic management' in the title, keywords, or the abstract. Further research is then required to analyze the field of strategic management with a more exploratory approach to find the variation of terms which are in use and analyze them with relevant bibliometric approaches, as for instance Nag et al. (2007) inductively developed a definition of strategic management based on exploratory word-analysis of a large number of relevant articles.

Our initial database search was for *articles* on 'strategic management' as a *topic* search-term (topic search includes title, abstract, keywords) in WoS (Core Collection) for *all years up to and including 2020*. The search yielded 4,330 articles in the categories of 'business' and 'management' (when referring to these two WoS categories together, we hereafter use 'BA' as short form), and 212 articles in the category 'public administration' (PA); a number of articles belonged to categories beyond these two; 7,133 articles were found in all categories. In the remainder, we focus on the two categories of 'business' and 'management' (BA) and public administration' (PA). The sizes of these separate fields are, as noticed, very different.

An initial analysis of keywords used in these separate strands of literature on strategic management showed that they use some similar keywords (notably 'performance'), yet most keywords are different – and a list of the most-used keywords displays evident differences.

Table A.1 displays the 15 most used keywords in the separate strands of literature on strategic management. Both strands list *performance* as the most used keyword (after 'strategic management' – cf search string). From there on, the differences are striking. For instance, *dynamic capabilities* is the tenth most used keyword in BA literature (9.1% of articles). In contrast, the same keyword is only used three times in the chosen corpus of public administration literature, taking the seventy-first place (1.4% of articles).

On the other hand, *strategic planning* is the sixth most used keyword in the PA-literature but takes a relatively obscure ninety-second place in business/administration. These observations indicate fundamental differences in the most common theoretical perspectives in studying strategic management. *Resource-based view* scores high in the BA literature, whereas *strategic planning* is high in the PA literature.

Table A.1 The 15 most used keywords (in addition to 'strategic management') in articles on strategic management in Public Management and Business/Management

BA – Business Administration and Management		PA - Public Administration	
Articles analyzed	4,330	Articles analyzed	212
keywords in all	11,312	keywords in all	812
Keywords used 10x or more	600	Keywords used 10x or more	18
BA – Business Administration and Management keywords	In % of articles	PA - Public Administration keywords	In % of articles
performance	24.6	performance	16
innovation	14.4	government	12.3
competitive advantage	11.5	management	10.4
resource-based view	10.9	organizations	9
firm	10.8	policy	8.5
management	9.6	strategic planning	8.5
firm performance	9.6	organizational performance	8
strategy	9.4	future	7.1
knowledge	9.2	innovation	7.1
dynamic capabilities	9.1	leadership	7.1
model	7.7	governance	6.6
capabilities	7.5	public-sector	6.6
impact	6.7	public management	6.1
perspective	5.5	implementation	5.7
industry	5.5	local government	5.7

A co-word analysis goes deeper into the relations of concepts. Co-word analyses are often displayed as a graphic network; however, a matrix can also display the data underlying such a network. Tables A.2 and A.3 show matrices of keywords in strategic management articles for BA and PA, respectively. The tables reveal how the same concepts appear in different semantic contexts.

Table A.2 Keyword-matrix for SM-articles in PA

	strategic management	performance	government	management	organizations	policy	strategic planning	organizational performance	future	innovation	leadership
strategic management											
performance	17										
government	14	7									
management	8	5	7								
organizations	11	6	3	4							
policy	9	3	4	1	4						
strategic planning	8	5	2	2	1	2					
organizational performance	9	0	4	2	0	0	2				
future	10	3	4	4	5	2	4	2			
innovation	7	6	3	5	2	2	1	1	3		
leadership	9	5	2	1	1	0	1	1	1	3	

Table A.3 Keyword-matrix for SM-articles in BA

	strategic management	performance	innovation	competitive advantage	resource-based view	firm	management	firm performance	strategy	knowledge	dynamic capabilities
strategic management											
performance	439										
innovation	278	186									
competitive advantage	254	84	87								
resource-based view	255	157	77	207							
firm	187	182	84	119	143						
management	118	118	69	32	31	36					
firm performance	194	28	84	84	80	6	37				
strategy	103	109	82	44	41	52	70	44			
knowledge	174	126	113	84	65	89	41	46	49		
dynamic capabilities	220	123	84	150	145	86	34	71	31	80	

The co-word matrices show that the concept of *performance* in PA-literature relates to keywords like *government, organizations, innovation, leadership,* and *strategic planning. In contrast, performance* as a concept in the generic strategic management literature in BA links strongly to innovation, firm, resource-based view, knowledge, and dynamic capabilities. The differences indicate that *performance* is semantically embedded somewhat differently in the two fields.

A cluster-analysis (Waltman et al. 2010) of the 50 most used keywords in each strand of literature, as shown in Table A.4, gives further insight into these differences. Clusters are constructed based on the bibliometric association strength of keywords

Table A.4 Cluster-analysis of keywords in Strategic Management literature

	Cluster 1	Cluster 2	Cluster 3	Cluster 4
	agency theory	capabilities	absorptive capacity	balanced scorecard
	corporate governance	competitive advantage	human capital	China
	corporate social responsibility	competitive strategy	human resource management	corporate strategy
	diversification	dynamic capabilities	intellectual capital	decision making
	family business	resource-based view	knowledge management	organizational change
	form performance	resources	organizational learning	strategic management
	institutional theory	supply chain management	organizational performance	strategic planning
	internationalization	value creation	social capital	
BA	stakeholder theory			
	sustainability			
	uncertainty			
	Cluster 5	*Cluster 6*	*Cluster 7*	
	business model	competition	corporate entrepreneurship	
	business strategy	competitiveness	entrepreneurial orientation	
	case study	leadership	market orientation	
	cognition	management	performance	
	entrepreneurship	project management	SMEs	
	innovation	strategy		
	learning			
	Cluster 1	*Cluster 2*	*Cluster 3*	*Cluster 4*
	competition	community sustainability	budgeting	Colombia
	contracting	cutback management	decision making	Latin America
	e-government	financial sustainability	learning	people management
	European Union	governance	public administration	performance
	federal agencies	innovation	public sector	performance management
	goal alignment	managerialism	strategic planning	sustainability
	organizational change	performance measurement	strategy	training
	organizational performance	Portuguese local government	value creation	

	Cluster 1	Cluster 2	Cluster 3	Cluster 4
PA	performance appraisal recruitment and selection strategic management	third sector		

Cluster 5	Cluster 6	Cluster 7
accountability	balanced scorecard	decentralization
complexity	implementation	homeland security
COVID-19	local government	national security
democracy	new public management	national strategies
emergency management	public management	NPM
leadership	strategy as practice	politics
public value		

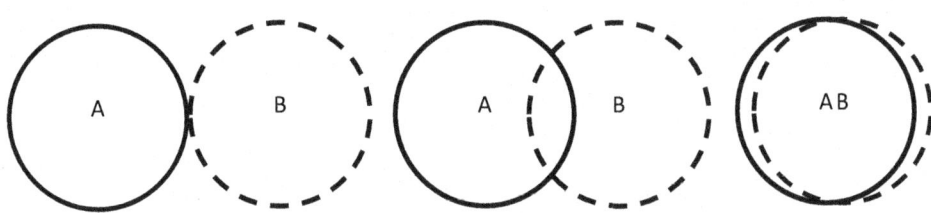

Figure A.1 How separate fields can have varying degrees of shared knowledge bases – depending on the references used

(Eck and Waltman, 2009 describe association strength as 'proportional to the ratio between, on the one hand, the observed number of co-occurrences of objects i and j and, on the other hand, the expected number of co-occurrences of objects i and j under the assumption that occurrences of i and j are statistically independent.' Eck and Waltman 2009, p. 1637). The analysis reveals that keywords such as *strategic management*, *performance*, and *strategy* are in very different clusters in the two strands of literature, further indicating that these concepts have different semantic nuances in the two areas.

An analysis of which references a scientific field uses can reveal the knowledge base which is employed (Zupic and Čater 2015). Comparing the use of references between two fields with a Venn diagram can indicate to which degree the fields share a common knowledge foundation (Figure A.1).

Table A.5 displays the shared knowledge foundation (column H) for the period 2010–2020. The mean of shared references per year (mean of column H) is 250 shared references per year, not counting the outlier of 2015 which shows an aberration with 643 shared references. This is also visualized in Figure A.2.

Relative to the fields' actual size (columns G and J), the shared knowledge foundation is relatively steady over time. The BA-literature on strategic management shared an average of 1.4% of their references with the PA literature on strategic management,

Table A.5 Analysis of references in common for BM and PA articles on Strategic Management. The dataset includes both articles and other document types.

A	B	C	D	E	F	G	H	I	J
Year	BA documents	References in BA documents	PA documents	References in PA documents	References only used by BA	% of BA references in common with PA	Shared references for PA and BA	References only used by PA	% of PA references in common with BA
2010	418	13,056	13	500	12,934	0.9	122	378	24.4
2011	279	18,679	16	960	18,409	1.4	270	690	28.1
2012	378	16,283	13	594	16,101	1.1	182	412	30.6
2013	274	13,978	13	854	13,692	2.0	286	568	33.5
2014	278	14,742	13	551	14,614	0.9	128	423	23.2
2015	396	20,636	20	1071	19,993	3.1	643	428	60.0
2016	461	24,268	21	835	23,943	1.3	325	510	38.9
2017	503	25,630	24	1,088	25,374	1.0	256	832	23.5
2018	487	26,558	18	1,127	26,223	1.3	335	792	29.7
2019	462	26,638	23	1,111	26,301	1.3	337	774	30.3
2020	358	24,538	27	1,283	24,284	1.0	254	1,029	19.8

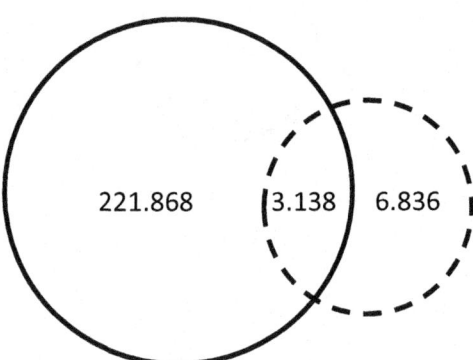

Figure A.2 Separate references and references in common used by BA and PA in strategic management articles (2010–2020)

whereas the PA literature, being much smaller, shared on average 31% of references with the BA literature. The more the PA literature references overlapped with the references in BA literature, the more similar the knowledge base is assumed to be. The year 2015 seems to be an outlier, with 60% of references in the PA literature in common with the BA literature from the same year. Apart from that specific year, the references they had in common lie steadily between around 20 and 30% of PA references. Stated differently, during the period 2010–2020, 70–80% of the knowledge base of articles on strategic management in Public Administration is separate from the knowledge base used by the general field of strategic management.

These data indicate a relatively stronger influence from the BA field towards the PA field than vice versa (Figures A.2 and A.3). However, the analysis does not reveal the direction of sharing – that is who cites whom.

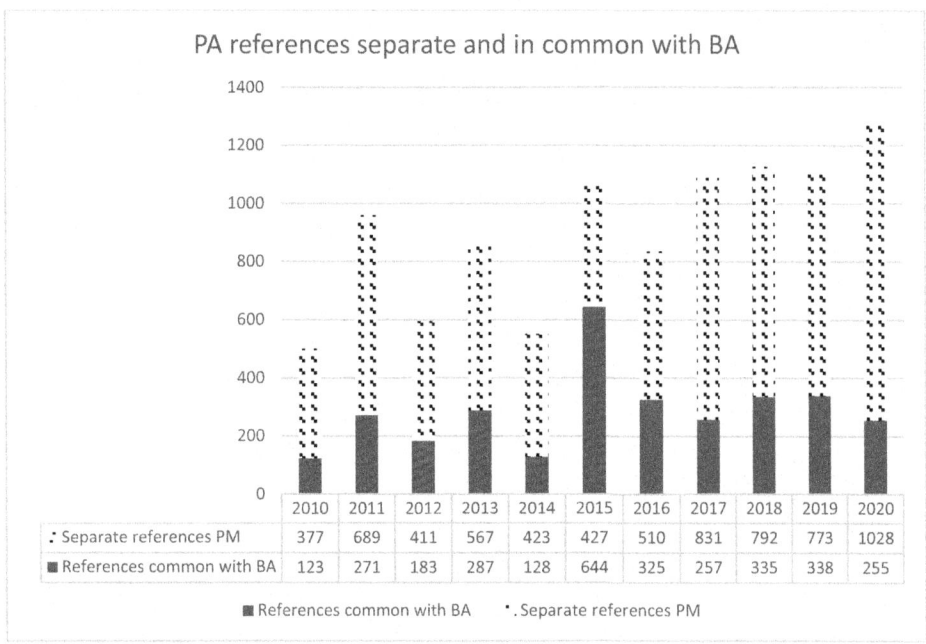

Figure A.3 Analysis of references separate and in common with PA and BA literature on Strategic Management

By combining the citation analysis feature in Web of science with category-analysis, we created a dataset spanning the years 2000–2020 which displays how the general field of BA has cited articles in PA on strategic management and, vice versa, how the general field of PA has cited articles in BA on strategic management. A benefit of including citations from the general fields of BA and PA (not only the segments focusing on strategic management) is that we thus extended the view of citing articles beyond limitations of our search string 'strategic management.' A closer analysis of the relations in this table shows that in the years 2000–2020, every 100 BA-article cited a PA-article on strategic management on average 0.14 times. On the other hand, every 100 PA article cited a BA article on strategic management on average 3.2 times. In other words, in the period measured, it was 22 times more probable that a PA article cited an article on strategic management in the BA corpus, than the other way round (Table A.6).

That is a significant difference and displays a strong influence from the BA literature towards the PA literature and a significantly smaller influence in the opposite direction. Only reporting the mean value of these data, however, does not reveal how the relationship has developed over time. An analysis of how many times BA articles referenced PA articles and vice versa for each year between 2000 and 2020 shows a downward trend especially for how much PA refers to BA literature (Figure A.4). The data show that over time, especially since 2010, the two academic fields are engaging with each other less and less.

Table A.6 Who cited whom? Annual analysis 2000–2020

A	B	C	D	E	F	G	H	I	J	K	L	M	N
Year	ALL BA Articles	All PA articles	All SM articles	BA articles on SM	PA articles on SM	BA cited in all	BA cited by BA	BA cited by PA	PA cited in all	PA cited by BA	PA cited by PA	For each 100th BA article, PA(SM) is cited x times	For each 100th PA article, BA(SM) is cited x times
2000	11385	821	74	54	0	9164	6099	63	0	0	0	0	6.58
2001	11038	872	81	49	2	11857	7952	92	23	10	1	0.09	10.55
2002	10606	849	85	53	0	5961	3945	50	0	0	0	0.00	5.89
2003	11268	968	82	56	2	4793	2922	38	29	5	1	0.04	3.93
2004	11741	917	115	77	2	5770	3705	46	38	7	12	0.06	5.02
2005	14172	1143	122	83	2	5441	3543	37	196	43	101	0.30	3.24
2006	16013	1511	126	80	2	5824	4070	48	26	10	10	0.06	3.18
2007	18074	1689	182	124	4	8658	6279	55	222	67	120	0.37	3.26
2008	21797	2383	190	132	7	6635	4575	95	173	52	63	0.24	3.99
2009	25442	2599	244	158	7	6961	4900	81	103	14	54	0.06	3.12
2010	26480	2586	319	188	10	7322	4984	52	338	109	188	0.41	2.01
2011	30907	2697	306	213	11	9766	7158	89	131	45	70	0.15	3.30
2012	28552	2704	303	194	9	7654	5565	59	232	55	148	0.19	2.18
2013	29636	2658	286	187	10	5476	3878	54	254	71	172	0.24	2.03
2014	31346	2699	287	204	8	7065	4721	47	64	12	25	0.04	1.74
2015	41863	3394	501	285	15	5303	3521	43	105	26	50	0.06	1.27
2016	43696	3799	576	350	16	5636	3890	72	93	32	42	0.07	1.90
2017	46017	4357	633	361	19	4436	3077	111	207	77	122	0.17	2.55
2018	47263	4126	643	366	15	2953	1897	24	38	16	24	0.03	0.58
2019	52770	4708	625	344	23	1355	860	29	44	13	25	0.02	0.62
2020	54561	4412	657	309	25	567	354	11	32	9	14	0.02	0.25

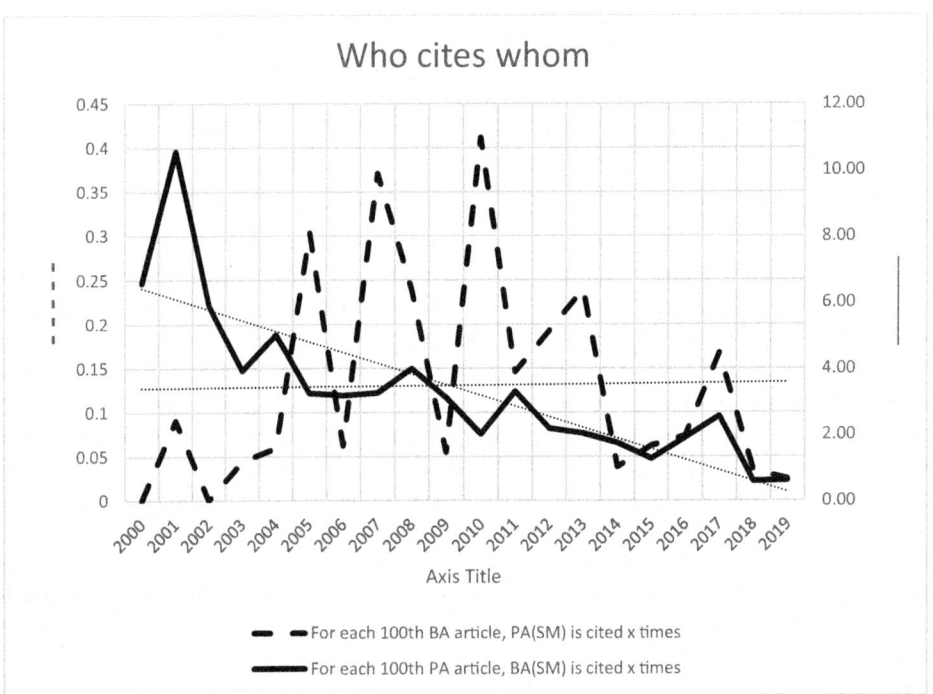

Figure A.4 Mutual citation (mean value per 100 article)

Our final bibliometric analysis applies the technique of bibliographic coupling, where assumptions of relationships between articles are made based on how often they cite the same sources. The more sources two articles cite in common, the stronger the association. This method can also apply to the respective countries where articles have been published. Thus, countries can be mapped in a network analysis based on the citation-praxis (the number of references they share). Seeing the differences between such maps (Figures A.5 and A.6) for PA and BA literature can contribute to our discussion.

In both maps, the US and England are dominant. However, sources from many more countries are involved in contributing about strategic management in the field of BA (107 countries) than the countries contributing to strategic management in the field of PA (39 countries). Furthermore, countries prominent on the BA-group are either far down or not at all included in the PA-group. Examples of this is Germany, France, and People's Republic of China, all prominently part of the BA discourse on strategic management, but low or absent from the PA discourse. This analysis indicates that there are significant differences as to which cultural-epistemic national communities are active in the respective discourses.

Our analysis reveals that strategic management in the separate fields of Business Administration and Management (BA) and Public Administration (PA) respectively are somewhat interlinked historically wise, but they are increasingly going down separate ways. The two fields include many of the same concepts (or at least use many of the same terms), but core concepts in one field are more peripheral concepts in the other one, and vice versa. These findings are especially significant when seeing which core theoretical approaches are employed, like *strategic planning* versus *resource-based view*: the former is centre stage in the PA literature, the latter is burgeoning in the BA literature. With separate journals and separate conferences, one can expect a diverging paradigmatic development and a trend towards continued separation, despite having an interest in the very notion of strategic management in common. However, it may be argued that it is especially for a relatively small field like strategic management in the public sector that there is a danger in distancing itself too much from

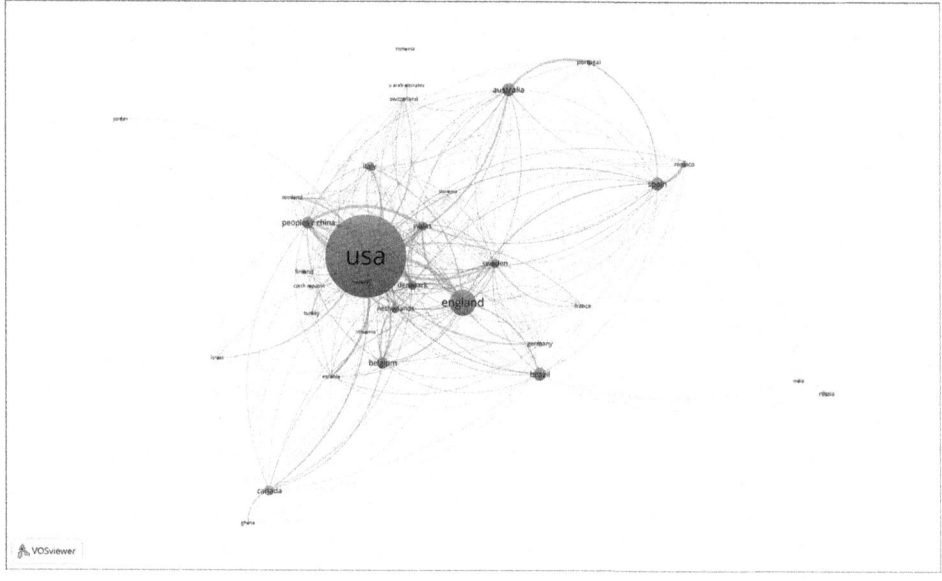

Figure A.5 Country-network based on citations in PA literature on strategic management‘

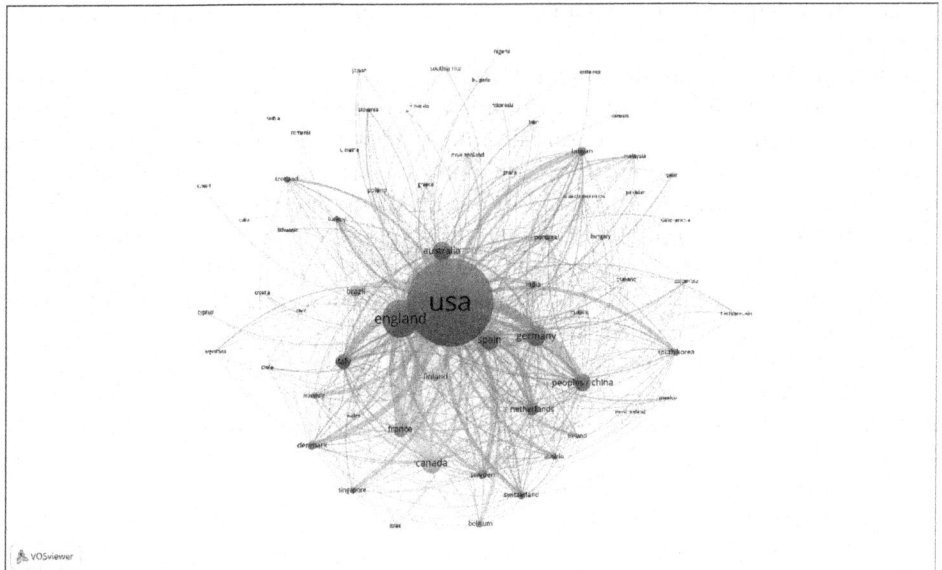

Figure A.6 Country-network based on citations in BA literature on strategic management

the 'main' field of strategic management in the BA literature. Substantial conceptual, theoretical, and methodical gains in the larger camp of BA can be overlooked and ultimately be deemed irrelevant or simply lost altogether for the discourse in the PA camp. True, certain developments of strategic management may be overly focused on for-profit organizations, and therefore be unusable for public services organizations (for reasons widely discussed throughout this chapter); and some developments in the BA literature may be hyperfocused on very idiosyncratic themes and thence of limited significance for both the research and the practice of public services organizations. The publications criteria in the BA literature may also have become more and more self-referential, shutting out valuable works from outside intellectual circuits simply because they do not conform to certain expectations and presumptive standards of rigour. However, there remains the key point that if the book's core argument holds, that generic strategic management models have enhanced applicability for public services organizations, then it is well worth the effort for public administration and management scholars to scout the BA literature for theories and models that can be applicable to public services organizations, as this book tries to do as systematically and comprehensively as possible. Such undertaking can contribute to attenuate the adverse effects of strategic management developing in siloed academic discourse-bubbles. (The reciprocal argument that it is a worthy undertaking for business administration and management scholars too to be heedful to PA scholarship also holds, because this would be beneficial to the BA scholarship, and ultimately because a functioning bridge between the two fields can only be built if both sides contribute to making it solid.)

Table A.7 Journals included in WoS category 'Public Administration'

ADMINISTRATION & SOCIETY
AMERICAN REVIEW OF PUBLIC ADMINISTRATION
AMME IDARESI DERGISI
AUSTRALIAN JOURNAL OF PUBLIC ADMINISTRATION
CANADIAN PUBLIC ADMINISTRATION-ADMINISTRATION PUBLIQUE DU CANADA
CANADIAN PUBLIC POLICY-ANALYSE DE POLITIQUES
CIVIL SZEMLE
CLIMATE POLICY
CONTEMPORARY ECONOMIC POLICY
CRITICAL POLICY STUDIES
ENVIRONMENT AND PLANNING C-POLITICS AND SPACE
GESTION Y POLITICA PUBLICA
GOVERNANCE-AN INTERNATIONAL JOURNAL OF POLICY ADMINISTRATION AND
   INSTITUTIONS
HUMAN SERVICE ORGANIZATIONS MANAGEMENT LEADERSHIP & GOVERNANCE
INTERNATIONAL PUBLIC MANAGEMENT JOURNAL
INTERNATIONAL REVIEW OF ADMINISTRATIVE SCIENCES
JOURNAL OF ACCOUNTING AND PUBLIC POLICY
JOURNAL OF CHINESE GOVERNANCE
JOURNAL OF COMPARATIVE POLICY ANALYSIS
JOURNAL OF EUROPEAN PUBLIC POLICY
JOURNAL OF EUROPEAN SOCIAL POLICY
JOURNAL OF HOMELAND SECURITY AND EMERGENCY MANAGEMENT
JOURNAL OF POLICY ANALYSIS AND MANAGEMENT
JOURNAL OF PUBLIC ADMINISTRATION RESEARCH AND THEORY
JOURNAL OF PUBLIC POLICY
JOURNAL OF SOCIAL POLICY
LEX LOCALIS-JOURNAL OF LOCAL SELF-GOVERNMENT
LOCAL GOVERNMENT STUDIES
NONPROFIT MANAGEMENT & LEADERSHIP
POLICY AND POLITICS
POLICY AND SOCIETY
POLICY SCIENCES
POLICY STUDIES
POLICY STUDIES JOURNAL
PUBLIC ADMINISTRATION
PUBLIC ADMINISTRATION AND DEVELOPMENT
PUBLIC ADMINISTRATION REVIEW
PUBLIC MANAGEMENT REVIEW
PUBLIC MONEY & MANAGEMENT
PUBLIC PERFORMANCE & MANAGEMENT REVIEW
PUBLIC PERSONNEL MANAGEMENT
PUBLIC POLICY AND ADMINISTRATION
REGULATION & GOVERNANCE
REVIEW OF POLICY RESEARCH
REVIEW OF PUBLIC PERSONNEL ADMINISTRATION
REVISTA DEL CLAD REFORMA Y DEMOCRACIA
SCIENCE AND PUBLIC POLICY
SOCIAL POLICY & ADMINISTRATION
TRANSYLVANIAN REVIEW OF ADMINISTRATIVE SCIENCES

Note

1 The journal *NONPROFIT MANAGEMENT & LEADERSHIP* appeared in both the 'Management' and the 'Public administration' category in WoS.

2 Schools of strategic management and their implications for contemporary public services organizations

Part 1 – from structure to culture

Over the decades since the 1970s and the 1980s, the discipline of strategic management has undergone significant expansion and is now a well-known staple of MBA courses. It also underpins much management consulting strategy activity (where some governments are as much an important customer as private firms, Saint Martin 2004; Steiner et al. 2018).

Whilst influential approaches of strategic management displaying strong roots in industrial economics (Porter 2004) may be seen as more suited to private firms than supposedly diverse public agencies (Allison 1983), we consider this view now to be dated, as argued in the introduction, given both the blurring of traditional boundaries between the public and the private sectors and because of the proliferation of novel models of strategic management, not all of which assume the presence of firms and of competitive markets.

Mintzberg et al. (2009) provide a lucid overview of various schools of strategic management, as does Pettigrew et al.'s Handbook (2006). Our objective is to build on this prior fine work by shifting the analysis towards the specific field of contemporary public services organizations (including also not-for-profit and 'third sector' organizations, now taking an important role in delivering publicly funded services) which was not a major focus in these earlier texts. This and the next chapter will provide a broad overview of different schools of strategic management – organized in the rough chronological order by which they emerged – and discuss their specific implications for public and not-for-profit organizations. A summative Table 2.1 provides an overview of the schools of thought of strategic management that we have identified and that are discussed throughout this and the following chapter, also pointing to the applicability of each school to public services settings.

In this chapter, we introduce and discuss some well-established schools: namely, strategic planning, design, strategic positioning, and the cultural schools, highlighting key texts and authors. The next chapter will consider more recent schools which have emerged as important. Due to reasons of space, we only examine what we see as the most relevant schools for current public and not-for-profit organizations and do not cover all those reviewed by Pettigrew et al. (2006) or Mintzberg et al. (2009).

One general question to bear in mind as the various schools are presented is whether they analyze the *content* of strategy, the *process* of strategy making, or both themes. A major divide in strategy studies is between studies focused on content (on what content of the strategy may lead to superior organizational performance), usually having an overall normative thrust, and studies focused on process formation (on how an organization's strategies form over time), often having an overall interpretive

DOI: 10.4324/9781003054917-2

Table 2.1 Key models of strategic management in private and public sector settings

School	Exemplary texts	Key public and not-for-profit sector texts	Comments
Strategic Design and Planning	Chandler (1962); Ansoff (1965); Andrews (1971)	Bryson (1988, 2018); Fretzel et al. (2000)	It can be adapted for public sector conditions (but note high politicization; pluralist power relations).
Strategic Positioning School	Porter (1980, 2004)	Porter and Teisberg (2006) – USA health care; Vining (2011)	Historically, private sector based and difficult to apply in public sector settings; may be more applicable within strong quasi markets; may still require adaptation.
Mintzberg, Learning, Emergent Strategy and Organizational Context	Quinn (1980); Mintzberg (1983); Mintzberg and Waters (1985)		Strong application to public sector settings;professionalized bureaucracy and adhocracy.
The (Public and Social) Entrepreneurial School	Mintzberg (1973)	Pettigrew (1979)	Strategy making in smaller scale settings; role of the founder of an innovative social setting; can apply to some social enterprises; it can also apply to core bureaucracies (e.g. EASA case) under certain conditions.
The Cultural School	Pascale and Athos (1981); Peters and Waterman (1982); Deal and Kennedy (1982)	Pettigrew (1979)	Japanese influence; reaction against structure; quality wave; it is significant both for commercial and public services organizations.
Resource-Based View	Penrose (1959);Wernerfelt (1984)	Harvey et al. (2010); Casebeer et al. (2010)	Knowledge-based view of strategy; widely applicable both to commercial and public services organizations.
Corporate Governance School	Jensen and Meckling (1976); Fama and Jensen (1983); Lorsch (1989); Charkham (1994)	Ferlie et al. (1996) (empirical study of UK NHS Boards)	A strong influence on NPM reforms; applicability to public services organizations broadly dependent on transformative effects of administrative reforms in the jurisdiction.
Network-Based and Collaborative Models of Strategy	Amin (1994); Child et al. (2019)	Rhodes (1997); Huxham and Vangen (2000); Newman (2001); Osborne (2010b)	A major strand in public management, puts emphasis on strategy as boundary-spanner and search for collaborative advantage.
Strategy as Process	Pettigrew (1985); Pettigrew and Whipp (1991); Van de Ven et al. (1999)	Pettigrew et al. (1992); McNulty and Ferlie (2002); Ferlie et al. (2013)	Broadly similar analytical logic can be applied to both sectors; both experiencing enhanced pressures for strategic change.
Strategy as Practice	Johnson et al. (2003); Jarzabkowski et al. (2007); Johnson et al. (2007)	Jarzabkowski and Wilson (2002)	Similar analytical logic applied to both sectors.
Public Value School	Moore (1995)	Benington and Moore (2011a)	Developed as a public sector model of strategy but influenced by other more orthodox models.

or explanatory thrust. We side with those advocating the perspective of overcoming the process-content dichotomy in the strategy literature and bridging the two (Chakravarthy and White 2006; Grant 2010; Johnson et al. 2003; Pettigrew et al. 2002; Sminia 2009). This book attempts to cover both dimensions in as much an integrated fashion as possible, though we are conscious this is a tall task (the two realms draw on distinct theoretical branches and use different languages, conceptual tools, and techniques of analysis).

2.1 The design school and strategic planning

The classic design school of strategy was first developed by American scholars in the 1960s, with a major monograph by Chandler (1962), and then texts by Ansoff (1965) and Andrews (1971). Chandler (1962) argued that a firm's strategy should then be reflected in its formal organizational structure: the famous dictum was that '*strategy determines structure*' – so there was a strong focus on the analysis of corporate structure. Chandler worked in a historically based case study tradition with intensive analysis of a small number of large American firms, with a particular interest in the relationship between a strategy of corporate diversification and associated structure in more decentralized organizational forms. Ansoff (1965) and Andrews (1971), by contrast, worked in a more deductive mode, bringing in modelling techniques from economics and operational research. These two different methodological approaches continue to be reflected throughout the development of strategic management as a discipline.

The design school essentially seeks to achieve a strategic fit between a particular organization and its environment (the 'matching of internal and external configuration' is also the terminology often used). Strategy making is normally seen as being led by senior managers and their advisers and then handed to middle management to implement. The 'strategic vision' (Mintzberg et al. 2009, p. 28) underlying the design should be kept simple, may be 'bespoke' to each organization (leading to 'case law' rather than abstract theory), and should be formulated so that it is easy to communicate to others.

The design school uses two well-known analytic techniques to assess the external environment (PESTEL) and the internal organization (SWOT) and then examine the fit between them. In conducting a PESTEL audit, the analyst should examine wider environmental trends in various key domains which can impinge on the firm: namely, politics, economics, sociological factors, technology, the environment, and law. Brief possible applications of the different domains to an analysis of the wider environment of a public services agency are given next.

(i)   *Politics*: an analysis of implications of an actual or a likely change of government; a reshuffle of ministers in the ruling party; the announcement of a major new policy direction and legislation on the levels of political support for an agency and its likely revenue flows;

(ii) *Economics*: likely growth and taxation rates; the effects of any economic crisis on public expenditure; an analysis of the prospects for public expenditure levels at both the macro- and then the individual agency levels;

(iii) *Sociological factors*: the effects of an ageing population, immigration, or changing family structures on the likely levels of demand for the services provided by a public agency;

(iv)   *Technology*: an analysis of how new information and communication technologies and the growth of e-government may be affecting the work of a public agency; a consideration of new technologies in health and social care and their effects on patterns of service delivery (e.g. telemedicine);

(v)   *Environment*: the impact of a push for more 'sustainable' public policies; the influence from the climate change agenda; how changing patterns of car use and public transport may affect service delivery; and

(vi)   *Law*: an analysis of a wider push either to regulation or deregulation; the legal effects of a country joining or leaving the EU (e.g. to social legislation); national changes to employment and trade union law and how they could affect the public sector employer and the worker.

Many public sector agencies could find such a PESTEL analysis a useful analytic tool as well as private firms, especially in periods of environmental turbulence; for example in assessing the effects of new information technologies coming downstream on work and service delivery patterns or the effects of potential political changes, as might be the case for one country joining – or leaving – the European Union, or the World Trade Organization, or a major reorganization of the territorial basis of a polity on a more – or less – decentralized basis. It may also be helpful to identify and explicitly prioritize the most important factors to avoid compiling a long 'shopping list' of descriptive factors and thus aid decision making based on the PESTEL analysis.

In certain application of the model, also an analysis of the industry (I) is encompassed: in this case, the technique is now called PESTELI. For example, Ahmad et al. (2019) conducted a systematic review using a PESTELI framework of existing studies on policy responses by health care systems to the growing policy problem of anti-microbial resistance. Ten studies were included in the final review ranging from single country (six) to regional-level multi-country studies (four). Eight studies carried out documentary reviews, and three of these also included stakeholder interviews. Two studies were based on expert opinion with no data collection. No study employed the PESTELI framework. Most studies (nine) included analysis of the political domain which emerged as highly important and one study included all six domains of the framework. Technological and industry analyses is a notable gap. Facilitators and inhibitors within the political and legislative domains were the most frequently reported. No facilitators were reported in the economic or industry domains but featured inhibiting factors including lack of ring-fenced funding for surveillance, perverse financial incentives, cost-shifting to patients, and joint-stock drug company ownership complicating regulations. They concluded that the PESTELI framework provides further opportunities to combat AMR using a systematic, strategic management approach, rather than a retrospective view.

In a SWOT analysis, the analyst should look at the distinctive strengths and weaknesses of the organization itself rather than the environment, and in addition to conceive of the opportunities and threats that environmental trends engender for the organization. The internal configuration of the organization (its strengths and weaknesses) should then match the external configuration represented by the opportunities brought about by environmental changes and counter the potential threats. While SWOT analyses are already used in public sector as well as private sector settings, it is also important here to move beyond the superficial and formulaic 'long list' often presented and to generate a smaller list of important factors. Ranking and prioritization of factors surfaced may help focus the analysis (Johnson et al. 2011, p. 106). Another criticism is that SWOT analyses are descriptive and not grounded in a coherent or cumulative theory (Grant 2008).

Example of UK higher education and MBA/MPA courses – a SWOT exercise

Let us take an example from UK higher education. Following a government policy decision which led in 2010 to the withdrawal of public funding for the teaching of non-science subjects, UK universities became increasingly reliant on private teaching fee income from overseas and postgraduate students, which are both deregulated sectors (e.g. MBA/MPA courses are highly market-based and there are no government scholarships). Universities have had to position themselves in these competitive fees markets based on a clear assessment of their market position. An individual university will now need to ask such questions as these: what fee level should it charge for its MBA and MPA courses? How does it benchmark against key comparators and which strategic group is it in? To what extent should it position itself in the more lucrative international market or confine itself to the UK student market? A SWOT analysis could enable it to assess the strength of its 'brand' *vis á vis* its key competitors and consider the extent to which it may be threatened by (or benefit from) liberalization of the higher education marketplace.

A brief example of the type of SWOT analysis that a UK-based university business school might use to assess its position in the MBA/MPA market is given next. Such a SWOT analysis might well produce a list of bullet points and key findings, covering the following domains:

Strengths/weaknesses

- An analysis could consider such questions as these: at the most macro-level, which strategic group of schools is in it (there may be distinct international, national, or regionally orientated groups; also research and teaching intensive groups)? What are the implications of such positioning for the fees that can realistically be charged and the recruitment strategies that may be advisable?;
- Regarding marketing data on the 'brand' of the university as a whole, is the profile (and hence market served) of the wider university regional, national, or international? Is it research or teaching intensive? Can it realistically charge a premium?; and
- How desirable is the physical and cultural location of the university in market terms (e.g. a Central London base can be thought to be able to more readily attract international students)?

At a more operational level:

- As regards rank and position in visible and influential 'league tables' (e.g. Financial Times league table of MBA programme): how leading or rather lagging behind is the school in the rankings for the wider sector as a whole? (the university-wide position in another set of key rankings (e.g. in the Times Education supplement) may also be important here);
- As regards the student feedback on courses (like quantitative evaluations, qualitative comments, and focus groups): is the student experience a positive one?;

- As regards the strength of networks the business school has with major employers (as seen in placements of students, internships, joint projects, and other links): how connected is the school externally with employing organizations and does it develop the career prospects of its MBA/MPA students?;
- As regards data on salary uplift three years after graduation (a key indicator in MBA rankings) and more broadly data on longer-term career trajectories of alumni: do former students go on to have successful and enjoyable careers?; and
- As regards data on the number of student applications and the entry tariff in terms of pre-existing qualifications which also reflect the school's position in the marketplace: is it in essence a 'selecting' (pick and choose) or a 'recruiting' (accept most applications) school?

Opportunities

- Opportunity to internationalize (e.g. ability to recruit more international students to the UK; consider and resolve visa issues; open a new campus in big, economically expanding countries like China);
- Opportunity to leverage any distinctive 'brand' in the wider university by putting on joint degrees with other well-known and reputable academic departments within the university to enter new market segments;
- An analysis of the local opportunities to develop new courses and degrees in key subject areas (e.g. accountancy; banking and finance; marketing) which can attract substantial numbers of new students;
- Local opportunities to develop further links with local employers and other stakeholders to improve the extent of connectivity; and
- Opportunity to build a 'cash surplus' for academic reinvestment by expanding new revenue streams in consultancy income or courses in executive education: do the academics have requisite skills to deliver such functions and if so, how can upskilling take place?

Threats

- At a macro-level, how are enrolments moving nationally and internationally in the sector? Is there a national or international decline in the number of MBA/MPA enrolments? Is there over or under supply from the sector?;
- What are the strategic moves from other business schools in the same group – will they launch new programmes too? Are they building new high-quality buildings? Are they opening a sub campus abroad? Do they have a dynamic capability in being more agile and responding more quickly in these areas?;
- The possible entrance of cost-effective and teaching quality assured private providers (e.g. BPP) into a more deregulated management education marketplace: what threats do they pose? What is the role of new teaching technologies – for example moving to online teaching? Can the business school respond quickly enough in this domain?; and
- At a micro- and individual level, is there a credible loss of individual academic 'stars' who are vulnerable to being poached in more market-like conditions by rival schools and take their reputation with them?

In conclusion, the design school analyzes the fit between the organization and its environment and aims to sensitize decision makers to (positive or negative) trends which may be occurring in the environment and which the organization should respond to. It uses the well-known SWOT and PESTEL models as two basic analytic techniques which help analyze the fit between the organization and a (changing) external environment. It is important that the use of these techniques does not just generate a long and descriptive 'shopping list' but also highlights a smaller number of key factors that should be considered in strategic decision making.

The strategic planning school

The strategic planning school develops the design school further, representing a greater move to formalization (Mintzberg et al. 2009). It fuelled the long-range planning movement evident in large mature corporations in the 1960s, reflected in influential texts such as Ansoff's (1965). It was also associated with the growth of corporate planning units and systems in these organizations. These tasks were often undertaken by specialist planning staff based in corporate headquarters, using long-range forecasting and operations management techniques, and then plans were passed down to middle management to implement.

Mintzberg (1994) considers its binary split between formulation and implementation (and therefore between thinking and doing) to be unhelpful, leading to loss of ownership of the strategic plan by the bulk of the workforce and then as leading to major implementation deficits as such an approach produces only 'paper plans' that have no basis in reality. Mintzberg (1994) traces the rise and then the fall of the strategic planning movement in the mid-1970s, as it encountered more uncertain and volatile economic environments, notably two oil shocks which made long-term forecasting hazardous. The political environment also became less consensual, with polarization between the Right and the Left and the possibility of radical shifts of public policy following a change of government. These developments had repercussions for the eclipse of large-scale and formalized governmental planning systems too.

Citing Koch (1976), Mintzberg (1994, p. 115) takes the example of the elaborate national system of 'indicative planning' developed in France after the Second World War which collapsed in the 1970s. Such a planning system was seen as lacking in democratic legitimacy, as it was taken over by technical elites, as lacking good long-run information and as incapable of coping with the radical environmental turbulence it encountered, or the behaviour of private sector actors beyond the direct control of government. Similarly, he considers the case of the comprehensive American Planning, Programming and Budgeting System (PPBS) system pioneered in the American Department of Defense by President John F. Kennedy's Defense Secretary (Robert McNamara) in the early 1960s. McNamara brought into government young staff members from Harvard University and the Rand Corporation (an important US organization with its roots in the defence sector and with much expertise in the strategic planning field) to support PPBS. PPBS was then generalized across the American government by President Lyndon B. Johnson in the mid-1960s, and it later diffused to some other countries. PPBS was supposed to herald a shift to a planning system based on programme outputs rather than budgetary inputs, with an explicit calculation of costs and benefits within an economics orientated mode of thinking. As a strategic planning tool, however, PPBS was tested to destruction during the Vietnam War, when its formalization, tactical unresponsiveness, and inability to deal with psychological factors encountered in warfare on the ground were seen as major failings.

Long-run strategic planning approaches were enthusiastically adopted by some UK public sector agencies in the 1960s, for example by the UK NHS and University Grants Commission with their five-year plans, in practice mainly used to guide major public sector capital investment decisions (e.g. the building of new hospitals and universities). UK local government experimented with more corporate forms of planning and management in the early 1970s, as an attempted antidote to historically strong departmental and professionalized dominated silos (e.g. social services; education). However, these long-term plans and corporate systems again collapsed in the turbulent years of the mid-1970s, when unpredictable and radical political, economic, and expenditure shifts all occurring at the same time made long-term planning assumptions unrealistic and the amount of capital monies available for public investment (their core purpose in practice) collapsed.

Similar deficiencies led to a decline in long corporate range planning systems in private firms in the early 1980s as they were cut back or even dismantled (the case of General Electric under Jack Welch, Mintzberg et al. 2009, p. 69). Increasing criticism (Mintzberg 1994; Wilson 1994) emerged in relation to the poor performance of elaborate strategic planning systems: specialist corporate staff took over the process (marginalizing line management) and the process then took over the corporate specialist staff who produced ever more elaborate plans but ones devoid of strategic insight. Those planning systems which survived tended to be decentralized to strategic business units (Wilson 1994). Some large and sophisticated companies (such as Shell) introduced new techniques such as scenario planning (more flexible planning for a range of different possible futures) to promote creativity and adaptability, but they were confined to a relatively small number of elite firms.

It can be argued historically that long-range planning had its earliest origins within government settings (including the planned socialist economies) and later moved into large mature corporations. After the 1917 communist revolution and the creation of the first socialist state, the USSR replaced a market-based economy with a planned and centrally directed economy. This required an agency to undertake this vast planning task. The new Gosplan (State Planning Committee, 1921–1991) was a special agency charged with compiling USSR-wide annual and five-year plans with the first Five Year Plan appearing in 1928. The New Deal in the USA of the 1930s led (Reagan 1999, pp. 186–187) to the creation of the National Planning Board (1933–1943). The Board had a special interest in planning public works as an integral part of the New Deal. Less dramatically, the European Union (EU) approach to long-range planning mainly in the form of seven-year plans (the early plans were five or six years long) has survived and even thrived across the decades till the present day.

Interestingly, Khurana (2007, Chapter 4.1)'s history of the evolution of American business schools characterizes their response to the New Deal during the 1930s as placing a renewed emphasis on applied and high-quality social science and a greater interest in public policy (was this a case of the early American business schools moving towards a greater embrace of government which seems to us distinctly odd today?). The attempted reconnection of business schools with a research base led to the formation of the still flourishing Academy of Management in 1936 as an academically based association for business school faculty.

The suggestion here is that there were rather few pronounced intersectoral differences in the openness to and experience of early strategic planning models which rather displayed a similar cycle – growth in the 1960s followed by decline in the late

1970s, with this pattern evident in both the private and public sectors. Their base in the private sector was in large mature corporations operating in relatively stable markets (which was a sector in relative decline from the 1970s onwards), as the approach was more difficult to apply to SMEs or to firms operating in volatile market conditions. Long-range planning in the public sector similarly became highly problematic in the turbulent and volatile decade of the 1970s as a number of political and economic shocks (e.g. rise in the oil price; high inflation and the Iran revolution of 1979) led to a new era of uncertainty and instability.

Bryson (1988, 2018) has more recently developed ideas from the design and strategic planning schools to propose an influential strategic planning change cycle for public and not-for-profit organizations. His approach is in multiple senses broader than strategic planning: it represents an approach to strategy as practical reasoning, encompassing both a number of schools of strategy discussed in this book (including but not limited to strategy-as-practice/strategizing, see also Bryson 2021) and a range of other approaches and strands of inquiry, including change management and collaborative leadership, drawing from public management, organization studies, and the social sciences more broadly. Strategic planning is here often seen as a lever for public service innovation (Berry 1994). Ultimately, Bryson produces an impressive synthesis of themes, integrated in a way that not just interconnects multiple strands of scholarly inquiry but also provides practitioners with a highly utilizable approach. Bryson originally (1988) advocated a structured process – formally organized into a series of distinct stages (although it is also recognized that there may be cycles of iteration between them) – to enable decision makers in such organizations to identify and resolve major organizational issues. The cycle starts with a clarification of agency mandates, missions, and values and would often be led by a strategic planning team. After a stakeholder analysis, core analytic techniques such as PESTEL and SWOT (along with a stakeholder analysis) are used to assess the environment and the organization. Potential strategic issues are then spotted in an inductive fashion, moving from the particular to more general themes rather than in a formal specification of goals at the start. Finally, a 'vision of success' should be agreed and widely communicated. Fretzel et al. (2000) provide a worked example of this approach to strategic planning in the US Navy, again including the heavy use of SWOTs.

Strategic planning models have also permeated reforms of the public sector, including at the EU level (Drumaux and Joyce 2020). Still, in a number of instances, the problem of a big gap between formalistic and actual adoption continues to be present, as illustrated in the case of Mexico reported in Box 2.1. We return on the interconnections between public management reform and the adoption of strategic management models in Chapter 7.

Box 2.1 Strategic Planning and Management in Mexico,
Mauricio I. Dussauge Laguna[1]

Since the mid-1990s, Strategic Planning and Management (SP&M) topics have been present in Mexico, both in government and academic circles. Concepts such as 'Vision,' 'Mission,' 'Values,' 'Strategy,' and 'Strengths-Weaknesses-

Opportunities-Threats' (SWOT) analysis, as well as cognate terms such as 'indicators,' 'benchmarks,' 'management,' and 'performance' have entered government discussions and documents. Similarly, the academic study of SP&M in the Mexican public sector has received some attention from public administration and policy specialists (Cabrero 1997; Arellano Gault 2004; Aguilar Villanueva 2006; Pardo and Velasco 2006; Ramírez and Arellano Gault 2014; Velasco 2010; Nivón 2020).

However, asserting that SP&M has an established presence in Mexico is quite different from providing a clear understanding about its significance or impacts on this country's public sector management practices. On the one hand, SP&M terms have gained currency in official documents and websites, at both federal and state governments levels. On the other hand, SP&M initiatives have been frequently overshadowed by other reform doctrines. Moreover, evidence is scarce regarding the systematic and careful application of SP&M within Mexican bureaucracies. Lastly, SP&M practices have in the late 2010s and early 2020s lost most of their logic and potential, given the presence of a populist government that cares little about plans, indicators, evidence, and related management tools.

In terms of government 'talk,' one could find some planning practices in Mexico since the 1980s. While not aligned with contemporary SP&M jargon and tools, a National Democratic Planning System was established back in the 1980s (Cejudo 2017). Since then, every new government has been legally obliged to involve citizens in the process of diagnosing national priorities and setting national goals. As a result, the incoming government must produce a 'National Development Plan' (NDP), as well as a series of policy sector or agency specific plans, all of which should be in line with the NDP. Over time, these plans have transitioned from rather general policy statements to more detailed actions, including specific targets and indicators for each policy sector.

In addition to this fairly legalistic and rigid planning process, SP&M principles have appeared in basically all administrative modernization initiatives enacted for the past 30 years. Particularly relevant were the two initiatives introduced during President Ernesto Zedillo's administration (1994–2000): the *Programa de Modernización de la Administración Pública 1995–2000* [Programme for the Modernisation of Public Administration 1995–2000], and the *Nueva Estructura Programática – Sistema de Evaluación del Desempeño* [NEP-SED, or New Budgetary Programmes Structure – Performance Evaluation System]. These initiatives introduced the concepts of 'organizational objectives' and 'management/budget indicators' that had to be 'aligned' with the institutional mission and vision of federal ministries and agencies, all of which required the introduction of strategic planning processes government-wide (SECODAM 1999; Chávez Presa 2000; Pardo 2003). Thereafter, government modernization plans up to President Enrique Peña Nieto's (2012–2018) *Programa para un Gobierno Cercano y Moderno* [Programme for a Closer and Modern Government] included SP&M jargon.

In more practical terms, SP&M principles have been widely disseminated both across federal institutions and government levels. Building on President

Zedillo's administration strategic planning efforts (Pardo 2003), federal institutions had to define their own 'vision,' 'mission,' and 'values.' Similarly, according to some surveys, SP&M principles have become more and more used by subnational governments. Indeed, some studies put SP&M as the second most widespread set of 'managerial' tools, only behind 'IT management' tools, but above others such as 'quality of service' or 'accountability' tools (Martínez Vilchis 2007, 2010).

Yet the dissemination of SP&M 'talk' and basic principles does not seem to have been followed by the systematic and regular application of a truly 'strategic' approach for the daily management of public organizations. After its heyday in the 1990s, various other administrative doctrines and reform initiatives became more prominent. For example, President Vicente Fox (2000–2006) was personally keen on SP&M practices, which featured heavily during his role as governor of the state of Guanajuato (1995–1999). In the first months of his presidency, Fox published a *Modelo Estratégico para la Innovación y la Calidad Gubernamental* [Strategic Model for Government Innovation and Quality]. However, this was quickly substituted by a broader *Agenda de Buen Gobierno* [Good Government Agenda], which included several initiatives on civil service reform, IT management, quality of service, and regulatory improvement, among others. This crowded the government's modernization agenda, divided up available resources and politico-administrative support, and undermined the relevance of purely SP&M-related activities (Dussauge-Laguna 2008).

Even more importantly, since the mid-2000s 'Managing for Results' (MfR) initiatives gained more prominence than SP&M among central agencies (Dussauge-Laguna 2013). In principle, MfR is clearly associated with SP&M (*e.g.* MfR activities usually take as a point of departure the need to 'align' performance indicators with institutional missions, visions, and objectives; Arellano Gault et al. 2012). Indeed, as part of the Mexican MfR approach, all logical frameworks and performance indicators used for evaluating public programmes are supposed to be based on agency-specific strategic objectives. Nonetheless, this has not necessarily strengthened a strategic management view among policy makers, whose attention tends to be mainly focused on complying with the evaluation process itself (Magaña 2021). In fact, evaluation findings and results are not systematically used, either in improving government programmes, or in adjusting budgetary appropriations. Thus, MfR has had a rather limited effect on how public managers adapt their organizational strategies to their environment, and very little (if at all) on their longer-term priorities.

With the arrival of President Andrés Manuel López Obrador (2018–2024), the use of SP&M has reached a new low, both in terms of 'talk' and practice. Rhetorically, López Obrador has often argued that 'neoliberal' governing practices, which include public management measures implemented in the past 30 years or so, have not reflected the 'will of the people' and have negatively affected the country's development (Gobierno de México 2019). Instead, the president has expressed his preference for a set of rather vague principles related to honesty, ethics, justice, etc. This change in rhetoric has been followed by a change in the government's approach to planning, as reflected in López Obrador's National

Development Plan 2019–2024. Indeed, while the Ministry of Finance drafted a conventional plan (which included strategic lines, objectives, and indicators; see Gaceta Parlamentaria 2019), the president publicly expressed his dislike for a document that seemed 'more of the same' (e.g. neoliberalism; see El Financiero 2019). He then asked his advisors to draft a new NDP to be submitted to the legislative power for approval (Diario Oficial de la Federación 2019). The final document is more a political manifesto than a plan. The episode led to the resignation of the then Minister of Finance, who would later state that 'one cannot draft a National Development Plan at the stroke of a pen' (Urzúa 2019a, 2019b).

The limited interest in SP&M practices during the López Obrador administration has been present at other levels. For instance, while the national planning law set a clear schedule for the submission of the national plan and complementary policy sector and agency plans, the federal government did not fully comply with the legal deadlines. By mid-2021 (almost three years into the administration's six-year term), not all plans had been published, and many had been published later than usual (CONEVAL 2020). Furthermore, the quality of available plans has been highly variable: some have reflected proper SP&M and MfR principles (clear objectives, links between public problems and proposed policies, measurable indicators, and targets, etc.), but many have lacked baselines, targets, or clear links between objectives and actions. A few actually completely lack an SP&M logic (CONEVAL 2020). In some policy areas, like the cultural sector, the planning process seems to have further contributed to the sector's 'crisis' by focusing on just one political objective, while sidelining other strategic areas (Nivón 2020). In other fields, like the energy policy sector, political considerations have taken priority over long-term strategic considerations. This has been particularly the case for the state-owned companies PEMEX (oil company) and CFE (electricity; Ballesteros and Moreno 2021; Interview 1). In cross-cutting sectors, such as civil service management and anticorruption policies, the drafting of an official strategic plan and related targets and indicators is yet to be completed (Interview 2). Thus, the populist tone set by President López Obrador has also had significant effects on administrative institutions and values, as well as on the application of SP&M routines and practices (Dussauge-Laguna 2021).

In closing, what could we say about Mexico's public sector experience with SP&M? How could we try to explain the latter's fate? Regarding the first question, it appears that whereas the *strategic planning* part of the equation did have some importance at some point in history (namely, through its legacy of mission and vision statements), the *strategic management* side has never gained much traction beyond very specific cases. For instance, the agency *Infonavit*, a semi-autonomous public agency in charge of providing credits for housing to workers, did develop a remarkable SP&M initiative throughout the 2000s (see Pardo and Velasco 2006; Ramírez and Arellano Gault 2014). However, the same has not happened in central ministries, nor in other semi-autonomous agencies. Moreover, government-wide, the introduction of MfR initiatives basically supplanted rather than complemented SP&M practices. Other reform trends, such as transparency and open government, have not been clearly linked to the use of SP&M practices during their implementation.

As for the second question, a first partial explanation might be found on Mexico's administrative tradition, including its history of strong legalism followed by a rather ambivalent attitude towards compliance. Given the formal mandate established in the 1980s (for plans) and in the 1990s (for mission/vision statements and indicators), federal ministries and agencies have kept their planning practices in place up to when this book goes to press. Furthermore, the national planning system legally requires ministries and agencies to align their actions with the National Development Plan (and complementary plans for each policy sector), as well as to submit progress reports periodically. Additional controls are exerted through the budget execution reports coordinated by the Ministry of Finances, and the audits developed *ex post* by the Supreme Audit Institution. Nonetheless, because of the informality which has also characterized traditionally government routines, both statements and managerial practices associated with SP&M have been mostly ignored in practice. Also, the NDP cannot be amended to reflect changes in the public sector's environment. Therefore, ministers and agency leaders may not think it useful (or might simply not be in a position) to follow a more strategically oriented management approach.

A second partial explanation can be found in the public/private sectors divide. At one level, one could think that SP&M principles and practices have not gained much relevance in the Mexican government because public sector managers lack the 'know how' on this subject and thus are not familiar with its benefits. At another level, one could refer to the organizational and institutional features of public organizations, such as the presence of ambiguous goals, red tape constraints, and a highly politicized environment. Indeed, the latter has been a prominent feature of Mexico's politico-administrative system, particularly in recent years with the rise of a populist government that has expressed its disdain regarding managerial concepts and tools.

In conclusion, SP&M talk and practices have had significant 'ups and downs' within the Mexican public sector. After a considerable expansion during the 1990s and early 2000s, the 'planning' side of the equation formally remains, albeit in a much-distorted version. At the same time, the 'management' side has become institutionalized in rather ritualistic practices that do not add much value to public managers. In the end, both planning and management practices inside the Mexican government have mostly lost their 'strategic' logic and purpose.

While this approach uses many private sector techniques (PESTEL, SWOT, scenario analysis), it can also be adapted to distinctive public sector conditions, namely, a highly political environment, lack of a strong hierarchy, and pluralist power relations. A stakeholder analysis should therefore be undertaken early on in the process to clarify which stakeholders are involved and how much power they have. The process of spotting strategic issues proceeds in an inductive and collaborative fashion, rather than simply being imposed from the top.

Bryson's (2018) most recent edition of his influential text responds to some earlier criticisms made of formal strategic planning systems and incorporates a greater emphasis on subjective factors such as effective leadership and vision generation. Learning processes now play a key role in this approach, as also argued also by Kools and George (2020, p. 262): 'For strategic planning to deliver on its promise of achieving organizational and societal change, it needs to be complemented with organizational learning.' It is claimed that the new model of a strategic planning change cycle championed by Bryson has moved significantly away from the old models of strategic planning which were too rigid and disconnected from implementation: in other words, the evolution of his text through five editions (1998–2018) suggests that the long-term planning school has itself learnt from and responded to earlier criticisms. Thanks to Bryson's and other scholars' work (e.g. George et al. 2020 also argue about the renewed significance of strategic planning as part and parcel of strategic management for public services organizations), a broader form of strategic planning has become a fixture of the strategic management of public services organizations and remains influential today.

2.2 The strategic positioning school

This major school is strongly associated with the work of Michael Porter (1980, 2004), with its disciplinary roots in industrial economics. The first edition of his key text 'Competitive Strategy' (Porter 1980) coincided with the start of the market-led decade of the 1980s in both the USA and UK, helping to make an academic wave of enduring significance globally. Porterian approaches remain highly influential within mainstream strategic management, emphasizing the importance of market structure and its analysis. They propose a clear and conceptually based framework to examine a firm's competitive strategy within a given industry, unlike the 'one off' analyses of the design school. However, the Porterian model assumes a highly rational analytic and top-down approach to strategy, then often given to middle management to implement (Mintzberg et al. 2009).

Key Porterian models and concepts include – as a first main contribution – the significant 'five forces framework' used to model competition at an industry level. This framework analyzes the dynamics of competition and (for example) the extent to which incumbents enjoy market power.

The five forces can be specified as follows:

(i)   *The threat of new entrants (or firms that may be able to enter the market)*: how strong are the barriers to any such market entry by firms? Such barriers include the need for large amounts of capital investment to enter a market and the need to comply with complex regulatory procedures or 'softer' factors such as well-established brands. The higher the barriers, the more difficult it will be to displace incumbents.

(ii) *The bargaining power of a firm's suppliers* (such as its various subcontractors and suppliers of raw materials): what is the nature of the relationship between the firm and these suppliers (e.g. over prices; the terms of subcontracts)? Who has most to lose from the end of any contracts and to what extent are substitute subcontractors/suppliers available?

(iii)   *The bargaining power of a firm's customers*: to what extent are customers (individual or corporate) able to put pressure on a firm to cut costs, raise quality, or launch new products? This will depend on how concentrated buyer power is, how well-informed buyers are and the extent to which they are prepared and able to switch to new suppliers.

(iv)   *Threat of substitute products* (products that can use new technology to substitute for a traditional product): given a high rate of technological change, it is possible that radical new products can emerge which can displace existing products (e.g. email replacing letters) through lowering costs or increased acceptability to consumers.

(v)   *Intensity of rivalry amongst competing firms*: the forces already reviewed taken together all influence the nature of competition and the extent of rivalry between firms in an industry. This may vary from relative cooperative strategies involving alliances or even cartels to more cut-throat competition designed to drive rivals out of the marketplace.

In contrast to the design school, Porter (2004) argues that there are only a small number of credible firm-level generic strategies (a second main contribution of Porter). The choices available are expressed in a two-by-two matrix, giving four possible boxes. A first dimension suggests a choice between a strategy based either on value-based differentiation (premium products or brands for premium prices) or cost leadership (low prices, generated by economies of scale, operational cost controls or tight subcontracts). However, firms should beware of being 'stuck in the middle' between these two choices, where performance is likely to be impaired (although this argument has been contested by Mintzberg et al. 2009, pp. 107–108). The second dimension of the matrix consists of the extent of focus where a firm could choose a broad strategy or alternatively a particular focus, either a cost focus in a key market or a differentiation focus on particular market segments, product lines, or geographical markets. A limitation of the five forces framework is that it appears especially suitable for single-industry organizations, but it may be more difficult to apply to complex organizations (both private and public sector), with large portfolios of products and operating across different industrial/service sectors and markets.

The value chain (Porter 1985) is Porter's third influential contribution to the mainstream strategic management literature, essentially modelling the production process which should in his view be seen as a whole. A set of sequential primary activities (ordered in the form of inbound logistics; operations; outbound logistics; marketing and sales; service) deliver products to the customer. They are supported by a variety of corporate support activities (firm infrastructure; human resource management; technology development and procurement). Taken as a whole, the primary and secondary activities produce the firm's profit margin.

The assumptions of the positioning school have been extensively critiqued by Mintzberg et al. (2009, Chapter 4), who see it as an extreme manifestation of the planning school, again leading to the separation of thinking and doing and of planning and acting. It is also criticized as over-dependent on a narrow set of rational analytic techniques (rather than creative and thoughtful synthesis which can produce a fuller strategic picture) and as advocating a highly top-down strategic process. Porterian analysis might be traditionally seen as assuming a competitive firm as its basic unit of analysis and hence as difficult to apply to public and not-for-profit settings. However, there appear to be various 'hybrid spaces' which cross public and private settings where recent attempts have been made to use them, as we explore next.

In the remainder of this section, we develop on the application of Porterian frames to public services settings, in broadly the reverse order in which we presented them. We thus start from considering applications of the value chain analysis.

Applying the value chain analysis in public services: example of the Porter and Teisberg (2006) book Redefining Health Care

Ideas of value chain analysis (including developing a related concept of a 'care delivery value chain' which combines a set of primary activities with secondary support activities across the health care process) have been developed by Porter and Teisberg (2006) in their analysis of the seemingly dysfunctional American health care sector, which historically displays a negative mix of high and growing costs, low access, and patchy health outcomes. This is a hybrid space as the USA government remains a major payer (through Medicare and Medicaid) for health care, but with provision delivered by a mix of public organizations, private firms, and not-for-profit organizations. Given the large flows of resources involved (an estimate, at the time the analysis was made, showed that health care accounted for some 17% of the USA GDP), this is an area with major policy implications (including for American firms with high health insurance costs to bear which can affect their competitiveness). These ideas about value chains in US health care have been further developed in Porter (2010), who outlines a method for developing and ensuring rigourous health care status outcome measures and also Kaplan and Porter (2011), who stress the need to measure accurately both costs and outcomes across the whole care cycle, using such re-engineering-based techniques as process mapping.

The cost containment strategy of American health policy since the 1990s (to build up a smaller number of larger and more expert insurers or so-called health maintenance organizations to challenge traditional provider dominance of the health care market) was here seen to have failed, leading only to continual 'salami slicing' of operational costs rather than the radical restructuring which could increase value for the patient. Porter and Teisberg (2006) argue the core problem is that the wrong kind of competition has been so far tried within the American health care market and that the focus now needs to shift from the previous emphasis on achieving incremental cost reductions to a new form of competition which seeks to maximize value for the patient, as expressed across the whole care journey (focusing on the so-called health care delivery value chain which is a variant of the generic value chain model found in private sector orientated literature).

In the health care delivery chain (Porter and Teisberg 2006, p. 397), there is a focus first of all on typical stages in the care process (preventing; diagnosing; preparing; intervening; recovering and monitoring). There are a number of secondary activities which support the primary care cycle (knowledge management; informing; measuring and accessing). The desired outcome is here specified as patient value (health results per unit of cost): there is here an important conceptual link with the Public Value school of thought in strategic management, which is examined further in Chapter 3.

To support this objective of increased value for the patient, improvements in outcome measurement and IT systems are needed so that information on outcomes and values is captured and made available to better informed consumers and payers. The implication is that health care providers should select areas where they are excellent and have high patient volumes and then concentrate in those sectors, rather than get 'stuck in the middle' with a broad range of low volume products of mediocre quality. Apart from supplying infrastructure and incentives to support such organizational reconfiguration, Porter and Teisberg (2006) see a relatively modest role for government and place greater faith in market-led restructuring. It is assumed that patients will be willing to travel long distances to access high-quality services, although possible equity issues here are not fully discussed (as poorer patients may find it more difficult to travel).

Porter and Teisberg (2006) give brief examples of good performers which are held up as role models. In cancer services, they draw on the case of the MD Anderson Cancer Center (a specialist centre of excellence) in Houston, Texas. They draw attention to its integrated practice model organized by tumour type, with a team of different clinicians and support facilities brought together in one specialist clinic, providing high volume and considerable experience. At the same time, the hospital reaches out to referring physicians to promote continuity across the whole care process (or care delivery value chain). Porter's ideas have proved influential in some parts in the UK NHS after the global financial crisis as value-based health care was seen as a more creative route to pursue under constrained financial circumstances than simple cost reduction, and some interesting local experiments were launched.

Applying the analysis of the competitive forces in public services: Vining (2011)'s modified framework

Vining (2011) has argued that public sector organizations can usefully adapt Porterian models of strategic management, notably including the five forces framework which we earlier introduced and discussed. While public managers do not seek to maximize profits, they may well seek to maximize their autonomy (we might add also the scope of their jurisdiction) and to avoid existential threats to their mandates. While there may not be day-to-day competition between mandates, there can be long-run contestability of mandates granted by political principals to public managers.

Citing Boyne (2006) and Andrews et al. (2006), Vining argues that public agencies that do not assess their potentially influential external environment lose 'strategic fit' (a classic design school concept) and face deteriorating levels of performance which will eventually push them into a crisis and a turnaround situation. Thus, public agencies face complex external political and financial environments which they need to assess so as to identify and then respond to any threats in good time. An example in point is provided by the strategic change that occurred at an Italian local health authority that struggled to regain fit, under conditions of tough financial and political pressures (see Box 2.2).

Box 2.2   The strategic management of an Italian local health authority: managing under conditions of uncertainty and political instability

By *Elio Borgonovi*

Responding to crisis circumstances: the forming of the strategic change

In September 2005, when the newly appointed director general of the local health authority 'Rome-E,' covering the northern territory of the city of Rome, the Italian capital and administratively belonging to a region named 'Lazio,' took office, he found that the organization he was responsible for had to face some critical challenges: first, an annual deficit that had continuously increased over the previous five years and that appeared out of control, from 118 million euro in 2001 to 145 million euro in 2004; second, a monthly cash flow from the regional funding coming from the Lazio Regional Government – regional governments are responsible for health care in Italy – that in July and November of that year was even lower than the personnel wages to be paid, with a negative forecast for 2006; third, a total lack of rules and instrument to govern the activities carried out by external providers: around 85% of the services were delivered by accredited private and public hospitals or autonomous ambulatory care providers, and the local health authority had virtually no control of such processes. Finally, to complicate matters, an absence of awareness of how critical the situation was, at all levels of professional and managerial responsibility: medics and managers alike were convinced that the region would cover the deficit incurred.

At a first meeting with the director of the Health Department and the administrative director, he first made manifest two key components of the strategy-based approach he envisaged, based on two pillars: organizational innovation and the introduction of an integrated system of managerial accounting and control and clinical governance. The strategic team was coaxed – or convinced, according to other interpretations – that time was the critical variable. So, in the first 100 days, they triggered a change process that involved all the organization.

In September–October 2005, an extended organization analysis was completed, adopting a participatory approach that involved the directors of all organizational units (clinical departments, functional areas, territorial districts). At the end of this phase, in November 2005, a diagnosis of the state of the art of the organization was shared with all the first line managers, to increase the awareness of how critical the situation was. The state of the art of the organization was discussed in many meetings, and the key issues could be summarized as follows:

• The organization was highly fragmented, and only vertical hierarchical relations – line management – was considered: horizontal relations among different departments, districts, health service delivery units were poor at most;

- There was an extensive duplication of activities that caused waste and inefficiency;
- Staff functions – administrative support activities – were dispersed across departments and district, with no economy of scale or specialization being reaped;
- Organization procedures were neither explicated nor formalized – indeed, they were often completely ignored: everything was done on informal behaviour or accordingly to consolidated habits;
- There was no organizational transparency, and no clinical objectives were assigned to the organizational units; middle and senior managers did not take responsibility for the outputs delivered, the levels of efficiency and cost control or, even less, for the health outcomes of treatments delivered;
- There was weak or no control on support services, like building and technology maintenance, cleaning, security, administrative services;
- Decisions on health processes and decisions on economic impacts were completely disconnected;
- A communication policy was noticeable for its absence, either internally or externally; and
- The control on resource utilization was weak or absent.

Nevertheless, some significant positive conditions could be detected:

- There was some significant professionalism in many staff: clinicians, nurses, other care givers, laboratory and instrument technicians, middle and senior managers;
- There was a strong and diffused expectation for an explicit recognition of professionalism and career development based on merit;
- Diagnostic and outpatient services were scattered throughout the territory, representing a highly valuable asset;
- Shared and organizationally embedded values about the pillars of the public health service were widely diffused and accepted, like health as a citizen right, equity in accessibility of services, an attention for the disadvantaged groups; and
- Real estate and technology assets were available and awaited to be better exploited, by adopting proper economic criteria.

In November 2005, after the organizational analysis and diagnosis were completed, the strategic team decided to prize on culture and values – the positive features in the picture that arose from the organizational diagnosis – to trigger strategic change: accordingly, the local health authority was to operate to effect an organization in which:

- People (patient and personnel) were at the centre;
- Health was first and foremost a right of the patient;
- Continuity of care between hospital and out-hospital health services was central; and

- Quality of services was to be pursued at any level, and innovation in delivery models to achieve higher effectiveness and efficiency was to permeate the whole organization.

In 30 November 2005, a formal three-year strategic plan (2006–2008) was presented to all relevant middle and senior managers, who were asked to diffuse the principles and guidelines in their units or responsibility. The strategic plan was based on clear objectives, for which few indicators were detailed; the priorities were:

(i)   To strengthen the network delivery model in order to overcome fragmentation;
(ii) To prioritize primary and secondary prevention and patient safety;
(iii) To strengthen the clinical governance, improving actual accessibility to services (for example, one indicator was the reduction of waiting lists); and
(iv) To strengthen cost control in order to gradually reduce the deficit.

Once formally approved, the strategic plan was communicated to the Lazio Regional Government, which had meantime been submitted to a special financial control procedure by the central government, because of the high level of total deficit accumulated over the previous ten years (even difficult to account for – some estimates spoke of a deficit close to the amount of ten billion euros).

Assigning organizational responsibilities

As a support tool to implement the strategic plan, in 2006, a formalized budgetary system – patterned on a Management by Objectives logic – was introduced: each organizational unit was asked to submit a proposal for the objectives to be achieved, indicators to measure the results, and amount of resources needed. The three components were discussed and negotiated with the director general, supported by a budget staff unit.

Moreover, several multidisciplinary task forces were set up, with the purpose of addressing a certain range of critical issues and proposing innovative solutions – to be evaluated in terms of improvement of health, quality of services delivered, efficiency and cost containment, and technical and economic sustainability. Examples of such task forces, by their mandate, were negotiation of new agreements with private accredited providers; integrated elderly people services; integrated information systems, rationalization of out-hospital delivery units to pursue economy of scale objective, legal disputes with services providers; sanitation procedures, patient and personnel safety; training and professional development for medical doctor, nurses, and other professional groups; primary care rationalization; and internal and external communication.

Auditing procedures to have a better recognition on hidden debt for 2004 and 2005 period were formally approved at the beginning of 2006. Accounting and financial reports for these two years did not recognize some debts.

A clear accounting of the situation was a condition for defining a reliable financial budget for year 2006 that was coherent with the Lazio Region guideline to reduce local health delivery organization expenditure.

At the end of the '100 days phase,' the strategic team completed the organization chart and appointed around 100 senior management who got the responsibility for the high-level organization units (hospital clinical departments, districts, administrative departments), who became the key actors and players for the change process.

They received the commitment to activate the objective-responsibility tree. They had the responsibility to define and negotiate objective and resource allocation for units, programmes, and activities carried out internally to their unit. Logically, the responsibility can be split as follows: implementation of organization guidelines and rules, personnel motivation, efficient use of resources, problem solving and innovation, integrated approach to patients' problems, results control, and internal and external communication.

The implementation of strategy

The first three-year strategic plan was renewed and extended till 2010. The implementation process was effected by focusing on the reorganization of services, the setting out of a formal, and gradually more and more detailed, programming and budgeting system, and the strengthening of the capacity to define clear objectives to be assigned to the external service providers (local health authorities in Italy are competent for the crucial public function of interpreting the patients' needs – and ensuring the 'insurance function' proper of a universal National Health Service; they often act also as service providers, but in many instances, service delivery is carried out by autonomous accredited health service providers, both public and private).

The implementation process raised harsh conflicts and passive or formalistic compliance – resilience behaviour – as many professionals holding personal and organizational power and connections with politicians and external lobbyists did not accept the kind of transparency, clear rules and evaluation based on results introduced by the new strategy.

Internal conflicts were made even harsher by the rigid financial constraints imposed by the regional government, which had in turn been submitted to a stringent 'financial recovery plan' negotiated with the central government. However, the director general – our main strategist, though in alliance with other key protagonists like the administrative director who together formed the 'strategy team' – utilized the external constraint imposing the redesign of the overall health services supply chain (in the direction of strengthening the primary and outpatient services) as a lever to speed up the implementation of the reorganization plan.

Yet the implementation process was negatively affected by external institutional and political condition – the outer context, characterized in Italy at all levels of government by frequent government turnover occurring before the natural end of the legislative period, dynamics that have a profound impact on public management (Mele and Ongaro 2014). In 2008–2009, the Lazio Regional Government experienced a political and institutional crisis. The governor was forced to resign, new elections took place, and the governmental majority changed. This also affected policy making and managerial structure, and the effect was that the strategic plan of the local health authority 'Rome-E' was never formally approved by the regional government; moreover, the procedure of appointment of the director general – who was in charge for four years – came to be legally contested. Notwithstanding such unfavourable circumstances, he and the strategy team went on with the substantive implementation of the plan they had decided in 2006–2007.

In 2008, the first results of the strategic plan started to become visible: new services for citizens has been set up, the trend in outlays appeared under control, a significant reduction of the delay in payments to the suppliers was achieved, which also enable to get lower prices and to activate the virtuous circle: respect of payment terms, reduction of prices, reduction of expenditures, availability of cash for timely payments; the local health authority 'Rome-E' could now guarantee payments within 180 days, while in 2005 payment time was over 360 days. In 2009, the diagnosis, cure, and care integrated processes approach was introduced, aimed to reduce duplication of activities and inefficiencies and guarantee the continuity of care. Moreover, new priority setting rules for different health needs were introduced, adopting as criterion the severity of the illness and a first step of health economic evaluation (benefit-cost criteria).

The strategic plan – developed and adapted *en route* – turned out to work. The local health authority acquired a stronger organizational identity; it was capable of strategically defining its positioning in the regional health delivery system, and notably in the hyper-complex Rome metropolitan area. The objective that it was capable of achieving can be summarized as follows:

- In the period 2006–2009, the respect of all the financial constraints negotiated with the Lazio Regional Government;
- The set-up and development of a budgeting and reporting system supported by a cost accounting system, based on cost centres and clear accountability lines;
- The strengthening of organizational units managers' capacity to monitor and evaluate costs in relation to the outputs and activity objectives;
- The integration of the cost accounting and the financial accounting system, enabling the director general to have a monthly monitoring and control;
- The revision of the revenue procedure, which led to increased revenues for some million euros and contributed to the reduction of the deficit; and
- The introduction of the debt management system that enabled a better cash management with the reduction of financial costs.

In 2010, the director general ended his mandate. An unplanned but lucky event led to him being replaced by another member of the strategy team, the previous administrative director, who was appointed by the new regional government as director general: he continued the implementation of the strategic plan he had contributed to design in 2006.

Vining (2011) then proposes an adapted 'public agency' Five Forces framework which specifically adds the extent of political influence as an extra dimension not considered by Porter. This analytic tool could enable public managers to think in a structured way about how to respond to this distinctive additional condition. Vining's Public Agency Five Forces model (2011) also considers and also modifies some parameters of Porter's original model to make them more appropriate to public services settings:

(i)   *Relation with suppliers*: also relevant to public agencies where there is some evidence they may be uninformed customers.

(ii) *New entrants/substitutes*: also relevant to public agencies where technological shifts (rise of email and the decline of the traditional role of the Post Office; electronically based 'self service' technologies, such as filing tax returns online) may be significant. In quasi markets, there may also be a more credible threat of new entrants than previously.

(iii) *Pressure from sponsors/customers*: may require some modification in the public services context, as often services are purchased by proxies and commissioners, rather than the end users, who may be relatively powerful.

(iv) *Intensity of rivalry*: this concept may be difficult to apply in traditional public services settings as many agencies have monopolies. However, we add that there has been some growth of long-term contestability of jurisdictions in some systems where poor public providers may lose their licence to operate (e.g. local education authorities in the UK).

Interestingly, it is further argued by Vining (2011) that different types of public agencies lie on a spectrum in terms of the intensity of their political control: from presidential/prime ministerial executive agencies on the highly politicized side of the spectrum, through conventional ministries/bureaux, down to corporatized agencies (like the UK executive agencies) and then state-owned enterprises or public/private hybrids where political control is weakest. These last two categories of weaker political control have in our view recently grown, reflecting a major NPM-based policy to reduce the scope of direct political control in favour of enhanced operational management that can deliver high 'performance' (e.g. executive agencies). In this model, the political centre 'steers but does not row': it agrees with a mandate and a performance contract with the newly spun out executive agencies but does not get involved on a day-to-day basis.

Vining (2011) makes the point that formal institutional reforms designed to isolate the bureau from operational political influence may still be counteracted by informal political influencing (including client lobbies). Indeed, studies on the autonomy and steering and control of public agencies point to a varied set of factors all dynamically interplaying in determining the 'actual' autonomy of public agencies (Laegreid and Verhoest 2010; Verhoest et al. 2012; for a country-specific case, e.g. Barbieri et al. 2010, 2013).

The nature and extent of political influence exerted on a public agency therefore remains an important factor within public services organizations and includes various subcomponents (Vining 2011), namely: (i) the political saliency of programme outputs; (ii) the diversity of the institutions seeking to influence; (iii) the number of institutions seeking to influence; (iv) the effectiveness of structural isolating mechanisms;

and (v) client lobbying capacity and effectiveness. This analytic framework can be used to assess the extent of 'strategic autonomy' experienced by a public agency in both policy and financial-organizational terms. The greater the level of such autonomy, the greater (in our terms) is the capacity for self-directed strategic behaviour by the agency (we return on this topic in Chapter 7).

2.3 Mintzbergian strategy: emergence, organizational learning, and context

Mintzberg is a major author who developed a set of ideas about strategic management which stand as an alternative to Porterian thinking. His 'emergent' perspective reacts against the premises of the earlier design and strategic planning schools, by drawing more on sociological and cognitive ideas than orthodox industrial economics.

Strategy is here defined as a process or as a 'pattern in a stream of decisions' (see Mintzberg and Waters 1985, an important article which first elaborated the notion) rather than as adherence to a fixed long-term plan. It may be easier to detect it in retrospect than at the time and does not depend on a formal long-term plan. It is not helpful to separate two distinct stages of formulation and implementation; rather, the process is iterative and not linear. Strategy making is seen in pluralist terms and can involve a greater plurality of actors than solely the CEO or top management. Strategies can be traced back to a stream of little or local decisions which only later build into a pattern and then go on to trigger major change, through a process of 'lock in' or path dependency. The school claims to have high descriptive validity – that is it captures how strategy is really made in organizations (Mintzberg et al. 2009, p. 187), partly because it uses field-based methods of research rather than axiomatic theory. While it is strong on description, it is reluctant to engage in prescription, much of which it is felt may prove unrealistic in practice.

The emergent perspective holds out the possibility that declared strategies may be not implemented or realized in practice. The formal strategic plans of the 1960s often led to major implementation deficits in the 1970s, in the public sector as in the private sector. This was a seen as a major phenomenon, the causes of which should be studied through a novel conceptual prism which did not assume perfect implementation. The perspective of strategy as an emergent pattern is sceptical of the top-down control of strategic planning and more interested in stimulating organizational learning (see also Mintzberg et al. 2009, Chapter 7) within ongoing strategy development. It places a greater role on experiential knowledge or even intuition as a source of strategic insight, as opposed to formal knowledge gained through specified analytic techniques. The strategists become 'whoever can learn' and creating the conditions for facilitating knowledge sharing takes centre stage.

The emergent perspective is linked to the learning school of strategic management. Mintzberg et al. (2009, Chapter 6) suggest that this school builds on the 'logical incrementalism' model of decision making (Quinn 1980). Incrementalism is a theoretical perspective which suggests that there are severe limits to rational analytic planning, both cognitively (no one can possess and process all the information required) and politically (strategy making is often a political process which involves bargaining and trade-offs between different stakeholder groups and which cannot be controlled in advance). The model of 'logical incrementalism' suggests that strategy formulation and implementation may rather evolve in a step-by-step and continual process but does not entirely rule out the role of senior management in a corporation or other organization in loosely guiding this process, albeit in an imperfect manner. The senior management team is still seen as the strategic core, although it is recognized that they have to struggle to guide a complex organization in part by building implementation capacity. From this perspective, a significant role is placed on conscious managerial learning over time about how to implement a strategy.

Mintzberg et al. (2009, p. 217) draw out the key axioms of the learning school. These include the idea that strategy takes the form 'of a process of learning over time in which, at the limit, formulation and implementation become indistinguishable.' This statement has implications for the changed role of strategic leadership: 'the role of leadership thus becomes not to preconceive deliberate strategies but to manage the process of strategic learning, whereby novel strategies can emerge.'

Senge and Suzuki's (1994) influential book on building a learning organization has important implications for a consideration of the nature of strategic management and leadership activity. It draws on interesting Eastern Asian ideas of the development of personal mastery and authenticity at work. In Senge's view, leaders should operate as coaches and stewards more than as conventional Western line managers. Much of the learning is seen as proceeding through teams rather than single individuals, no matter how senior.

Mintzberg's (1983) has also developed important work on the impact of organizational context on patterns of strategy making. Building on extensive case-based empirical work, he proposed a typology of five different organizational archetypes into which, he argued, all organizations would fall. Importantly, strategy making could proceed differently in each archetype, as it was related to the context of the organization. Strategy could not be based on highly generic and acontextual prescriptions in a Porterian manner.

Two of his five archetypes are drawn from distinctive public sector settings and exhibit idiosyncratic strategy processes. The first archetype of special interest to us is the *professionalized bureaucracy*. Many routine public sector functions have now been privatized, downsized, or automated (e.g. in social security), but much of that which remains is highly professionalized (including professions in health, education, science, or law). As the contemporary public sector is now highly professionalized, the influence of the public professions in strategy making is an important theme, with medicine and law being the ideal typical examples of traditionally powerful professional groups. Yet earlier schools of thought did not consider the influence of professionals on strategy making in any depth. An example in point is the development of strategic thinking in the French defence administration over the years (Box 2.3).

Box 2.3   Strategy in the military field: politics and the weight of De Gaulle's inheritance in France

By *Robert Fouchet and Marius Bertolucci*

The etymology of the word strategy reminds us that this 'art' originated in the military field, where it was a primary concern well before it became of interest for other public and private organizations. Facing the complexity of contemporary world, over the past few years, the defence organizations in France have manifested a renewed attention to how strategic thinking is produced. Defence organizations operate at the crossroads of the weight of the past, of past choices that shape the range of the available options; the contingencies of the present, with its requirements and operational constraints; and the need to prepare for an unknown future. Politics and political responses to budgetary pressures powerfully affect the way in which strategic thinking unfolds.

Major events in recent world history (the fall of the Berlin Wall, the 9/11 attack, the 2008 financial and economic crisis, the Arab spring) have put pressure on defence organizations to adapt to a changed world. The acceleration of the frequency of these changes is matched by a shortening of the time of issuance of the main formal strategic plan in the sector: the White Paper on Defence (1973, 1994, 2008, 2013). Because of changes in international relations, but also because of the dynamics of the budgetary policy, strategy and strategy making have taken a new significance in France.

The 2008 White Paper established a new strategic function, named 'knowledge and anticipation,' renewed in its 2013 version, in charge of providing the 'intelligence and foresight that enables the strategic anticipation that informs action' (p. 70). However, doubts have been raised as to whether such act of establishing a new entity may be more a pretext than an effective response to the perceived weak influence of the French army strategic thinking on the international scene. The academia and private sector actors (like think tanks) are often ignored in favour of historical experts, who remain the key source of policy advice in France, and this may have occurred to the detriment of novel and bold ways of thinking strategically about the future of the French army. To cope with this perceived weakness, since 2008, the Ministry of Defence initiated a consolidation across the different services with the purpose of increasing coordination and mobilizing more interdisciplinary cognitive resources, which resulted in the establishment in 2010 of the *Comité de coherence de la recherché stratégique et de la prospective de défense* (CCRP, Committee for the consistency of strategic research and the perspective of defence). Defined as a 'governance' body embedded in the very heart of the Ministry of Defence where the organizational principle of hierarchy and a hierarchical culture are at the core, it was intended as a structural arrangement for coordinating various organizations (the *Direction des Affaires Stratégiques* – DAS – or Direction for Strategic Affairs; the *Etàt Majeur des Armées* – EMA – or Chief of Defence Staff; the *Direction Général des Armament* – DGA – or Directorate General of Armaments; and others). To the same end, resorting to external advisors was deemed crucial, as this represented an opportunity to gain information and otherwise unattainable analyses within the institutional hierarchical structure. As part of this process, a number of military organizations were charged with forward-looking tasks: the same DAS, the *centre interarmées de Concepts de Doctrine et d'Epérimentation* – CICDE – or Joint Forces Centre for Concept Development, Doctrine and Experimentation, set up in 2005 and entrusted tasks encompassing, interestingly, 'knowledge management and the learning from field operations,' the *DGA*, that became responsible for the 'technological outlook, development and forecasting.' A major concern in both public and behind-the-closed doors debates was decoupling long-term planning – embodied, inter alia, in the 30-year prospective plane (*PP30*) – from what was dubbed 'the tyranny of the urgency.' The specificity of the French administration dominated by the glue formed by the high-flyers belonging to the *grand corps de l'État*, present also within the Defence Ministry, was deemed to constitute an obstacle to foresight and forward-looking exercises (Mérindol 2008), also because of the limited channels for policy advice from outside the bureaucracy, a feature of the French public sector (Pollitt and Bouckaert 2009).

Perhaps surprising is that the majority of strategic studies in the military field are available to the public, thereby including the White Paper on Defence, which is the most prominent example. It appears that events closer to the time of issuance of this document may have a disproportionate influence in the drafting of it. For instance, the intervention in Mali that occurred in January 2013 influenced the writing of the last 2013 White Paper. The lessons learnt concerned the importance of armed forces already deployed on the operational theatre, the role of special forces and the device called *Guépard*, alongside a wider set of considerations about a future in which the army would be smaller in size, but highly trained and well-equipped.

Yet politics and the dynamics of administrative reforms and of the budgetary policy burst into the scene – bringing into it their much shorter temporal horizon. The *General Review of Public Policies* and subsequent reforms, aimed at introducing a form of systematic 'spending review' tightly led by politicians, had a deep impact. Such interventions were temporally ill-matched with the burst of the 2008 financial crisis, and ultimately led to drastic reductions to recruitment and its corollary of brutal deep reorganizations. Senior military authorities, including the Chief of Defence Staff, the Admiral Edouard Guillaud, publicly spoke of serious risks of a loss of morale and spotted the high turnover of non-commissioned military personnel, causing thereby a loss of irreplaceable expertise gained in operating land. A clear split between young officers and the top brass also became evident. In 2013, a group of a dozen lieutenants of the French army, dubbed the collective Marc Bloch,[2] upon request of anonymity, reported to the press their discontent, regretting that strategic thinking was conceived of as an exclusive prerogative of the top tiers of the military organizations, and arguing for enlarged participation and more inclusive processes. Perhaps this was revelatory of a perceived need, if not an outright shift, from a conception of strategy as rational planning (echoing the precepts of the planning school) to a learning school approach whereby the contribution of 'whoever can learn' gets to be recognized, also in a hierarchical organizational culture like the military one.

One final question deserves consideration: is partisan politics influential on strategic thinking in the defence sector in France, or is there one basic strategic stance (of which the army is the custodian, on behalf of the nation)? It appears that there is one basic strategic stance (see e.g. the general recognition of the function performed by the nuclear deterrent, which was never questioned). The shadow of General De Gaulle, who used to say: 'I am on neither side, I am on the side of France' is perennial in this ministry. Non-partisanship seems also a dominant note of the budgetary policy for this field. Thus, the downsizing of the army occurred by means of the RGPP effected under the government of Nicolas Sarkozy, in line with the 2009–2015 military budgetary law curtailing 54,000 jobs was matched by a further staff reduction of 24,000 by the subsequent Socialist government that took office in 2012. The combined effect might be for the French State all-powerful during the 'Glorious Thirty,' to give way to a light(er) State that will need to rely more on rapid learning, in conditions of shrinking resources and increased uncertainty.

Mintzberg's (1983, Chapter 10) analysis of strategy making in professionalized settings fits such settings as universities and teaching hospitals well. It predicts a decentralized and incremental approach to strategy making, with localized goals of continuing subgroup expansion espoused by professionals. It is in one sense bureaucratic with a strong set of rules and regulations which govern (for example) transactions between different professional groups (e.g. surgeons and physicians). Yet it is also strongly influenced by the key professionals that it nominally employs but who retain important sources of dominance (Freidson 1970).

Professional segments (e.g. different academic departments) remain 'pigeon holed' in silos and tend to have a weak corporate overview. There can be dense and time-consuming inter-segment conflict and bargaining over turf and the extent of jurisdictions (Abbott 1988). So, for example if an academic department proposes a new teaching programme in a contested field, neighbouring academic departments in the university may suspect encroachment and demand more time for 'consultation.' Administrative elements are here weakly developed and facilitative rather than directive in nature so cannot countermand these time-consuming processes of inter-professional negotiation.

Within this configuration, severe problems may arise in relation to the handling of radical or urgent organizational change (including corporate-wide change, retrenchment, or crisis management) and also in the handling of 'difficult colleagues' who do not engage in effective self-regulation and who are resistant to challenge from their peers. Power lies in the hands of a college of senior professionals rather than the workforce as a whole, which is seen as deeply stratified: so, the form is more an oligarchy than either a monarchy or a democracy. The wider professional fields (professional and epistemic communities) outside the organization also exert strong influence on their members inside the organization: Mintzberg (1982, p. 262) notes: 'in the professional bureaucracy, the strategy formation process is controlled primarily by the professional associations outside the structure, secondarily by the professionals of the operating core themselves and only after that by the administrators.' An example would be the various Royal Colleges in UK Medicine which help define field-wide norms and expectations.

The second archetype of particular interest to public services organizations is the *Ad Hocracy* which characterizes highly creative organizations (he analyzed such public services organizations as NASA and the Canadian National Film Board) which need to support sophisticated and complex innovations over a long period. The retention of flexibility is a key objective, pursued within a highly organic and project-based form of working. Power is delegated to a wide variety of staff including key experts and creative personnel, but with fewer rules and regulations than in the professionalized bureaucracy as there is a premium on radical and fast innovation. Multidisciplinary teams are assembled to work on particular projects, disbanded, and then regrouped. In terms of strategy formation, there is unlikely to be an explicit strategic plan; rather, strategies emerge in a stream of decisions about which projects to support and fund. For example, Mintzberg (1983) found that two-thirds of the projects commissioned by the Canadian National Film Board were proposed by the Board's own employees and funded from its general budget. Projects were approved by a standing committee, but proposals come from the creative filmmakers. Some trends and groupings in commissioning decisions may be apparent after the event, but they are relatively weak and may shift from one period to another. We note that this form could well be present in various media (e.g. the BBC), cultural (e.g. Arts Council), and science-based organizations.

Mintzberg's work is attractive to public management scholars because he develops a wide typology of different organizations rather than assuming a competitive firm operating within a market structure. He is actively interested in the analysis of public services settings, rather than treating them as residuals. His argument that the nature of strategy making varies by organizational context is furthermore operationalized within a range of major settings. His analysis of professions and 'creatives' and their strong influence on strategy making is additive (Porter's analysis of health care, by contrast, is light on exploring the role played by clinical professionals). Critics argue that Mintzberg is strong on the analysis of strategic process, but weaker on the content of strategy (so what would be a good strategy for this organization?) and consideration of the impact of strategy on performance.

2.4 The entrepreneurial school and social enterprises

The Entrepreneurial School of strategy is here introduced with regard to entrepreneurship in the public sector. This school is further developed in more detail in Chapter 5, with particular reference to not-for-profit organizations.

Accounts of strategy making in small and medium enterprises (SMEs) often highlight the strong, personal, influence of a founder or entrepreneur rather than formal corporate or business planning systems. Within novel human services settings or small non-profit organizations, similar processes may be evident but dependent on 'social' rather than economic entrepreneurs with the vision and energy to construct new social settings: Pettigrew (1979)'s longitudinal study of the strategy of an unusual boarding school highlighted the imprinting role of the founding headmaster in setting its educational ideology and culture over a long period. Ormrod et al. (2007) similarly explored the enduring role of founding psychiatrists in innovative mental health settings in setting a collective clinical ideology. These studies were influenced by a now unfairly neglected American literature developed in the 1970s on the creation of enduring and alternative social settings (Kanter 1972; Sarason 1976), which examined the role of founders and of collective commitment mechanisms they developed within these settings to sustain their development.

An entrepreneur is often seen as an individual who accepts a high level of personal risk to launch a new product or service, acting as a founder and an owner manager of an SME. Mintzberg (1973) characterized a distinctive form of strategy making in the entrepreneurial organization. First, it would be dominated by the search for exciting new opportunities rather than dealing with existing operational problems. Second, power lies in the hands of the CEO/founder, often unwilling to delegate operational responsibilities (possibly leading to overload and bottlenecks at the top). Third, strategy making tends not to be incremental, rather to take the form of 'bold strokes' with the possibility of high payoff: the CEO thrives in conditions of high uncertainty and risk taking. Fourth, the strategy is driven by the goal of growth, in part to satisfy the high ego needs of the CEO. The disadvantages of this form include difficulties in succession planning; an over-concentration of power in the hands of one person (especially if that person is also the founder of the organization), a quirky tone, and over-involvement in detail by the CEO perhaps to the point of obsession.

Mintzberg et al. (2009, Chapter 5) sees the entrepreneurial perspective as highlighting the role of a single individual (like the design school), but also the importance of experience and intuition in generating a strategic vision (unlike the rational analytics of the design school). 'Vision' is seen in lying in the mind of the leader, and it may be a semi-formed general idea or an image of a desired future rather than a fully formed plan. Entrepreneurial strategists typically seek to grow the organization by occupying a distinctive and protected niche which fits with their vision.

McGrath (2006) reviews the academic literature on entrepreneurship and its relationship with strategy making. The field is important as some entrepreneurs can make a substantial or even stepwise contribution to economic change and wealth creation through start-ups in a way that would be difficult for mature corporations to do. Spotting a gap in the market and launching a new product or service which fills it is the core of the entrepreneurial process, as in the early high-tech firms in Silicon Valley. However, such 'high impact' start-ups are rare and the failure rate for new ventures is high, especially after an initial honeymoon period, given frequent resource constraints (such as lack of access to working capital or of experienced management if they expand).

We argue (Ongaro and Ferlie 2020) that the entrepreneurial school as explicated by Mintzberg may be applied to public services organizations too, provided qualifying conditions are taken into account. A key condition to consider concerns the statutory limit to the term of office in the public sector, a feature of most public posts, at least in liberal-democratic regimes which somewhat restricts the power of senior management.

We seek to develop our argument about the applicability and explanatory usefulness of the entrepreneurial school for public services organizations, and notably also for core public agencies whose organizational model and governance arrangements are bureaucratic-Weberian, through the case study of how the director general of the European Aviation Safety Agency (EASA) led this public sector organization, an agency of the European Union (EU), to become the second most important player on the world stage in civil aviation, after the US Federal Aviation Administration (FAA), over the relatively short time period 2003–2012 (see Box 2.4 and more widely Ongaro and Ferlie 2020, from which the case analysis and this elaboration are drawn). The case shows how the entrepreneurial school of strategic management helps explain the behaviour of 'core' public bureaucracies – organizations established by and operating under the regulation of public and administrative law – provided the distinctive conditions for *public* entrepreneurship to occur are appropriately profiled.

What are such conditions? Two are especially relevant. The first is that the chief of the organization comes to be identified and perceived as, in a certain sense, also the 'founder' of the organization: in the EASA case, its 'founding director' was the first person to be hired by it and for some time the only one; he also had the opportunity to have a certain time frame ahead as the chief executive (a five-year renewable once term of office) and to have concentrated multiple organizational powers in his hands, not least by having been in charge of human resources and the recruitment process since the inception (at the beginning directly by performing also as director of human resources – HR – later indirectly by supervising the HR director). Entrepreneurs need a time horizon ahead of them to make their organization grow.

The second condition lies in the director of the agency enjoying a high degree of formal authority similar to the concentration of executive authority generally entrusted by commercial law to the entrepreneur in a privately owned organization – conditions which were detectable in full in the EASA case (given the corporate governance configuration of the agency).

In sum,

> under the combined conditions of, first, circumstances which may replicate the role of 'founder' of the organisation, and, second, a power base (formal authority over her/his own organisation) that resembles that of an entrepreneur in the business sector, if the top official of the public agency is also endowed with the leadership skills providing the required authoritativeness, the strategy process in public agencies may potentially unfold along the pattern of the entrepreneurial school in strategic management, marked by one person, the entrepreneur, leading the organisation in a visionary way, by exploiting the opportunities that arise in the environment (also by taking the appropriate dose of risk), envisioning the future of the organisation, energising and mobilising the people in and around it – all such things being done in a public sector organisation in ways broadly similar to those detected by the literature on the entrepreneurial school for private sector organisations.
>
> (Ongaro and Ferlie 2020, p. 370)

There is, of course, one fundamental difference between the narrative from the entrepreneurial school as it has been applied so far to commercial sector organizations (see the account of the retail chain set up by Sam Steinberg, starting from a small grocery in Montreal, Canada, by Mintzberg and Waters 1982) and the narrative developed for the public sector: office holding expires in public sector organizations, differently from the private sector entrepreneurs who 'own their creature' (not always and necessarily, but quite often). In fact, differently from the entrepreneur who establishes her or his own business through a private law act, the public entrepreneur has to be appointed by an external appointing authority; to recall Lynn (2006), '[the public sector] is constituted through sovereign mandate, the [private sector] through individual initiative.' Therefore, the main difference between entrepreneurs in the private sector, especially when they are the founder of the enterprise and property rights ensure them legal control over their creature, and entrepreneurs in the public sector lies in the statutory limitations to office holding. Public entrepreneurs have an 'expiry date' as well as generally no entitlement to organize succession, and they must act within such time frame: they have to deploy their skills and energies within such horizon and are faced with the challenge to 'act within constrained time frame.' This is a defining feature of entrepreneurship in the public sector. The specifics of how it is articulated in actual cases hinges upon the governance structure of the organization under consideration (like e.g. for how many terms of office the general director may be renewed).

There is an important link between the profile of the public entrepreneur as outlined here and the notion of the 'entrepreneurial public manager' as developed in the Public Value school of thought of strategic management, which we examine in Chapter 3. In that school, public managers are considered 'entrepreneurs' in that, like their counterparts in the private sector, they create value – specifically *public* value – through innovation in policy and public services: in the Public Value school, their attribute as entrepreneurs lies in their value-creation orientation, in being the 'creator of public value.' It follows that in the Public Value school, the analytical emphasis is on how to define and measure public value, and issues of definition and measurement of public value are centre-stage; also central in the Public Value school is the relationship between public managers turned innovators and elected officials: this is a question of the authorizing environment which provides legitimacy to public managers in operating in an entrepreneurial fashion.

Conversely, and in many regards complementarily (and not unproblematically, see Bellone and Goerl 1992), the application of Mintzberg's entrepreneurial school to public services organizations enables to focus especially on the issue of the entrepreneurial skills that are required of public entrepreneurs to succeed 'on their own terms,' that is in the terms of getting their organization to grow and thrive in bureaucratic environments which can be as 'threatening' to the long-term survival and prosperity of the organization as industrial competitive markets are, albeit for different reasons. The answer to the question 'Are Government Organisations Immortal?', famously asked by Herbert Kaufman in a 1976 book, is negative, and survival skills in the form of entrepreneurship are required for public organizations to continue in existence and to thrive, as illustrated by the EASA case (see Box 2.4).

Box 2.4   Public entrepreneurship at the European Aviation Safety Agency (EASA)

In the field of air transport, in the first decade of the 2000s, the EU has brought about a major change globally. In fact, in air transport

> The European Union has brought about a revolution . . . before the creation of the single market, European aviation was characterized by protectionism, collusion, fragmentation [where] Governments used their authority to promote the interests of state-owned 'national champions of the air.' . . . Action by the Union has transformed the regulation of the sector. The EU . . . has displaced a state-centred regime with a multilateral framework of rules that are enforced by a supranational regulatory authority' (Kassim and Stevens 2010, p. 1). . . . As a consequence, 'the Union is an international actor in aviation and not merely an international presence' (Kassim and Stevens

2010, p. 156). Internally, the EU developed a new regulatory architecture with 'impact on national policy, policymaking, and the structure of the European industry.'

(Kassim and Stevens 2010, p. 216)

The strategic behaviour of the European Aviation Safety Agency (EASA), notably its drive towards impressive organizational growth under the leadership of its 'founding director,' Mr Patrick Goudou, powerfully contributed to make such a revolution happen. In fact, EASA has grown in less than ten years (from its establishment in 2002 to the end of second mandate as director of Mr Goudou) into a well-established organization on the international stage, having dramatically expanded its tasks and assigned competencies. With its annual budget of about 130 million euro and more than 600 staff, EASA has grown into one of the largest EU agencies (Barbieri and Ongaro 2008; Ongaro et al. 2012; Ongaro et al. 2015).

EASA underwent such an impressive growth in large measure, thanks to the strategic guidance of its executive director since its establishment. It is a story of how a public entrepreneur led a public agency, whose future was at the time of its establishment highly uncertain, to become a central institution in air transport, at European and global levels. EASA can be seen as an organization permeated by a clear sense of direction and perspective ('to become the Federal Aviation Administration of the EU') and equipped with the capacities to implement such vision, a state of affairs that reflected a set of consistent decisions taken in a fast-moving and often not benign environment.

The European Commission played a key role in the structural design of establishing an agency replacing a looser network among national aviation authorities (Pierre and Peters 2009), but the impressive growth of EASA owes extensively to the bold entrepreneurial approach by Goudou, a French national, with a degree in engineering at the prestigious *Ecole Polytechnique* and significant experience in the French public administration, notably in the defence sector. A military by training and career, before joining EASA he had reached the higher tiers in the French *Armée* (the army). He held previous responsibilities in procurement and ran a large service organization in the defence sector.

The newly appointed director imagined a vision for EASA. There was an exemplar at hand: the FAA of the United States of America. Whilst the differences between a composite supranational politico-institutional architecture like the EU and a nation state (and the world superpower) like the US were crystal clear to the director of EASA, the FAA was taken as an aspirational model to look at, a perspective that might inspire behaviours and provide consistency to organizational decisions over time: 'to become the European FAA' became the shared motto and narrative for the future of EASA. The FAA was not only an inspiration from far away: the FAA was factually supportive to EASA, and it signed up an agreement for setting up a close collaboration with EASA in 2005, when EASA was moving its first steps. The significance of such agreement can hardly be overestimated: it did not just constitute a working partnership, but it signalled to EASA's stakeholders the model towards which the agency was heading – it provided the vision for EASA. The agreement struck with the FAA was put in frames and hanging to be very visible to whoever visited the executive director or his close aides in the director's corridor at the sixteenth floor of the Cologne headquarters of EASA. This vision of EASA as the European FAA and the imagery associated with it powerfully contributed to legitimizing the new vision broached by the director, and to win consensus both 'downwards', within the rank-and-file of the agency staff which had started to recruit only a couple of years before, and 'upwards', in the Management Board where Member States are represented.

At about the same time (2004), the process of recruiting the staff of the agency started, and the director was heavily engaged in the selection process, chairing all the competent committees: a very hands-on approach to choosing the new collaborators and the staff of the agency at large. Due to his unique status of having been the first person to be hired by the agency after its establishment, and to have directly or indirectly supervised the process of appointment of each of the staff that entered the agency over the subsequent years, Mr Goudou came to be perceived not just as the formal hierarchical top of the organization but also, and significantly, as 'the founder' of the organization, the one that everybody when joining the agency recognized as the ultimate boss, the leader which moulded the organization, 'authoritative' due to his charismatic leadership, alongside the formal status of being the top hierarchical authority.

The organizational development of EASA may be interpreted as unfolding along four phases, in each of which Goudou's leadership proved decisive. The first one started in 2003, with the establishment of EASA in provisional premises in Brussels, and ended in 2006, when EASA overcame a financial crisis, determined by a tough confrontation with National Aviation Authorities about the system of fees in place. By that time, the agency, operating at full steam in its Cologne premises, had gained the legitimacy of its main stakeholders and interlocutors: primarily the aircraft industry and the same national aviation authorities. Pierre and Peters (2009) studied the recognition and acceptance of EASA by its environment, seen as a process of institutionalization paralleled by deinstitutionalization of the previous institutional arrangement, namely, the loose networking of national authorities. In leading EASA through this phase, Goudou's leadership style was daring in terms of risk-taking (notably as seen in the significant administrative risk he took upon himself by signing off thousands of aviation certifications, in the absence of a fully operational supporting administration); it was also confrontational with national authorities, yet displaying authoritativeness, enabling EASA to carve its space and assert itself in the now 'Europeanized' policy subsystem.

The second phase spans 2006–2008, a period marked by a turbulent and impressive growth in the competencies and decision powers of the agency, epitomized in the 2008 recasting of the mandate of the agency and accompanied by significant increases of the financial and personnel resources administered by the agency, and concluded by the renewal of the executive director, Mr Goudou, in the stint for the subsequent five-year term. The leadership style was 'empire-builder mode' in the way magnificently depicted by Mintzberg et al.

(2009), whereby organizational growth and institutionalization of the standing in the organizational environment became the overarching goal driving organizational efforts under the direction of Goudou.

The third phase encompasses 2008–2010 and may be placed under the label of the 'consolidation' of the agency in its recognized role in aviation safety and the running of its operations with a significant component of in-house activities (initially when the agency started, it had to outsource all its tasks, with the sole exception of the key act of issuance of authorization to fly, as it had no internal capabilities to execute the tasks). The leadership accompanied the transition from 'heroic' to 'normal' times also by increasing delegation to managers.

The fourth and final period (2011–2012) was one of looming budgetary cuts, which had however not prevented further growth of the agency into the subsequent decade and beyond.

Source: based on Ongaro and Ferlie (2020)

This entrepreneurial perspective may be relevant also to strategy making in social enterprises, NGOs, and novel human services settings which also often grow up around one inspirational leader or founder. The quantity and quality of technical and management support may here be more uneven than in corporate settings, accentuating the power of the visible leader and reducing checks and balances (Hatten 1982) on one-person control. However, the level of energy and inspiration may be higher in these settings than in public bureaux, displaying a more vital organizational culture. In Chapter 5, we will consider the implications of the literature on entrepreneurial strategy making for social enterprises and other not-for-profit settings in more detail.

2.5 The cultural school

The design school puts emphasis on the alignment of strategy and structure, and it draws its inspiration and imagery from the large and decentralized American corporation as a preferred organizational form (e.g., Chandler 1962). Its prescription (often diffused through expanding and increasingly influential international management consultancies, McKenna 2006) was frequently one of structural reorganization to converge on this multi-divisional form. In the 1980s, this perspective was radically challenged by the very different cultural school, working in an anthropological tradition, fuelled by the rise of the Japanese economy with its very different model of the firm.

The growth of the cultural school was then fuelled by the changing economic circumstances. By the early 1980s, traditionally dominant American firms faced a growing challenge from a resurgent economy in Japan, with leading firms such as Honda and Toyota emerging. Such Japanese firms often did not have a reputation for radical technological innovation; so why were they so successful? They appeared to be organized in a very different way from Western firms, able to ensure consistently high quality (using such devices as quality circles) and displaying strong and positive work group cultures based on lifelong employment, rather than the Western pattern of adversarial industrial relations.

The influential text by Pascale and Athos (1981) provided intensive and reflective case studies of distinctive Japanese and American firms. Their writing emphasized the role of strong cultures in guiding high performance in Japanese firms, such as the 'spiritual values' which appeared to underpin the example of Matsushita. Japanese culture (including in the domain of corporate culture) was less short termist and action orientated than Western culture and more reflective, balanced, and deft. It was also less individualistic and more collectivist.

Pascale and Athos' (1981) academic research was supported by McKinsey's who used it to develop successful new 'post structural' products in the cultural arena. With the relative decline of American companies and the rise of Japanese firms, interest in the consultants' old product of structural reorganization on American lines declined so new consulting products were needed.

Two McKinsey consultants (Peters and Waterman 1982) built on this work by Pascale and Athos (1981) to produce a best-selling global book: *In Search of Excellence*. This text provided examples of continuously innovative big American companies (such as Hewlett Packard) with the underlying message that 'soft is hard,' given the core role of organizational culture. Building on concepts developed with Pascale and Athos (1981), the famous McKinsey's 7 S model was developed as a diagnostic tool (Peters and Waterman 1982, p. 10), namely, structure, systems, style, staff, skills, strategy, and (placed in the centre of the diagram and so in a privileged position) shared values.

So shared values were here seen as more fundamental than both structure and strategy. Their second clear message was that such corporate culture could be managed: that managers should seek to manage corporate meaning and had the prospect of success in doing so (the theme of the management of culture is discussed more at length in Chapter 7). However, they argued that management (pp. 82–83) in excellent companies moves beyond a 'transactional' focus on operational decisions to more ambitious and 'transformational' leadership which raises levels of motivation and morality from the workforce and engages with their perhaps unconscious emotional needs.

A case of managing cultural change in public services organizations provided by the German city of Mannheim is reported in Box 2.5, although it should be noted that the cultural school was indeed present but was only one of the models of strategic management evident in the case which rather showed a mixed or multi-school pattern.

Box 2.5   Squaring as a programme – the German city of Mannheim's approach to strategic management

By *Isabella Proeller*

A leading German national newspaper has referred to Mannheim as the *nerd* of German local governments, because the city government was not satisfied with merely *good-enough* management reforms but has reached beyond expectations and set a new standard for German local government (Crolly 2011). Over the past 15 years, Mannheim has succeeded in positioning itself as a best-practice benchmark for local government reforms in Germany (Färber et al. 2014; Salm and Schwab 2016). Even more importantly here, its approach is a rare example in Germany of a deliberate strategic management approach in local government (Weiss 2017, pp. 1404–1405).

The turn to a strategic management approach is closely linked to the era of Mannheim's Lord Mayor, Dr Peter Kurz. In 2007, Dr Peter Kurz came into office as newly elected Lord Mayor and is still in office to date in 2021. He initiated a change process with the proclaimed objective of making Mannheim the most modern city government in Germany. Labelling the reform this way flirts with the unique historical city planning of Mannheim, in which the streets in the city centre are all laid out in a square. *Change² — Change in squares*, the official programme name, has become a standing reference, even a vision, for Mannheim's management approach. One of its core ambitions has been to enable behavioural changes towards a more outcome-oriented attitude (also see www.mannheim.de/de/stadt-gestalten/verwaltungsmodernisierung). In 2016, Change² was complemented by the *SHM²* programme (2017–2020 – Stadt Mannheim 2016), which stands as an abbreviation for *strategic budget management* and aims to consolidate the city's finances. SHM², which also uses the squared symbol in its acronym, is regarded as a continuation and update of the ongoing modernization process of Change².

Since the beginning, the Change² process has been built on two main pillars: a master plan compiling core objectives and measures, and a second stream of initiatives aimed at cultural change under the motto 'effecting more together.' The first project out of the initial 36 master-plan projects was the development of an overall strategy for the city, which specified seven strategic objectives around the overarching goal of creating a 'growing city.' In the years that followed, Mannheim institutionalized a two-year budget in which departments and offices discuss and establish management objectives to contribute to achieving the strategic objectives, and resources are presented alongside the objectives and measures. In the course of SHM², the budget preparation for 2018/2019 was further strengthened in the direction of the strategic priorities. All local products were prioritized and rated against the strategic criteria, and a set of selected measures was presented to realize directly felt improvements for citizens and adhere to the strategic priorities. This again led to the SHM² masterplan (Stadt Mannheim 2016) structured around topical projects, retaining some of the preceding topics and projects while also identifying new ones.

Cultural change and the corresponding measures have been explicit and prominent core objectives and ambitions of both the Change² and SHM² programmes. To make the importance and meaning of the envisioned new culture understood, Mannheim set up an extensive array of dialogues, communication platforms, and feedback surveys. A series of 'Lord Mayor dialogues' was conducted:

- Several times per year, the Lord Mayor invites small groups of employees of the city administration who have been selected by random sampling to attend a personal meeting. The Lord Mayor informs them about the objectives and background of Change^2 and SHM^2, and they discuss the process and the employees' experiences.

- In the 'management circle,' the Lord Mayor regularly meets with the management staff of the departments and offices and discusses the modernization process, as well as management issues.
- There are also regular and intensive meetings with union representatives.

The intensive use of 'dialogues' is a unique feature of the reform approach in Mannheim. It has proved to be an effective and successful means of communicating the necessity, direction and objectives, and challenges of a complex change project and reaching – rather directly – the approximately 8,000 employees of the city administration. Besides the dialogue, feedback on the process is also collected via an employee survey every one or two years, as well as via a 'climate check,' an ongoing, short, 'smiley'-based feedback format.

To ensure the development of management capacities needed for Change^2, the functions of management recruiting and training were structurally decentralized and organized in a newly established agency called the Competence Center for Management Development. The Competence Center for Management Development is in charge when management functions need to be filled. It has established a new selection process that uses potentials analysis and assessment centres to guarantee that not only expertise but also leadership competences are ensured at the management level. This innovative approach to leadership development and recruiting has had a major effect, as corroborated by the evaluation of the Change^2 programme in 2014. The quality of management has improved, more positions have been filled with external applicants and candidates from the private sector, and motivation in management has risen (Färber et al. 2014, p. 32).

The initial phase of the Change^2 modernization process was formally evaluated at the end of 2013 and confirmed that substantial changes in employees' behaviour and the city management have been made (Färber et al. 2014). The SHM^2 formally ended in 2020, a mid-term report was published, and the final report is expected soon. Mannheim has received several national and international awards in recent years for its city management and Change^2 process. Bearing in mind that institutional context matters a lot for public management, those successes must be interpreted against the German local government context and its reform practices. Over the past 15 years, Mannheim has earned – and maintained – a stellar position with regard to local public management in Germany and has set a new benchmark for objective-based management, but also personnel and leadership management – as well as its persistent and authentic focus on cultural change and organizational development.

How should Mannheim's modernization process be characterized and analyzed from the perspective of strategic management? The case displays various features that are typically analyzed and highlighted by various 'schools,' like the learning, cultural, entrepreneurial, and planning schools. So, the focus of Change^2 on enabling cultural and strategic change refers to the emergent approach theorized by Henry Mintzberg and the Learning School in the sense of strategists as coaches and supporters of strategy and strategic change, but also to the Cultural School in the sense of shaping (new) values as an important task of the strategy process and the managers involved. The prominent role of Lord Mayor Dr Kurz draws attention to the perspective of the entrepreneurial school. In line with this perspective is the figurehead function that Dr Kurz has taken on in the process as initiator and founder of the process, and more 'bold strokes' than logical incremental patterns of change. However, in the Mannheim city council, we find clear references to planning school approaches, such as with the declared mission, the strategic goals, and the master plan. The melting of approaches – and the eventual stronger explanatory power of one over the other – can be analyzed from the longitudinal perspective. The entrepreneurial school highlights the risk of loss of momentum when a strong leader leaves the scene, while the learning and cultural schools emphasize the importance of routines and values in institutionalizing organizational change. While Lord Mayor Dr Kurz has been and continues to be a strong leader and central actor for both Change[2] and SHM[2], institutionalization has progressed substantially as well. Lastly, Mannheim's continuing efforts to enhance leadership and management capabilities might also be interpreted and analyzed using the *dynamic capabilities approach*.

The argument that corporate culture could be purposefully managed is controversial and relates to an internal controversy within the cultural school (Smircich 1983) between those who see culture as what an organization *has* (culture as more akin to an independent variable which could be measured and changed through a planned or managerial intervention) and those who see it as what an organization *is* (so that culture had an autonomous element, a tendency to self-reproduce and to lie beyond direct managerial control).

Deal and Kennedy (1988) developed the cultural school further by looking at the 'rites and rituals' of corporate life. One could learn much about the underlying culture of an organization by examining the nature of the office layout (do senior staff get larger offices or is it entirely open plan?; is the décor grey or colourful?) or dress code (how informal is it?; who has to wear more formal clothing?). Tracking the stories or myths which are often told in the organization and who is portrayed as a corporate hero or villain could also be insightful, as could examining key organizational rites of passage, such as induction or awards ceremonies (what is valued within the organization in terms of getting an award?) or retirement parties.

Taking a more social psychological perspective, Johnson (1992) argues that managerial experience filters complex internal and external stimuli, in turn reflecting a prior set of taken for granted assumptions, beliefs, and values within the organization's managerial community. This is less a purely rational perspective on strategy than a cognitive, cultural, and political one. The 'interpretive paradigm' of the organization operates as a deep cognitive structure. It may even be unconscious in nature, so being easier for outsiders than insiders to decode. Citing UK case-based work (Pettigrew 1985; Johnson 1987), he argued that (p. 29): 'the 'guidance' that gives rise to strategy is, then, most likely to do so with the taken for granted assumptions, beliefs and values that are encapsulated within the idea of managerial experience and organizational culture.'

What are the implications of this cultural perspective for progressing strategic change? Johnson (1992) notes that the first task of the analyst is to make the tacit paradigm explicit, perhaps using the cultural web tool (discussed next) as a diagnostic instrument and then generating a debate within the organization about the cultural obstacles to significant change. Another task for managers is to seek to 'manage meaning' by providing signals and symbols for change, such as the closure of special dining rooms for senior managers, changing the dress code, or socially constructing a performance crisis.

Johnson et al. (2011, pp. 176–177) offer the cultural web tool as a diagnostic instrument, visualized in the manner of the McKinsey 7 S framework. While *the interpretive paradigm is placed at the centre* of their framework, it is surrounded by six circles representing respectively:

(i)   *Routines and rituals* are 'the way we do things around here' on a day-to-day level. They are often taken for granted and may be an obstacle to significant change. Rituals, on the other hand, are special events which dramatize what is important in organizational life, such as induction processes, retirement parties, promotion or assessment panels, or after works drinks for junior staff where they can be frank without the bosses being present!

(ii) *Stories* are an important part of an organization's life; there may be stories which circulate widely within an organization and which are passed onto new recruits. They often dramatize successes, disasters, heroes, villains, and mavericks.

(iii) *Symbols* are objects, events, acts or people that convey, maintain, or create over and above their functional purpose, such as the way in which office layout conveys power differences or the (in) formality corporate culture. The nature of the language used within the organization also helps construct groups in particular ways. There may be symbolic events (such as an annual founder's day) where speeches and presentations reveal the cultural core of the organization.

(iv) *Power* is defined by Johnson et al. (2011, p. 177) as the ability of groups and individuals to persuade, influence, or coerce others into following certain courses of action. So, the nature of power relations within the organization needs to be considered. Usually, powerful groups will be closely attached to the core paradigm and a paradigm shift may require changes in underlying power relations too.

(v)   *Organizational structure* is the more formal manifestation of power relations. For example, what is the extent of (de) centralization? Are there strong vertical reporting relations or more flexible and network-based forms of working?

(vi) *Control systems* are formal and informal ways of monitoring and supporting staff such as reporting requirements, sign off systems, audit systems, and systems for awarding performance-related pay.

Because the paradigm itself is tacit and 'taken for granted,' one way of surfacing it is to conduct initial analysis of these six more visible dimensions and then infer from that analysis key properties of the underlying paradigm. A common argument is that the underlying paradigm is highly change resistant. We comment that undertaking a full cultural web analysis in a large and complex organization may be an ambitious task and that more worked examples would be useful.

Some applications to public services organizations

The cultural school has been applied to and also developed within the analysis of public services organizations since about 1980. Andrew Pettigrew is a major researcher in this field, and his work and his 'process school'-based work will be considered in more detail in a later chapter.

Here we briefly highlight Pettigrew 1979's early and influential case study-based work on the creation of a strong and enduring culture by a founder to help underline a distinctive vision and pedagogic ideology in an innovative school setting. Concrete commitment-building mechanisms were identified which helped in culture creation. The distinctive vision made the school exceptional and helped create its enduring educational identity.

Pettigrew et al. 1992's later model of receptive and non-receptive organizational contexts for change in the UK health care sector (explored in more detail later in the chapter on strategy as process) also included as one important feature the presence of a 'supportive organizational culture.' Such a culture (pp. 281–282) included a focus on skill rather than rank or status; an open and risk-taking approach; openness to research and evaluation; a strong value base and a strong positive self-image and sense of achievement. While culture was seen as one of a number of positive dimensions, it was not accorded primacy over other factors.

Some cultural questions are also explored empirically within the field of health care organizations (UK NHS hospitals) by Mannion et al. (2010), using a combination of a quantitative tool over three time points between 2001 and 2008 (based on the Competing Values Framework) and qualitative case material to assess cultural types and how they may be changing. The most dominant cultural form in the surveys was found to be the 'clan' culture (as indeed would be expected in a traditional professionalized bureaucracy where professional groups demonstrated intense solidarity internally), although its prevalence was declining. There was a growth over time of both hierarchical and rational culture types (more consistent with NPM reforms). The qualitative material revealed a messy picture of different but coexisting subcultures organized by hierarchical level and occupational group.

Strong cultures can also have a negative aspect. The enduring 'canteen culture' found in many policing organizations (Loftus 2010), for example amongst rank and file officers celebrated masculinity and punitive views about offenders, making a formidable but invisible obstacle to liberalizing but top-down reforms announced by senior management.

Professional cultures espoused by the rank and file may also effectively resist top-down and managerialist reforms in other sectors. The following example is taken from the UK health care sector, where embedded and powerful professional cultures helped blunt and reshape a top-down re-engineering change programme sponsored by senior management (Box 2.6).

Box 2.6   Business process re-engineering in the UK NHS and the role of professional and sub-professional cultures

While much of the culture change literature advocates a transformative and inspirational approach to leadership in public services settings, it may underestimate the potential for resistance from embedded professional subcultures.

Some empirical studies have found more nuanced impacts from transformational change efforts than originally proclaimed.

Business process re-engineering (BPR) was an influential corporate change programme of the 1990s, originally tried in private sector manufacturing settings but which later diffused into public sector settings (see, for example Ongaro 2004), aided by important diffusion agents as management consultants, central government, and blockbuster texts (Hammer and Champy 1993).

McNulty and Ferlie (2002) examined the implementation of a BPR corporate change programme in a large NHS acute hospital supported by external management consultants: while the initial ambitions were transformational, the long-term impact was assessed in the end (McNulty and Ferlie 2002) as patchy and incremental. BPR texts such as Hammer and Champy 1993 had proclaimed the transformational impact of re-engineering on organizations. As well as streamlining work practices and introducing new ICTs, the ambition was to achieve radical cultural change, specifically by moving from a producer to a customer-centric culture and from a task-bound mode of thinking to a lateral process mode of thinking. In the hospital studied, however, entrenched agency and professional jurisdictions and cultures heavily blunted these transformational ambitions so that change was in the end more incremental in nature and heavily shaped by powerful and continuing professional (medical) jurisdictions that damped down external threats.

Source: McNulty and Ferlie 2002

In concluding this section on the cultural school, we note its radically different orientation from the prior schools, notably the design school, which was focused on the strategy-structure nexus. Its openness to perspectives drawn from non-Western and specifically Japanese firms is interesting and additive: this school makes a distinct contribution to our understanding of strategy. We suggest it has clear relevance to the public and not-for-profit sector: it does not assume strong market forces.

The cultural school also balances a narrow focus on the top management team of previous schools with the awareness of the possibility of the role played by a strong collective culture and professional groups. The cultural perspective also highlights the strong and collective values which may well lie at the base of (for example) social movement-based NGOs in social or development work. Such values may underpin organizational development and desired forms of organizational change (e.g. developing a client orientation; fostering a learning culture), acting as a positive base underpinning strategy formation.

However, we should not assume that there is always a consensual culture, despite these examples of unitary value-driven organizations. Organizational and professional subcultures (Deal and Kennedy 1982) in public services settings may often be diverse, competing and even conflicting, orientated to defending their tasks and jurisdictions. They may operate across whole fields rather than be confined to a single organization (as Mintzberg 1983 argues in his analysis of the professionalized bureaucracy), hence making them less malleable by managerial action from inside the organization. Many public services settings are pluralist and display distributed rather than centralized forms of power relations. They may have a range of coexisting or even competing stakeholders, external as well as internal which have to be held together in tension in fragile processes of strategic change (Denis et al. 2001).

It is important to notice that the Japanese ideas of management highlighted in this chapter rapidly diffused into many public sector organizations from the mid-1980s onwards, often under a 'quality' umbrella one can think of the 'Quality Conferences' promoted by the Departments for Public Administration of the Member States of the EU, or the quality awards for public service innovations like the European Public Sector Award promoted by the European Institute for Public Administration.

2.6 Summing up on the 'Early' schools of thought in strategic management

This chapter has reviewed some important early models of strategic management (from the 1960s to early 1980s) and considered their applicability and implications for current public services organizations. In summary, the early design school contributed important analytic techniques (e.g. SWOT) which have diffused into the public services and are part and parcel of the taken for granted toolkit for strategic management in public services organizations. Formal long-range strategic planning rose and declined in government as in private firms (and then re-picked up momentum and diffusion in public services organizations, thanks to the work of scholars like Bryson), yet the influence of these early models continues through the continuing production of strategic plans within many public agencies.

The chapter then considered the influential strand from industrial economics and Porter's work which has more potential application in public services which have been radically reshaped by reforms inspired by the New Public Management, notably because of the diffusion of market-type mechanisms in these settings. It then reviewed some of Mintzberg's ideas which appear widely applicable to public services settings as they do not assume the operation of strong market forces and two of his five archetypes (the professionalized bureaucracy and the adhocracy) derive from the study of public services settings. His notion of the 'entrepreneurial organization' can be applied to the analysis of strategy making of public sector organizations, under certain conditions, as well as more broadly to social enterprises, which are also a key actor in public services.

Finally, the rise of the Japanese economy and relative decline of American large corporations provoked a rise of interest in distinctive cultural approaches in the 1980s which also diffused into public services settings. By the 1980s, therefore, the process of school proliferation was already evident, a trend which was to accelerate in future decades and which is considered in the next chapter.

Notes

1 Professor-Researcher (Public Administration Division) and Academic Coordinator of the PhD in Public Policy Programme, Centre for Research and Teaching in Economics (Centro de Investigación y Docencia Económicas, CIDE). E-mail: mauricio.dussauge@cide.edu.
2 Marc Bloch was a great French historian and officer of the French army during the two world wars. In his book, *Strange Defeat* written in 1940, he denounces the dysfunctions of the army and the disastrous consequences of the collapse of morale.

3 Further proliferation of schools of strategic management
Part II – the 1980s onwards

This chapter continues the chronologically organized review of more recent schools of strategic management. From the 1980s onwards, the proliferation of schools of strategic management appears to have accelerated, bringing in new disciplinary perspectives. While mainstream industrial economics-based approaches have remained influential, they have been complemented by a range of alternative prisms drawn from other social sciences, even including 'exotic' candidates such as complexity theory (Stacey 1995).

The chapter will start by examining the increasing influence of the resource-based view of the firm/organization (3.1) which comes from an alternative branch of industrial economics and has had increasing applications in the arena of public services organizations, for example in the arena of knowledge mobilization. It then introduces the corporate governance perspective (3.2) (which has some links to the academic discipline of law) with its special focus on the role of the Board. There are brief introductions to the network governance (3.3) and strategy as process schools (3.4), but these themes are picked up in more detail in later chapters in their own right.

The chapter then reviews the more recent and increasingly influential strategy as practice school (3.5), which is informed by more sociological and practice-based approaches. It concludes with a review of the Public Value school (section 3.6), closely associated with the work of Mark Moore, which is distinctively developed within public services settings, such as American local government. The threads of both Chapters 2 and 3 are then drawn together in an overview section which provides comparative discussion of all the different schools and what they can contribute as we conclude these two chapters which have been dedicated to provide an overview of the schools of thought of strategic management for application to public services organizations.

3.1 The resource-based view of the firm/organization

This originally private sector-based school, termed the resource-based view (RBV) of the firm (Barney 1991; Barney and Clark 2007), has been of growing importance over the last 20 years within mainstream strategic management and should now be seen as a major strand. Crilly et al. (2013) have developed a structured literature review of this important stream of literature and drawn out some implications for application in the health care sector. We will here consider the potential applicability of this school for a wider population of public services organizations, alongside private firms.

The 'firm' (its original focus) is in this school seen in terms of its tangible and also (important) intangible resources, including its underlying knowledge bases, which

DOI: 10.4324/9781003054917-3

taken as a bundle produce competitive advantage in an advanced economy (Eisenhardt and Santos 2006). While Porter looks at the firm within its sectoral context, RBV looks at the internal capacities of the firm. Firms have different resource profiles and are hence heterogeneous, with such variation between them even in the same sector exerting performance effects. So, the existence of heterogeneity or differences between firms' resources within the same industry is a fundamental assumption of this school.

Penrose (1959) is credited as the founder of the school. She asked this basic question: why do firms grow? Her approach stresses the internal capabilities of the firm (in particular, expert management capability which cannot be acquired readily on the open market) rather than external market structure. A firm – but more broadly any organization, including in the sphere of interest of this book 'corporatized' public services organizations – can be seen as a 'bundle of resources' under internal managerial direction which develops an idiosyncratic profile over time. If a firm has underutilized human assets, then there are internal incentives for growth. Successful completion of growth adds to the skills and experience levels of management, making further expansion easier. Such management knowledge may be experiential and tacit in nature, difficult to codify or transmit but becoming in its own right an important source of competitive advantage and of growth. Pitelis (2009)'s review suggests her work has had more long-term impact in strategic management than in her original field of economics.

Wernerfelt (1984) developed the term 'resource based theory' in a brief but influential article which switched attention from a conventional product perspective to examining firms' resources within their diversification decisions. So, a decision to acquire a firm in a new market could be seen as buying a 'bundle of assets' in a highly imperfect market: such acquisitions were more successful if they included rare resources which then represented an invisible barrier to entry for potential competitors. Lockett et al. (2008, p. 1136)'s review suggests Wernerfelt's core ideas have proved to be highly influential in the field, namely that:

(i)   Firms are fundamentally heterogeneous;
(ii)   A firm should base its strategy on its strengths;
(iii) Tomorrow's strengths are likely to be based on today's strengths; and
(iv)   Knowledge about market structure, market allocation, and industry positioning may tell us little about an individual firm.

Barney (1991) notes that resources may be imperfectly mobile across firms with the implication that their resource profiles may be long lasting. These resources are not just physical but also human and organizational in nature. The VRIN model – acronym for Value, Rarity, Inimitability and Non-substitutability – is a core analytic technique used within this school (see Barney 1991; also Barney and Clark 2007; Johnson et al. 2011, pp. 90–91) as it is claimed that 'resources and capabilities which are simultaneously valuable, rare, imperfectly imitable and non-substitutable – the VRIN conditions – are the main sources of above normal rents and competitive advantage' (Easterby-Smith and Prieto 2008, p. 236). They can be explicated as follows:

Value: some strategic capabilities enable a firm to increase its efficiency and effectiveness and to win competitive advantage (Barney 1991). They will of course need to be valued by the firm's customers as well as managers (Johnson et al. 2011).

Rarity: rare capabilities are possessed by a small number of firms and cannot be easily acquired. Excellent managerial talent is given as an example by Barney (1991). Johnson et al. (2011, pp. 90–91) cite further examples such as patents, branding and reputation, intellectual capital, prime location, and special relations with suppliers or customers. Some rare capabilities can only be built up over time (e.g. reputation; good relationships).

Inimitability: a firm's competitive advantage will only be sustained if it is difficult for competitors to imitate readily. Barney (1991) suggests why some resources may be difficult to imitate.

(i)   History and path dependency; firms are shaped by their place in time and space and such features cannot be readily transferred; for example, it would be difficult for UK firms to replicate the successful German model of medium-sized firms in what is a very different political and financial context.

(ii)   Causal ambiguity in that it is not clear precisely how these capabilities act (often in combination) to promote competitive advantage; therefore, it is difficult for an imitating firm to know what it should try to imitate.

(iii)   Social complexity: these resources may be based in complex social processes, such as a firm with productive working relations, a positive organizational culture and good external reputation. As already remarked, it may be highly challenging to try to create a positive organizational culture in what has previously been a dysfunctional setting. These social processes may influence the 'pay off' from new technologies: for example a firm may introduce a new knowledge management system, but the workforce be reluctant to use it.

Non-substitutability: to endure, these core capabilities must not be at risk of ready substitution by rival firms. Barney (1991) gives the example of within category substitution where a firm tries to develop a similar high-quality top management team to a rival (if say a direct poaching strategy has failed). There may be also cross category equivalents: thus, a clear vision for the firm's future could either be developed by a charismatic individual leader or a formal strategic planning system, but the key output is a high-quality vision in both cases. Either option could be adopted by a rival firm as a form of substitution. Johnson et al. (2011, p. 91) give examples of technological substitution (such as new email-based modes of communication displaying letters) or competence substitution (automation of traditional craft skills).

An important development within this school, which may possibly go on to form a sub-school in its own right, has been the concept of '*dynamic capabilities*' (Teece et al. 1997; Teece 2007), capabilities which are seen as evolving, rather than operating as a static form of analysis. This notion refers to the evolution of the firm's competences and capabilities over time. Such evolution could enable it to create new products and processes and respond to rapidly changing and discontinuous market conditions, reflecting a contemporary world of rapid and innovation-led competition and the credible threat of the market-led extinction of existing competences. This concept overcomes criticism of RBV that it is too static (Easterby-Smith and Prieto 2008), bringing in concerns for skill acquisition, knowledge management, and organizational learning over time: 'if control over scarce resources is the source of economic profits, then it follows that such issues as skill acquisition, the management of knowledge and know how and learning become fundamental strategic issues' (Teece et al. 1997, p. 514).

Another important concept in this perspective is that of '*absorptive capacity*' (Cohen and Levindhal 1990). This notion is used to examine the three stage process of knowledge transfer and application 'which posits that firms need to (a) recognise new, valuable and relevant knowledge (b) assimilate it into their processes and (c) apply it commercially' (Bierly et al. 2009, p. 482). The ability to sense, import, and then use external knowledge effectively may be a core organizational competence. In its turn, the firm's level of absorptive capacity is affected by the level of the firm's prior related knowledge (Cohen and Levindhal 1990). For example, firms that conduct their own research and development may be better able to sense high-quality R&D in external firms. As well as acquiring such information, a successful firm also needs to develop capacity in transferring this information effectively across different subunits internally (Zahra and George 2002).

A final conceptual development in this perspective has been that of '*ambidexterity*' or the balance between future-orientated exploration and day-to-day exploitation. Raisch and Birkinshaw (2008) define the term as 'an organisation's ability to be aligned and efficient in its management of today's business demands while simultaneously being adaptive to changes in the environment.' While it could be argued that there is a trade-off between exploration (seeking resources beyond the firm) and exploitation (using resources within the firm), the ambidexterity premise (Tushman and O'Reilly 1996) suggests that firms capable of pursuing both exploration and exploitation at the same time should perform better than firms that focus on one or the other. Indeed, this capacity to do both may lie at the heart of effective dynamic capabilities.

The RBV approach has influenced a growing stream of work on Knowledge Intensive Firms (KIFs) (Karreman 2010), which include such settings as management consulting and law (Brivot 2011). Given that knowledge (rather than capital or technology) is here the key basis of corporate advantage, the nature and effectiveness of organizational systems for knowledge management and mobilization assume great importance (readers will note that this perspective assumes an explicit and Western notion of knowledge, unlike the different processes evident in Japanese firms, as discussed earlier).

Grant (1996) developed a knowledge-based view of strategy further. Assuming hypercompetitive economic environments, the traditional focus on established market structures becomes less appealing than an examination of the firm's internal resources. Knowledge – and in particular tacit knowledge – is now seen as a key internal resource. The key question is how firms access and integrate perhaps multiple knowledge bases, overcoming organizational barriers to capture, transfer, or replication. This view of the firm as an integrator of knowledge may explain recent trends in organizational design such as cross functional product development teams or corporate change programmes aimed at broadening and 'empowering' workers' roles away from narrow specialization. While the knowledge-based view is intuitively appealing in the analysis of advanced post-industrial economies, Eisenhardt and Santos (2006) note that it requires more empirical testing and theoretical development (what does a knowledge-based organization really look like?). It may not be a new theory in its own right but merely an outgrowth of RBV.

Applications of RBV to public services settings

Theoretically, we argue that the RBV/knowledge theory can be applied to a subset of knowledge intensive organizations in the public sector which have some scope for autonomous action at the operational level. These would include such settings as autonomized hospitals, universities, or science- and engineering-based executive agencies (a large number of which were for example created in the UK Defence sector, like QinetiQ, which is now a private firm but still with a long-term partnership agreement with the Ministry of Defence). Much of the contemporary public sector appears to be knowledge intensive, given trends to the privatization and outsourcing of more routine and lower skill work but the preservation of high skill work in house, so the RBV perspective potentially has wide application.

While there has historically been little empirical exploration of RBV in public services settings, that picture has started to shift. For example, Bryson et al. (2007) operationalize the perspective in a consultation process to identify a 'livelihood scheme' in a UK public sector agency (a health care consulting unit): 'a livelihood scheme – that is the public sector equivalent of a private sector business model – to show how distinctive competences are directly linked to meeting organizational aspirations' (p. 703). They ask: what might distinctive competences look like in this setting? The consultation process identified distinctive competences where the unit was already in a strong position (e.g. partnership skills; it was well networked and had a collaborative relationship with the regional health and social care economy) but also areas where it needed to develop new core competences. This diagnosis led to corrective actions being undertaken (e.g. partnering with a university to develop new knowledge and eventually products in the field of team-based working).

Pablo et al. (2007) apply the concept of 'dynamic capability' to the analysis of organizational change in a Canadian case: the Albertan health care field after the election of a radical right and NPM friendly provincial government that wanted greater efficiency but also accorded management teams some discretion as to how to achieve this overall political objective: 'public sector managers are increasingly expected to use managerial strategies to improve organizational performance – even in times of decreasing financial resources' (p. 687). They looked at the reconfiguration of internal decision-making routines as a key area (p. 688):

> we studied a public sector health care organization as it responded to demands for improved performance, while simultaneously being constrained by diminishing financial resources. The organization's executive team wanted to find ways to continually improve the delivery of health care services in response to continually changing conditions.

Pablo and colleagues (Pablo et al. 2007) argue that RBV is a particularly helpful model of strategy to apply in this context, as it does not assume strong competitive forces but does relate strongly to change management. The decision to develop 'learning through experimentation' core competence as a performance improvement strategy seemed suitable in that context, as it had high legitimacy with key stakeholder groups such as the clinicians.

Casebeer et al. (2010) later saw 'organizational learning' as a second dynamic capability for this agency, involving a 'bundle' of enablers, including leadership, trust, team working, and boundary spanning. To have real influence, these forces need to be enacted at the middle and lower levels of the organization as well as at the top. Their case study also examined the enactment of the policy of Calgary Health Region to rebalance the health care system and make it more cost effective, in part by developing more primary care capacity as an alternative to expensive hospital-based care. A specific policy was to improve health system performance through promoting a strategy of continual improvement in primary care based on new research to health conditions. These objectives were pursued by launching a number of experiments: (p. 282) 'Overall CHR focussed on the dynamic capability of learning through experimenting as a route to continually improving the organization's ability to perform.' Developing this learning style in turn depended on a supportive style of leadership which moved across traditional professional boundaries and a platform of high trust behaviours within the system.

Not all empirical studies using RBV concepts to examine strategic behaviour in public services organizations have been so positive. This theoretical perspective was also used to look at poor levels of 'absorptive capacity' by failing UK public organizations selected from different sectors which were moving into crisis based 'turnaround' situations (Harvey et al. 2010, building on a generic model by Lane et al. 2006). These organizations often failed to acquire knowledge from publicly available external reports which signalled concerns about poor performance and experienced continuing deterioration in their performance. There was little benchmarking with external comparators. There were few explicit internal systems evident which might help assimilate any such knowledge. Nor were there well-designed internal change management processes to help turn such knowledge into action: instead, there was organizational change – often of a sudden or dramatic nature – but often imposed on these public sector organizations by outside actors such as inspectorates or management consultancies. Moreover, neither many of these organizations, nor their regulators, nor higher-level service improvement bodies generally seemed to consider the development of such absorptive capacity important.

'Knowledge mobilisation' strategies by public services organizations represent a further area where RBV concepts may be helpfully employed to tackle questions like: how can public sector organizations translate new knowledge and evidence into action, for example for changing historic patterns of service delivery in line with new evidence? What organization-wide systems and processes may be helpful? Another way of reading Casebeer's et al. 2010 study from Alberta is as an analysis of an attempt to develop such an organizational capacity to turn primary care research evidence into practice through local experiments.

The well-developed literature on the relationship between social research and public policy making (Davies et al. 2010) suggests that it is often not linear but context dependent, complex, and indirect in nature. Often, the literature focuses on the national or macro-level of public policy making, highlighting such factors as interests and ideologies (Weiss 1999), but Davies et al. begin to explore implications for research uptake at the meso or organizational level:

issues of interests, ideologies, information and institutions still apply, albeit these will operate around local issues and with local stakeholder groups. One of the central issues at the meso level of policy making is however the potential for tension between national policies and legislation and local needs, priorities and agendas.

(Davies et al. 2010, pp. 208–209)

Negative aspects of a local organizational context may be a barrier to research uptake, for example where heavy short-term demands squeeze out the space for longer-term and more reflective work (we add there is a link here to the receptive contexts for change model developed by Pettigrew et al. 1992).

Can implications for appropriate organizational design which better supports research uptake at the meso level be brought out further? Davies et al. (2010, p. 217) cite Walter et al. (2004)'s review of the literature on supporting research uptake in UK social care settings which outlined three alternative models:

(i) *The research-based practitioner model* which tends to be individualistic in focus, apart from the provision of education and training programmes by the organization. Despite its flaws, it is widely used in practice.

(ii) *The embedded research model* in which research enters practice more systemically, through pressures and levers developed at the national level through research-based guidelines, codes of best practice, inspection bodies, performance management regimes, and incentive-based funding; and

(iii) *The organizational excellence model* which is the most closely related to RBV. Here, the organization does not simply receive external guidance but is also the internal locus for research, evaluation, experimentation, and practice development, working in partnership with universities and other knowledge producers. There are links here with wider quality improvement and collaborative ideas (e.g. Continuous Quality Improvement programmes).

Health care policy is another important arena with (at least in the UK) a strong national policy level push towards the development of 'translational research' capacity to shorten the time span in moving new scientific knowledge 'from bench to bedside' (HM Treasury 2005), that is from discovery to wide application in routine clinical practice. What implications does this national policy push have for the meso level of the health care organization? Crilly et al.'s 2013 (p. 80) review of the RBV literature draws out some implications for health care providers and reflective practitioners. One is a push to specialization to develop deep reputation and expertise – and we would add more potential for integration and cross working between on-site clinical academic researchers and clinical practitioners – across a narrower range of patient groups. These organizational conditions are indeed rare, difficult to imitate or substitute. Strangely enough, there is an overlap here with the Porterian analysis of health care (Porter and Teisberg 2006) which similarly advocates against getting 'stuck in the middle,' although RBV and Porterian perspectives are often seen as at odds. Crilly et al. (2013) also suggested that 'organizational slack' may be functional in protecting local innovation and experimentation, arguing against an entirely efficiency/productivity-led policy agenda.

These are clearly only preliminary studies and much more conceptual and empirical work is needed to apply the RBV perspective to knowledge-based public services organizations, but, as some authors (Pablo et al. 2007) have highlighted, it is a school with strong applicability at least selectively to certain public services settings.

3.2 The corporate governance perspective: the strategic role of the board?

The board formally sits at the apex of many organizations, especially private limited companies, and increasingly has, at least formally, a governance role in many public services organizations. In NPM regimes in particular (such as the UK), there has often been an adoption of firm-based models of corporate governance (with a reduction in staff or trade union representation and less role for elections to seats on the board) within public services organizations given an attempt to empower the board as a directing centre, moving it away from its old decorative, honorific, or 'rubber stamp' role and increasingly the 'governability' of public services organizations. These trends in governance are also apparent in some not-for-profit organizations, as explored in a later chapter.

The formal role of the board

In its basic structure and composition, the main board of a firm normally comprises a number of full-time senior managers employed by the organization (executive directors or EDs) and part-time independent directors from outside (non-executive directors or NEDs). There are often two key leadership roles expressed in a 'duo' of a non-executive chairman and a chief executive officer (CEO), although sometimes these two posts may be combined. The working relationship between the CEO and the chairman is critical to the functioning of the board, as is the extent to which NEDs are effectively involved.

The board is supposed to take responsibility for the overall governance of the organization, reporting to shareholders/constituents at a general assembly. It may well set up subcommittees to pursue particular tasks (e.g. audit committee) which then report back to the main board. Chambers (2010) summarizes the main role of the board in the three core functions to determine strategy (direction); assess performance (control); and shape organizational culture (values, rules, tone). In our view, it might be expected also to have a leading role in the handling of any mergers or acquisitions; ensuring overall financial control and probity; and deciding the dividend policy (in private limited companies).

Within the board, non-executive directors are supposed to have a leading role in the hiring and (if need be) firing of senior management; agreeing compensation arrangements for senior managers, perhaps through a compensation subcommittee, and monitoring their performance; and also in supplying individual expertise in particular areas important to the organization beyond the executive directors' knowledge base (e.g. accounting; law).

Formally speaking, therefore, the board is supposed to have a major role in the formulation of strategy, appointment of senior management, and performance monitoring. However, there have been many cases of weak corporate governance systems in practice in the private sector: for example the rash of ill-advised mergers and acquisitions decisions signed off by the boards of banks before the 2008 financial crash. There has also been criticism that boards are too ready to agree lavish compensation packages for senior management on a 'going rate' basis rather than on successful performance. Successive enquiries into scandals in some UK public services organizations (especially in the health care sector: Chambers 2010; see also Mid Staffs NHS Foundation Trust, Francis Report 2013, p. 44) found a marginal or even negative role for the board, which often failed to set up effective governance systems or to grasp the enormity of the clinical service failings unfolding around them. It may therefore be questioned how developed the actual effectiveness of the board is in strategically steering the organization, private or public. This consideration has driven a series of proposals for certain reforms of the role of the board.

Taking the example of the UK, from the 1990s onwards, various reports and policy initiatives in the UK sought to improve corporate governance systems within publicly listed firms to combat senior management domination to prevent reoccurrence of corporate scandals. Cadbury Report (1992) made recommendations in relation to changes in board level 'best practice' for the private sector then adopted by some public services organizations. The Higgs Review (2003) later considered how to enhance the role and effectiveness of NEDs in the private sector. The recommendations of these committees often diffused into UK public services settings (perhaps uncritically so, Chambers 2010). These reforms were often structural: the separation of the roles of chairman and CEO; an increase in the proportion of NEDs and an insistence that NEDs dominate key specialist subcommittees, including audit and compensation committees. The question to which these structural reforms need to be complemented by an awareness of board process will be considered later on in the chapter.

To draw lessons from the vicissitudes of the private sector for the strategic management of public services organizations, we would argue that an analysis of the role of the board is part and parcel of any understanding of how strategy forms, but particularly so as it is found in practice, rather than within normative or prescriptive accounts, as the chasm between the two may be especially wide. Not only the role of the board may be ineffective, it could also be marginal (acting as a mere 'rubber stamp') or even negative (ignoring alarming developments occurring in the organization). The argument has been put forward that boards in public sector organizations may still be more constrained and have less 'strategic space' than in private firms (Abbott et al. 2008), so that there may be good reasons why public sector boards find it more difficult to operate effectively.

After having briefly reviewed the role of the board in practice, we now turn to discuss the corporate governance school from an academic standpoint.

Some academic writing on corporate governance and the role of the board

We now introduce and discuss the corporate governance school of academic writing, additional to those schools considered in Mintzberg et al. (2009), although well discussed by Davis and Useem (2006). This school sometimes brings in economic and also legal perspectives to the analysis of corporate governance and strategy, further complemented by critical and sociological approaches (Davis and Useem 2006) which investigate the impact of the political economy on preferred corporate governance forms. There is a long-standing debate in the generic corporate governance literature about the 'managerial hegemony thesis,' that is whether non-executives are in effective strategic control, or whether senior managers remain hegemonic actors: are non-executives 'pawns or potentates' (Lorsch and McIver 1989)? If senior managers do remain hegemonic, the question arises: is it possible to redesign the corporate governance systems to increase the role of non-executives?

The corporate governance literature grew substantially in the 1990s as interest in the role of the board both in the private firm (partly in response to corporate governance scandals) and in newly created NPM-style public services settings increased. Ever since the classic American study of Berle and Means (1932) into the governance of large corporations, there has been concern that a powerful corporate class of senior managers has taken informal control, insulated from both shareholders (nominally their principals) and the wider public interest. This 'managerial hegemony perspective' suggests that ownership of the means of production no longer accords shareholders effective control. Reinforced by the wide dispersal of stock holding, ownership has rather become increasingly divorced from effective control. The senior managers in a firm can often accrue more income (and also 'perks') from their salaried positions than from personal ownership of stock in the companies they are directing.

More sociological accounts, for example examine behaviours in the boardroom in terms of the working relationship between executive and non-executive directors (McNulty and Pettigrew 1999). They could examine whether non-executive and executive directors are drawn from the same basic social groupings and the extent of interlocks (membership of multiple boards). They might examine whether more diverse boards (with more of a gender or ethnicity balance) produce a greater range of perspectives and more acute questioning.

Coming from a different intellectual tradition, 'contractarian' models of the firm (where the firm is seen as a 'nexus of contracts') also responded to managerial hegemony theory (Davis and Useem 2006) in an attempt to protect shareholders, even where stock ownership was widely dispersed. Agency theory (see Jensen and Meckling 1976; Fama and Jensen 1983) suggested 'contractarian' reform doctrines (Davis and Useem 2006; Mizruchi 2004) to realign literal and psychological contracts between senior managers and the board, now seen as a proxy for shareholders. Roberts et al. (2005) suggest both that agency theory is highly influential and that it is subject to critique for remaining at too great a distance from the study of real world directors' behaviour.

An influential doctrine within agency theory is to compensate senior managers with shares in the company as well as salary, in order to align incentives between principals and agents (performance-related pay could be another mechanism, as could tying salary levels to share price or appointment of senior managers on short-term and renewable contracts). A second doctrine is to increase reporting to and oversight from directors, perhaps by setting up a specialist compensation subcommittee of the board and increasing the proportion of external directors on the board. A third is to increase the external market for corporate control so that a company with a falling share price is more likely to become a takeover target, after which there well may be a clear-out of senior management (in other words, their positions become riskier and more contestable): while top management talent is head hunted and rewarded, managerial failure is punished more brutally. Such a package of reforms could combat managerial dominance and increase shareholder value. Pettigrew and McNulty (1995) note that the agency theory's perspective is focused on the exercise of control rather than seeing strategy making as a shared function of the board. Agency theory insists on a controlling and monitoring role for NEDs, rather than a stance of complementary or shared tasks with the EDs.

Stewardship theory (as reviewed by Donaldson and Davis 1991) represents a theoretical alternative to agency theory. While agency theory argues that a shared chair/CEO role will tilt decisions away from owners and towards managers, stewardship theory argues that it may be more helpful to combine chair/CEO roles. It takes a more optimistic view of the motivations of senior managers, suggesting there is no major problem with executive motivation. Executives may be intrinsically motivated to do a good job and to be a steward of corporate assets, perhaps seeking to gain influence or a good personal reputation on that basis. Long-standing managers may identify with their firm, merging their individual ego with the corporation. Under these circumstances, combining CEO and chair roles could create an unambiguous leadership role helpful to the firm. Testing these ideas against some empirical data gave somewhat more support to stewardship theory than agency theory.

Interlocks at board level represent another major theme in the literature on private sector corporate governance (Mizruchi 1996). All American publicly traded companies are required to have a board. One intriguing is in relation to the extent and significance of any interlocks. A high degree of interlocks may facilitate possible collusion in the marketplace, against the American tradition of strong antitrust legislation. From a neo-Marxist perspective, interlocks could represent a high degree of social cohesion amongst a ruling elite or 'inner circle' who capture multiple roles at the governance level (Useem 1984). Empirically, for example it appears banks have a high degree of centrality in such networks, suggesting the power of finance capitalism.

The 1990s saw increased empirically orientated work on (flawed) corporate governance systems in practice and how to reform them (reviewed in Ferlie et al. 1996, Chapter 5). Lorsch and McIver's (1989) empirical research on USA directors suggested their basic functions were overseeing the management of the company, review of its performance, overseeing the company's social responsibility, and ensuring compliance with the law. They found that real power lay with the top management team (TMT) and that outside occasional crises (such as the replacement of the CEO), NEDs found it difficult to influence major decisions. Dealing with gradual decline was especially difficult.

Charkham (1994, p. 4) suggested two basic principles of corporate governance in the private sector were first, that management should be free to manage but second, that it should exercise this freedom within a system of effective accountability to shareholders and the board. Pearce and Zahra (1991) argue that powerful boards are associated with better corporate financial performance.

Some analyses stress the potential strategic function of the board (Charkham 1986; Zahra 1990), especially in NPM-rich public sector settings (Ferlie et al. 1995, 1996) which supposedly have more scope for operational autonomy. However, some empirical studies in the UK public sector suggested such a strategic role is still limited in practice (Peck 1995) even in NPM-based settings (here a NHS Foundation Trust).

Taking an international perspective, Davis and Useem (2006) suggest different varieties of capitalism clearly evident internationally (such as Anglo-American, continental European, and Japanese variants) may produce different corporate governance systems: for example reflecting ownership by families (as in Germany or Spain) rather than by many shareholders in the Anglo-American model. Much of the governance literature reviewed so far is Anglo-American and somewhat parochial. They suggest

(p. 241) that investor power may be rising internationally, combined with the impact of financial globalization:

> the rising power of investors has made for greater director focus on creating value and less cosiness with top management. American and British directors, following the Anglo Saxon model, are already focussed on value than most. But directors in other economies can be expected to slowly gravitate toward the mantra of shareholder supremacy as well.

The structural perspective on board composition has been complemented (Pettigrew and McNulty 1995; McNulty and Pettigrew 1999; Roberts et al. 2005) with more qualitatively and empirically based work to uncover influence processes and behaviour patterns in the boardroom. These strategy process scholars investigated the role of the board as a (at least potentially) major site for strategic decision making but where there were also challenges. McNulty and Pettigrew (1999)'s empirical UK study argued that some non-executive members were able to influence strategic choice, change, and control. They did this by shaping the ideas, methods, and processes by which strategic ideas emerged. However, their influence level was associated with various contextual features: changing norms about corporate governance; the history and performance of the company; the processes and conduct of board meetings; and the extent of informal dialogue between board meetings. This 'shaping' interpretation is at variance with both agency theory and the managerial hegemony school.

Roberts et al. (2005) suggest three couplets express the appropriate balance which in their view NEDs should demonstrate on the board of a publicly quoted firm: (i) engaged but non-executive – a NED should take an active interest in the firm and seek to learn about it, but not try to make micro-level decisions (this may be difficult if they come from a career in executive roles previously); (ii) challenging but supportive – to challenge the executives when necessary but to do this in a way which is helpful rather than obstructive; (iii) independent but involved – maintaining a critical distance from the executives and not 'going native' but without getting out of touch with what is going on in the firm.

Having reviewed some of the key concepts and academic debates of the corporate governance literature, we now discuss its application to public services organizations, drawing in particular from evidence from the UK.

Applications of the corporate governance literature to public services organizations

Corporate governance reforms along private sector lines have been a major strand in NPM-led restructuring in the UK. For example these reforms ensured that boards in such sectors as health care and higher education became smaller, less representative (with fewer staff members and local councillors) and with more private sector business appointments. These reforms were designed to ensure that such boards became more strategic in their operation and with greater influence on the workings of the organization, rather than undertaking decorative or symbolic functions. The old 'members' were relabelled as 'Non Executive Directors' on private sector lines, also now typically appointed rather than elected.

Within the UK public sector, a parallel the rise of the so-called appointed state marked the progressive transfer of powers from elected bodies to appointed bodies known as quasi autonomous non-governmental organizations (or QUANGOs) (Skelcher 1998). NPM reforms are here seen as undermining democratic practice and good governance within an opaque system of 'quasi government' and as leading to a 'democratic deficit.' Further questions emerge as to who is appointed at the board level in UK NPM-style agencies (Skelcher 1998) and how. Multiple interlocks at the board level, that is, where boards are linked to each other through cross representation, were apparent in the public management domain too. Is a party-based political patronage system in operation which controls appointments to these boards (Skelcher estimated at that point that there were 70,000 such posts available to be filled) or are appointments made in a transparent way and on merit? The extent of diversity (e.g. gender and ethnicity) on these public sector boards is an important one, as a highly homogenous board is unlikely to exhibit much creative challenge and fresh thinking.

Skelcher (2000) explores the nature of governance in the post NPM state, given later network governance ideas and then subsequent reforms such as more inter-agency and cross sectoral partnerships designed to handle many 'cross cutting issues' which go beyond the jurisdiction of any one department (e.g. whole area strategies, 'Strategic Partnership Boards'). He distinguishes between elected bodies (at the primary level), appointed bodies (at the second level), and now an increasing number of inter-agency partnerships (at the tertiary level) at the middle or meso level. They are seen (p. 4) as a 'dense, multi layered and largely impenetrable structure for public action.' There are accountability issues to consider in Network Governance-based structures too as (p. 13):

> overall, the transfer of responsibility and power to tertiary bodies poses major issues both for the theory and practice of public governance and management. It removes centres of decision making further from elected political structures, increasing their distance from citizens and often becoming invisible to public view.

This dense web of partnerships exhibits a high level of complexity, opaqueness, and weak accountability (except perhaps upwards to central government in meeting performance targets).

Key examples of NPM-style reforms to corporate governance can be found in UK higher education where the Lambert Review (2003) recommended smaller and more 'business like' boards to govern universities that had become highly complex organizations with large budgets effectively. The recommendation was that university councils should become smaller and more strategic, with non-executives brought in to advise in areas where they had special expertise (e.g. finance). The division of decision making with senior academics (still represented in an academic board) was not always clear: who was to have prime responsibility for academic (as opposed to financial) strategy in practice?

In a critical policy review, Buckland (2004) considers these recommendations of the Lambert Review (2003), based on its adoption of agency theory, to be flawed and contextually inappropriate, given the academic work process (this goes back to Mintzberg's argument about the distinctive nature of strategy making in a professionalized organization). Buckland recommends a shift away from this conventional corporate governance approach to a more pluralist and stakeholder-based model and a looser and broader approach to strategy as appropriate to these more loosely coupled settings (Buckland 2009).

Lambert (2003) built on a prior history, including the removal of staff, trade unions, and local government representatives on the boards of the old UK polytechnics when they became new universities in 1992. In the UK, non-executives on university councils typically appoint the vice chancellor, whereas in some other countries candidates to the post of 'Rector' or 'President' (as they are generally called) of the university run for election in a constituency made up of staff members. The balance between non-executive vs staff-led influence in the procedures for selecting (also the decision between appointment vs election) the president/rector/vice chancellors of universities is thus an important indicator of governance systems in the higher education sector internationally (Ferlie et al. 2009).

Major New Public Management-style corporate governance reforms in the United Kingdom National Health Service (NHS) introduced in 1990 also restructured NHS boards on more private sector lines, with an equal mix of NEDs and EDs. Chambers (2010) describes this model as reflecting the Anglo-Saxon model of the unitary board of the firm. Chairman and CEO roles had always been separate in this sector. Staff, union, and local government representatives were removed, and NEDs were appointed rather than elected. These reforms were designed to create smaller and more cohesive boards and to reduce producer dominance and increase 'governability.'

However, Peck (1995)'s case study of a new NPM-style board in a single NHS Trust found it still had only a marginal impact. In a much larger study, Ferlie et al. (1996, pp. 160–161) discussed the 'funnelling process' which shaped and limited what went to NHS boards from the senior executives. They developed a four-tier model of board effectiveness based on their study of 11 new style NHS boards as a diagnostic framework for board members to help them assess their own effectiveness:

- *At Level A*, the board acts as a conventional 'rubber stamp.' Although some questions of clarification may be asked, executive recommendations tend to go through with little real debate.
- *At Level B*, non-executives are more probing, questioning proposals and sending them back for reconsideration. However, the non-executives are still not involved in the formulation of strategy.
- *At Level C*, there would be substantial non-executive involvement in deciding strategic options and in an early stage of the process.
- *At Level D*, the board debates and delineates a vision of strategic priorities for a future period. The NEDs are involved in shaping this vision, which underpins medium-term statements of strategy. The shape of the vision and the timetable for its achievement may be flexible, but its assumptions act as a foundation.

Ferlie et al. (1996) suggested that boards may move from one level to another over time (upwards or downwards), although moving up from the moderate Level B may involve complex, hard, work. Two factors were essential in moving on from this level: having NEDs in post who have experience, expertise, and confidence and also EDs who genuinely want to make this shared transition. Their judgement was that at the end of fieldwork, none of the 11 sites could be seen as at Level A. Most were at Level

B, with some moving to Level C but one site only (a focused NHS Hospital Trust as opposed to more diffuse health authorities) to Level D. The possibility of achieving Level D did, however, appear to be a real one in a few more promising sites.

After this initial burst of research interest into the post-1990 NHS boards, there have since been fewer large-scale studies. However, there is a small but continuing stream of more recent work on health care boards that can be usefully reviewed here. Abbott et al.'s (2008) exploration of decision making in so-called UK NHS Primary Care Trusts (which were at this stage responsible for primary care rather than hospital services) found that their scope for local strategic direction remained constrained by continuing strong central government control and direction, and they were more likely to discuss what they termed 'second order' functions (e.g. finance) than 'first order' functions (e.g. clinical services, including their reconfiguration); moreover, there was little overt challenge of senior managers and they displayed a 'high trust' culture; they were also overloaded with paperwork and had limited decision-making capacity, while some of the most useful work went on in subcommittees rather than the main board. In many ways, they concluded that 'little seems to have changed from previous studies.'

A more recent reform to NHS governance systems marks a limited tilt back to a more stakeholder-based model (Buckland 2004): there are now 'community' governors appointed and mechanisms in place to promote local public and patient involvement as well as a conventional NPM-style board of directors. Chambers (2010) refers to this pattern as a hybrid whereby an Anglo-Saxon unitary board is now nested inside a more pluralist Continental (European) style supervisory board. The wider and larger set of governors (about 50 of them) who represent many local constituencies is in theory now able to replace the CEO and NEDs (rather than this being done by the Department of Health). But we need to know: how are these governors constructing their role in practice?

Empirical research (Allen et al. 2012) suggested there were frequent perceptions amongst their respondents that these governors and wider stakeholder representatives had as yet only limited impact in governance and that their skills were being underutilized by senior executives. Dixon et al. (2010)'s exploration of accountability for NHS Foundation Trusts also found that governors had only a marginal role as they lacked (or were kept hidden from) key sources of information. In addition, their legitimacy was contested by senior managers. There remained only a weak sense of accountability in these Foundation Trusts as expressed downwards to the local population, yet a strong sense of accountability upwards (to the Department of Health), so that in practice little had changed in developing a more 'downwards looking' accountability.

Two studies examine the correlates of higher levels of 'performance' (whilst recognizing such definitions may be contested) in UK NHS boards. Chambers (2012)'s empirical work suggested that their 'performance' is likely to be higher where (i) the CEO has been in post for more than four years; (ii) there are more women on the board; (iii) there is a greater contribution of NEDs found at board meetings; and (iv) in specialist hospitals.

Another potential cleavage on NHS board is between those EDs who are general managers and from clinical (medicine or nursing) backgrounds. Storey and Holti's (2009) case study-based investigation of two boards in London NHS Trusts found some differences (the general managers emphasized financial control more) but also that the comparison was more nuanced than expected – the general managers acknowledged multiple objectives and forms of accountability; whilst the clinicians had moved on from merely being representatives of the profession to take a somewhat more corporate approach.

There has been increased concern that health care boards have neglected their core oversight role in the field of patient quality and safety which has been displaced by a preoccupation with financial control or mergers and acquisitions. Millar et al.'s (2013) review of the (mainly American) literature on the role of hospital boards in the domain of quality and patient safety surfaced four themes which appeared to be correlated with higher performance: (i) strong and committed leadership from the CEO and board with a strong focus on quality and patient safety rather than finance; (ii) measurement metrics (dashboards; checklists) in the field of quality and patient safety going to the board, and being read, understood, and used; (iii) implementation of board-level oversight; ensuring there are regular agenda items in this field, setting up a quality subcommittee rather than delegating the issue to clinical staff; and (iv) relying on external sources of external regulation and accountability that require the board to sign off returns (e.g. national systems of external regulation in the domain of infection control). Chambers et al.'s (2013) literature review of this patient safety theme in the UK health care context suggests that higher level NHS board performance in this domain is likely to be positively correlated with a quality subcommittee of the board and higher physician involvement, but negatively correlated with a strong focus on financial agenda items; marginalization of the board; and a failure of the board to tackle underlying organizational culture issues.

We have mostly drawn in this analysis from UK examples, because they have been widely studied in the public management literature. Boards are, however, ubiquitous in public agencies across countries and jurisdictions (e.g. nearly all the agencies of the European Union have a governing board, where often sit representatives from each Member State of the EU), and understanding their role in decision-making processes is part and parcel of any study of strategy formation.

We also suggest more work is needed in this important area of corporate governance systems in current public services organizations. Examples of fine empirical works on different countries already available include Allix and Van Thiel (2005), and Verhoest et al. (2012). We need to know more about the involvement of non-executives and the board in strategy making in these settings and the extent to which (and where and why) non-executives are able to combat senior managerial hegemony and to carve out an effective role. It would be interesting to explore further the correlates of higher board 'performance' (although there is unlikely to be one best way): Chambers (2012) suggests a pattern of 'high trust, high challenge and high engagement' is promising. More comparative research exploring alternatives to the operation of the Anglo-Saxon unitary board model evident in NPM-based settings would also be useful for advancing knowledge on the role of the board in the strategy formation process.

Some of these governance themes re-emerge and are further developed in Chapter 5 on strategy making in third-sector organizations.

3.3 Network-based and collaborative models of strategy: an introduction

Since the early 1990s or so, a stream of private sector-based management literature has increasingly moved away from a central assumption of the firm as a large vertically integrated organization (the so-called Fordist mode of production) engaged in mass production of a small number of standard goods to a 'post Fordist' model of specialist and flexible production by leaner firms, often set within larger networks (Amin 1994; Boltanski and Chiapello 2005, Chapter 1). Whereas it used to be assumed that large firms would consolidate and drive out small firms, that trend now appears to have gone into reverse, at least in some important sectors.

In public management and public policy too, there has been a major movement emphasizing the significance of networks and asserting their growing significance, also replacing and displacing more hierarchical modes of governance, as well as an emphasis on collaborative arrangements and more broadly the importance of developing forms of collaborative governance.

The question thus emerges: are similar moves to network-based forms and strategy evident in current public services settings, particularly with the rise of post-NPM 'network governance' orientated (Rhodes 2007) models of public management? And what can this perspective teach us about the strategic management of public services organizations? These important questions are explored in Chapter 4, which is devoted to an in-depth analysis of this perspective.

3.4 The strategy as process school: an introduction

The strategy as process school became prominent in the 1980s and 1990s, being typically interested in processes of attempted large-scale strategic or transformational change (that is, broader than the previous focus on incremental change) that occurred in large organizations particularly since the 1980s, which was empirically evident in both firms and public agencies. Why did this school come to prominence in this period? From the 1980s onwards, both private and public sector organizations in many countries came under intense environmental or political pressure to manage strategic or even transformational forms of change (rather than the more traditional forms of incremental change), given globalization, marketization, and New Public Management reforms in many public sectors worldwide. So, the old presumption of gradual forms of change such as logical incrementalism (Quinn 1980) now appeared dated.

A major focus was on large and mature organizations facing pressures to 'revitalise' (e.g. Pettigrew 1985; Pettigrew et al. 1992), rather than on SMEs or small NGOs. There is here a strong interest in the definition and explanation of organizational 'performance,' often defined in public services settings through proxy or intermediate indicators (e.g. ability to meet stated national policy objectives such as hospital closures or internal market development, see Pettigrew et al. 1992; Ferlie et al. 1996) rather than (say) return on capital or indeed final clinical outcomes. So, it is a form of *management and public management* research. This school is alert to the study of major organizational change in its organizational and social context, including the outer context of the political economy (Pettigrew et al. 1992) as well as the inner context of the firm or organization. Resistance to change is always seen as possible, and attempted strategic change processes may produce implementation deficits which are of interest in their own right.

A later chapter (Chapter 6) will consider the strategy process school (Pettigrew et al. 1992; Van de Ven et al. 1999; Garud and Van de Ven 2006) in more detail, in part because one of the authors of this book (EF) has written in this tradition and has a particular interest in this stream of work. This school brings context systematically into the analysis, and hence it also provides a link to the consideration of context in strategic management which is more systematically discussed in the subsequent Chapter 7.

3.5 Strategy as practice

The comparatively recent strategy-as-practice movement has many links with the strategy-as-process approach in its focus on the inner dynamics of change processes and methodological emphasis on thick, in-depth, often qualitative exploration of selected cases. Its analytical unit is however different: it advocates the micro-level study of concrete and local strategic practices in use (reflecting the wider 'practice turn' across many social sciences, Jarzabkowski et al. 2007). Authors writing in this tradition use the term 'strategizing' to reinforce the notion of human activity which makes strategy in practice. This shift undercuts the old macro-level approaches to strategy which led in their view to a 'cul de sac of high abstraction, broad categories and lifeless concepts' (Johnson et al. 2003, p. 6). Johnson et al. (2003, p. 6) originally defined their approach as follows:

> an emphasis on the detailed processes and practices which constitute the day to day activities of organizational life and which relate to strategic outcomes. Our focus is therefore on micro activities that, while often invisible to traditional strategy research, nevertheless can have significant consequences for organizations and those that work in them.

A later definition (Johnson et al. 2007) extended the focus from day-to-day activities to include more episodic activities, such as board meetings and away days. Second, there was now a more explicit recognition of the connection between activity and its wider context(s): 'a concern with what people do in relation to strategy and how this is influenced by and influences their organizational and institutional context,' perhaps in response to criticisms that the strategy as practice perspective was too micro and disconnected from higher-order trends and shifts.

It is evident in this approach that there is a reprise of many of the themes and the overall thrust of the strategy as process approach (already briefly previewed and to which Chapter 6 is dedicated), which emerged earlier (in the 1970s and 1980s), and this tradition may have been re-energized by the rise of the strategy-as-practice approach, which presents many points of intellectual affinity. There is also, however, in this later school a sense of remedying some perceived failures of the process (and other) previous schools.

What is in fact, it may be asked, the difference between strategy as practice and strategy as process? The strategy-as-process school is here critiqued (Johnson et al. 2007) for moving back from promising early case study work (e.g. Pettigrew 1973) to cross-sectional studies (although we will later argue that they underestimate the extent that the comparative case tradition continues to flourish in the process school). Another difference may be that the process school has a rather narrower view of the cast of actors involved in strategy making, given its increasing focus on the board and NEDs as a prime area of investigation (McNulty and Pettigrew 1999); whereas the strategy-as-practice school has retained a more pluralist focus, including middle managers, management consultants, and boundary spanners.

Johnson et al. (2007) also argue that a practice perspective can remedy deficiencies in newer schools of strategy as well as those classic rational analytic approaches which fail to consider the role of human action. So, the strategy as practice perspective may not just address failures of the rational analytic schools like planning and positioning, but it could also, for instance, illuminate the 'untradeable assets' which are emphasized theoretically but rarely concretely traced by RBV, and in this perspective, it could help RBV deliver on its own manifesto.

Furthermore, Johnson et al. (2003, 2007) argue the case for a shift to a strategy as practice perspective has been reinforced by the emergence in the economic domain of open markets and mobile labour, which means that old barriers to entry are being eroded. As markets open up, sustainable competitive advantage now lies in 'micro' assets that are difficult to detect and trade. Complementing RBV theory, a practice perspective could investigate empirically what these 'micro assets' really are. These 'hyper competitive' markets also produce organizational settings in which strategic responsibilities are now increasingly decentralized from the corporate centre to line managers who are closer to markets and customers and who can react more rapidly. Inherited formal and episodic cycles of strategic planning here give way to strategy making seen as a continuous process. As a result of these shifts, more people within organizations are involved in strategy making and more frequently.

Also writing in this tradition, Jarzabkowski et al. (2007, p. 6) react against the dominance of economic and Porterian approaches in conventional strategic management, seeking to bring human agency back in: 'in order to understand human agency in the construction and enactment of strategy, it is necessary to focus on the actions and interactions of the strategy practitioner.' The strategy-as-practice perspective emphasizes 'strategizing' or the 'doing of strategy' by people. Moreover, a broader range of actors – including middle managers, consultants, and business gurus – has the potential to emerge as strategists than what is allowed by top-down models which privilege the CEO and the top management team. Jarzabkowski et al. (2007, p. 6) stress, however, the need to link the micro-level of strategy with macro-contexts in a multi-level mode of analysis (in response to a critique from Contu and Willmott (2003), of a lack of consideration of power relations in practice based modes of analysis): 'micro phenomena need to be understood in their wider social context: actors are not acting in isolation but are drawing upon the regular, socially defined modes of acting that arise from the plural social institutions to which they belong.' This institutionalist perspective suggests that the macro field produces a menu of possibilities (e.g. use of management consultants; formal strategic planning; culture change programmes) which are selected, used, and possibly adapted by strategic actors in particular organizations. The strategy-as-practice approach, like the strategy as process, place 'context' and the analysis of it centre stage. We shall discuss in Chapter 7 that, in our view, context ought to be considered by all schools of thought in strategic management, because context shapes the very premises, in terms both of autonomy and of what is expected of strategy and of strategists, of strategy making in public services organizations.

The analysis in the strategy-as-practice approach is still pluralist in nature and discounts the possibility of a strongly directive power centre emerging. A further challenge for strategy as practice research (Jarzabkowski et al. 2007; Jarzabkowski 2008) is to ensure that highly detailed and localized empirical research characteristic of the school does indeed connect with the study of outcomes that are consequential for the organization.

What are the strategic practices in use that might concretely be studied? Jarzabkowski et al. (2007, p. 6) mention meetings, workshops (e.g. away days), analytic tools
(such as the use of SWOT), management processes (such as annual plans or investment decisions), and rhetoric or discourse (such as top management's attempt to
project a vision). Accordingly, this school tends to draw on qualitative and in particular ethnographic and anthropological methods, with immersion in field settings and
direct observation, to investigate the career and fate of such techniques in action. In
the following case study (Box 3.1), we see how a series of meetings – regular gather-
ings of stakeholders – were events that played a key function in enabling a major
strategic transformation of a public services organization, the European Training
Foundation.

This example also introduces us to the application of the strategy as practice perspective to public services organizations, to which the remainder of this section is
dedicated. The logic of strategizing seen as an integrative approach for thinking of
strategic management for public services in a more holistic way has also been developed by John Bryson and other leading scholars in a set of publications: we return to
this broad conception and approach of strategizing towards the end of this section,
through a dedicated box prepared by Bryson elaborating on this perspective.

Box 3.1   The European Training Foundation (ETF): combining the design and the strategy-as-practice schools to explain strategic change

The ETF is an agency of the European Union (EU) which was formally established in 1990 – one of the first, as most EU agencies have been established
since the 1990s – and became operational in 1994. In its early years, its core
competence was one of project management, delivering technical assistance
services in education and vocational training in third-country recipients of EU-
funded programmes. Then, a major strategic turn occurred, and between 2000
and 2010, the tasks and the very position of the agency in the EU institutional-
administrative environment changed dramatically. ETF became a provider of
high-level policy advice and a major actor of vocational education and training
policies in third-country recipients of EU funding; its staff have since been operating as policy advisors to governments in Asia, the Caucasus, the Near East, the
Mediterranean basin, and the Balkans.

How did such major strategic change occur? How did it happen that this
public agency changed its mandate, core tasks, and capabilities as well as its key
relationships and interdependencies with EU institutions (chiefly the Commission)? A set of actors both within and outside the agency jointly operated to
steer the re-orientation of ETF. They managed to achieve legitimacy from key
external stakeholders for such a turn.

This process occurred in an environment fraught with threats for the very
survival of the agency. In fact, when ETF became operational, developments in
the EU-funded programmes aimed at supporting the transition of former Soviet

bloc countries to democratic institutions and free market economy provided the frame in which ETF found its well-recognized original function, namely, delivering technical assistance in vocational training (chiefly monitoring the execution of EU-funded programmes). But soon after, the circumstances changed dramatically: following up the resignation of the European Commission executive led by Jacques Santer (in the year 1999) due to a financial scandal, reform of the governance and management of the Commission gained prominence and led to various interventions in financial and personnel management. Under new regulations, the Commission was forbidden to outsource tasks in external relations, including the technical assistance ETF was providing. So, some in the Commission (and elsewhere) raised the issue of 'what to do with ETF? Kill it?' Moreover, some countries originally recipients of EU technical assistance were on their way to completing EU accession, hence becoming State Members of the EU and no longer clients of it (ETF provides services only to third, namely, non-EU, countries). The situation had suddenly become fluid and had at stake the role and the very survival of the agency.

However, the transforming environment was bringing not just threats, but potential opportunities as well: the nascent European Neighbourhood Policy would make new countries enter the scope of EU external policy. At the same time, the European public discourse known as the 'Lisbon agenda for the competitiveness of Europe' outlined a programme of reforms marked by concepts such as 'lifelong learning' and 'lifetime education,' which opened up a new policy space for the agency.

How was then ETF to cope with the transforming environment? A decisive intervention came from Mrs Catherine Day, a high official representing the Commission in the governing board of ETF, later to become the secretary general of the Commission. The move that turned out to be a watershed event occurred when she sent a letter – specifically, an email – to various officials within the Commission, which circulated widely and in which she outlined a 'vision' for ETF. The main thesis was that ETF should become a source of expertise and support to Commission Delegations (EU 'embassies' in third countries) and that its task should be to shape the education policy of the recipient countries, so that they were 'aligned' with EU goals. Project management tasks would be outsourced for the most part to the recipient countries' governments.

Actors in different DGs of the European Commission reacted differently; but a decisive intervention came from within the agency. An external evaluation had been commissioned to a consultancy; the central evaluative question was the future tasks and mandate of ETF: 'what does ETF have to do?' The final report was delivered and officially discussed at the Governing Board meeting in late 2002. The then director Peter De Rooij and his aides exploited the opportunity to comment on the evaluation report before its final adoption to stress the passage about the opportuneness to cast a new mandate for ETF. Soon after, the director of ETF of the time intervened in front of the Education Committee of the European Parliament, one of the two EU legislative bodies. The other legislative body, the Council of Ministers, which is formed by the governments of the EU Member States, was also targeted by the ETF director. This process eventually led to both legislative organs recasting of the founding regulation and setting the new competencies that were incorporated into the mandate of the agency.

Such a 'proactive' stance from ETF, however, was not the initial one, and it was supported by an unexpected event: a gathering in November 2003 the Advisory Forum held with partner countries, member states, and the Commission. The topic of the meeting was 'learning matters' and suggested ETF could showcase – and was on that occasion recognized to have the legitimacy to provide – three kinds of knowledge: of vocational training and education policies, of the recipient countries, and of the administrative functioning of EU programmes. The event marked the collective perception about the need to change and gave shape to a shared sense of direction for ETF and what it was to become.

A second forum was held three years later, in 2006: the 2006 forum demonstrated the importance of consulting and of networking in the EU neighbouring countries where ETF was active. The third forum held in 2009 formalized the so-called 'Torino' process (ETF is located in Turin, or Torino in the Italian language). In sum, the 2003 forum performed a catalytic function for the initial strategic turn, whilst successive events and the triggering of the Torino process performed the complementary function of developing and consolidating the new 'vision' of ETF as a provider of policy advice.

The unfolding of the strategic change that occurred at ETF requires the recounting of another event when the execution of a major funded programme was taken back from ETF reassigned to another agency. The ETF on that occasion eventually managed to keep the posts in the staffing and to replace the departing personnel with people with new and different skills, more attuned to the new advisory role. This event occurred in 2005–2006, and in hindsight it provided a key moment for ETF to be able to build its skills base and organizational capabilities to sustain its new role, thus aligning strategy and structure.

How can we interpret strategic change? What form did strategy take in this case? The new strategy on one hand was explicit and formalized in documents exchanged with the Commission and other EU institutions and approved by the governing board and in legally binding EU acts. It may also be interpreted as deliberate: from the letter sent out by Mrs Day and addressed to the decision makers involved in recasting the mandate of ETF, to the public hearings made by the *pro tempore* ETF director in front of the competent parliamentary committee. A clear vision for ETF was championed by certain key actors from the early phases of the strategic change process. In other words, strategy in the case appears to be both formalized and deliberate.

Content-wise, the novel and threatening circumstances that took shape around 2000 were mostly regarded as provoking a misfit between the changing environment (interpreted as a set of external threats and opportunities) and the internal configuration of ETF (seen as no longer adequate to the environment), for which a bespoke solution was sought. The subsequent changes to the statute and hence mandate of ETF are a reflection and embodiment of the strategic turn that occurred, hence in a sense 'policy change' was driven by strategic change, rather than the other way around.

Put together, these elements – strategy as a deliberate attempt to lead the organization by certain key actors, strategy as searching for a proper fit between the organization and the environment, strategy as 'bespoke' and unique to the organization – fit well with the design school of strategic management.

However, the original design school often assumes one individual (typically the CEO) to be the pivotal actor and the architect of the strategy. In this public agency setting, the initial framework has to be amended to accommodate the presence of a collective actor – some individuals composing it even being institutionally affiliated to other organizations – as 'the strategist.' Importantly, in fact, the story points to the *joint* action of actors who entered (and exited) the decision opportunities at different points in time as having steered the agency's re-orientation. *Jointly*, they imagined, built up capacity, and legitimated a 'new vision' for the agency as an EU centre of expertise in education and vocational training. In other words, these actors acted collectively to design the new strategy: this is a case of design strategy with a collective strategist, rather than a single individual.

On the other hand and complementarily, this major strategic change would have not been sustainable without the building up of organizational capacities and, especially, without the legitimacy and recognition that came from aptly exploiting the 'Torino process,' both symbolically and practically, for getting full recognition and legitimacy by all the agency's stakeholders. The theoretical underpinnings for the interpretation of 'practices' as embodying or making the strategy (rather than just being a manifestation of it) are indeed provided by the strategy-as-practice approach.

Summing up, it is a combination of the design school with the strategy-as-practice approach that provides a theoretically based interpretation of how strategy unfolded at ETF: strategy was both a matter of 'fit' between internal configuration and external configuration, deliberate and unique, and at the same time strategy was significantly made through key events and practices, notably the Torino Process.

Source: elaborated from Ongaro and Ferlie 2019

Strategy as practice in public/not-for-profit settings

The strategy-as-practice perspective has a strong alignment with public and not-for-profit settings, perhaps because it does not assume the presence of strong competitive forces shaping the organization and in its openness to pluralist forces such as influential professionals who may counterbalance the traditional power of top management.

Jarzabkowski and Wilson (2002) provide a longitudinal case study of strategy making in a major UK university (Warwick), combining strategy-as-process and strategy-as-practice perspectives. The empirical findings were complex and nuanced. This single case study suggested a different pattern from the conventional literature on universities, which sees them as weakly organized or 'loosely coupled' (Weick 1976), thus challenging some established assumptions. One explanation for this shift was that the university had developed major streams of income from non-governmental sources so that it was an exemplar of a new form of an 'entrepreneurial university.' It both needed to protect these sources of extra income at a corporate level and then had the benefit of making university-wide decisions about how to reinvest them.

Jarzabkowski and Wilson (2002) concluded that the top management team at Warwick was a cohesive group which undertook a stream of intended strategic activity, and while the cast of strategic actors was broader and included heads of some large academic departments, such a broadening was still relatively contained: (pp. 375–376) 'we found a University where the goals were clearly articulated and actions were consistent with those goals over time. This consistency was based on dirigiste formalised procedures which supported the decision making and action process.' There were local routines and practices which supported this strategic style, such as the important doctrine of short lines of communications between 'strong centre and strong academic departments,' notably a subset of large and powerful academic departments. The intermediate faculty tier appeared less well developed. In addition, many key role-holders had built up long experience in post and there was interlocking membership of the key committees (critics might argue that the degree of pluralism in this case appears highly bounded).

Other important practice-based studies referred to in Johnson et al. 2007 include Gioia and Chittipeddi (1991), who analyzed the initiation of a strategic change process in an American university setting by a new president, using a cognitive framing of cycles of sense making and sense giving to explain attempts by the new leader to develop and then to communicate a new strategic vision for the university.

Oakes et al. (1998) examine the introduction of new forms of 'business' planning in museums in the mid-1990s in Alberta, Canada. Such planning systems are seen not as neutral techniques but as a form of 'pedagogy' which attempted to teach new NPM-based work practices to museum curators (an interesting and understudied group of public services professionals), following the election of a radical right provincial government and its fundamental review of the scope and nature of the public sector. This article is unusual in its ability to draw strong connections between new micro-level planning and a changing macro-level political economy which translated itself into practical meso-level reform doctrines.

Strategizing

Prominent scholar John Bryson has made a major contribution to conceptualizing strategizing as an organizing and integrating concept, intended in a broad and encompassing way that in a certain sense 'upgrades' this notion and brings it to bear as a general way of conceiving of human activity, rather than as an approach to strategic management 'strictly intended.' This conception is wrought out by John Bryson in the following Box 3.2.

Box 3.2 Strategizing as an organizing and integrating concept

By *John M. Bryson*

Strategizing is such a basic part of being human that it can be easy to overlook as a concept. A variety of formulaic step-by-step guides and stand-alone tools and techniques are available to help with strategizing in, for example, personal self-help guides, leadership training programmes, and organizational management textbooks. At the same time, careful studies of the actual process and practices of strategizing are surprisingly rare (though that is changing). How odd, given strategizing's significance as a pervasive organizing and integrating concept!

As an organizing concept, strategizing links aspirations and capabilities, issues and answers, and problems and solutions (Ackermann and Eden 2011; Gaddis 2018; Bryson 2021). This includes forming, deciding on, or changing aspirations and strategies. It also includes developing or acquiring capabilities, and it includes learning-by-doing and changing your mind (Ansell 2011). Where in the world would we be without aspirations, capabilities, and the linkages among them?

As an integrating concept, strategizing cuts across levels from societal to organizational to individual, and it pulls from multiple fields and disciplines, in much the same way that concepts like leadership, collaborating, resourcing, planning, and implementation do. The world comes at us in a holistic way far differently than the disintegrated worlds of academia, journals, professions, and practices. We need integrating concepts to pull together what otherwise is excessively fragmented. Strategizing is such a concept.

Strategizing is a response to challenges and opportunities. If one is to address the challenges effectively and take advantage of opportunities, while minimizing or overcoming weaknesses and threats, strategizing is certainly necessary, since there are undoubtedly more ways to fail than to succeed. Even though strategizing can never guarantee success, at least it may reduce the risk of failure, or if failure does occur, it can help increase the likelihood of drawing the right lessons from failure, so that success is more likely in the future (Bryson 2021).

Strategizing in practice necessarily involves thinking, acting, and learning (Ferlie and Ongaro, this volume) in a politically astute way (Hartley et al. 2015), and is, for those reasons, a vital source of the effectiveness of public and non-profit organizations. My colleague Bert George and I define strategizing as 'consisting of the activities undertaken by public organizations or other entities to deliberately and emergently (re)align their aspirations and capabilities, thus exploring how aspirations can actually be achieved within a given context – or else need to be changed – taking into account current capabilities and the possible need to develop new capabilities or to change the context' (Bryson and George 2020, p. 1). Learning, of course, is an integral aspect of effective strategizing and is focused 'pragmatically on what works, which likely includes knowing something about what doesn't; learning of this sort doesn't have to be by design – much of it will be tacit and epiphenomenal' (Bryson 2018, p. 14).

Strategizing doesn't assume some organization, group, or person is necessarily in charge, nor does it assume that strategies are deliberately set, though some can be. Strategizing instead typically is taking place in the flow of time, where some strategies are deliberately set, but others are emergent; some strategies are realized in practice, while others are not (Mintzberg et al. 2009). Strategizing as a concept is more about seeing organizations (or other entities) as flows through time that are or are not, will or will not, accomplish some proximate or distal, explicit or implicit, purposes. Strategizing is about trying to alter something about those flows, meaning their volume, speed, shape, content, or direction. There are lots of ways to alter those flows, for example, leadership changes, funding changes, strategic planning, organizational redesigns, competition, and collaboration. A focus on strategizing opens one's eyes to what all of these flows and interventions are for, what they consist of, and how they work. The focus helps organize attention and integrate knowledge for action.

3.6 A public sector-based school of strategy: the public value approach

Before concluding this chapter, we finally consider a school of thought in strategic management which originated in the public sector, rather than in the private sector to be then adapted for public services organizations.

The Public Value school (Moore 1995; Benington and Moore 2011b) is an explicitly public sector management-orientated model (Moore is an academic at the Kennedy School of Government at Harvard rather than Harvard Business School), whose origin can be traced in Moore's important 1995 book. His work has also been developed through extensive interaction with public managers in many executive education programmes and so has a strong practice connection. Its intellectual roots lie more in applied public management than conventional political science or economics, and it is open to an adapted version of some generic strategic management concepts. Other key authors in the origin of the Public Value school are John Benington and Jean Hartley in the UK and John Alford in Australia.

The Public Value school offers reflections on and a response to the New Public Management reform wave. On the one hand, the Public Value school is based on the claim that the NPM has in important respects been superseded, because of its own internal weaknesses. On the other hand, it accepts some of NPM's criticisms of the 'old' public sector and searches for better social value through accelerating more entrepreneurial public managers' capacity to engage in innovation (Benington and Moore 2011a), armed with their 'restless value seeking imaginations.'

Moore contests the traditional American public administrative doctrine that sees public managers as highly constrained (p. 17):

> this doctrine produces a characteristic mindset among public sector managers: the mindset of administrators or bureaucrats rather than of entrepreneurs, leaders of executives. Their orientation is *downward* toward the reliable control of

organizational operations rather than either *outward,* toward the achievement of valuable results, or *upward,* towards renegotiated policy mandates. Instead of viewing their task as initiating or facilitating change, they tend to see it as maintaining a long term institutional perspective in the face of fickle political whims.

Where legislative mandates are weak, ambiguous, or flexible, public sector managers have scope for taking strategic action to expand the wider public value of their organizations. Moore (1995) starts with a simple example/homily of a town librarian wondering about whether to expand the traditional scope of the library's services to meet the wider needs of local children who need more intensive support, and in essence whether to act as a social innovator or to remain within a narrower prescribed role. Public managers are here seen as stewards of public value more than as loyal/ unimaginative (depending on one's view) agents of politicians. Central to this school is the notion of 'creation of public value,' defined as the impact on public needs (collectively identified and selected through democratic means). Such notions of how the political system might operate have been criticized on the ground that they are Western-centric or even American-centric (Rhodes and Wanna 2007).

The Public Value school is friendly to some (adapted) notions of corporate strategic management developed by private sector writers, while seeking to maximize public value rather than shareholder value (p. 70). Its concept of a public value chain, for instance, echoes Porter's idea of a value chain. Indeed, the notion of public value may be coupled with the analytical apparatus of the value chain, suitably adapted for public services organizations. The approach of the value chain (one of the key concepts introduced by Porter, see Chapter 2) consists of the analysis of processes in the organization, or across a network of organizations, to identify what activities add value for the final user of the public service. The overall thrust of the value chain analysis in public services is to prioritize activities that 'add value' to the services delivered to the users and concentrate all organizational efforts on improving them, and also to assess activities that do not add value, to find out whether their costs may be reduced, or even whether they may be eliminated altogether. Defining and measuring public value is the obvious underpinning of this entire approach.

Within a public value perspective, also, the RBV-based concept that the public organization might have a distinctive competence wider than its current use may be a helpful one. The drive to increase agency performance considering the preferences of external stakeholders can help increase public value. RBV-based concepts of agency flexibility and adaptability may help a public agency survive and flourish more than rigidly focusing on a specified mandate.

The strategic triangle model is a key analytic technique and heuristic presented within this school (Moore 1995, p. 71; Moore and Benington 2011a, pp. 4–5; also Stoker 2005). Public sector strategy making rests on three fundamental tenets which need to be aligned together to create public value:

(i) *Defining public value:* clarifying and specifying the strategic goals of the organization (cast in terms of important public values and appraised against the benefits that could have been gained through alternative private uses of the resources employed to reach those goals);

(ii) *Authorization:* creating the 'authorizing environment' necessary to achieve the desired public outcomes; building a coalition of stakeholders from the public, private and third sectors (importantly, this coalition includes but is not restricted to elected politicians and appointed overseers), whose support is needed to sustain the necessary strategic actions; and

(iii) *Building operational capacity*: harnessing and mobilizing the operational resources (finance, skills, staff, technology), both inside and outside the organization, necessary to support the achievement of desired public value outcomes.

The public value perspective goes beyond the state/market binary divide, examining the possibility for networked community governance (Benington 2011), with some affinities with the post-NPM network governance model of public policy reform already reviewed. It certainly presents itself as a post-NPM model (Benington 2011, p. 46), including a novel focus on environmental value: 'adding value to the public realm by actively promoting sustainable development and reducing public "bads" like pollution, waste, global warming.' An interesting chapter by Swilling (2011) develops this sustainability perspective on public value further, with a particular focus on developing countries at risk of ecosystem breakdown.

Clearly, this strategic triangle model (Moore 1995, p. 74) differs from standard public administration accounts in advocating public managerial action and in particular their sponsoring of social innovation within crowded and complex policy arenas where elected politicians are seen as only one of many legitimate stakeholders. As such, it has been critiqued by political scientists (Rhodes and Wanna 2007, 2008; see also Alford 2008 for a rejoinder) for its blurring of the politics/administration divide and for taking an overly optimistic view of the motivations of public managers depicted as unselfish 'platonic guardians' and neutral defenders of the public interest, rather than seen as a special interest group with its own expansionist agenda (on empirical grounds, one might also consider the levels of governmental corruption as measured by the international non-governmental organization 'Transparency International' in a number of countries, some of them explicitly encompassed in our work, and query on this terrain as well the extent to which public managers may be regarded as platonic guardians of the public interest, anywhere and anytime).

Critics could also argue that its discussion of public value remains at a very high level (Benington 2011) and embeds a range of different dimensions, and it can thus turn out to be difficult to operationalize. This consideration links to a further point about their recommended decision-making process: who decides what adds to public value and how are such decisions made? Could public managers become over-dominant in such decisions and use their dominance to promote the expansion of their own organizations as argued by Niskanen (1971)? And also, while it presents itself as a post-NPM model, is it more NPM-like than it itself recognizes? Its emphasis on the potential role of public managers as self-directed social entrepreneurs under loose political constraints appears as a soft, public sector version of the NPM doctrine that 'managers must manage' ('let managers manage' coupled with 'make managers manage'). The Public Value school undoubtedly imports and also adapts concepts from mainstream private sector-based models of strategic management, notably Porter and RBV. Its assessment of political legitimacy may be seen in this critique as representing a variant of the external environmental analysis often found in conventional strategic analysis; while its consideration of internal operational competences – or lack of them – is another form of internal analysis. In its overall thrust, however, the Public Value school appears as original and distinctive in its origins within government settings. Developments more recently like the adoption of the intellectually sophisticated lens of 'political astuteness' by public managers (Hartley et al. 2015) have led to a refinement of the propositions of the Public Value school in ways that address at least some of the criticisms that have been put to it.

Finally, the Public Value school has powerfully contributed to defining the notion and the profile of the 'public entrepreneur': the public entrepreneur is in this perspective the public manager who acts as creator of public value. The public entrepreneur is in problematic and dynamic relationship with politicians/elected officials/the authorizing environment. We have already seen the notion of the 'public entrepreneur' from a different theoretical angle, that is, when applying Mintzberg's notion of the 'entrepreneurial school of thought in strategic management' to the public sector and public services in Chapter 2; that perspective emphasizes the skills required of the public entrepreneur to be successful in its own terms, that is, in growing a public services organization and making it survive and thrive in its environment, while the Public Value school problematizes notably the 'outcome' of public entrepreneurship, namely, if it ultimately creates public value (and therefore discusses what is public value and how to measure it), as well as its legitimacy (and therefore the authorizing environment and the relationship between public managers turned entrepreneurs and elected officials/politicians). The two approaches – the Public Value school and Mintzberg's entrepreneurial school – should in our view be seen as complementary, as they focus different profiles of the same phenomenon. A third 'declension' of the notion of the public entrepreneur, notably the social entrepreneur, is discussed in depth in Chapter 5.

3.7 Concluding discussion

This chapter has reviewed some recent schools of strategic management, considering their application to current public services and not-for-profit settings (on the latter, we further develop our argument in Chapter 5). We observe that the number of schools of strategic management is increasing over time, as newer ones emerge and then coexist with older ones rather than displacing them entirely. While the Porterian models of the 1980s remain influential, there are a growing number of alternatives. These newer models exhibit different disciplinary roots from conventional industrial economics (Porter), including heterodox economics (Penrose, RBV), anthropological, historical, and longitudinal approaches (strategy as process), and cognitive/micro sociological (e.g. strategy as practice) and a network-based and collaborative approach to strategy. The Public Value school has originated and developed within public service and government settings.

These theories may indeed be complementary as well as competing and enable us to understand complex empirical cases in a variety of different ways. We illustrate this observation with two cases here. The combined use of some of the cited schools sheds helpful light on the strategic management of universities in Finland operating under changing environmental conditions (Box 3.3). Policy and organizational changes in the public employment services in the Netherlands can also be seen through a variety of theoretical prisms (Box 3.4) as can the strategic management of the Quebec health care system (Box 3.5).

Box 3.3   Pursuing strategic research management – prioritizing research areas in Finnish universities

By *Turo Virtanen*

The global trend of reforming universities incorporates attempts to deploy more business-like management practices – including strategic management. In many countries, this has been part of the reforms of public administration and followed NPM ideas. Such ideas have spilled over to universities, which are heavily dependent on governmental funding. Universities' autonomy in academic and scholarly affairs is a commonly accepted value. Although the autonomy may be formally organized with a variety of organizational parameters, there is a tendency to expect that the use of governmental money for education and research is based on strategic planning executed both by government and universities themselves.

In Finland, universities have autonomy based on the constitution, and since 2010, universities are no longer part of regular state organization and budget. However, most of the funding comes as governmental subsidies (not as appropriations) from the state budget. The dialogue between the state and universities takes the form of performance contracts established for four-year periods. The contracts include goals and performance targets and resources for both education and research. The Ministry of Education and Culture confirms the contracts that are expected to implement governmental policies of higher education, research, and innovation. In this case study of the University of Helsinki, the focus is on research, the core of the academic freedom enjoyed by universities. Academic research has been traditionally left more or less untouched by explicit organizational strategies, but many countries have reformed their research and innovation policies to include stronger measures of creating critical mass and research profiles for universities.

The Finnish government decided in 2005, as part of the structural development of the public research system, to allocate resources to bigger entities and to strengthen networks, management, and performance evaluation of public research system. The governmental development plan for education and research 2011–2016 set the goal that universities would profile themselves according to their strengths to improve their competitiveness. Since 2009, the Ministry has explicitly expected the universities to set prioritized focus areas for academic research.

For example, the strategic research areas of the University of Helsinki, as specified in the performance contract between the Ministry and the university for 2010–2012, were (i) the thinking and learning human being, (ii) health and welfare, (iii) climate and environmental development and natural resources, and (iv) culture and society. In its feedback, the Ministry recommended more specified foci. In 2011, the university agreed on ten focus areas of research: (i) the basic structure, materials, and natural resources of the physical world, (ii) the basic structure of life, (iii) the changing environment – clean water, (iv) the thinking and learning human being, (v) welfare and safety, (vi) clinical research, (vii) precise reasoning, (viii) language and culture, (ix) social justice, and (x) globalization and social change.

The focus areas are not part of the university's strategy but of the annual targets programme, as the university wanted to keep it open the option for yearly updates. The university strategy for 2013–2016 set some guidelines regarding research focus areas: 'the University's focus areas will draw on high-quality research and societal impact'; the focus areas 'are based on proven excellence, social significance and emerging fields of importance'; 'the University will establish transparent quality criteria for allocating research resources to relevant areas'; 'departmental and faculty-level profiling will be used to increase investment in top-quality research'; and 'resources will be systematically directed to both focus areas and new initiatives.'

The formulation process of research focus areas included planning processes in each 11 faculties of the university. This material was used for designing both the focus areas of the whole university and those of the faculties. The latter can be understood also as instruments in the implementation of the university-wide focus areas, as faculty-level areas were the basis for university-level synthesis.

In the interviews conducted as part of a larger study, the university leadership pointed out that given the large scope and intention to be a full-scale university with all major disciplines also in the future, the leaders of the university were hesitant in specifying focus areas. It is fair to say that without the pressure from the Ministry, research focus areas would not exist, or their design would have started later. Focus areas were seen as more important for smaller universities, rather than for the only major university in the country. However, the process was carried out, and it was considered beneficial. Also the focus areas as such were considered handy in the communication with potential international partners. However, certain constraints turned out to be obvious: the formulations are bound to be very general, and their impact faint if not negligible, as resources were bound by already existing activities and extra government funding appeared unlikely.

The leadership team emphasized that choices between possible focus areas should be made at faculty and department levels, as the university has no resources to pursue the internationally renowned research in all areas. In practice, the implementation of focus areas turned out to be slow, partly because of the inherently difficult reallocation of resources within the university.

The university executives aimed, however, to be consistent with the plan, as the focus areas were paid attention to in the allocation of resources. Nonetheless, the amount of allocated resources was small. The proposals for allocations came from the faculties, which tended to refer to the focus areas with the hope of increasing the likelihood of positive decisions. Small amounts of funding were allocated also to proposals of new initiatives. At the same time, the university was inconsistent with its plan, because all 'good' applications for external research funding tended to get the recommendation from department heads and deans, although the application might not be sufficiently connected to the focus areas. In the age of austerity, the university simply needs all the money it can get.

One can interpret the observed process of setting focus areas for academic research (at least on paper) through the lens of a number of schools of strategic management, or the critiques thereof. The split between formulation and implementation of a strategy, one traditional critique of the *strategic planning school*, is clearly detectable. Research focus areas existed as a choice on paper, and only relatively faint implementation could be observed, mostly on paper as argumentation justifying applications and decisions, many of which would have taken place anyway. What is astonishing is the readiness to update research focus areas annually. The idea of long-term planning with effective implementation would imply more permanent choices. This suggests a perception that research is too dynamic to be steered in long term.

The *strategic positioning school* also played in, at least formally: the University of Helsinki set an officially declared goal to be among the 50 best universities in the world (without specifying how this is measured). The university executives understood that this required building on strengths and also on new initiatives, but setting research focus areas was not, at least openly, a key instrument in pursuing this goal.

The *entrepreneurial school* emphasizes bold strokes which seem to be non-existent in pursuing a research profile in the university. Research strategies are easily conservative, not innovative, at least when they are built on the existing research strengths consolidated over the years by and with the support of senior colleagues and without resources to recruit 'stellar academics.' This does not prevent individual scientists from taking risks in the pursuit of innovation, but the organizational support in terms of money may be negligible.

The *Mintzbergian* ideas about emergent strategies and learning come out of the 'rationality box.' The role of research focus areas in university research strategy can be understood as a pattern in the stream of decisions – an emergent pattern to be found only retrospectively. The research strategy is largely based on reactions to environmental and cognitive limitations. The formulation of focus areas was considered an important learning experience, and not a long-term commitment, as the option of annual updates was kept open. This confirms the existence of learning aspect connected to even the formal stages of strategic planning. Finally, the *cultural school* raises issues going beyond rational behaviour. Perhaps the most visible belief in the NPM-inspired tenet of strategic choices assumes that also universities may flourish only if academically free research is managed more 'rationally.' This may be a cultural fad (story and ritual) that universities need to pay attention to, at least formally (symbolically), to make the appearance of an advanced and legitimate consumer of public and private money for research.

Box 3.4   Strategic management in reforming the Public Employment Service in the Netherlands

By *Nicolette van Gestel*

During the last decades, the Public Employment Service (PES) in the Netherlands went through several radical reforms. The first reform was the introduction of a *network model* in 1991, wherein the PES was governed by central and regional 'tripartite' boards, with representatives from the government, employers' associations, and unions each having an equal say. In 2002, the network model was replaced by a *principal-agent model* wherein the government acted as a principal and private bureaus for employment services were contracted as agents. The third reform in the Dutch PES was introduced in 2009, when the two national agencies for social security and for job services were merged to a single *hierarchy,* followed by a *digitizing of services* (called operation 'Redesign') and a restriction of the usual face-to-face contacts in job services to only 10% of the clients since 2012. Despite the various modes of governance in this turbulent history of reforms (network, market, hierarchy), all reforms had similar aims: to increase the efficiency of the PES services, to improve the number of job placements and reduce social expenditures, and to enlarge the user-friendliness of the services. The strategic management of the PES in the Netherlands thus seems steady in what they strive for, but rather unsettled in how to reach these aims.

The background for the subsequent reforms is a continuous dissatisfaction about the PES performance, in particular the number of job placements, and the difficulty to reach a political solution given the various preferences of political parties and other interest groups (Van Gestel and Hillebrand 2011). The main actors behind the first reform (the network model) were the Christian democrats, both the political party (CDA) and the Christian democratic union (CNV), who thought to engage employers' associations and trade unions directly in the governing boards of the PES in order to improve the PES performance. About ten years later, the second reform (the principal-agent model) was supported by the Liberals who were keen on the privatization of the job services to private bureaus and framed the principal-agent model as marketization. The Liberals got support from the Social Democrats, who did not like the privatization but enjoyed the government being in the role of principal. The third reform had its main background in the government's deficit: the PES budget for job finding was downsized severely, which led to the government's strategic decision for the merger of two national agencies and a few years later to the decision to digitizing the PES services for the unemployed. With the third reform, the PES management also decided to keep face-to-face services restricted to a small group of clients that were supposed to be in need of intensified assistance (e.g. some of the elderly, migrants, disabled workers).

The reforms took place in a highly political environment, with pluralist power relations. The context of the reforms was characterized by regularly changing political coalitions: the first reform was prepared and supported by Christian Democrats and Liberals (during the 1980s), the second reform by Liberals and Social Democrats (2002), and the third one by Christian Democrats and Social Democrats (2009), respectively, Liberals and Social Democrats (2012).

Theoretical lenses

The first reform of the PES towards the network model can be perceived as an example of the *classical design school* in strategic management, where the strategy of an organization should be reflected in its formal structure ('strategy determines structure,' Chandler 1962). The main rationale behind the design of the tripartite network model (the first reform) was to improve employment rates. Given this strategy, it was presumed that a network structure where the government collaborates with employers' associations and unions would be most appropriate. The first reform thus looked for a strategic fit between the PES organization and the major players in its environment. In contrast to the first reform, the next two reforms were not inspired by a strategy for the labor market, but by the government's aim for efficiency of the PES services. The principal-agent model emphasized the assumed lowering of prices by competition between private providers, and the digitizing of job services was first and foremost a solution for severe budget cuts of the PES.

The *strategic planning school* emphasizes long-range planning and resists a binary split between (policy) formulation and implementation, as 'paper plans' without a basis in reality would lead to major implementation problems. One of the main reasons of the government for the first PES reform was to avoid this binary split between policy formulation and implementation. Employers' associations and unions were involved in the governing structure of the PES in 1991, to stay away from 'paper plans' that were disconnected from real life problems at the labor market. Moreover, the governing power of the government was decentralized to regional, tripartite boards to solve regional labor market problems. However, an evaluation of the Dutch welfare state between 1980 and 2008 found that the successive reforms were badly informed about the implementation process, leading to a recurrence of policy problems and ineffective reforms (Van Gestel et al. 2009). Following this critical evaluation, strategic planning should focus less on changing governance structures, and more on improving collaborative processes, with an in-depth reflection on performance, decentralized leadership, and innovative experiments.

This comes close to a *Mintzbergian strategy*, as opposed to the Design school and Porterian thinking, where an emerging strategy by plural actors in an iterative process of organizational learning is put central. In the 25 years of PES reforms, we can observe a short period where Mintzberg's strategy seemingly influenced the ideas about strategic management. It was after the second reform of the PES, in particular between 2002 and 2006, that a bottom up 'chain collaboration' started between the national agency for social security and the remaining PES office, together with the local governments, while all parties realized that the frequent structural changes had not brought them any further. In this period, the emphasis was on the *process* (improving collaboration between the different agencies) rather than on structural reform.

The *Entrepreneurial School* only influenced the strategic management of the PES during the first reform. Interestingly, at that time the entrepreneurs in strategic management of the PES were three people who worked closely together while each was connected to a particular group of stakeholders: the director of the PES dealt with the ministry and its bureaucrats; the minister of Social Affairs and Employment discussed the PES strategy with the Parliament; while the project manager of the first PES reform kept the social partners involved.

After the first reform was realized, this type of entrepreneurial managers or leaders of the PES was no longer accepted by the political environment. Public managers with an entrepreneurial style, such as the new director of the PES in 1991, or in 2002, received a low response on their entrepreneurial actions, e.g. to introduce channelling in public services.

Finally, the *strategy-as-practice perspective* advocates a research agenda to explore what people do in terms of strategic activity at a micro-level (in day-to-day activities such as meetings), while considering their institutional and organizational contexts. The need to connect these micro- and macro-levels in analysis is also emphasized by *neo-institutional theory*, which traditionally tends to focus on institutional structures rather than on agency and action. The many reforms of the PES during the past 25 years cannot be understood without taking this connection between micro- and macro-analysis seriously.

Box 3.5 Strategic management and Quebec health care administration

By *Johanne Préval and Jean-Louis Denis*

École nationale d'administration publique – Canada

This case outlines a recent strategic reform in the health system in Quebec and then considers how it may be understood using several schools of strategic management.

The Quebec health care system is structured around three levels of governance. The Ministry of Health and Social Services (MSSS) of Quebec is the provincial authority that oversees 18 RHAs which have governance responsibilities over the delivery of care and services within their territory. RHAs and health care organizations have their own governing board but are at the same time hierarchically related to the superior level of governance. Each level of governance has its own set of priorities that are communicated through strategic plans and can be agreed through contracts.

In 2004, the government of Quebec undertook a reform which consisted of the reorganization of its health care system. Two bills, numbers 25 and 83 respectively, were adopted in 2004 and 2005 and targeted the boundaries of public health care organizations with the aim of improving the integration of health and social services and ultimately the health of the population. This major policy transforms the structural landscape of the health care systems by creating Health and Social Services Centres (HSSC) in 95 local health territories. Their creation was based on a recommendation from a public commission, the Clair Commission, and its final report in 2000 recommended merging institutions on a sub-regional basis to create integrated care delivery systems and to place value on the management of performance within the system (Sutherland et al. 2013).

The reform was guided by two principles: population-based responsibility and the hierarchical provision of services and service programmes. Regional health agencies had the mandate to implement the HSSC, and the responsibility to manage, coordinate, and deliver health care to the population of their region.

The HSSC are created as a result of a merger between long-term care facilities, local community services centres, and small hospitals. Formally, the HSSC represent the head of local health networks with a capacity to contract services or make service agreements with a variety of providers like family medical groups located in public or private structures, community groups, diagnostic services, and other specialized services. The HSSC are in charge of a geographically defined population and have the responsability of providing a broad range of services to its population. To ensure access across the territory to specialized care and support from teaching hospitals to other providers like primary care physicians, four integrated university health networks (RUIS) were created based on a close collaboration between universities and health care organizations.

This reform was conducted in response to different challenges faced by Quebec's health care system such as demographic changes (e.g. aging of the population), changes in disease pattern (increasing prevalence of chronic diseases and multiple chronic diseases in an aging population), and growing demand for health care services. The reform aims also to contain the increase of health care cost by providing more services within community or primary care settings in a context of severe constraints on public finance (70% of health care costs are assumed by the public purse).

How does strategic management fit in the context of this Quebec health care reform? The main strategic approach behind the transformation of the health care system is the implementation of a major structural change coupled with a vision that privileges the role of primary care as one of the main drivers of the system. With this reform, the legislator forces different providers to increase their level of communication and coordination and to better coordinate their practices around patients' needs. The challenge of implementing this reform is significant because structural change and the promotion of a vision are probably not sufficient to transform the system in order to offer better care and services. We will now explore how these major changes resonate with some key schools in the field of strategy.

Conception school: a new model of service delivery was conceived based on structural reorganization and a territorial and population-based approach within the HSSC. The regional health authorities were granted with the responsibilities to develop and manage local network services including community organizations and to make sure that the population is involved in the planning process. A shift has been made from planning from the point of view of health care providers to a public health perspective incorporating the voice of users of services and non-users within pre-defined local territories. Each HSSC has their own structure of governance and develops their own local health plan with the objective to increase the accessibility and quality of care and to increase the coordination and integration of care. Results of evaluation suggested that various health care institutions are more integrated than before as a consequence of the development of both horizontal and vertical collaborations among health care providers (Breton et al. 2013). But the HSSC need more support and input from the RHA to develop stronger mechanisms of coordination like clinical information system and incentives to collaborate. Three main challenges are at the core of the implementation of a vision that incorporates public health logic and objectives: 'the low level of physicians' involvement, the competitive behaviours among health care providers and the NGOs' fear of losing their autonomy' (Denis et al. 2011) through their participation in local health networks under the impulsion or leadership of HSSC.

Cultural school: Population-based planning into health care and services delivery introduces a dual responsibility for the HSSC: delivering health and social care and developing interventions to improve the health of the population like community-based preventive intervention (Breton et al. 2013). These two responsibilities are somewhat in tension because they value different views of health priorities and of the kind of interventions that should be implemented. Furthermore, within local health networks, the participation of different providers brings to the forefront various pattern of values and interests including divergent views around the allocation of resources. In addition, some organizations or providers may be more inclined to value patient-centred care and broad interventions to improve the health of the population; while others are more aligned with increasing the supply of acute care for the population. While a cultural shift is not easy to operate, there is the emergence of a territorial-based vision of care that fosters the coexistence and possibly more synergy between a provider-driven and a population-driven system. In addition, at the organization level, teamwork or inter-professional collaboration for integrated health services have developed and reflect some changes in mindsets. The issue of the autonomy of professionals and particularly of the participation of physicians in broad organizational or system goals is still a challenge despite interesting developments around teamwork and inter-professional collaboration. 'Family physicians play a fundamental role in the delivery and co-ordination of care within local health territories. Yet, HSSCs have only limited resources through their different programs to attract physicians and make them collaborate with their programs' (Denis and van Gestel 2015).

Entrepreneurial school: the reform process consisted of a reorganization of health care services based on a population approach, and integration of services for more accessible, coordinated and quality of care within an entity, namely, the HSSC. Such transformation depends on physicians and other health care professional and implies their collaboration. These professionals can play a key role in the design and implementation of innovative health care delivery arrangements and the improvement of health care quality. The entrepreneurship of professionals and clinical leaders, and more specifically clinical leaders, may foster the development of a more collective leadership where managerial and clinical leaders work in collaboration to innovate and improve care and services within their local territories. The role of so-called institutionnal entrepreurs at a meso level of the system in the development of agreements and alliances with differents public and private providers to improve the overall supply of primary care services, specialized services, care for more vulnerable groups, and health promotion and social services appears critical (Breton et al. 2013). The role of such entrepreneurs creates variations across local health territories in term of health priorities and ways of responding to the needs of the population.

Learning organization: Since its creation in 1970, the evolution of the public health care system in Quebec was marked by different waves of reforms. A sense of continuity can be seen through this evolution where governments and providers try with different perspectives and various level of commitment to find solutions to the challenge of improving care and the health of the population.

Numerous reforms and legislative policies have been implemented, based mostly on the principles of universality of care and the primacy of primary health care in the structuring of the system. The Quebec public health care system was formally created in 1970s. At that time, the Ministry of Health created local community service centres (CLSCs) to provide integrated health and social services across the whole province. Efforts have been initially made to develop and strengthen primary health care structures but with not much attention paid to integration of care across providers and organizations partially due to less pressures to improve the coordination of care. In 1990, the focus of reforms was more on regionalization of the system with the creation of regional health authorities (RHAs) to improve the coordination of care among primary care resources (CLSC and private medical clinics, for example) and between primary care and more specialized car (CLSC and hospitals, for example). It was expected that a stronger governance body at the regional level will be in a better position to act upon the health of the population and to improve the planning, the organization, and the delivery of care. While RHAs have levers to affect the delivery of care and services, they have limited capacity to improve the delivery at the point of care and to create local health networks that efficiently connect health care providers within each local territories. Reforms in the 2000 aims, as we described earlier, to consolidate resources within local health territories and to improve integration of care across the system. Overall, there is a strong sense of continuity through the various reforms within the Quebec health care system but a difficulty to move beyond structural reorganization and to mobilize a broader set of levers to operate changes.

The received wisdom that strategic management models cannot be readily applied to public services settings also has to be questioned as newer schools do not always assume competitive markets. In some streams (e.g. strategy as process; strategy as practice), there are already interesting and important empirical studies applying them to public settings, alongside private sector settings.

Finally, marketizing and NPM-based reforms inside the public sector have increased the potential of orthodox strategic management models, as seen in Porter and Tesiberg's (2006) analysis of the American health care system or principal-agent approaches to the redesign of corporate governance systems which have been influential inside the public as well as the private sectors (although also subject to critique). These orthodox models can no longer be dismissed as entirely irrelevant to public sector settings.

4 Collaborative and network-based forms of strategy

We have already briefly introduced in Chapter 3 the concept of collaborative and network-based forms of strategy. Public sector organizations appear to be increasingly collaborating with other public, private, and not-for-profit organizations to create joint policies or services, especially in complex policy arenas (e.g. child poverty; obesity; an ageing society) where many different bodies from various sectors need to come together to generate effective solutions. Public agencies are also now seeking to collaborate 'downwards' with users or citizens to co-produce services or co-design public policy. The vertically integrated and 'silo-ed' public agency is clearly not nowadays the only unit of analysis when seen from a strategy point of view. There is instead a manifest and sustained growth of various forms of partnerships, alliances, and networks across the whole cycle of public services, from their design to delivery and evaluation. Local 'whole systems' are also becoming an important focus for policy interventions. All these developments change and broaden the traditional role of the State and move local public agencies away from a 'standalone' mode.

These developments have also been picked up in various academic literatures. For example, the influential 'Triple Helix' model of scientific knowledge production (Etzkowitz and Leydesdorff 2000; Etzkowitz 2003) argues that national and regional knowledge production systems emerge as a result of interactions and co-evolution from the three helices of government, industry, and universities. They then suggest there is a transition from early state-centred models of knowledge production to more co-equal ones, where the university plays an enhanced role in its own right. Hybrid and novel arenas and organizations emerge (such as science parks or technology transfer units) which bind the different helices together. The implication is that the State (both national level and also regional and local government which may well play a key role in seeking to drive local economic growth) is only one player. The government therefore cannot simply command but has to negotiate with the other helices, with their own self-direction and autonomy.

Within the public management literature, these wider developments are best addressed in the Network Governance (hereafter NG) narrative apparent from the 1990s onwards which takes a more decentred view of the State. This perspective moves beyond the traditional concept of the unitary national State exerting strong command and control towards accounts that highlight many non-State actors. This chapter introduces and reviews key features of the NG model of public management, including more networks and partnerships, as seen from a strategic management perspective. We ask: how can inter-organizational and cooperative strategy in such a 'network governance style world' be understood?

DOI: 10.4324/9781003054917-4

The chapter starts by outlining a brief review of recent texts from the private sector-orientated strategic management literature which indicates cooperative strategy is now a theme of broad interest there too. A subsequent review of another social science-based stream of literature explores trends towards network-based modes of economic organization, notably in 'Post Fordist' (Amin 1994) literature. Jessop's 1994 characterization of the post-Fordist State and its increased interest in promoting economic growth in partnership with others is particularly interesting.

Third, the chapter considers literature on novel forms of leadership activity which may also be an important resource to promote such cooperative strategies.

Finally, the chapter proposes some strategic redesign implications from recent literature on so-called co-production and co-creation approaches, where public agencies work cooperatively 'downwards' to co-produce services and also co-design public policies with groups of users and citizens in a cooperative fashion.

The chapter's concluding discussion picks out some implications for practitioners and considers issues for the future.

4.1 Network governance and public services management: some key features

We start by considering a high-level trend towards more collaborative government which has been evident from the 1990s onwards (Huxham and Vangen 2000). Theoretically, key authors (including Rhodes 1997, 2007; Newman 2001; Osborne 2010b) have advanced a 'Network Governance' (NG) model of public management seen as an alternative paradigm to both hierarchically based Traditional Public Administration (TPA) and more market-orientated New Public Management (NPM) approaches.

NG ideas have been influential internationally. Taking for example the UK, they were influential under New Labour governments (1997–2010). While this early history seems to have partly fallen into oblivion, some key NG reforms were important and enduring, including devolution of policy responsibility to subnations and strong regions; greater multi-level governance; the use of managed networks to reconfigure public service delivery; greater engagement with civil society and the third sector; the early emergence of e government; the modernization of the machinery of government and a move to evidence informed policy making. So, it is argued here that NG ideas have had an important legacy that needs to be better recognized and considered.

What are the broader themes in the bundle of specific NG reforms mentioned previously? First, there is a shift from 'government to governance.' 'Governance' is a broader and looser concept than 'government' (Rhodes 1997, 2007; Newman 2001). The old presumption of a centralized and unitary nation state no longer held; instead, a more plural and pluralist state (Osborne 2010b) emerged which incorporates a broader group of actors in the public policy process, including partners from the private and third sectors as well as the traditional public sector. The remaining elements of the public sector became smaller but also established more partnerships with non-public sector actors both to make policy and to deliver services.

Second, there was a shift from 'competition to collaboration.' There was a push-back against the reforms of the earlier NPM era in the UK which were now seen by some key authors as producing major dysfunctional effects (Dunleavy et al. 2006a, 2006b), including an over-fragmentation of government, too many siloed agencies, and a hollowing out of creative policy-making capacity which in turn reflected NPM's excessive concern with short-term and efficiency-orientated operational management. The NPM doctrine of competition also meant that the more strongly incentivized public agencies were reluctant to cooperate with each other to tackle complex public policy problems. This entailed some rowing back from earlier NPM reforms. The favoured governance mode of these new collaborative settings shifted to the use of networks (albeit with the State trying to manage them, Ferlie et al. 2013) and the hierarchy and markets mix found in NPM regimes became less important. There was also a greater emphasis on 'joined up government' whereby different levels, agencies, and functions of government would work more closely together, both vertically (central and local government) and horizontally (e.g. greater cooperation between linked ministries such as health, education, and the interior on social policy problems).

A debate, noticeable e.g. within UK political science, is whether the increasing number of policy networks are largely autonomous or whether they can still be steered or even be commanded by the State. Rhodes (1997, 2007)'s Differentiated Polity model takes the view that the core central executive has been effectively 'hollowed out' and retains little effective command or steering capacity. By contrast, Marsh et al. (2003) and Marsh (2011)'s Asymmetric Power model argued this view overstates the extent of the diffusion of power and that traditional and central 'power hoarding' UK political institutions remain dominant. Many of their arguments appear to relate to the national level, however, and different and more pluralist behaviours may be observed at subnational or local government level. This academic debate is also a very British one and alternative federal or politically more consensual political regimes in Europe (e.g. Germany) and elsewhere may exhibit more pluralist behaviours, a bigger role for social partners and more autonomous policy networks.

Third, there is a move away in the Network Governance model from the traditional centralized and unitary national state towards a focus on multi-level government (Rhodes 1997, 2007) and multi-level governance (Enderlein et al. 2010; Ongaro 2015a, 2020b), including through the important and enduring reform of devolution of powers to Scotland, Wales, and Northern Ireland). Governmental functions have moved from the nation state upwards to multilateral arenas and bodies (including the European Union, at least until Brexit in the UK case), sideways to private firms and executive agencies, and downwards to increasingly strong sub-nations, regions, and cities. The UK devolved some significant policy-making powers to Scotland, Wales, and to a lesser extent London around 2000 with new parliaments and assemblies being set up there. The devolution of health policy competences has, for example been important and led to differential responses to the recent COVID epidemic, with Scotland and Wales taking a more cautious line than England and imposing stronger control measures. Mayors have been directly elected in some large metropolitan regions in England (e.g. the Greater Manchester Region) to strengthen visible regional political leadership and reduce the economic and political dominance of London within England.

As well as these UK examples, some important European countries (including France, Italy, and Spain) have over the last 30 years or so devolved powers to regions, cities, and mayors in a reaction against the traditional centralized 'Napoleonic' model of State (Ongaro 2009, 2010, 2018; Peters 2008). In Spain, for example, the Basque and Catalan regions have secured extensive devolved powers, although some political parties there continue to press for more devolution and even independence.

Germany since the late 1940s has operated a highly devolved system where the regions or Lander have extensive discretion over public management and service delivery.

Fourth, there is increased emphasis in the Network Governance model on government partnering with civil society and the third sector and over a broad range of policy areas. Whereas earlier NPM reforms saw third-sector service providers rather narrowly as a flexible and cost-effective alternative to rigid and high-cost public provision, NG values them more as partners in their own right and as valuable contributors to society which can contribute to civic participation and social inclusion.

Fifth, NG shifts emphasis from the building up of general management roles as public service change leaders (it was termed the New Public *Management* after all) to developing wider *leadership* as a change strategy, supported by investment in national leadership development agencies and bespoke training and development programmes for aspiring senior leaders (Newman 2005; O'Reilly and Reed 2010). 'Leaders' can come from many roles and backgrounds, including public services professionals, as well as solely managers. The prospect is one of a softer, transformational, authentic, and inspirational leadership style (Newman 2001, 2005; Ferlie et al. 2013) rather than traditional role-based or transactional forms. Leadership may well come from small mixed teams – including professionals – as well as from single general managers (Ferlie et al. 2013). The attempted re-involvement of public services professionals in leadership marks a retreat from presumed managerialist excesses of the earlier NPM wave.

Finally, NG doctrines are committed to the 'modernization' (in itself a key NG word) of government, in part to retain legitimacy with governments' publics as many citizens are now used to radically new and user-orientated new technologies as consumers of private services (e.g. Uber; Amazon; e banking). This modernization project may involve recourse to longer-term planning and budgetary time scales as well, supporting less ideological approaches to evidence-based policy (an important mantra was 'what matters is what works'). Historically, the period of NG influence coincided with the start of a radical technological shift which made e government and the digitalization of public services delivery possible. NG would clearly emphasize as a goal e participation by citizens and users in digitalized arenas in addition to NPM style goals of cost saving and better access for routine services by digitally aware users (e.g. applying for car parking permits in local government remotely).

Pollitt and Bouckaert's (2017) comparative analysis of public management reforms in 12 countries suggests that Network Governance (or what they term New Public Governance) ideas have had as yet only rather broad and diffuse influence internationally, while also addressing important contemporary issues and problems in public management (pp. 126–127):

> while the NPG model may at present appear to be rather vague and idealistic, it is nevertheless focussed on some core contemporary features of politics and society (governments sharing power with other social actors in a range of informal ways). It may yet be developed into something more theoretically precise and operational.

As well as the UK in the New Labour period, the Netherlands was a pioneer of NG ideas (partly due to its historical evolution and political culture). Kickert (1997b) indeed sees the Netherlands as an alternative to 'Anglo Saxon managerialism' in its attachment to public governance. Kickert (1997b) presents various case studies of NG in action in the Netherlands, including in the important education and welfare sectors.

Summing up this initial reconnaissance of the NG model and field, some key messages are that the network governances perspective suggests a likely growth of alliances, partnerships, networks, and the increased use of local systems to tackle many and important 'wicked' public policy problems, with the implication that the single agency will become less central; so that strategic management in such multi-actor and networked settings may become more important: there is a shift from directive government to an indirect form of 'governance' which may still seek to shape and steer, often through the use of networks rather than market or hierarchy.

However, this fundamental development also poses various issues, challenges, and questions for governments, both central and local. At the level of central government, questions that arise include these: how can the different ministries and departments work together in a more 'joined up' way and pool their knowledge and resources? How much influence can the central coordinating departments at national level (e.g. Treasury; Ministry of Public Administration; Prime Minister's/President's office) exert on the major spending ministries (e.g. Health and Education) to cooperate more broadly? How does central government seek to engage in multi-level governance, both upwards (to multinational organizations), sideways (to executive agencies, private firms, and NGOs supplying public services) and downwards to devolved jurisdictions and local government? Does central government try to structure how local networks and partnerships function (this question of 'meta governance' will be considered later), perhaps through using specific policy instruments and steering devices? This final question brings us to questions pertaining to the local level: how does strategy form in the many alliances, partnerships, networks, and local system-based approaches likely to emerge within localities? Is one agency designated as a lead agency or 'system builder' within public policy responses at local level and if so, do other partners accept their role? Or does strategy emerge in a more collective and emergent way across many agencies and other organizations within local territories? If so, how?

We now consider other streams of academic literature which help make sense of an NG-style world in which cooperative strategy is more important. We start from exploring cooperative strategies between private firms.

4.2 Cooperative strategy between private firms

Long-term developments are also increasing the importance of cooperative and network-based strategy between private firms. This trend is not confined to public agencies, and there may be some lessons to be learnt from private organizations of relevance for public services (and vice versa). The assumption that firms would always compete with each other may be dated, and the search for cooperative rather than competitive advantage may be preferred, at least under certain circumstances.

Some business school-based writers have explored what collaborative strategy might mean in private firm settings. For example Hansen and Nohria (2004) analyze 'how to build collaborative advantage' but define the term narrowly in relation to greater collaboration *within* complex and multi-unit firms. Kanter (1994) takes a broader view in looking at alliances *between* firms (p. 96): 'being a good partner has become a key corporate asset. I call it a company's collaborative advantage. In the global economy, a well developed ability to create and sustain fruitful collaborations gives companies a significant competitive leg up.' Kanter plotted a continuum of such alliances, moving from the early stage of mutual service companies, through joint ventures to more elaborate value chain partnerships.

Kanter empirically found three factors produced productive partnerships, especially when firms were operating across conventional national and cultural boundaries. The first was a longitudinal element: successful alliances are not just one-off deals but 'living systems that evolve in their possibilities' (p. 97). Second, they involved collaboration (creating new value together) rather than mere exchange (getting something back for what you put in). Partners valued the different skills each brings to the alliance. Third, they could not be controlled just by formal systems but required many interpersonal connections and internal infrastructures to enhance mutual learning.

Child et al. (2005) have written a whole book on private firms and cooperative strategy. Their overall argument is as follows (p. 1):

> cooperative strategy is the attempt by organizations to realise their objectives through cooperation with other organizations rather than in competition with them. It focusses on the benefits that can be gained through cooperation and how to manage the cooperation so as to realise them. A cooperative strategy can offer significant advantages for companies that are lacking in particular competences or resources to secure these through links with others possessing complementary skills and assets; it may also offer easier access to new markets and opportunities for mutual synergy and learning.

Cooperative strategy often produces 'strategic alliances' between two firms. While these alliances were previously (in the 1990s) seen as difficult to manage and displayed a high rate of termination, Child et al. (2005) argue they have recently re-emerged, linked to more joint ventures engaged in foreign direct investment. They also argue many strategic alliances still present challenges and have a short average life, perhaps reflecting underlying tensions between partners. Enduring strategic alliances require genuine cooperation between diverse groups, based on high communication and trust levels: managers need to be able to build relationships skilfully and have a broad strategic awareness of the deep rationale for the alliance. The authors then suggest that the nature of cooperative strategy may have recently evolved (Child et al. 2005, p. 5), and the effective use of information and promotion of innovation have become key competitive factors. There is also a movement from traditional bilateral partnerships (joint ventures and strategic alliances) towards more complex networked forms including innovation chains, global value chains, business ecosystems, and ICT-led alliances.

They take a specific interest in government (Child et al. 2005, pp. 429–446) by noting the growing number of public–private partnerships (PPPs) linking government and business, especially in long-term financing and provision of infrastructure in the health and education sectors. There have been many such PPPs in UK public services over the last 20 or so years. We add also that large-scale projects involving public and private actors may come together in mixed teams for a short or medium time, for example in transport (e.g. for upgrading rail or metro services). They (p. 439) also argue that in some cases, PPPs have failed to deliver value for money for the taxpayer and call for a strategic approach to their management based on key principles, including ensuring that there are complementary assets between government and the private firms contracted with; that government has well-developed contracting and negotiation skills; and an appropriate distribution of risk/return to the various parties throughout the life of the PPP (findings in line with what emerges from the recent public management literature looking at PPPs, Vecchi and Hellowell 2018).

In summary, the key point from this review is that this private sector literature similarly suggests that competitive advantage may increasingly be pursued within joint ventures or strategic partnerships between firms – or even within diffuse networks or value chains – rather than within the single firm, and these novel organizational forms depend on building effective collaboration. Such alliances also present challenges in their management and some will fail. There are also a growing number of PPPs where the overall interests of government and private firms need to be aligned to protect the interests of the taxpayer. There may be some learning points here for the public sector, and indeed it may fruitfully be two-way learning.

4.3 Post-Fordism and the post-Fordist state

Another and extensive stream of academic literature drawn from political economy and human geography explores changing forms of work organization. It suggests a long-term shift from the dominant large, stable, and vertically integrated firm (the so-called Fordist mode of production) to an alternative 'post Fordist' model based on networks of smaller firms and flexible specialization. Some specific implications for the changing post-Fordist state are also discussed in this literature.

Amin (1994)'s reader on post-Fordism contains several relevant chapters. Amin's (1994) introduction argues for a shift since the 1970s from the old 'Fordist' form of the mass production and consumption of a limited range of standard products to 'flexible specialization,' where more broadly skilled workers produce a greater variety of highly value adding and customized goods. Firms decentralize decision making to these upskilled workers and pursue job enrichment strategies to motivate and retain them. Second, the power of the traditional nation state is in decline, being 'hollowed out' from above by globalization and from below by stronger regions and cities. Third, the concept of the 'industrial district,' in which there is a strong geographical clustering by firms – large firms but also small start-ups – in certain favoured and high economic growth areas, re-emerges as important. These new industrial districts are knowledge intensive in form and produce high-value products and services. Amin (1994, p. 21) suggests they display: 'a culture of cooperation, trust and negotiability between firms trading with each other, as well as within firms, as a key condition underpinning the interdependence and flexibility demanded by this model of industrial organization.'

Examples of high-growth regions include Silicon Valley in California (information technology (IT)-related and seen as a classic case), Route 128 around Boston, Massachusetts (again IT driven), and 'the third Italy' (based on fashion) in Reggio Emilia. A good London example is the 'Silicon Roundabout,' north of the City of London, with an agglomeration of high-tech-related start-ups. These high-growth industrial districts are often supported by a local and major research-intensive university within a wider economic and knowledge 'eco system.' A major UK example is the 'Silicon

Fen' area (based on software and bio technology) situated near Cambridge University and with close links with its scientists.

Jessop's (1994) chapter in Amin's edition specifically analyzes the changing nature of the post-Fordist state. Clearly, if the nature of the state changes in a fundamental sense, then there may also be changes to fundamental models of public management and some associated approaches to strategic management, as reviewed earlier in book. The question of any such change in the basic mode of the state is then a major one with important 'downstream' effects.

Jessop distinguishes first between two radically different models of the state and argues that important transition between them took place in the late 1970s and 1980s. On the one hand, there is what is termed the 'old Keynesian welfare state' (dominant from the 1940s to late 1970s) and on the other the 'new Schumpeterian workfare state' (emerging from the 1980s onwards).

The Keynesian (named after the famous interwar economist Maynard Keynes) welfare state was strongly associated with the post-war economic boom (1945–1975). It was 'corporatist' in nature, so that government-brokered national level partnerships and agreements with key producer interests (employers' associations and trade unions) within what was a relatively consensual regime of national planning. There was both a large nationalized and a private industrial sector which coexisted with each other within a mixed economy. This Keynesian state also pursued goals of full employment (using macro-economic stabilizers such as demand stimulation to reduce unemployment) and a well-developed welfare state to protect workers.

The tendency of a large public sector to generate demands for further expansion and the commitment always to maintain full employment led eventually (late 1970s) in the eyes of critics to a pattern of excessive powers for the public sector trade unions, higher taxation, and a danger of the expanding state crowding out a beleaguered private sector. These political and economic conditions eventually produced a taxpayers' revolt which fuelled the electoral rise of the New Right (as expressed by such major political leaders as Ronald Reagan in the USA and Mrs Thatcher in the UK) around 1980. The economic, political, and ideological crisis of the Fordist state in the late 1970s was then profound. Jessop (p. 260) argues three forces helped drive the transition to a new mode of the state: (i) the rise of new technologies (including ICTs); (ii) a process of internationalization, and (iii) a general paradigm shift to post-Fordism as already discussed.

The successor form is termed the 'Schumpeterian workfare state.' Schumpeter was an Austrian economist who worked on then novel questions of entrepreneurship, the dynamics of radical innovation, and the 'creative destruction' of old forms of economic organization. This model's key features are described by Jessop (1994, p. 263) as follows:

> to promote product, process, organization and market innovation in open economies in order to strengthen as far as possible the structural competitiveness of the national economy by intervening on the supply side and to subordinate social policy to the needs of labour market flexibility and/or the constraints of international competition.'

In this transition, traditional welfare state services operating to a social logic were subordinated to the rising economic logic of productivity and national international competitiveness.

In addition, there may well be changes to the traditional nation state consistent with Network Governance (Jessop 1994). The first trend is the 'hollowing out' of the traditional nation state and a move to multi-level governance with power shifting to multilateral bodies operating above the nation state (e.g. the European Union, World Trade Organization, and International Monetary Fund), reflecting economic globalization.

Another major shift refers to the devolution of jurisdiction and power downwards to stronger regions and cities (e.g. to Scotland, Wales, and London within the UK, as previously discussed). The agenda of these new parliaments or assemblies is likely to be dominated in this view (p. 272) by how to secure economic regeneration and greater competitiveness rather than a traditional social policy agenda. One further implication is that these sub-national policy networks and communities become increasingly complex and also important in addition to traditional national policy networks.

A third long-term shift suggests the more lateral linkages between strong cities and regions, often brokered in the European context by the European Union but also by political sentiment (e.g. between Scotland and Catalonia). We comment that these internationalist links may have been recently eroded by emerging and more nationalist governments within some national states inside and outside Europe.

Finally, Jessop (1994, p. 274) considers the current shape of the nation state. It has not died in his view but has been 'hollowed out.' Yet it retains core competences in house which include the steering of multi-level governance systems. The nation state is still interested and capable in 'managing the political linkages across different territorial scales and is expected to do so in the interests of its citizens.' It can, at its best, stand for transparency, democratic accountability, and proximity against shadowy but powerful forces of economic globalization.

We now introduce a vignette taken from the English NHS which illustrates the use of regionally based managed networks with a variety of partners (including private firms) to progress an economic growth-orientated (rather than traditional health improvement) agenda in a region, consistent with many of themes in the model of the Schumpeterian state addressed earlier.

Box 4.1 NHS Academic Health Science Networks and regional economic growth strategies in England

Regional Academic Health Sciences Networks (15) (AHSNs) (Ferlie et al. 2017) were set up by the English Department of Health in 2013 (Department of Health of the United Kingdom 2011). AHSNs are coordinated by the NHS but are complex networks which involve various private and public sector partners, including local government, large private firms, and SMEs. They are part of a developing regional infrastructure in the English health care system which expresses a long-running national 'health and wealth' policy stream tying the health care system more firmly to economic objectives and partners as well as traditional health improvement ones. Their aim is to diffuse health care innovations more rapidly and speed up their commercialization, thereby contributing to high-value employment and economic growth. AHSNs are also managed rather than self-organizing networks, as they are performance managed by the Department of Health and face periodic central review.

We now present a vignette of one region which was attempting to develop a regional life sciences strategy and promote a science park by involving a range of different collaborators but where the AHSN played an important coordinating role.

Aims and content of the innovation

This innovation was a large-scale initiative with two related foci: (i) a strategy to expand a regional life sciences cluster and (ii) within that, the associated redevelopment of a science park in a rural site, previously used by public sector research agencies with a long tradition of excellent scientific research, but now with spare capacity. A policy decision had recently been taken that a number of within region scientists would relocate to refurbished science labs out of the region so there was an economic concern regionally about the loss of well-paid science jobs.

Stakeholders and partners

An initial coalition of partners was formed which included the research and innovation division of a regional research-intensive university, a County Council and Local Enterprise Partnership which brought together different agencies to promote economic growth, and the AHSN (which undertook a review and proposed the idea of a regional life sciences cluster). This core grouping enrolled further support from leading scientists across the region; vice chancellors (presidents) of local universities; a well-informed and sympathetic local MP; and senior directors in the public research agencies currently on site. Support was also secured from government nationally. So, a wide and disparate array of stakeholders was involved from various sectors and which included political as well as administrative champions.

AHSN knowledge mobilization strategy and contribution

There was a strong concern locally to strengthen excellence in the life sciences and in selected priority areas across the region. The region could then position itself to receive economic 'refugees' from what were now seen as saturated science parks and clusters out of the region (e.g. some of which had difficulties in getting planning permission for new science parks and further expansion in their original sites). This would also stop the drain of pre-existing regional scientific talent to other high-profile clusters and raise the identity and profile of the area so as to attract a significant number of firms from outside, along with inward investment.

This tracer is 'macro' and strategic in nature and heavily focused on life science policy and wealth creation (with a target to create over 2,000 new jobs and attract £100m of investment within five years). There are many players involved from different sectors of which the AHSN is only one. The AHSN helped build regional collaborations with other players (e.g. a Local Economic Partnership which is a vehicle for getting a multi-sectoral network with an interest in promoting economic growth together in a locality; a county council; a regional research-intensive university) and write the initial vision. At an operational level, pump-priming money from the AHSN helped resource a well-established scientific group to prepare successful bids for larger awards from prestigious outside funders.

Source: based on Ferlie E., Nicolini D., Ledger J., D'Andreta D., Kravcenko D., and de Pury J. (2017), **Chapter 7**

The post-Fordist perspective on the changing nature of the state suggests some important implications and raises various questions. It implies that the national state increasingly has to negotiate with other social and economic actors, some of which have substantial autonomy in their own right (e.g. the universities in the Triple Helix model), and that it cannot simply direct them; it also implies that there is a trend to 'multi level' governance above the level of the nation state (e.g. multinational organizations) and also below it (the rise of strong sub-nations, regions, and cities), raising issues of what theoretical perspectives can usefully be employed to make sense of it (Ongaro 2015a). At another level, it points to a switch of attention away from a traditional welfare state agenda based on public spending and towards a public policy agenda based on the pursuit of productivity and international competitiveness. As a result, economic and productivity-orientated policy networks become more important (e.g. AHSNs in the UK health care sector) and receive greater attention.

Some key learning points and implications which emerge from this changed model of the state are:

- The state (national and regional) is increasingly interested in promoting economic growth in conjunction with economic, university, and other partners;
- Novel arenas emerge to link these key actors;
- Favourable pre-existing organizational characteristics and high levels of social capital are likely to be evident in successful high-growth regions;
- Where these conditions are not present, this model may struggle to establish itself and some regions may be much less successful;
- International as well as national linkages and networks may be important as well as national and regional actors; the EU is a good example to look at, as would be the World Health Organization;
- While regions play a key role, the nation state may well still seek to orchestrate a process of multi-level governance involving regional actors. It may well seek to devise and steer regional or local networks (as seen in the AHSNs case).

Finally, we ask: does the nation or devolved state still effectively advocate for principles of transparency, accountability, and public value against opaque forces of financialization and globalization, as sometimes claimed in the literature (Jessop 1994)? It would be good to have more concrete examples and case studies to test this bold claim.

4.4 Importance and nature of leadership in collaborative strategy

Some Network Governance writing suggests that active and motivational forms of leadership are a strategic resource which can help implement desired public policy objectives in what are now much more dispersed organizational arenas, with weak line management hierarchies (Newman 2001, 2005; O'Reilly and Reed 2010; Ferlie et al. 2011, 2013; Torfing and Ansell 2017; Sørensen 2020; Bryson 2021). There is a shifting emphasis from narrower 'management' characteristics of the New Public Management to broader 'leadership,' notably in performing its integrative function across dispersed policy arenas. Thus Newman (2001, p. 24)'s list of propositions on NG includes 'the role of government shifting to a focus on providing leadership, building partnerships, steering and coordinating and providing system wide integration and regulation.'

But what form of leadership may be favoured? Given the stress within Network Governance on integrating the responses of many public agencies and other organizations to tackle complex problems, a shift to more lateral and distributed leadership and away from individualized or role-dependent models (e.g. a dominant CEO in a single agency) can be expected. Theoretically, some different models of leadership might be applied in such cooperative settings. One likely change is moving from transactional to transformational or 'authentic' models of leadership that can persuade and inspire rather than simply direct. Another expected shift may be from individualistic to distributed leadership, as a mixed team may have broader credibility with varied constituencies.

Some studies have suggested some empirical evidence for such shifts. For example, Denis et al.'s 2001 study of leadership in Canadian health care organizations highlighted collective or distributed forms of leadership where different role holders (e.g. managers; professionals) take on different leadership tasks as a range of different forces need to be aligned to permit complex service change to happen. Newman (2005) analyzed the relationship between network governance and a recourse to transformational leadership in the UK under New Labour to promote its project of modernizing government. At one level, top-down central targets for the localities continued and even intensified. Yet at the same time, traditional single agency-based line management became less powerful so there was recourse to 'soft leadership' to tackle complex public policy problems and stimulate service improvement.

What Newman terms the 'ethic of office' also changed (p. 721) in a post-bureaucratic direction:

> the practitioner is viewed as facing outwards, building partnerships and engaging communities for the purpose of delivering 'joined up' and sustainable policy outcomes. The release from the bureaucratic ethos of office, coupled with the emphasis on policy outcomes, opens up new forms of social agency.

The pattern was one of 'decentralised centralisation': the centre set an overall vision and targets but accorded substantial discretion to local adaptations and encouraged active leadership to 'make things happen' in the localities. This leadership style (Newman 2005) heralded was now more affective than rational cognitive in style, emphasizing feelings, reflections, and emotions. There was greater use of soft leadership development technologies, such as 360-degree appraisal (where a staff member gets feedback not just from superiors but also from colleagues and subordinates, along with providing a self-evaluation) and action learning sets (which are facilitated small groups of staff which diagnose collectively problems at work, take actions and interventions and then reflect on and discuss the organizational process and outcomes evident over several meetings). The preferred leadership style becomes in this perspective more transformational than transactional, value laden rather than value neutral, emphasizing such qualities as enthusiasm, integrity, vision, and charisma. It is also broad rather than siloed within particular functions and dedicated to achieving cultural change as well as undertaking single transactions. Managers are in this perspective supposed to be supported by national (and resource-intensive) national leadership development programmes set up in various sectors, including local government in the case of Newman's study.

Drawing on an American case study work on the Urban Partnership in Minneapolis-St Pauls, Crosby et al. 2010 similarly argue that approaches to solving complex public policy problems with many different actors and in a shared power and highly diverse environment require a leadership style that is both integrative and visionary and which crosses traditional boundaries. By integrative leadership, they suggest (p. 200):

> we see the leadership practice of these leaders as integrative – that is, they help integrate processes, structures and resources in semi permanent ways. Integration is similar to collaboration, but we think the former term captures more directly the need for leaders and constituents to move back and forth across boundaries and build linking pathways and other communalities.

They build on Crosby and Bryson's 2005 'Leadership for the Common Good' framework which highlights the visionary, ethical, and political aspects of public leadership. The main contribution of visionary leadership is the creation and communication of meaning (sometimes termed 'sense giving') in formal and informal forums (p. 201) to create common understandings. Forum and communication design is thus an important skill for visionary leaders.

More recently, Hartley (2018) has advanced ten propositions on leadership in public services settings to stimulate debate. The underlying work context is in her view highly pluralist, with multiple goals, diverse publics, and varied stakeholders. Thus, public services leadership has to navigate and influence multiple arenas, where ideas and actions are often scrutinized, contested, and debated (Hartley 2018). Leadership may here be political in nature (e.g. from elected ministers, mayors, and councillors) as well as coming from managers, professionals, or other staff, or indeed represent a mix of political and managerial sources within a distributed leadership form. The handling of contest and conflict within a deliberative process becomes a prime skill for public leaders.

But is a leadership perspective by itself too narrowly subjective in orientation? Authors also point to broader factors in organizational change in public services organizations which include contextual or structural conditions as well as action or leadership-related elements. For example, Pettigrew et al.'s (1992) model of 'receptive contexts for change' in English health care includes an attention to 'objective' factors such as the complexity of the organizational context and environmental pressure as well as 'subjective' leadership. In a similar vein, Huxham and Vangen (2005) provide an account of 'Collaborative Advantage' in case studies of local partnerships between various public, private, and third-sector organizations. The subtitle of their book echoes but also challenges Porter's classic book on private sector firms' strategy: 'Competitive Advantage.' Huxham and Vangen (2005) outline a model of leadership for collaborative governance in these partnership-based settings – but importantly, they also argue (and in this sense recall Porter's lesson) that structure is important in their view as well as action, and the two dimensions could interact so both needed to be considered. While leadership activity was certainly important, therefore, it also interacted with structural forces. There is here an intellectual affinity with the argument about human action deploying 'in context,' being always contextualized: a point to which we return in Chapter 6. Huxham and Vangen (2005) then suggest that leadership can be exercised through design of structures (e.g. open/closed) or processes (e.g. communication processes) as well as by direct actions taken by participants. Many structures and processes appeared, however, to be mandated from above by central government, leaving less room for local discretion. This observation links to the notion of steering or 'meta governance' discussed later in this chapter.

In summary, the following key learning points emerge from this brief review of the leadership literature in NG settings:

- The section started by asserting that some Network Governance writing suggests that active and motivational forms of leadership are a strategic resource which can help implement desired public policy objectives in what are now much more dispersed organizational arenas, with weak line management hierarchies; there is a now a shift of interest from management to leadership.
- Much of the literature reviewed suggests a significant move away from traditional command and control to more networked styles of leadership. Also 'hard' leadership is likely to give way to a 'soft' leadership style. Visionary and transformational styles of leadership may now be preferred.
- The core competences and skills required of public managers may increasingly emphasize partnership building skills; this agenda may increasingly feature in the management development programmes offered to public managers.
- The literature suggests both managerial and political forms of leadership may be important and indeed there may be a mix, with political leaders (such as elected mayors) potentially offering an important source of leadership.
- Wider context and structure may still matter in determining the outcomes of complex collaborations. There may well be limits to what subjective leadership can do by itself to make such partnerships work. We need more evidence including well-designed case study work to test these arguments.

We now move on to consider some implications of the recently increased interest in questions of co-production and co-creation in public services organizations.

4.5 A shift to co-production and co-creation? Some implications for strategic management

As already suggested, the Network Governance model stresses the need for public services organizations to work in partnership with a variety of different stakeholders, including with citizens, service users, and their representatives in civil society and the third sector.

Building on and developing these earlier broad NG ideas, there has recently been rapidly growing interest in 'co creation' and 'co production'-based approaches to public policy and management (Osborne et al. 2016; Ansell and Torfing 2021; Ferlie 2021), where public services organizations work 'downwards' more with citizens and services users who become important social partners in their own right. These trends can be seen both in the narrower redesign of frontline service delivery processes and more ambitiously in open public policy making.

First, we need to define the key terms of 'co production' and 'co creation' and be aware of differences between them. Co-creation is seen as a higher-order concept than co-production by Ansell and Torfing (2021). They first highlight the increased role of users/consumers in co-producing services at the operational level of public service delivery (similar to the marketing informed redesign of forms of private consumption which enables customers to add value to goods and services purchased).

However, co-creation is a higher order and more systemic process (p. 6):

> hence we shall define co production as a basically dyadic relation between private service users and public services providers that allows both parties to make good use of their experiences, competences and resources in the service delivery process. . . . By contrast, we define co creation as the process through which a plethora of public and private actors are involved – ideally on an equal footing – and in a collaborative endeavor to define common problems and implement new, better, yet flexible public solutions.

Such efforts may involve challenging common wisdom to produce innovative solutions and to generate public value. These large-scale changes could lead to redesigning whole public policy and service delivery systems. Note the affinity with the public value model of strategic management here (Chapter 3).

Ansell and Torfing (2021) also observe an expanding scope of initiatives from individualized service co-production to more ambitious collective problem solving. This shift may be especially important in addressing 'wicked problems' (such as climate change or an ageing society) with high interdependence between many social actors (including between policy makers and citizens and/or service users), where policy problems are multifaceted and complex and where simple market or hierarchy-led solutions are ineffective.

There are, of course, also many barriers to such changes so that 'strategic visions, institutional designs, organizational structures, and the mindset of key actors must be transformed to support co creation and to allow the upscaling of local experiments' (Ansell and Torfing 2021, pp. 7–8). At present, co-creation experiments may be confined to interesting pockets but not be mainstreamed, creating a gap that strategic management approaches can address.

Torfing et al. 2019 consider how a shift to co-creation in public services management might occur. They identify important potential drivers which include support from a political leadership which wants to reconnect with the citizen base (so top-down support and an overall framework may be helpful). There may also be a push from middle ranking public managers and professionals who see co-creation as a mechanism for sourcing new ideas to help solve intractable problems. This may be combined with bottom-up pressure from citizens and also a desire for strategic alliances from private sector firms looking for partnerships with government (e.g. pharma and vaccine production). We add these pressures may need to be strong and sustained to be influential and that multiple pushes from different sources may be helpfully reinforcing each other.

Torfing et al. 2019 also explore the system-wide institutional redesign which may be needed to foster larger-scale co-creation. They introduce the notion of the 'meta governance' of public policy networks (pp. 813–814):

> meta governance is concerned with affecting the process and outcomes of network governance without reverting too much to traditional forms of command and control that are likely to scare off network actors or create fierce opposition . . . as such, meta governance aims to design, frame, support and intervene in governance networks while respecting their capacity for self regulation.

This concept has clear similarities with using managed networks as a governance mode as discussed earlier (see also Baker 2015).

Torfing et al. (2019, p. 816) further suggest other system-wide changes are needed to sustain a paradigm transition to co-creation. For example they suggest a move away from performance management systems based on top-down control of inputs and outputs (New Public Management style) to a 'more trust based steering based on learning enhancing self evaluations of the outcomes provided by public organizations and the inter organizational networks of which they are part.'

We will now present a brief worked case study of a turn to co-creation and co-production in a major organization in Wales to explore how such processes can take place. Interestingly, the case combines a long-term strategic plan with a major local innovation in co-production, indicating that different models of strategic management may be combined fruitfully.

Box 4.2   Co-creation in Welsh Water

By *Irene Pluchinotta, Hannah Williams, Ewan Ferlie, and Martin Kitchener*

This case study gives an account of a participative and organization-wide strategic planning process together with a turn to co-production within a major local innovation. Welsh Water is an interesting hybrid organization: it is a public limited company but also took the decision in 2002 to operate without shareholders (most unusually in the UK water sector which was privatized in the 1980s), and it since has had a strong stakeholder and public interest orientation, perhaps reflecting distinctively Welsh political and management values. Any surplus is reinvested in the organization. This earlier shift in overall governance seems to be correlated with important later initiatives to promote participation and co-production.

First, Welsh Water launched a long-term strategic planning process to create its 2050 plan (Welsh Water 2018) (https://corporate.dwrcymru.com/en/about-us/our-plans/water-2050). This plan was designed with Cardiff University and Arup, an independent firm of designers, planners, engineers, and consultants. They also consulted widely with stakeholders (p. 26) and synthesized views received to inform the plan: 'We received over 20,000 responses from customers through the Welsh Water website; public events; an online chat bot; an 'online community' panel, and in-depth interviews, all developed and applied in cooperation with our Customer Challenge Group. Thirteen stakeholders provided their written feedback and we connected with many more at a launch event.'

Alongside the 2050 plan, WW works in five-year business planning cycles, which set out short- to medium-term plans. In 2016, a customer consultation was conducted (face-to-face and online) to decide how the £30 million of surplus should be spent. Customers were given several options: reduce their own bills; reduce the bills of struggling customers; spend to save, for example invest in renewable energy; help the worst-served customers, that is those with repeat debt problems; or invest in community education and recreation. Twelve thousand customers took part and wider goals of community development and helping less advantaged customers were strongly favoured. As a result, the next five-year business plan was designed around customers' responses.

Second, Welsh Water promoted co-production ideas within its 'Water Resilient Community' initiative in a deprived area (the Rhondda Fach). The project involves a large capital investment (around £23 million) for upgrading the main water pipes. WW used this project to open an honest relationship and dialogue with customers. WW decided to add value by using participative approaches, helping customers who have problems with water debt with the special social tariff, promoting affordability targets, working with other organizations trying to deliver local projects (such as a major housing association and a health board), consult with businesses customers (traders, independent shops) to make sure the works did not affect their trade.

This innovative project used community meetings, stakeholders' workshops, events, the 'community van,' publications, and school educational programmes. To promote this service, WW co-produced a leaflet with local customers. WW's Education Team provided outreach sessions to local schools. Instead of visiting a school once (which was common practice), the team sustained an ongoing relationship with each school and visited three times. Moreover, WW hosted Facebook live Q&A sessions and town hall meetings, created a programme for young people to tackle unemployment, worked out of Jobcentres, and redesigned their communication strategy based on customer feedback.

Source: Pluchinotta et al. 2020

Some key learning points which emerge from this review of the co-production and co-creation literature analyzed in relation to the field of the strategic management of public services include the following. First, there is increased interest in co-production and co-creation ideas in public agencies which can be seen as an extension of NG approaches. Second, there is an issue about how public agencies go beyond small-scale pilot projects and make a more strategic turn to co-production and co-creation. The literature suggests there are barriers to a turn to co-production and co-creation as well as drivers and such barriers should not be underestimated. Third, there may be a role for the 'meta governance' of these agency-level change processes from above, as some literature suggests; if so, the national level state may have an important role in designing them. Finally, certain more conventional strategic management models or approaches (such as a long-term strategic plan) may be valuable in supporting a wider transition to co-production within public agencies, as seen in the Welsh Water case presented.

4.6 Concluding remarks: similarities and dissimilarities between Networked Governance and the other schools of strategic management

This chapter has argued there is a growth of interest in collaborative and network-based forms of strategy which complement received models centred on competitive advantage or top-down, line management-based models. The chapter also reviewed the literature on the Network Governance model of public management which reflected but also helped fuel such developments.

It was also discussed that NG is a more 'decentred' model of public management whereby traditional Weberian line management hierarchies and NPM-style markets and quasi markets are eroded. More and more varied actors now inhabit the public policy process, including those from civil society. A range of 'wicked' or highly complex public policy problems may call for better inter-agency and intersectoral cooperation. Concrete and enduring NG reforms from the UK in the New Labour period (1997–2010) were presented, including important examples of managed networks and devolution, as well as examples from the Netherlands.

The chapter has then considered several different academic literatures which help us make sense of strategy making in an NG-type and more collaborative world, also drawing out questions and implications for policy and practice in discussion. A possible implication from the post-Fordist literature reviewed is, for example that economic networks and partnerships may displace traditional social policy-orientated ones as the old welfare state shrinks, becomes more conditional, or is subordinated to a productivity agenda. Post-Fordism also highlighted the growth of 'strong' sub-nations, regions, and cities below the traditional nation state, as well as more international linkages between nations and between strong regions.

Strategy in these multi-actor settings may take the form of steering or influencing rather than directing. At national level, there is an intriguing notion of 'meta governance' from above which seeks to influence the behaviour of local public policy-related networks (e.g. see the example of managed networks in the UK health care sector). Public agencies are encouraged in this cooperative perspective to become more outwards and also downwards facing. The building of enduring partnerships with other public agencies, private firms, and civil society organizations on a whole area basis becomes more critical.

The co-production and co-creation stream of literature has then been considered, which suggests that public agencies need to become better at working together with users and citizens. Doing this on an organization-wide level requires a strategic approach which gets beyond small-scale pilot projects in receptive but atypical contexts (Pettigrew et al. 1992). Strategic management-based models and approaches may be helpful in such 'scaling up,' notably when processes of co-creation are aimed for (Ongaro et al. 2021).

Authentic and transformational leadership that can influence and inspire across conventional boundaries has also been highlighted as potentially an important resource to help manage any strategic transition to more cooperative forms of strategy. More empirical work is needed to test these assertions. The point was also made that leadership 'cannot do everything' and that context and structure are also important.

In concluding this chapter, we can now query whether cooperative and network-based strategy has an affinity with other schools of strategic management, or whether it represents a radically different approach. We explore whether some models of strategic management reviewed earlier in the book could be associated with developing a cooperative strategy. The public value model of strategy recurred in some literature reviewed (Ansell and Torfing 2021) as a helpful background prism for developing cooperative strategy and may even be regarded as a prime resource in this regard.

Some other models of strategic management may also be useful in NG settings. Specifically, rather conventional strategic planning exercises may usefully express top-down support and provide resources for cooperatively orientated innovation in the field, as in the Welsh Water case (Box 4.2). The cultural school could well be important in stressing the importance of a positive set of underlying and outward-looking values that opens an organization to wider influences both sideways to other agencies and organizations and 'downwards' to user and citizens. The planning and cultural school were detected to have been evident in a recent article delineating how models of strategic management can be applied to shed light on the dynamics of co-creation processes, based on the Welsh Water case already illustrated in Box 4.2 (Ongaro et al. 2021). Decentralized forms of strategy driven from the field in a bottom-up way might also be thought to indicate the adoption of a strategy as practice approach. Finally, a Mintzbergian process of emergence and learning might fit well with a network-based setting where partners need to develop reciprocal knowledge and co-evolve.

There are finally some practical implications of this cooperative and networks-based perspective for the preferred style, requisite knowledge, and skills bases of public managers. The skills needed may well include a strength in building high trust and long-term relationships; coalition building; influencing rather than simply directing; an authentic and emotionally intelligent leadership style; being able to understand and empathize with the perspectives of others and to communicate effectively with them; ensure that there is a broad base for the exercise of leadership rather than reliance on one individual, however charismatic. These ideas could also usefully inform the redesign of education and training programmes in public management to reorientate them towards the knowledge and skills bases required for the managing of networks and systems rather than just directing single agencies.

5 Strategy making and governance in the third sector

This chapter continues in the emphasis as in the previous chapter on how a plurality of actors operating in networked and collaborative governance arrangements are central in the delivery of current public services, as we have previously argued in Chapter 4. In particular, we consider moves beyond any crude state/market binary divide to explore questions of strategic management and governance within a growing arena of 'third sector' organizations, neither part of traditional government (though often now funded by it) nor conventional firms with shareholders. This increasingly important hybrid group of non-governmental organizations (NGOs) includes various subcategories: voluntary and 'social movement'-based organizations (where the organization is aligned with a social group with a strong identity, e.g. voluntary organizations that work against racial discrimination or for better health services for people and families affected by mental health problems), worker-owned cooperatives and mutually owned organizations, and a new wave of social enterprises which may be more 'business like' in nature.

As these organizations have grown in scale and professionalized their management, so they have adopted more generic management models, including some strategic management practices. However, there is a lively debate as to whether such strategic management practices can be readily transposed, or whether the distinctive and mission-driven identity of NGOs makes such intersectoral diffusion problematic.

The chapter starts with an overview of recent policy and organizational developments in the NGO field. It then examines the simplest case of the entrepreneurial school (seen in Chapter 3), which is also applicable to some social enterprises. It moves on to consider the extent to which generic strategic management models may be appropriately adopted in these NGO settings as they grow their scale and commercial operations or whether they require customization (and concluding they still require substantial adaptation to the mission-based nature of NGOs). It finally highlights governance and accountability mechanisms – and their possible weaknesses – as a theme of great interest in this sector (some introductory elements of the dilemmas faced by small NGOs are highlighted in the US-based case reported in Box 5.1).

5.1 Overview of policy and organizational developments in the NGOs sector: scaling up, convergence, and possible mission drift

Billis (2010)'s overview of developments in the UK voluntary sector policy and organizations suggests that this field has grown markedly in scale and also in its public policy profile over the last 20 years or so. In the USA, by contrast, voluntary sector provision

DOI: 10.4324/9781003054917-5

has traditionally been more extensive, notably so in such sectors as health and welfare and also the arts (e.g. museums; Foundations). The UK voluntary sector has faced similar challenges to UK public services organizations in being subjected to NPM reforms and so exposed to models and thinking originally developed for the private sector: 'for better or worse, third sector staff – in common with their colleagues in the public sector – became increasingly subjected to the virtues of concepts originally developed for the private sector' (Billis 2010, p. 7). Within the domain of public policy, the third sector was favoured by UK New Labour (1997–2010) governments' 'partnership' discourse which incorporated the third sector, given its move away from uncontested reliance on traditional public sector providers. This policy level support has been continued under centre right UK governments from 2010 onwards, but it combined with budgetary policies in the era of austerity which have created a tighter financial context for NGOs. Cornforth (2014) also highlights a different policy stream evident in the New Labour period which emphasized the broader role of NGOs in promoting social capital and social inclusion, to tackle problems of antisocial behaviour. The implication of this social capital perspective is that NGOs should develop as 'self steering' and downwards-looking organizations, facing out to local communities or client populations rather than upwards to government as a letter of contracts.

However, some NGOs have recently evolved to become large-scale service deliverers to government under contract, as an outcome of NPM reforms (Rathgeb-Smith 2005) which have included outsourcing to the third sector, given a perceived legacy of a failed public sector (e.g. in social housing) which then opened a gap that was filled by new forms of provision. Such trends pose dilemmas as well as opportunities for NGOs, as too close a funding relation with government and working to onerous contracts may erode their distinctive mission and diminish their wider expressive (traditionally non-contractual) contribution to social capital and civil society (Billis 2010). They are also caught in an increased blurring of traditional sectoral boundaries which may erode their traditional identity and volunteer-based culture (Billis 2010). Harris (2010) explores possible negative effects of such loss of their traditional identity on these organizations' ability to attract and retain volunteers, given disorientating changes in basic culture and ethos. These conditions accord NGOs a strategic choice or rather a dilemma (Van de Pijl and Sminia 2004) between corporatist co-option by government on the one hand and a stance of oppositionist activism on the other. A possible tension emerges between the base of volunteers in the traditional local associations and the increasingly dominant paid hierarchy of executives.

There appear to be expanding commercial operations located within ring-fenced subunits in a number of major NGOs (Parsons and Broadbridge 2004) and a professionalization of NGO management (e.g. more highly paid CEOs) as these organizations grow in scope and scale. There also appears to be an 'isomorphic' (or 'same shape') convergence on the private firm as a preferred role model (Steen-Johnsen et al. 2011), just as in NPM-based public services: perhaps even to a greater extent given the NGO sector is less likely to contain powerful public services professions (such as medicine) as a countervailing force. The increased interest in models of strategic management in NGOs reflects these wider developments and convergence process. Corporate governance arrangements in NGOs have been explored in the literature as an important theme. Rathgeb-Smith (2005) highlights potential weaknesses in the governance dimension (board level) as of key importance to the proper functioning of NGOs. Cornforth and Spear (2010) note current but controversial suggestions in the third sector that private sector corporate governance practices (e.g. paying board members; allowing executives to serve as board members) might now be usefully imported to upgrade perceived board effectiveness. We consider these governance issues in more detail next.

It is possible that the 2008 financial crisis and later public policies based on public expenditure reductions and financial austerity may have reversed taken for granted assumptions of never-ending growth and increased financial support from government for NGOs (Cornforth 2014). If so, then such NGOs may now face difficult strategic choices in relation to questions of downsizing and diversification, reflecting possible over-dependence on government funding. The case reported in Box 5.1 – drawn from a real case based in the context of the United States of America and anonymized for purposes of publication – is illustrative in this regard.

Box 5.1   The Happy Days Café

By *Jeffrey Straussman*

The Happy Days Café is a bakery and restaurant that serves breakfast and lunch, Monday through Friday. It is located in an upscale business district of a medium-sized city, and it is managed by *Helping Hands*, a local non-profit agency that provides services to people with psychiatric disabilities. Like other restaurants, the Happy Days Café is financed by the sales of bakery goods and meals served to its customers. Prices for baked goods and meals are based on market conditions and the prices at the Café are similar to the prices found at the other small restaurants that serve breakfast and lunch in the area. Since the Happy Days Café employs people with developmental and psychiatric disabilities, it also receives funding from the Ministry of Labor's *Office of Supported Work Programs* in the form of an annual grant. The grant constitutes one-third of its total revenues. A small percentage of its funding comes from charitable contributions to its parent organization, Helping Hands.

The Happy Days Café opened on 2 January 2003. The Café started with 20 programme participants in 2003. Eight moved on to competitive employment; four of them were still employed after 12 months. After the first year of operation, the Café annually employed about 69 people, with approximately 32 employed at any given time. The Café employs five professional staff: a programme director responsible for both the business and the therapeutic dimensions of the Cafe, a bakery manager, a restaurant manager, and two employment specialists. The bakery and restaurant managers are responsible for teaching cooking and baking to the programme participants. Employment specialists train individuals in waitressing and counter skills, along with doing interviewing, hiring, counselling, and service planning. The programme participants all receive mental health services from Helping Hands. They are called 'trainees' and work in a variety of roles including dishwashers, janitors, bakers, breakfast and lunch cooks, and counter people who work directly with the customers. Trainees are paid the government minimum wage of $6 (USD) an hour with the expectation that the work experience gained will eventually translate into competitive employment in the private marketplace. Timelines for programme completion and transition to competitive employment ranged from six to 18 months, depending on the needs of the individual.

The Happy Days Café, as a supported work programme, is a far cry from its predecessor employment programme known as the 'sheltered workshop.' Sheltered workshops have been the prevailing model for providing employment experience to people with disabilities. Developed originally to serve people with developmental disabilities, sheltered workshops typically paid below government minimum wage levels and offered a limited range of job options. Most were assembly line, production-related repetitive work, and the workers were isolated from the non-disabled. Socially acceptable behaviours and work skills learnt in the sheltered workshop were not transferable to typical work environments. For example, piece work contracts that consisted of redundant tasks offered little opportunity to expand skills that would increase a person's future employability. In short, workers in sheltered workshops were rarely able to secure competitive, non-subsidized employment.

Trainees at the Happy Days Café have the following characteristics:

- A serious psychiatric disability that prevents them from gaining competitive employment on their own without substantial support and coaching;
- A lack of social skills necessary to relate to co-workers and supervisors;
- A deficit in the coping skills needed to manage stress in the work environment; and
- An inadequate network of social supports from their family and their community.

The supported work programme at the Café receives referrals of potential trainees to the Happy Days Café from various inpatient facilities, private therapists, group homes where people with psychiatric disabilities live and from the families of people with psychiatric disabilities. All of these referrals are screened by staff at Helping Hands.

After the first year of operation, the Office of Supported Work Programs doubled its grant to Helping Hands because it was impressed with the new therapeutic and employment model represented by the Happy Days Café. Meanwhile, a very favorable restaurant review of the Café in the local newspaper pushed sales up significantly. The fact that the Happy Days Café was actually a supported work programme for people with psychiatric disabilities was not mentioned in the article.

Dealing with the press for the first time underscored the emerging tension between managing the mental health needs of the trainees and trying to operate a business in a competitive environment. While the primary goal has been to offer a quality vocational training programme to individuals with psychiatric disabilities, the demands of the business sometimes supported and sometimes actually dominated the programme goals. Some mental health specialists claimed that a restaurant environment was too stressful for the trainees.

Sometimes trainees became agitated when the professional staff was not always available to do situational counseling on the spot when the immediate demands of customer service or production took priority.

The tension of pursuing a social mission while trying to manage a financially sound business was evident in the decision to offer approximately 30 part-time jobs to trainees. In particular, this decision meant that the Happy Days Café departed from the pure business model since there is a significant difference in the labor cost of operating the Café compared to the labor cost of operating a comparable competitive business. In a typical business of the size of the Happy Days Café, six to eight full-time employees would be able to operate the business. Furthermore, a competitive business would not have two employment specialists on staff to do situational counseling, goal planning, and coordination with other service providers. The kitchen at the Happy Days Café is about twice as large as what is needed since the Café trains and employs many more people than one would find in a normal restaurant. This also means that the rent for the Café is higher because of the extra space and, had the space been used for customer seating, this could have produced additional revenue.

Clearly, the Happy Days Café has had positive impacts on the trainees. Trainees began to develop an identity that was not connected solely to their psychiatric disability. Instead of describing their daily activity as going to day treatment mental health programmes, they now said that they were going to work. From a therapeutic sense, the ability to picture oneself in a role other than disabled is a key step in the long process of recovery. Socialization is a second therapeutic outcome of the Happy Days Café. Trainees accompanied one another to work, played card games, and sometimes even romantic relationships developed among them. Confidence and self-esteem improved for many of the trainees.

While the jobs at the Happy Days Café are all connected to the restaurant and the bakery, trainees were more likely to get a job in a field other than food service when they transitioned to unsubsidized employment. Trainees found that generic work skills such as reliability, punctuality, appropriate dress and hygiene, and relating effectively to supervisors and co-workers were learnt at the Happy Days Café.

After several years of operation, it became clear that many trainees did not want to leave the Café. Some said that they wanted to retire from the Happy Days Café, and still others said that it was the only job that they had ever been successful at. But not everything was unambiguously positive. Staff felt increased pressure to demonstrate higher numbers of competitive (unsubsidized) placements in the marketplace. On average, eight individuals per year would transition on to competitive employment, with three additional trainees leaving to further their education. The average length of time a person stayed in the programme at the Café was two years, but a few remained for as long as six years. About half of the placements were in jobs unrelated to food service.

While it was hard to say whether the Happy Days Café was successful or not, things began to change starting in 2008. A new conservative government took charge with a mandate to trim overall government spending and Helping Hands was not immune from budget cuts from the Office of Supported

Work Programs. Its grant was reduced by 10% a year for three consecutive years. Meanwhile, the Happy Days Café faced growing competitive pressure. When the Café opened in 2003, there were six restaurants operating in the area; by 2010, there were 15. The programme's revenue peaked in 2007 and then began to decline. Finally, the central government increased the minimum wage to $7 in 2008, and it was supposed to further increase. By 2011, the future of the Happy Days Café was less bright.

5.2 The simplest case: the entrepreneurial school and social enterprises

The first and simplest approach apparent within this sector draws on the entrepreneurial school of strategy (Mintzberg et al. 2009; McGrath 2006), already considered in Chapter 3 for application to public *sector* organizations (see the example of an EU agency like the European Aviation Safety Agency – EASA, in Box 2.4). Accounts of strategy making in small and medium enterprises (SMEs) typically highlight the strong, personal influence of a founder or entrepreneur rather than formal corporate or business planning systems. Within novel human services settings or small nonprofit organizations, similar processes may be evident: Pettigrew (1979)'s longitudinal study of the strategy of an unusual boarding school highlighted the leadership and indeed imprinting role of the founding headmaster in setting its basic and long-enduring educational ideology and culture; a similar experience, in the social sector, is that of the House of Charity in Milan, Italy, which received its imprinting and grew impressively under the leadership of its de facto founder and first and only president, Fr Virginio Colmegna (the story is recounted in Box 5.1). Mintzberg et al. (2009, Chapter 5) argue that the entrepreneurial perspective emphasizes not only the role of a single individual (as is seen already in the design school, at least in its initial and more traditional versions, but see the case of the European Training Foundation for an example of a collective strategist, Box 3.1), but also the importance of experience and intuition in generating a guiding strategic vision (unlike the rational analytics or formal techniques apparent in the design school). 'Vision' is rather seen in lying in the head of the leader, and it may be a semi-formed general idea or an image of a desired future rather than a fully formed plan (like in the planning school). Entrepreneurial strategists typically seek to grow the organization by occupying a distinctive and protected niche which fits with the general vision.

Box 5.2   The role of the social entrepreneur at the 'House of Charity' (Casa della Carità) in Milan, Italy

Established in 2002 by the then archbishop of Milan, Cardinal Carlo Maria Martini (1927–2012 – a highly influential Jesuit and leading figure in the theological debate worldwide), the Casa della Caritá (hereafter House of Charity) is a foundation active in Milan (northern Italy) supporting the homeless and facilitating social cohesion and reintegration. Since 2002, it hosted thousands of people, singles as well as families. Since its establishment, the leadership of the House of Charity was entrusted to its president, Fr Virginio Colmegna, who previously had experience as the director of the Caritas of the diocese of Milan. Resourced with an initial endowment (the bequest of an affluent donor) and with premises in the outskirts of Milan, and initially also supported by the municipality of Milan (a change of the mayor later radically reverted the relationships with the local government), it grew impressively in terms of volumes of services delivered, range of activities, and influence on the policy debate (this includes the setting up of the 'academy of charity,' through which the Foundation undertook a significant participation to the local and national public debate on such issues as housing, migration, security, employment). The burst of the 2008 financial crisis (soon followed in Italy by a deep economic downturn) further accentuated its levels of activity, whilst the reduced flow of resources coming from public funding (also as an outcome of the fiscal crisis that put strains on public budgets) multiplied the challenges faced by the House of Charity. Its impressive development was undoubtedly the outcome of the bold leadership and strong vision of the founder, as was its turbulent growth that in many respects stretched to its limits the financial and organizational capacities of this charity.

In earlier work, Mintzberg (1973) characterized key features of strategy making in an entrepreneurial organization. First, it would be dominated by the search for exciting new opportunities more than dealing with existing operational problems. Second, much power lies in the hands of the CEO/founder, who is often unwilling to delegate operational responsibilities (possibly then leading to overload and bottlenecks at the top). Third, strategy making tends not to be incremental but rather take the form of 'bold strokes' with the possibility of high pay-off: the ever-active CEO/founder thrives in conditions of high uncertainty and risk taking. Fourth, the strategy is driven by the goal of growth, in part to satisfy the high ego needs of the CEO.

The disadvantages of such an approach to strategy making include difficulties in succession planning; an over-concentration of power in the hands of one person (especially if that person is also the founder), a quirky tone, and over-involvement in detail by the CEO perhaps to the point of taking an obsessive and maniacal style.

Social enterprises represent an emergent hybrid sub-form within the third sector. Rathgeb-Smith (2005) highlights undercapitalization as a serious weakness in traditional NGOs, addressed in this recent turn to more business-like 'social enterprises.' These settings may display more private sector-style thinking and have better access to large-scale flows of finance so may need to be analyzed as a distinctive subset where two alternative modes of governance can clash (Aiken 2010), with an inherent danger than a strong business focus could crowd out the original social mission. Billis (2010) traces the emergence of the social enterprise movement to the US and Italy in the 1990s.

Bloom (2006) considers which strategic management literature may be most relevant to social enterprise settings. Plausible models highlighted include first Moore's (1995) strategic triangle (as reviewed earlier) and the public value perspective, seen as applicable to non-profit organizations as well as the public services. It is clear that while Moore's (1995) analysis deals mainly with strategy in public agencies, there is indeed overlap with the encouragement of community-based organizations (e.g. discussion of the creation of tenants' groups in Boston housing projects, Moore 1995, pp. 250–253). As public organizations downsize, decentralize, and outsource to the NGO sector, so such community-based organizations could take on more service delivery functions. Second, Oster's 1995 six forces chart for non-profit industry analysis is commended as a strategic tool, in essence adapted from Porter's basic five forces model originally developed in the context of private firms. We will review these important texts from Moore and Oster in more detail later.

Third, Bloom (2006) supports the use of the basic logic model developed by the Kellogg Foundation (2006) for programme implementation and evaluation by non-profit organizations. It is seen as helpful in modelling a value chain and as supplying a 'theory of change' and a method for estimating the extent of societal impact. Kellogg's basic logic model introduces concepts of leverage and of high-scale impact seen as particularly important in social enterprises:

> each social entrepreneur's theory of change ideally embeds an understanding of how to create public value in a leveraged manner, recognising the realities of allocating scarce resources and the often critical demands of time, especially in projects involving life threatening situations.
>
> (Bloom 2006, pp. 288–289)

Summing up, the entrepreneurial perspective may be relevant to strategy making in small-scale social enterprises, NGOs, and novel human services settings (see Ormrod et al. 2007, on the role of founders in shaping innovative mental health settings) which grow up around one inspirational leader or founder. Entrepreneurial theories of non-profits (Anheier 2005, p. 127) provide such a supply side explanation for their growth, although social entrepreneurs may be more interested in pursuing non-monetary objectives (e.g. in faith-based organizations) than the usual monetary reward goals espoused by conventional entrepreneurs.

However, the quantity and quality of technical and management support may be more uneven in NGOs than in corporate settings, accentuating the power of the visible leader further and reducing operational level checks and balances (e.g. formal HRM policies and procedures) (Hatten 1982). Should these small-scale organizations go into rapid growth, for example winning contracts for large-scale service delivery from public sector commissioners, the transition from personalized to bureaucratic forms of governance may be challenging, as operational management capacity may be weak, and developing it may challenge the concentrated authority of the visible founder. The role of the founder, however, may linger for a long time, and its bequest may be extremely influential: this is illustrated in Box 5.3, which also links to our next theme: strategic management in large NGOs.

Box 5.3   Grant-making foundations for global health: governance and the role of the founder in the *Gates*, the *Rockefeller*, and the *Wellcome Trust* Foundations

By *Elisa Ricciuti*

Global health is a difficult to define, yet tremendously important area generally intended as having characteristics of both public health and international health (Koplan et al. 2009); global health is a highly complex and multidisciplinary field (Lee et al. 2002). One of the main novelties of the global health world is the intervention of the *private* sector in what has traditionally been a *public* area of action, and the increased interconnections between actors of different nature – public–private partnerships (PPPs), non-governmental organizations (NGOs), and transnational corporations (TNCs) (Buse and Walt 2000; Dodgson et al. 2002; Buse and Lee 2005; Cohen 2006; The Lancet 2009a; Smith 2010).

Among the new ensemble of private, not-for-profit actors intervening in the policy process, there are the philanthropic foundations. They are not 'new' actors, not even in the global health field (Birn and Fee 2013): what is new is the relevance they seem to have acquired recently, due also to the creation of the Gates Foundation and its primary role in the current debate (Brown 2007; The Lancet 2009b), and due to recent studies on 'new' forms of philanthropy, such as 'philanthrocapitalism' or 'venture philanthropy,' which have elicited a debate on the topic (Bishop and Green 2008). Foundations intervene in the global health field in terms of giving additional resources to health (Ravishankar et al. 2009; Murray et al. 2011; IHME 2012) but also through a more and more relevant influence in priority-setting at the global level (Ollila 2005). They also contribute to health and development aid by fostering innovation and social change, funding education institutions and capacity-building in developing countries (Sulla 2006; Birn and Fee 2013). Whatever their focus areas, they act indeed beyond the public sector's action, with different roles and intensity (Fleishman 2007; Marten and Witte 2008; Moran 2011).

If this is the broader scenario and so significant and varied are the contributions foundations make to the field of global health, a legitimate question is *how do foundations make their grant-making strategies?* If the board is the place where strategic decisions are made, it is exactly in the governance and accountability that the Achille's heel of foundations lies. As studies report, foundations have been often criticized for being secretive and highly unaccountable in their decision making, not open to external criticism and even not responding to the needs of the final beneficiaries (Anheier and Hammack 2013).

The roots of the debate on the accountability of foundations can be found in their peculiar nature and governance structures, considered by many as unacceptable in our democratic, globalized era. Like other non-profits, foundations have a public or social-related mission and deploy private resources to advance their strategic objectives. Unlike other non-profits though, grant-making foundations generally do not seek public money, being based on a completely private endowment – often formed by the personal wealth of a funder, or family, or originated from a company, and continuously invested in the stock market. Accepting that foundations are *private*, but their impact is *public*, how do private foundations make their strategies?

Foundations are not all the same; even within the one big category of grant-making foundations, governance structures are indeed very different from one another. This does not depend on the size of the organization or the nature of the activity, but on the governance structures that leaders have designed for their own foundation (in case of living founders, like Bill Gates), or have inherited from the original founder's will (in case of long dead founder, like John D. Rockefeller and Henry S. Wellcome). Beyond governance structures, the autonomy of foundations' leaders is extremely important to set out rules for the inclusion of external inputs and advice to strategic decision. To show how both governance structures and the degree of openness to external inputs are different in foundations, we discuss three foundations, which are among the most relevant private donors in global health nowadays. They are all grant-making and with the same main focus, which is health research: the Gates Foundation (based in Seattle, US), the Rockefeller Foundation (based in New York, US) and the Wellcome Trust (based in London, UK).[1]

The Gates Foundation is the largest private philanthropic foundation in the world. It counts 37.2 billion USD of endowment (as of the year 2013), an average expenditure of 3.5 billion USD per year and over 1,000 employees. Moreover, it is one of the youngest foundations in the field of global health, created in 2000 from the merger of the William H. Gates Foundation and the Gates Learning Foundation and initially run only with part of the personal fortune of Bill and Melinda Gates, then favoured by a pledge made by Warren Buffet in 2006 which almost doubled the original endowment. The Gates Foundation is a family foundation: its board members (called co-chairs) are Bill Gates, his former wife Melinda, and his father, late William Gates Sr. They make decisions over the foundations' strategies. Moreover, Bill and Melinda Gates are also very active in the grant-making process, fully committed to the organization's activities, participating in review meetings, and performing several trips on the field. The foundation used to have a stable group of external experts for the Global Health Program (the Global Health Advisory Board), but it has been dismissed in 2007 and external advice to the co-chairs on the foundations' strategies and grants' proposals are now given on a random, informal basis.

The Rockefeller Foundation is the oldest foundation in the field of global health, established in 1913. Although its endowment is not among the first US foundations (around 3.7 billion USD in 2012), it has been and still is one of the major private players in global health around the world. Its prestigious history has contributed to funding major health institutions, like the WHO, to building public health schools around the globe and to promoting public health campaigns in developing countries (Birn and Fee 2013). Founded in 1913 from an oil magnate, Sir John D. Rockefeller, it was set up with the idea of 'promoting the well-being of humanity,' as written in the Foundation's mission. It counted (as of the year 2013) approximately 130 million USD of average expenditure and around 200 employees. The Rockefeller Foundation went through a massive reorganization after a new president took office in 2006, changing the governance structures and decision-making procedures. The board came to be composed of 13 people, including the president (as ex-officio member), all prominent figures in the American public, non-profit, and corporate world. Nonetheless, the foundation's strategy and all grants must get clearance from the president. The Rockefeller Foundation also uses external advice in random, informal ways, and it's up to the directors to decide where and to what extent external advice is needed in the grant proposals' review process.

The Wellcome Trust is less known outside the UK compared to the US-based foundations, although with its asset base of approximately 22 billion USD, it is currently the second-largest foundation in the world after the Gates Foundation. The Trust has a long tradition, established in 1936 by the will and the bequest of Henry Wellcome. Wellcome, an American businessman, collector, and philanthropist, moved to England to set up a multinational pharmaceutical company in 1880. The Wellcome Trust has a completely different decision-making process compared to the US foundations mentioned. It has (year 2013) ten board members (called governors), who steer the organization, approving annual strategies and multi-annual strategic plans. The most peculiar characteristic of the Wellcome Trust board of governors is that they participate in specific panels set up for the evaluation and approval of grants' proposals. Usually at least one member of the board is present at panels' meetings, although it has no voting power. Moreover, the Wellcome Trust has a peculiar 'response mode' grant-making model, whereby the first steps of proposals' evaluations are conducted with a strong participation of external contributions, mainly academics. There are stable groups (the Expert Review Groups) involved in the review of grants' proposals, in different steps up to the final decisions where both governors and directors are involved.

As we can see from these brief accounts of the boards' structures and involvement of these three foundations, the role of leaders is indeed extremely relevant in determining both governance structures and decision-making mechanisms of philanthropic foundations. External contributions can be either stable or random and the extent of the discretional choice of leaders over funding decisions may be extremely varied. The relevance of foundations' leader, with both its positive and negative implications, has been noted to be one of the most important features of new foundations in the so-called philanthrocapitalism (Bishop and Green 2008; McGoey 2012). The debate is open on the extent to which an often unclear, strongly internally driven, and potentially self-interested decision making can have a positive impact into making strategic decisions in the interest of global public health.

5.3 Large-scale third-sector organizations and dilemmas in their strategic management

While the entrepreneurial school may fit well with small-scale and founder-based NGOs or social enterprises, it may be less relevant to NGOs which have grown in size, professionalized, become service deliverers to government, and increased the scale and scope of their commercial operations (see the cases of three 'global' NGOs reported in Box 5.2). The question is whether such large third-sector organizations could usefully employ generic models of strategy drawn either from the private or the public sectors.

As an example of such major organizational changes, Parsons and Broadbridge (2004) trace the professionalization, commercialization, and bureaucratization of the UK charity shop sector since the 1980s–1990s. There has been a growth of paid senior staff (often recruited from the for-profit sector), along with the importing of private sector practices (e.g. sales targets, incentive-based bonuses, and the poorly received introduction of inter-shop league tables), with a danger of a culture clash between the new professionalized line hierarchy and the traditional volunteer base embedded at local level. Increased centralization to head office and the standardization of shops' work practices devalued traditional 'local knowledges' and was resented at the bottom of the organization (Parsons and Broadbridge 2004).

Examining the experience of NGOs in one American district, Mulhare (1999, cited in Parsons and Broadbridge 2004) found a close relationship between the increased influence of professionalizing management staff in NGOs and recourse to strategic planning models from the 1980s onwards (e.g. citing Bryson's well-known book as an example). Such practices were seen as a guarantor of professional approaches to fund-raising and more business-like working generally (Mulhare (1999, p. 327): 'strategic planning had become a symbolic demonstration of management competence, whether or not planning benefitted the non profit organization in other ways.' Mulhare suggests that the emergent occupational segment of NGO managers looked more to the business sector than government for role models and guiding texts, within their professionalization project.

By 1990, it had become clear that such strategic planning attempts had worked best in large and already bureaucratized settings (such as universities and major hospitals) with pre-existing and highly formalized approaches to decision making and poorly in smaller and more fluid NGOs (Mulhare 1999). There was some disillusion evident in the field with highly formalized and rational analytic approaches to strategic planning. Mulhare (1999) called for NGOs to develop management practices which reflected their own cultures and contexts, perhaps using Mintzberg's (1983) typology of organizational archetypes as a diagnostic instrument.

Along with a greater focus on the possible benefits of strategic planning and management, there may also be more emphasis on the 'management of change' within large NGOs, which could, however, negatively affect their fundamental ethos alongside the declared objective of improving the efficiency of their operations. Parsons and Broadbridge (2004) cite Salipante and Golden-Biddle (1995)'s discussion of the importance of retaining 'traditionality' in non-profits which can (in their view rightly) restrain such attempts to change management, where they could erode basic culture and mission. Such a traditionalist stance could even protect NGOs from experiencing a dysfunctional series of managerial 'fads and fashions,' so evident in the private sector.

Salipante and Golden-Biddle (1995) argue that 'improperly applied, concepts of strategic management represent a serious threat to non profits' basic character and identity.' They argue that enduring 'advocacy based missions' should remain at the core of non-profits' strategy and that 'traditionality' should be highly valued in the sector. Young (2001) similarly emphasizes that its underlying identity provides internal guidance capacity for an NGO:

> in short, non profit organizations must know who they are to make successful strategic and structural choices. At the same time, the flexibility of form allows non profits to choose who they are, often from among several possible 'organizational identities.

Traditional missions should (they argue) guide such organizational adaptation as is required, but in an incremental way and with dialogue with the whole of the organization rather than being proclaimed from the top. Given that many social needs and missions of NGOs are enduring, a strategic stance of 'greater continuity and less frequent and sweeping changes' may be preferable. Furthermore, the retention of a distinct organizational identity and high levels of trust are long-term assets in terms of underlying social capital for non-profits which could be jeopardized by excessive reorganization and shifts of strategic focus.

We infer from their analysis (with which we would broadly agree) that the articulation and retention of a strong, clear and stable mission statement which can readily mobilize public, donor, and volunteer support may be one strategic management technique that would fit with the basic characteristics and needs of NGOs (as Oster 1995 also argues). It may be that some other aspects of the strategic management corpus – broadly understood – can also be used appropriately, as we explore later.

5.4 A discussion of whether distinctive characteristics of third-sector organizations still shape their strategic management

Van de Pijl and Sminia (2004) argue that third-sector organizations (which they term 'public interest organizations' (PIOs)) could well benefit from more strategic management ideas and techniques, yet they also caution that many strategic management models were first developed within the private sector and may not travel well into the third sector where distinctive conditions still apply. They note that there can be a tension between the logic of the paid staff who are primarily concerned to achieve externally facing objectives or organizational 'interests' (notably the lobbying of government) and that of the base of the volunteers which needs to be explicitly handled within strategy making. Thus, a third-sector organization presents a 'representation vs. control' dilemma as it needs to balance the interests of a line management hierarchy of paid staff on the one hand with a representative constituency of members and volunteers on the other. While a control orientation may lead to a narrow and top-down approach to strategy and an emphasis on achieving a unified position, a representative orientation may lead to a bottom-up, more diffuse, and heterogeneous mode.

Van de Pijl and Sminia (2004) then theoretically draw on a distinctive strand of paradox-related thinking in organizational analysis (Hampden-Turner 1990), including Poole and van de Ven's (1989) argument that 'dilemma, contradiction and paradox' can under certain circumstances produce positive organizational learning, as long the tensions are handled to create a virtuous rather than a vicious cycle. A third-sector organization has to pay attention both to conventional questions of resource flows and strategic management but also the special internal dynamics of a volunteer-based organization which offers a different logic (Van de Pijl and Sminia 2004,

p. 138). Indeed, a third-sector organization which does not address this basic tension between such dual logics as a strategic issue in its own right may suffer 'a PIO whose design inhibits confrontation along the two dilemmas will lack the ability to learn and develop, with eventual dire consequences' (Van de Pijl and Sminia 2004, p. 141).

Van de Pijl and Sminia (2004) applied this dilemma-based perspective to a longitudinal exploration of decision making in the Dutch Federation of Parent Associations, a national voluntary organization active in the field of the welfare of people with mental handicap. Over time, it appeared that the 'bottom up' counterforce provided by the parents' membership disappeared from the equation and the more conventional control end (associated with the paid staff) became (over) dominant. A key learning point is that approaches to strategic management in the third sector may need to be adapted from public as well as private sector settings, as they have many volunteers as well as some paid staff.

Adapting private sector models of strategy for NGOs

Oster's (1995) important text essentially developed private sector-based strategic management/industrial economics thinking and techniques to make them relevant to the world of (American) non-profits, increasingly operating in competitive markets and facing demanding customers, just as private firms do. Like private firms, they are seen as facing generic management challenges in such areas as HRM, corporate governance, product mix and pricing decisions, programme evaluation and change management, as well as sectorally specific challenges in the field of fund-raising and relations with major donors.

A key chapter (Oster 1995, Chapter 3) outlines an industry-level analysis in which a sample non-profit organization might operate. It takes a Porterian approach, adapting his five-forces model into a six-forces chart for non-profit industry analysis. The major difference is that the Porterian notion of 'customers' is decomposed into an analysis of two separate demand side groups: users and donors. Users may be paying customers (e.g. the local Red Cross branch may sell blood to a local hospital), where it would be important to establish the degree of buyer power. Users of non-profits may also be non-paying 'clients' where consumption can be imposed (e.g. prisoners), which provokes complications in a Porterian analysis.

The second group on the demand side is identified as 'donors,' an idiosyncratic feature of the non-profit sector. The power of the donor increases with his or her share of the revenues. In major museums, for example, much of the income stream may revolve around the wishes and tastes of a small number of major benefactors.

This perspective can then be used to refine operational-level analytic tools. Specifically, the *product portfolio map* technique (Oster 1995, p. 93) enables boards of non-profits to make decisions about how much an organizational activity (i) contributes to the achievement of the core mission and (ii) contributes to economic viability, or to both or neither of these core dimensions through a visually appealing matrix. The advice is that non-profits should balance their mix of activities to ensure a focus on both the mission and economic viability.

Oster (1995) recognizes some enduring differences between the firm and the NGO, especially in the centrality of mission (Chapter 2) as NGOs often operate in hard-to-monitor markets where trust is an important source of competitive advantage and hence an organizational 'core competence.' On the whole, however, Oster's discussion tends to skate over important sources of difference, in our view, from private sector firms. There is little discussion of the cultural aspects of NGOs, likely demands in these settings for participative modes of strategy making from the volunteer base, and their consequences for likely recourse to emergent and bottom-up forms of strategy making.

Adapting public sector models of strategy for NGOs

Another view from a different group of public management-orientated authors is that there are relatively few differences between current public and not-for-profit organizations in their rightful approach to strategic management. These authors have furthermore drawn on generic strategic management concepts in devising their strategy models for the public sector, albeit in a customized manner.

The title of Nutt and Backoff (1987, 1992)'s texts on strategic management clearly suggests they are aimed at third sector as well as public sector organization; indeed it is assumed that these organizations are similar forms. They suggest using generic techniques, such as the SWOT analysis. Bryson (2018) also argues his model of the strategic change cycle is applicable both to public sector and non-profit/third-sector organizations, which he too groups together within the same broad family.

Moore's (2000) interesting cross-sectoral discussion of the organizational characteristics and of strategy making in the for-profit, non-profit, and governmental sectors is worth examining closely. These three sectors are seen by him as having different logics in terms of revenue streams and underlying conceptions of value creation. His account of strategy making in the private firm draws on essentially Porterian concepts. Moore (2000) then acknowledges important differences between non-profits when compared to governmental bureaux: their mandates are not generally specified in legislation; they are not dependent on collective and Parliamentary deliberative processes; and they are financed through donations rather than taxation (although this distinction may be eroding as service delivery functions are outsourced from government to non-profits). Yet Moore argues that there is 'close kinship' between the non-profit and governmental groups as they both define value in terms of social mission rather than profits and their flows of revenue come from broader social groupings than direct customers. So, the two groups can both be placed in a combined mission based 'public services organization' box which remains distinctive from private firms.

For Moore (2000), enacting the underlying 'mission' – and considering how it can legitimately evolve over time – is core to strategy making in non-profit settings as well as achieving financial sustainability (the so-called double bottom line). An important question is how broadly or narrowly the mission should be expressed within a mission statement: a broader definition provides for more interpretive flexibility, although also more scope for contest around (re) interpretation. On the other hand, donors and volunteers may be suspicious of very broad goals and prefer a greater level of specificity. A not-for-profit organization is likely to be interested in specifying clearly how its mission can create social value. So, the mission statement is an important strategic technique in this sector as it is 'the story that organizations tell to sustain a flow of resources to them' (Moore 2000).

Moore (2000) reports of his executive education work with executives in American non-profit organizations suggested that aspects of the public value strategic triangle originally developed for executives in the government sector also had resonance for them, namely:

(i)   Social value is defined in terms of mission achievement rather than primarily in terms of financial performance;

(ii)   The (wider) authorizing environment is an important source of support and legitimacy; non-profit managers fully appreciate the importance of building coalitions, and working with interest groups and media as part of politically informed advocacy work; and

(iii) Building such wider legitimacy and support is seen as an end in itself by such managers as well as a means.

Moore (2000) looks at non-profit organizations from a wider perspective rather than merely seeing them as a production function as they may also produce wider social value in indirect ways. They may, for example, enable individual donors to express their charitable aspirations or build social capital, social inclusion, and trust: so, understanding the experience of the volunteer and the impact of volunteering on wider stocks of social capital may be important as well as objectives of revenue generation and cost effectiveness. For example volunteers excluded from the mainstream labour market may see working for an understanding non-profit as a supportive step back into the world of paid work.

Within this public value perspective, Benington and Moore (2011a) develop an expanded concept of the 'public sphere.' It is argued (Benington 2011) that there is an emerging paradigm of 'networked community governance,' consistent with a higher-level shift from traditional top-down 'government' to a wider and looser form of 'governance.' Within this new paradigm, civil society (rather than the state or market) plays an enhanced role, perhaps operating in partnership with a facilitating State and through forms of co-production. This perspective might well support the outsourcing of poor-quality public provision to local community and social groups or the creation of hybrid governance structures.

But are there also enduring differences between the public and not-for-profit sectors which should be considered within strategy making? Some non-profit organizations are highly value- or mission-based, to a greater extent than supposedly neutral and process-based Weberian public bureaucracies. This is particularly significant where NGOs reflect religious or ideological positions, or where they are linked to 'social movements,' that is, value-laden and ideologically informed action group aimed at achieving social and attitudinal change. Various major not-for-profits in the health sector relate to traditionally marginalized or stigmatized social groups and have a strong advocacy and lobbying role as well as a service delivery function (e.g. the large UK NGO which is called MIND in mental health services has strongly supported increasing the influence of the user movement in redesigning services; the Terrence Higgins Trust in the field of HIV/AIDS promotes a strong user voice in the conduct of randomized control trials for new drugs as well as in other services). Social movement organizations may seek to promote social and attitudinal change to combat traditional stigma, marginalization, and power inequalities: understanding their underpinning ideology, social values, and collective culture may be critical and may lead to a more bottom-up and emergent form of strategy and approach to securing societal change (Bate et al. 2004).

5.5 Questions of NGOs' governance and accountability

Potentially problematic governance and accountability mechanisms in NGOs are well explored in the sectoral literature, in particular the role of the board (Cornforth 2014). Rathgeb-Smith (2005) argues that as NGOs have no pressures from share-holders (unlike firms) or voters (unlike the public sector), so their governance level of voluntary trustees and board members may be largely self-appointed (or elected with low levels of rank-and-file member or user engagement). There may be little contest for seats on boards of NGOs as such roles may be seen as an honorific but time-consuming duty. Board members are themselves normally unpaid volunteers, prohibited from any financial gain from their involvement with the NGO, may have low levels of managerial skills and experience, or may occupy many such non-executive posts for reasons of social standing and prestige (with the implication they have little time to dedicate to anyone). The outcome may be weak scrutiny by the trustees of the executive employees and poor levels of organizational performance which go unchallenged.

Steen-Johnsen et al. (2011) argue that the governance of what they term 'civil society organizations' is a growing and multidisciplinary field. They distinguish between, first, an interest in an external governance perspective (i.e. how they interact with other organizations within complex and intersectoral policy fields), most evident in the political science literature on network governance and, second, an interest in their internal governance (i.e. the role of the board and of trustees; the nature and extent of democratic accountability to members), more evident in the management literature. They argue that the two foci need to be brought together in a multi-level analysis, as in an exploration of the increasing tendency to import corporate governance models from the for-profit sector, in part to satisfy societal demands for greater accountability and received notions of 'good governance.'

Whether such importing is appropriate is a subject of lively debate. On the one hand, it is argued that NGOs have become more 'firm like,' have expanded in scope and scale, and hence require board members with senior level business skills. Anheier (2005, pp. 206–207) suggests many non-profits have entered into a long-term process of product diversification, complementing original activity orientated to the social prime mission with more secondary business activities (e.g. a museum deciding to expand its café to generate income to cross subsidize core cultural objectives). Given such product diversification, the board members of non-profits now have to make 'business like' strategic decisions about which programmes to wind down or invest in (rather as a firm or public agency has to decide where to allocate scarce capital).

On the other hand, other authors argue the special ethos and identity of NGOs needs – perhaps above all – to be reflected in its governance arrangements, potentially threatened by an all-powerful board at the strategic apex of the organization on the model of the private firm. Elstub's (2006) account of the increasing involvement of UK NGOs in public service delivery in the New Labour period highlights their potential contribution to overall policy goals of democratic renewal, empowerment, and social inclusion (rather than, say, an alternative overall goal of cost-effective production; see Elstub 2006). Such primary goals have implications for legitimate forms of internal decision making. It is evident, first, that such NGOs need to be constituted as devolved power centres in their own right, rather than appendages of an over-mighty state, so that they can contribute as autonomous and self-steering organizations to enriching civil society. Second, Elstub (2006) argues that it follows that their own decision-making structures should then be based on the norm of deliberative democracy which advocates 'the making of decisions through dialogue between affected parties.' In other words, there should be an internal process of democratization, helping the empowerment of minority and subordinated groups to challenge the dominant social policy agenda. Guo et al. (2014) similarly argue that the existing NGO corporate governance literature marginalizes important themes of representation, participation, and power and call for the greater use of democratic and critical perspectives.

Historically, there has been a strong focus in the sectoral literature on formal board structure. The governing body of a non-profit organization would often be elected by all members in 'private' elections and confined to volunteers/trustees rather than paid professional staff, but there now appear to be various alternative forms. For a 'unitary organization' (that is, a not-for-profit organization without commercial subsidiaries), Cornforth and Spear (2010) suggest three options. The first is the classic membership association-based structure, where the board is elected by all the members, usually at an Annual General Meeting and is formally accountable to them. The disadvantages of this option may be that members without relevant skills or experience may be elected or that participation levels may remain low. The second option is where the membership is closed to board members only, who are therefore effectively self-selecting. The board may here become undemocratic, narrow, oligarchical, and inward-looking, but this option also offers the possible advantage that board members can be co-opted on the basis of relevant skills and experience. Cornforth and Spear (2010) raise the possibility that grass roots energy and participation levels may decline in NGOs as they advance through their life cycle, possibly leading to an increased use of the second mode. The third governance structure is the mixed mode, where some board members are elected but others co-opted.

Increasingly, some non-profits have expanded their trading arms for income-generation purposes, sometimes spun out into separate commercial subsidiaries for legal reasons. This trend leads to more complex governance structures, as each subsidiary (as well as the main charity) will need to have its own board (Cornforth and Spear 2010), placing additional oversight demands on charity trustees (who have to handle any reputational damage from over-commercialized subsidiaries, even if they are formally legally separate entities).

Cornforth (2014) further argues that this established sectoral literature on corporate governance contains a number of flaws: it has been too top-down, has neglected what actually happens in the boardroom from a process perspective, and has been only weakly informed by organizational or other theory. He calls for the development of new methods and theories, such as the processual, longitudinal, and case-based form of research which some process scholars have developed in the study of private sector boards (McNulty and Pettigrew 1999).

5.6 Concluding discussion

The application and development of strategic management literature appears as yet limited in the not-for-profit sector. Some authors do not consider it as an important block of literature: so Helmig et al.'s (2004) overview of existing management research in the non-profit sector distinguishes between economic theories (e.g. principal-agent theory as a possible prism for conceptualizing governance regimes within non-profits) and sociological theories (e.g. institutionalist perspectives on mimetic 'fads and fashions' which sweep across the sector) but says little about strategic management models. Instead, a marketing-based perspective is held out as more useful.

We agree with writers (e.g. Salipante and Golden-Biddle 1995) who are cautious about the literal and overzealous importing of private sector-based and Porterian models of strategy into the sector, given NGOs' enduring and distinctive conditions of social mission. But this chapter has highlighted other schools of strategy which may usefully be brought in (even if in an adapted form) to help NGOs think more clearly about their long-term and overall direction, which we feel may be helpful to them. We now summarize the key arguments developed in the chapter.

First, Mintzberg et al.'s (2009) entrepreneurial school may well be applicable to strategy making in small and recently founded not-for-profits, especially those with a dominant founder. It clearly informs the developing social enterprise stream of work. But the entrepreneurial school fits less well in 'scaled up,' professionalized third-sector organizations, perhaps now delivering large-scale contracts for government.

Which texts and models of strategy making might be most useful in these larger-scale third-sector settings? Moore (2000)'s discussion of the similarities and differences between strategy making in the private, public, and third sectors suggests lines of analysis which may in our view be helpful. Moore and Bennington (2011) continue to move public value analysis out of its original base in the public sector into an expanded realm of civil society/community-based organizations.

We further suggest that if the question of mission (or its erosion) remains the defining question for the sector, the cultural school of strategy could usefully be brought in more systematically. Questions from this perspective include the role of strong collective values and ideologies in shaping strategies. Specific techniques including the use of mission statements and cultural web analysis may here be indicated.

We also suggest that NGOs may well want to pay careful attention to the *process* as well as the *content* of strategy, keeping the rival claims of the professional executives and the rank-and-file volunteer base in balance. They may well wish to ensure that the claims of the former do not crowd out the legitimate involvement of the latter within strategic management exercises (contra Mulhare 1999).

Note

1 Data reported in this case study derive from the author's doctoral research work on the three foundations. Data on assets size, expenditures, and numbers of employees are drawn by accesses, occurred between 2011 and 2014 to foundations' websites, annual reports, as well as the Top Funders statistics page freely accessible from The Foundation Center (www. foundationcenter.org).

6 Strategy as process

A review and prospective agenda

In Chapter 3, we briefly introduced the organizational process school of strategy, associated with major authors such as Pettigrew (1979, 1987, 1992), Hinings and Greenwood (1988), Greenwood and Hinings (1993), Van de Ven et al. (1999), and Garud and Van de Ven (2006), which became prominent in the 1980s and 1990s. Miller and Freisen's (1984) 'quantum view' of organizational change has similarities with this approach, positing the idea of periodic radical reconfiguration or paradigm shifts rather than continuous or incremental change. One of the present authors has written in this tradition (see Pettigrew et al. 1992; McNulty and Ferlie 2002; Ferlie et al. 2013), so this chapter both takes a retrospective review and provides a stocktake of this strand of research. It also looks forward to a prospective research agenda and considers some implications of this approach for the practice of strategic management.

One explanation for the rise of the process school is that it addressed and commented on the major economic and public policy phenomena of the 1980s and 1990s, leading to major shocks and discontinuous change in the private and public sectors alike in many countries, and certainly in the UK case. Old established British firms such as ICI were coming under challenge from globalization and marketization (Pettigrew 1985) with a loss of their traditional and protected markets. British firms were increasingly under pressure to become more internationally competitive in a variety of sectors (Pettigrew and Whipp 1991), presenting an opportunity for analysis of the micro dynamics of how they sought to achieve this state. Top-down shocks were also apparent in the UK public sector, given a sustained period of radical right or Thatcherite governments (1979–1997). There were major NPM-style policy shifts within the UK public services towards managerialization (Pettigrew et al. 1992), performance management, and then the introduction of quasi markets and corporate governance shifts to strengthen the role of the board (Ferlie et al. 1996).

This chapter will first outline and discuss some key texts and authors of the process school, followed by some applications to the study of public services organizations. It will draw out the wider contribution of the process school to the strategy field more broadly. It will finally outline a prospective research agenda.

6.1 Some key texts and authors of the strategy as process school

The central focus of this school is the behaviourally and historically informed explanation of forms of – and also resistance to – *strategic change* across whole organizations as seen over time. The focus moves beyond the previous concentration on incremental change (Quinn 1980) or localized change or pilots within particular settings

DOI: 10.4324/9781003054917-6

to examine the dynamics of large-scale and systemic change. Change and metamorphosis (the radical changing of shape) is a major theme across many academic disciplines: taking biology, for example a phenomenon to be explained is how a caterpillar mutates into a butterfly. Garud and Van de Ven (2006, p. 207) provide a definition of the basic term of organizational change by suggesting that 'most organization scholars would agree that change is a difference in form, quality or state over time in an entity.' Authors in the school draw on interesting wider social science theories and ideas (Garud and Van de Ven 2006) to construct a typology of different change categories (e.g. planned vs unplanned; incremental vs revolutionary) which gets beyond a simple linear model of planned and perfectly implemented change. This intellectual curiosity and roots in wider social science is an attractive feature of this school which helps reconceptualize strategy processes in imaginative ways.

Van de Ven and colleagues (Van de Ven et al. 1999) represent an important set of American process researchers who examined patterns in the diffusion of innovations, including some in health care. Here we will review their theoretical work on generating a typology of different perspectives such as a longitudinal or a more dialectic prism (see next). Garud and Van de Ven (2006) thus access and examine different theories of organizational change from a process perspective. They note the increasing pace and complexity of current organizational change processes, seeing them not as a discrete shift but rather (p. 206) 'as nested sequences of events that unfold over time in the development of individuals, organizations and industries.' How should such sequences be analyzed?

To give one example of broader theoretical thinking, Garud and Van de Ven (2006) discuss a family of 'dialectical' theories of organization change (taking basic ideas from the discipline of philosophy) which assumes (p. 209) 'the organization exists in a pluralistic world of colliding events, forces, or contradictory values that compete with each other for domination and control.' There is here a contest between different power blocks, interpretations, and rationales, the outcome of which may be unpredictable. Dialectical process theories explain stability and change with reference to the changing balance of power between opposing entities. The status quo or thesis (A) may be challenged by an antithesis (not A), and it is possible that the resolution of the conflict produces a new synthesis, which incorporates both A and not A yet is beyond both (a theoretical frame patterned on Hegel's philosophical conception of dialectical becoming; for a discussion in relation to its applicability in the field of public administration, Ongaro 2020a, Chapter 4). The synthesis becomes the new status quo/thesis and then the cycle of dialectical change may start again. The creation of a desired synthesis may be an optimal win/win situation but is not ensured as either the status quo or the antithesis may win (so these are possibilistic as opposed to necessitated dialectical processes).

Applications of dialectical thinking to organizational analysis (Garud and Van de Ven 2006, p. 214) place limits around the search for consensus, and internal cohesion often held up as a preferred organizational goal, at least where environmental conditions are fast moving, uncertain, or ambiguous. Under these more complex conditions, disagreement may provide a helpful resource for innovation, radical change, or renewal (p. 215):

> dialectical change processes are becoming increasingly relevant as organizations become complex and pluralistic. Dialectical processes are generated as actors

with different bases of power and from different cultures interact with one another to influence organizational directions and compete with one another for scarce organizational resources. In a multi cultural context, a change effort may produce counter reactions that affect the balance of power and associated social structures.

Informed by this perspective, Garud and Van de Ven (2006) move beyond a unitary view of the firm to a stakeholder model where multiple constituencies are seen as legitimate. It is recognized their interests and viewpoints may be in tension with each other (e.g. shareholders, workers, customers, local communities around the firm's plants). In these situations, the recognition and handling of disagreement may introduce a greater range of perspectives into the decision-making process, help foster creative syntheses and avoid narrow groupthink or entrenched thinking and over-dominance from one stakeholder group. The construction of pluralistic leadership processes is advocated (Van de Ven et al. 1999; Denis et al. 2001), suggesting (for example) a need to balance sponsors and champions by licensed critics to set up a dynamic of creative tension.

The process school came to prominence in the 1980s, as part of the wider movement (including Mintzberg) away from the early rational analytic approaches to strategy which had then run into major implementation deficits. Such gaps drew attention to underlying cognitive and behavioural blockages which limited perfect rationality and the scope of intended action. Andrew Pettigrew is a major author in this school with continuing impact and influence.

He is one of the first major *qualitative* UK management scholars, with a radically different approach from the earlier well-known work of the so-called and influential Aston School in the 1960s which had rather explored the formal structural properties of organizations, using quantitative and scaling techniques. By contrast, the process school which emerged from the 1970s onwards brought in strong concerns for then novel themes such as organizational culture as seen through an interpretive and anthropological perspective (Pettigrew 1979) and also (and this is novel) for the influence of internal organizational politics (Pettigrew 1973). So, the school lies more towards the emergent than the rational analytic camp of strategy (although it does not totally preclude the role of data collection and analysis in strategy formation). In terms of its overall approach, 'a view of process combining political and cultural elements evidently has real power in explaining continuity and change' (Pettigrew 1987, p. 658). Pettigrew's work is highly contextualized, arguing that change processes must be understood in their wider and societal contexts: for example micro-level NPM reforms of the 1980s apparent within public services organizations can only be understood given macro-level shifts in the wider political economy.

The process school typically focuses the analysis of strategic change processes in large and major organizations selected as interesting or 'strategic' case studies in their own right (such as Imperial Chemical Industries (ICI), Pettigrew 1985 or the NHS, Pettigrew et al. 1992). To increase external generalizability and to establish low-level patterns (rather than the predictive laws of natural science), comparative designs are used, often with six or eight purposefully selected and contrasting cases (Pettigrew and Whipp 1991; Pettigrew et al. 1992; Ferlie et al. 1996, 2013). The empirical ambition and sophistication of these field studies is extensive (Marinetto 2012) (often dependent on securing a large research grant to employ full-time researchers).

Preferred research methods are to investigate a small number of organizations inten-
sively and over-extended time scales; rather than more organizations in less depth. It
typically uses longitudinal case study methods, veering away from the 'variables paradigm' and the formal modelling of positivist social science.

The process school often uses retrospective methods and analysis for those cases
in which there is a clear end point or decision organizational outcome to explain
and draws on historically informed methods of analysis (such as archival material or
interviews with long standing personnel) to track the process. There is an interest in
linking the study of organizational process to performance and to specific 'outcomes'
(perhaps to counter the criticism that the process school was all process and no outcome). 'Outcomes' may be defined in intermediate terms such as the organization's
ability to implement nationally espoused policies (Pettigrew et al. 1992) rather than
in final terms of citizen well-being and can be criticized on that basis. Organizations
that can manage such desired strategic changes more effectively are described as
'higher performers' (Pettigrew et al. 1992), so it is fair to say that the school maintains
a subtly managerialist perspective and can in the end be seen as a branch of management research

The style of writing tends towards the discursive rather than being hypothesis-
based. The major theme in the body of work is exploring the dynamics of strategic change and also resistance to it. There is no assumption that strategic change
exercises will always be successful. Continuity always lies alongside change (Pettigrew
1987) and may indeed suffocate it. There may be an initial appearance of organizational change in the early stages of a longitudinal analysis but only to be followed
later by a regression back to the *status quo ante*. Such false starts only become apparent
through tracking an organization over time to test early claims of instant success. The
process approach can be attractive in studying implementation deficits and resistance
to large-scale organizational change where these have emerged as significant problems in the field (as in the late 1970s in UK public sector management).

Two important overview articles offer useful high-level methodological and epistemological reflections on the strategy as process approach. Pettigrew (1987) (discussed by Sminia and de Rond 2012) suggested that too much strategic management
research had so far been rational analytic and 'ahistorical, aprocessual and acontextual' in character so that 'there are remarkably few studies of change that actually
allow the change process to reveal itself in any kind of substantially temporal or contextual manner' (p. 655). A broadly cultural/political framing is here used for theoretical emplacement.

Pettigrew (1987) also outlines 'the change triangle' as a helpful and accessible heuristic which sees the analysis of organizational change as best informed by an awareness of three core dimensions, namely, content, context, and process. The three key
points of the triangle can be summarized as follows: (i) the content of change; (ii) the
context of change (inner and outer); and (iii) the process of change.

The *content of change* refers to the particular areas of transformation under consideration which in the public services might include a particular policy area (e.g.
social security; local government); clearly some policy areas may be more complex to
manage in the sense of the number of stakeholders involved, the degree of contest
between them, the nature of power relations in the field; the strength of the evidence
base behind the policy seen as a legitimating resource and resource requirements for
policy implementation.

The *context of change* refers to both the inner level – within the organization – and outer levels – strongly connecting to shifts in the wider social, economic, and political context: the process school is probably the one approach to strategic management that is most sensitive to the need of bringing the wider social, economic, and political context into the picture explicitly; in this sense, it provides a key link to the broader understanding of how context affects the very premises of strategy and strategy making, beyond the analysis of the immediate environment: this topic is systematically discussed in Chapter 7. For instance, wider and deteriorating economic circumstances helped create a crisis in ICI to support the case for its strategic reorientation, also orchestrated within the firm by effective senior leadership (Pettigrew 1985). Within the UK public sector, the new New Right-influenced political economy of the 1980s led to a set of top-down NPM reforms (Ferlie et al. 1996) within local public agencies designed to shift power relations, increase central strategic control, and reduce implementation gaps. Specifically, new general managerial roles in the NHS in the mid-1980s were designed to enhance managerial direction (as opposed to traditional administrative facilitation) and accelerate the rate of politically desired but controversial strategic changes, such as hospital mergers and closures (Pettigrew et al. 1992). Tracing such links between the different levels in a multi-level system is not easy and needs to be handled with care (explored more fully next).

The *process of change* refers to tracing 'the actions, reactions and interactions of the various interested parties' through a period of time. It is suggested that such longitudinality in analysis matters as 'snap shot' analyses suggest more change; whereas historically grounded studies often suggest more continuity.

Pettigrew et al. (2001) offer general reflections on this school and more detailed arguments about contextualist analysis which we here outline and discuss.

Multiple contexts and levels of analysis

While a core tenet remains that organizational change should be seen in its wider context, this later article gets beyond the original crude dichotomy between inner and outer contexts (Pettigrew 1987) to develop a more nuanced analysis of multiple contexts.

We suggest this is not an easy perspective to operationalize in empirical cases. For example, how should one handle the need for complexity reduction within process analysis and to retain rich data but at the same time reduce it to establish broader themes? Specifically, how many levels of analysis should concretely be included in a treatment of context? How can the multiple processes at work at these different levels and the interactions between them be realistically studied? How can the constitutive role of the macro context (including nebulous changes in received political ideas about government should be organized) be actively brought into the study of a local organization being studied and a causal chain established between the macro- and micro-levels established?

Time, history, process, and action

Contextualism pays strong attention to the specifics of time and place in influencing organizational change processes, with an associated move away from single snapshot methods (such as one-off surveys) to longitudinal case studies. It sees change as a sequence of events over time rather than a one-off 'jump' from one state to another (before/after comparisons). Time can be experienced not just as an objective chronology but also be socially constructed within the organization through subjectively meaningful 'phases' which represent experienced organizational transitions.

We comment that there are dilemmas about how far back one should go in tracing the change process and when it starts. While periodization is one effective way of 'telling a story,' the establishment of meaningful periods may only be induced after intensive study and reflection.

Change processes and organizational performance outcomes

There is a concern to tie process analysis to assessment of outcomes and organizational performance: Chakravarthy and White (2006) argue too much strategy process research has concentrated on process and not enough on strategy content or performance outcomes. Pettigrew et al. (2001) suggest that the explanation of an observed organizational outcome (or even better variable outcomes across a set of organizations) might well be a focal point of analysis, seeking to link these outcomes to an influence of context and process.

We suggest some tricky issues remain in terms of method. It may not always be easy to specify clear and non-contestable performance outcomes as different stakeholders may have different ideas about what makes for success. Empirical study may not discover a neat set of lower/higher performers which can be subjected to comparative analysis but rather reveal a mixed or volatile pattern ('one day is good; the next is bad').

International comparative research and organizational change

Writing in the context of the study of the firm, Pettigrew et al. (2001) assert that too much process research has been bounded by national boundaries and there is now a need (given globalization and the existence of powerful multinational companies) for more ambitious forms of comparative management research which cross national jurisdictions. The 'varieties of capitalism' perspective (Hall and Soskice 2001) suggests that distinctively different types of firms may be evident in the USA/UK, Western Europe, and Japan, and beyond those areas in other parts of the world, that are best apparent in international and comparative studies.

Similar observations underpin much of current public management research which is often too parochial and nationally bounded. However, undertaking well-designed comparative studies of public management is not simple, given the need to reduce complexity and institutional detail in analysis and to establish a cross national analytic framework.

Some 'comparativists' who study public management trends across national borders derive typologies or 'ideal types' to group clusters of countries together (Painter and Peters 2010; Pollitt and Bouckaert 2017), reduce local detail, and explore tracks of development within each grouping. A major comparativist question is whether there is likely to be global convergence on an NPM master paradigm or not. Against this view, Pollitt and Bouckaert 2017 suggest continuing local 'path dependence' which creates continuing divergence at a national level. Another approach is to compare a set of countries in relation to a well-defined theme, region, or particular sector: thus

Paradeise et al. 2009 explore various country-specific chapters on higher education reform strategies across Western Europe, specifically benchmarking them against the NPM and NG reform narratives outlined here. Ongaro (2009) examines underlying trajectories of public management reform within a previously overlooked cluster of Southern European states hitherto accorded less attention in the public management literature than Anglo-American or Northern European clusters.

Receptivity, customization, sequencing, pace, and episodic versus continuous change

Despite the rapid growth of a change management 'industry' and associated change products launched by management consulting firms, the effects of temporal and situational issues in organizational change are still not clear. One possible contribution of process research is providing a scholarly base for the design of such management of change interventions. For example, how can the degree of receptivity for change (Pettigrew et al. 1992; McNulty and Ferlie 2002, Butler 2003) be practically diagnosed in a setting? What is the evidence in relation to the best sequencing of actions and the appropriate pacing of change? How can the tendency to the loss of momentum over the long term be managed and 'change overload' be prevented? The process literature also addresses issues of historical legacy, such as the fateful and imprinting role of founding conditions (Pettigrew 1979; Ormrod et al. 2007). One important implication is that organizational change programmes may need to be adapted and customized to the particular characteristics of the organization (here, a public agency) rather than imposed in a top-down and uniform way. Such local adaptation (customization) is here seen as helpful in increasing the probability of adoption, even at the cost of the loss of some fidelity to the original model in its entirety.

There is also an interesting debate in the field between episodic and continuous models of organizational change. Episodic models (Miller 1993, 1994) of change (Pettigrew et al. 2001, p. 704) focus on 'organizational changes that tend to be infrequent, discontinuous and intentional.' A growing process of strategic drift and of declining performance eventually and rarely opens up a gap which can be filled by strategic and motivational change leaders. By contrast, continuous models of change are ongoing, evolving but in the end cumulative or even transformational (Orlikowski 1996): 'the distinctive quality of continuous change is its small, uninterrupted, adjustments, created simultaneously across units which create cumulative and substantial change' (p. 704). We explore this debate in more detail later.

Engagement between scholars and practitioners

An interesting question is the espoused relation between academics and managerial practitioners within the different schools of strategy: where on the spectrum do they place themselves between strong engagement on the one hand and critical distance on the other?

The strategy as process school has a presumption of greater engagement. Pettigrew et al. (2001) note the emergence of new forms of research 'co production' across many sciences and social sciences. Here there is a shift from detached and unidisciplinary academic research and a turn to the production of knowledge 'in the context of application.' Research teams become more multidisciplinary and may include more representation from the practice field. Pettigrew et al. 2001 warn against scholarly overdetachment and the drift to mega theory (reflecting a common inwards-looking orientation of academic disciplines, perhaps being replicated in the more technical or abstract branches of strategic management). They call for more engagement with practice. Van De Ven (2007) also advocates the notion of 'engaged scholarship,' with stronger participation from non-academic stakeholders and more collaborative modes of research design.

But what form does such engagement take within this school? Does it indeed produce 'useful' modes of research and writing? The core written 'outputs' of process research (Pettigrew 1985; Pettigrew and Whipp 1991, Pettigrew et al. 1992, Van de Ven et al. 1999) often take the form of peer-reviewed academic articles or even more challengingly long research monographs published by academic publishers, reflecting the discursive style of writing and its attachment more to the tradition of the humanities than of natural science. These publications are typically based on the findings from long-term empirical projects, often with relatively little interim feedback for the field. It may take six or seven years between the start of a large-scale strategy as process project and the final monograph being published. The academic writing style in these core outputs is not easy for many busy practitioners to read. These publications do not take the form of short-term cycles of 'action research' often desired by the management field and there is little joint writing with practitioners. There is a stress on strong theorization of empirical findings (as is needed to be accepted in top journals).

Yet a defence is that such fundamental work and peer-reviewed publications create a solid academic base from which further engagement with practitioners can take place on a more academically secure basis. Narrative-based case study research is more accessible to many non-academic readers than other approaches such as econometric modelling: vivid stories are an effective mode of communication. Heuristics such as the 'Pettigrew triangle' usefully effectively convey key messages to the field.

We know from the research policy literature that interactions between scholars and practitioners may be long term and indirect, rather than short term and direct (Weiss 1979). So, the academic base can lead to later writing of more applied and policy-orientated pieces within a gradual process of 'enlightenment.' An example would be Roberts et al. 2005's overview of existing academic research which informed the Higgs Review's policy work on corporate governance. Process scholars may also be used as speakers and advisers to consultancy firms and government on the basis of reputation generated by their academic outputs; although the basic projects appear to be largely funded by public science (including the National Institute for Health Research in the case of health management research) rather than consulting firms (unlike work in the cultural stream, Pascale and Athos 1981).

6.2 Applications of the strategy as process perspective to public services organizations

The strategy as process school clearly sees public services and not-for-profit settings as well as private firms as sites of interest; indeed it is unusual in its breadth of interest. Two monographs by Pettigrew et al. (Pettigrew and Whipp 1991, 1992) (see Box 6.1 for a more detailed analysis) constitute a purposively designed pair of cognate studies of strategic change processes, one in UK private firms and the other set in the UK NHS.

Van de Ven et al. (1999) examine patterns and phases in the career of innovations in various USA settings, including a focus on health care (many of the major authors in the school tend to be UK/North American) which can be seen as a hybrid sector in the American case. Scott et al. (2000) focus on institutional changes in the American health care field, taking the example of the San Francisco Bay Area as a health care field as it evolved and changed over several decades. Their unit of analysis is a regional field and the population of health care organizations within it. They examine empirically the extent to which organizational change within the field from professional dominance to managed care should be seen as incremental or rather profound/discontinuous, the latter being associated with the emergence of new organizational forms (health maintenance organizations) on the purchaser side less tied to traditional behaviours and assumptions.

Reay and Hinings (2005, 2009) examine long-term change processes across the health care field in Alberta, Canada, seen in terms of a basic and long-lasting tension between an established professional dominance model and a rising NPM archetype which was sponsored actively by a radical right wing and newly elected provincial government and to some extent counterbalanced the traditional power of clinicians.

In other sectors, Butler (2003) examined the differential long-term trajectories of two English Local Authorities in terms of marketizing their housing services, developing the analysis of their receptivity to change. Van Gestel and Hillebrand (2011) conduct an analysis of oscillating change patterns (consistent with dialectical approaches) within Dutch public employment services, again linked to different political values systems and parties.

Box 6.1   Example of a process study in the public services field: Pettigrew et al.'s *Shaping Strategic Change* (1992) in UK health care

Using comparative and longitudinal case study methods, Pettigrew et al. (1992, p. 274) (we should declare that the team included one of the present authors) studied the ability of eight District Health Authorities (DHAs) in the English NHS to implement major national health policies (e.g. merger and closure of hospitals), finding substantial local variation. Four 'pairs' of DHAs were studied over time. Pettigrew et al. 1992 inductively derived a model and heuristic of Organizational Receptivity to Change (ORC), based on their analysis of 'receptive and non receptive' contexts for strategic change as revealed in the cases to explain such differences. This study has been highlighted as one of the few case-based studies in UK health management research (Marinetto 2012) to have achieved empirical scale and hence a greater degree of external generalizability than the typical single case.

The heuristic figure somewhat resembles the McKinsey 7 S model in its thinking and pictorial representation, except that 'culture' is not privileged with a special status in the centre in the diagram. It similarly eschews linear thinking to suggest a broad 'syndrome' of a cluster of interrelated factors. Pettigrew et al.

(1992) also note that receptivity to change is a dynamic rather than a static concept: organizations could build it up over a long period but then lose it suddenly in, say, a crisis or a reorganization. The title of the book *Shaping Strategic Change* deliberately suggested the role for influencing forms of action (more than direct command) under conditions of high pluralism and of uncertainty, rather than the operation of a predictive management of change science. The construction of a general model helpfully reduced the large amount of local detail thrown up by such a large-scale empirical study into a smaller number of cross site themes.

Here we explicate the model outlined in Chapter 9 of Pettigrew et al. (1992) which distinguished those organizations with greater strategic change capacity from those with lesser capacity. They can be divided in two groupings of internally facing and externally facing features.

Internal factors

The quality and coherence of 'policy': analytic and process components

The health care organizations studied varied in their ability to conceptualize the policy areas they were working with and to construct coherent local policy frameworks to frame general national policy in a way that was credible in their locality. Local policy making certainly included an element of support generation and coalition building prior to implementation (as would be expected in a political perspective) and initial recourse to a broad vision rather than a detailed blueprint, fitting with a more emergent approach. However, this feature also included a stress on the importance of data collection and clear analytic framing locally: it did not support the radically constructionist 'paralysis by analysis' argument against data collection and for immediate action.

Availability of key people leading change

This feature plays into the leadership debate referred to earlier. Higher performing organizations tended to display strong (and stable) mixed leadership teams at the top. The study did not support the proposition of a heroic and charismatic general manager as an effective leadership configuration, but rather a small mixed team, perhaps including a general manager, a senior clinician, and a senior nurse that could reach out to various constituencies and parcel out key tasks according to skill base. The second point related to the need to select, develop, and sustain these teams over a long period: paradoxically, there was a need for some stability in senior personnel to effect strategic change. This point tells against frequent reorganization and movement of senior personnel currently so often found in public services agencies.

Supportive organizational culture

The study concluded that 'more successful' health care organizations in terms of strategic change were characterized by a 'supportive organizational culture.'

In what sense was this term being used? While the NHS should be seen as a collection of different subcultures (medical, nursing, political, and managerial), the analysis identified some positive manifestations of an energized managerial subculture: flexible working with purpose designed structures rather than formal hierarchy; a focus on skill rather than rank; an open risk-taking approach so that failed risks are not heavily punished; an openness to research and evaluation; strong collective values; and a positive self-image and sense of achievement. From an RBV viewpoint, some of these internal factors could be seen as underlying organizational core competences.

Effective managerial clinical relations

The relationship and possible tension between managerial and professional elements in public services organizations has already emerged as a major theme in this chapter. This health care study also found that the nature of the managerial/clinical interface was critical in influencing the extent of strategic change achieved and furthermore varied markedly from one site to another (undermining highly structural explanations which tended to stress pervasive conflict across the whole field). Where clinicians had gone into opposition, they could exert a powerful block on change. Perhaps more surprisingly, general managers varied in the extent to which they saw relationship building with clinicians as a core part of their brief. These relations were not fixed as upwards and downwards spirals in such relations were evident: they could quickly sour but were slow to build up.

Managerial/clinical relations were easier where negative stereotypes had broken down, perhaps through the development of mixed roles or perspectives. The advantage of managers with a background in the health sector – rather than being brought in from outside – was that they were more likely to understand the world of clinicians and what they valued (one could add that from a NPM point of view, they were also less likely to challenge clinical dominance, at least directly). A positive profile was evident in some localities where managers had managed (for example) to secure a newly built hospital for clinicians.

There was a subgroup of senior clinicians who combined a medical background with part time managerial roles, and this was a critical subgroup that general managers needed to ally with and indeed develop capacity in this area. Members of this group could produce general, strategic, ideas rather than remain embedded in clinical detail. The nature of clinical/managerial relations has been found to be a critical factor in other studies of change processes in health care fields (Reay and Hinings 2005, 2009).

Simplicity and clarity of goals and priorities

This focusing issue arises from the danger of the multiplication of ever-shifting policy priorities and therefore of change overload. General managers varied in their ability to narrow their change agenda down into a set of key priorities and to insulate this core from shifting short-term pressures. So, persistence and patience in the pursuit of a small number of objectives were associated with higher levels of strategic change. It appears managers may be wise to ignore or minimize some short-term pressures, while using others to amplify the case for their pre-existing change objectives. Skills in complexity and conflict reduction could be important here in trying to contain complex problems in simpler frameworks.

External factors

Environmental pressure – intensity and scale

The observation was made that those health care organizations that experienced a moderate, stable, and predictable degree of environmental (specifically financial) pressure appeared to manage strategic change more effectively. Organizations experiencing growth had no incentive to make complex and difficult decisions; while organizations that experienced a financial crisis could 'implode' and lose their ability to make strategic decisions by moving into tactical and short-termist crisis management mode.

Cooperative inter-organizational networks

A number of major policy and service changes (for example, in mental health and learning disability) were not only the responsibility of the health care sector but involved other actors such as social care (a responsibility of local government in the UK) and also voluntary organizations. In these fields, strategic change was dependent on the development and use of cooperative inter-organizational networks which in their turn managed to retain a sense of purpose and forward movement.

Health care agencies had little direct power in these wider settings but had to win influence by promoting boundary spanning and clear communication and education channels. Trading between the different agencies also helped establish norms of reciprocity and trust.

The fit between the change agenda and the locale

It appeared that some locales were more complex than others and therefore it was here more difficult to achieve large-scale service change. Features of complexity included the scale and complexity of the locale (number of organizational players; number of medical schools), whether there was one or rival centres of population (such as two medium-sized towns) and whether there was a local political culture which contested top-down and retrenchment-based national changes to health policy (e.g. left wing councillors who opposed hospital closures and associated public sector job losses).

Hunter et al.'s (2015) comparative case-based study of change processes in the NHS North East transformational change programme used the Pettigrew et al. 1992 receptive contexts for change model as a theoretical framing. They concluded all the factors identified were still relevant but felt that four were especially relevant (in descending order of importance): environmental pressure; quality and coherence of policy; key people leading change; and a supportive organizational culture.

Hunter's (2019) short paper then re-presented these earlier empirically grounded conclusions in a readily accessible form that could be used by health care policy makers and managers in a project funded by WHO Europe to support health systems transformation efforts. We comment that it is unusual and encouraging that the Pettigrew et al. 1992 case-based study was repeated nearly 30 years later by another team of researchers in a different locale and many of the factors still found to be valid.

This 1992 monograph also informed a later stream of process research on UK health care and local government organizations to build more cumulative knowledge. Bennett and Ferlie (1994) attempted to replicate the model from Pettigrew et al. (1992) in looking at innovation processes in the development of new services for HIV/AIDS, so adding to the extent of external generalizability. Some later work on UK local government (where the content of change was intended outsourcing strategies in two housing departments) confirmed and developed this Organizational Receptivity to Change model further (Butler 2003; Butler and Allen 2008).

For example, Butler (2003) identified four receptivity factors which explained the two trajectories of the local councils studied:

(i)   *Leading change:* the extent to which there was an active leadership group championing the change process, either senior officers or elected councillors;
(ii) *Institutional politics:* or how the broader coalition of forces in the locality (including tenants of social housing) lined up against the change agenda;
(iii) *Implementation capacity:* or the extent to which those leading change were able to construct a viable implementation strategy;
(iv) *Ideological vision:* the espousing of a clear ideological vision (especially by locally elected politicians) to animate the change process; thus, the council with the fastest pace of movement contained a political grouping with a stable majority that was strongly committed to NPM-style reforming in its services and indeed had a national profile in that respect as an outlier.

These 'asymmetric features' distinguished between these two public services organizations operating in the same broad institutional field yet displaying distinctive local trajectories. We comment that the 'ideological vision' feature is distinctive and additive and draws attention to the potential role of political and ideological vision in driving forward strategic change processes in the public services and especially in local government, with its strong basis of political as well as managerial leadership, in the cases reviewed here from the radical right (as in the Alberta studies also reviewed in this chapter); similarities may be drawn, *inter alia,* with certain episodes of change in the 'NPM period' of reforms in New Zealand (Boston et al. 1996).

6.3 Institutionalist perspectives as an important theoretical influence on streams of investigation into strategic change

As we have seen, the process school draws on various organizational theories to conceptualize its qualitative and case study-based empirical data. So-called institutionalist perspectives are an important theoretical influence on strategy process research. Institutionalist perspectives typically examine processes of continuity and change in well-embedded organizational fields (rather than a single organization), where conventional market forces are weak. An organizational field can be described as: 'an embedded set of organizations engaged in a similar purpose or in related activities which together shape and give meaning in that field' (Van Gestel and Hillebrand 2011, p. 232). This approach to organizational analysis operates at the level of the organizational field such as the whole health care or criminal justice sector: organizations are seen as embedded in fields which exert powerful pressures for conformity (Di Maggio and Powell 1983; Zucker 1987) or so-called isomorphism.

Public sector and professionalized fields are typically highly institutionalized, with many barriers to rapid market entry or exit and only weak market forces. These are mature fields shaped by institutional forces such as the professional or governmental regulators (which control accreditations and resource flows) and fashion setters (such as reports from enquiries or management consultants). Decision makers in these organizations are less driven by the search for market *efficiency* than for *legitimacy* in the eyes of such influential external stakeholders.

Within conventional institutionalist analysis (Ferlie and FitzGerald 2002), organizations can be expected to move to adopt similar designs and activities across a whole field. The work activities undertaken are stable, repetitive, and enduring across the field, and institutionalized within 'taken for granted' rules. Inertia is therefore common and radical change rare. Local strategic choice by a particular organization to diverge radically from field-wide norms and to launch experiments in work design is seen as unlikely: we assume convergence is more likely than divergence.

How does major organizational change ever take place in highly institutionalized fields? A first possibility is that these organizations are incapable of change, even in the face of deteriorating environmental conditions and weakening resource flows. Taken to its logical conclusion, there can be a mass extinction event (as in the end of the age of dinosaurs, in an example drawn from natural history) with whole populations of organizations disappearing and being replaced by smaller and nimbler forms (such as small mammals, to pursue the natural history analogy).

A second possibility is that there are successive waves of managerial 'fads and fashions' (Abrahamson 1991, 1996) which diffuse rapidly, have short-term impact and are then quickly dropped in favour of the next fad, such as the move from Total Quality Management to Business Process Reengineering (McNulty and Ferlie 2002; Ongaro 2004) and now Lean Production. These short-term fads may be diffused across the field by centrally located and high-status knowledge diffusers such as leading management consultants or may diffuse out from prestigious early adopting sites to more peripheral sites: again, the motive for later adopters being to acquire legitimacy and the trappings of progress.

A third but rare possibility is one of fundamental 'archetype change.' In an influential book, Hinings and Greenwood (1988) argue that organizations tend towards coherent deep patterns or 'archetypes,' consisting of three distinct but interrelated components: formal structure, processes, and the underlying interpretive schema (including culture, beliefs, and ideology). For a radical reorientation to take place, simultaneous change is needed along all three dimensions, but notably in the interpretive domain which is the most difficult to shift. Such rare moments of transition open up a space for ideological change agents who can supply new narratives and 'manage new meaning.' Without such interpretive change, shifts and reforms in formal structure and processes are likely to have limited impact as the organization eventually gravitates back to the original archetype.

Hinings and Greenwood (1988) here take powerful ideas previously developed in the sociology of science about the periodic epistemological transition between scientific paradigms (Kuhn 1962) – such as the move from Newtonian- to Einstein-based models of physics about 1900 – and move them into organizational analysis. The paradigm shift perspective suggests the sequence of a long period of 'normal science' or within paradigm stability, an increasing number of anomalies leading to interpretive contest and then a short and sharp transition to a successor paradigm, which finally ushers in a new period of stability and taken for granted assumptions.

Hinings and Greenwood (1988) and Greenwood and Hinings (1993) identified a variety of possible alternative organizational tracks, including successful archetype transition (as described earlier), but also a failed transition which leads to regression back to the original archetype; continuing oscillation between the two archetypes (closer to dialectical notions of organizational change); and finally a possible track of an 'unresolved' discursion between two alternative archetypes. We comment that it is theoretically unclear how this lack of resolution could last over an extended period as at least the initial statements of archetype theory predicted a gravitation to underlying paradigmatic 'coherence' and a dislike of mixed forms.

Some important empirical studies, however, suggest a more complex and hybrid picture. Cooper et al. (1996) examined strategic change processes in two large Canadian law firms through the lens of archetype theory (Greenwood and Hinings 1993). Law represents a powerful profession which has traditionally been self-managed through a partnership form. In these sites, there were two competing value sets apparent, namely, one of traditional professionalism (the old Professional Partnership Form) and a new market-based and 'business like' customer service ideology or Managed Professional Business (while they did not explore societal reasons for the rise of these new values, one could speculate that it was related to an underlying process of globalization and the marketization of segments of the Canadian economy). Key customers in large law firms were likely to be corporate counsel acting for other firms, rather than private individuals. Respondents reported that a shift towards the MPB form was significant both culturally and in moving away from the highly decentralized mode of strategy making in traditional professionalized organizations (Mintzberg 1983) to more corporatized approaches, with the growth of corporate planning, marketing, and HRM functions.

Cooper et al. 1996 found that these two different forms appeared to coexist over an extended period, suggesting that the 'unresolved excursion' track might be an empirically found practice. Their concept of 'sedimented change' allows for the persistence of some of the old values associated with law as a traditional profession alongside rising new business-orientated values: 'these two powerful schemes can co exist, fuse and conflict within the sedimented structures of large law firms' (p. 635), like layers on top of each other in geological formations such as cliffs.

Within public management studies, archetype theory has similarly been employed to examine a possible transition from a professional bureaucratic to an NPM paradigm. Such analyses often highlight the remaining power base of some public sector professions and the way their remaining power can still shape the new equilibrium emerging from the period of radical change.

Using Hinings and Greenwood (1988) for their initial theoretical direction, Denis et al. (2001) present process-based case studies of organizational change in Canadian hospitals, which are seen as pluralistic settings where power is diffuse and objectives between the different stakeholders divergent. The content of the change process studied varied from relatively minor changes to internal work processes to major mergers between hospitals mandated by government. The focus of their study is on how organizational change takes place in such pluralistic and complex settings. For example, power appeared to be spread widely between the chief executive officer, the board (and especially its chair), the medical executive council (which reported to the board and not the CEO), and the director of professional services, a senior clinician taking on a managerial role and reporting to the CEO. Nursing appeared less visible than they had expected. Nor did patients' groups appear to be influential. So, the pluralism is highly bounded between three alternative elites: the governance structure, senior managers, and senior medical staff.

Denis et al. 2001 concluded that strategic change was feasible under these conditions but also sporadic and unpredictable. They found a collective (rather than individual) leadership constellation was critical to success but that also such groups are themselves fragile and change over time:

> in fact, strategic change in pluralistic contexts is viewed as a succession of episodes in which leadership group members may promote change through their actions, but where these actions simultaneously alter the future form and viability of the leadership group because their legitimacy is constantly being reevaluated by powerful constituencies.
>
> (Denis et al. 2001)

If a leader made too many concessions to external constituencies, there might be growing opposition from internal constituencies, and vice versa. Opposition to merger proposals or crises could suddenly lead to the departure of key decision makers so that a new phase now began, and a leadership constellation needed to be rebuilt. The change process around the mergers did not have a clear final resolution but rather 'change staggers through a series of shifting alliances and momentary compromises. However, it is difficult to achieve irreversibility in such a fragile context' (Denis et al. 2001).

Theoretically, Denis et al. (2001) moved away from archetype theory at the end of their analysis which rather painted a picture of an uncertain and boundedly pluralist bargaining process. They suggested that a novel complexity theory-based approach to strategic management (Stacey 1995) might be fruitful to explore with its move away from the assumption of finality towards seeing change as a complex and dialectical process between opposing forces and characterized by non-linear relationships, feedback loops, and unpredictable or cyclical patterns of change.

Reay and Hinings (2005) also examined processes of strategic change across the whole organizational field of health care (producers, consumers, regulatory and financing agencies, and alternative suppliers) in the oil-rich Canadian province of Alberta. A radical and NPM-friendly provincial government was elected there in 1993 which quickly introduced major structural and centralizing reforms (moving from 200 local health care boards to 17 Regional Health Authorities) to facilitate the introduction of cost-cutting and business-friendly measures. Within the domain of corporate governance, for instance, physicians were removed from holding board-level positions and pro-business appointments made. At an ideological level, policy documents began to refer to the 'consumer' rather than the 'patient,' and values of efficiency and effectiveness were strongly espoused.

Using documentary sources as data (rather than interviews), Reay and Hinings (2005) see the central issue as a contest between the old dominant institutional logic of clinical dominance upheld by physicians and a new NPM logic supported by the elected provincial government. They look in particular at the reinstitutionalization stage towards the end of the change process, rather than the usual focus on its initiation. Archetype theory would indeed predict that a brief period of radical change would normally be followed by reinstitutionalization and a new long period of stability.

The key question is whether and how the traditional dominant logic of the field can shift away from a previous pattern of medical dominance. The possession and use of organizational power are important and may lead to resistance as 'field level actors (especially those with high levels of power) do not naturally accept a new dominant logic' (p. 352). On the other hand, the radical right and ideologically coherent provincial government consistently used its power position to reinforce these structural changes and introduced new legislation, despite continuing opposition from the physicians.

While physicians made tactical adjustments to the new order (for example signing a new contract), many of them continued to resist the new market-friendly logic over a long period (the study covered seven years after reorganization). Reay and Hinings (2005) suggested there was an 'uneasy truce' between the two logics where the old professional dominance logic had been 'subdued but not eliminated.' In other words, two competing institutional logics coexisted over an extended period. They concluded (p. 375):

> the Alberta health care field moved from one dominant institutional logic (medical professionalism) to a new logic (business like health care) through the government's use of restructuring and constant assertion of its power through action. Even though the dominant logic for the field changed, the previously dominant logic of medical professionalism remains strongly entrenched for one important actor in the field – physicians.

How can the rivalry of competing institutional logics be managed? Reay and Hinings (2009) examine this question given that day-to-day work somehow continued across the field. So, the question was 'how actors within organizations accomplished their day to day work when there was no clearly dominant logic to guide their behaviour' (p. 630). They discovered four mechanisms which enabled the RHAs and doctors to work together at a day-to-day level (i) *differentiating medical decisions from other decisions*: a Physician Liaison Council was established to give (strong) advice on clinical matters; (ii) *seeking informal input from physicians as part of the decision-making process*, with evidence of growing RHA/physician interactions and rapprochement over time; (iii) *working together against the provincial government*: while RHAs were originally seen as the creatures of the provincial government, over time they began to assert their independence and even lobby upwards for more resources. As a consequence, relations between the RHAs and the physicians improved; (iv) j*ointly innovating in experimental sites*. The RHAs were charged with increasing the efficiency and effectiveness of health services. As a result, small- to moderate-scale organizational experiments were launched in such areas as service redesign or relocation or the expansion of multidisciplinary teams. In these novel and experimental sites, there was often joint sponsorship and leadership from both the RHA and from physicians.

So 'this sense of separateness combined with collaborative work appears to have resulted in relative stability in most settings' (p. 643). The rivalry between competing logics was in essence managed through pragmatic collaboration. Theoretically, these findings suggested that institutionalized conflict could in the end produce 'creative tension' between the two separate logics. There was a striking emphasis on the continuing independence of physicians (with no move to a unified superordinate identity or hybrid roles), yet a division of labour with the RHAs was in the end agreed, but as a pragmatic accommodation rather than as a high trust alliance.

Van Gestel and Hillebrand (2011) examine change processes in the different organizational field of public employment services in the Netherlands over an extended period (over 20 years). They note (p. 231) 'such processes are usually considered as struggles between competing institutional logics, as dialectical in nature and as involving many individual and collective actors.' Van Gestel and Hillebrand (2011) suggest that both the old punctuated equilibrium view of periodic radical change leading to one clearly dominant institutional logic and a long period of stability and more recent studies (Reay and Hinings 2005) which suggest that competing logics can coexist over an extended period in tension may be limited in scope. They (p. 633) suggest a third possible outcome of oscillation or switching:

> outcomes may also be characterised by ongoing change rather than stable fields with one dominant or multiple competing logics. In other words, while one dominant logic may emerge, it does so only temporarily and one change is followed by another.

They use the image of 'fields in flux' to characterize this third scenario.

Their case study data of the evolution of the Dutch public employment services field since 1980 suggested three possible logics which were all associated with different governments, political parties, and economic interest groups: the original statist bureaucratic model (evident since the 1930s and dominant before 1991); a corporatist network model (dominant 1991–2002); and a capitalist market model (dominant from 2002). There appeared to be continuing contest between these three models with only temporary truces after which contest quickly re-emerged. In part, this was due to periodic shifts in political control and governing party, associated with different public policy reform ideas. In addition, the field was relatively pluralist without one dominant actor able to impose a definitive solution.

6.4 A critical discussion of the process school

In discussing the long-term impact of Pettigrew's work, Sminia and de Rond (2012) see the 'Pettigrew brand' of strategy as lying in characteristically large-scale, contextualist, and longitudinal process-based studies, asking '*why, what and how*' questions. Perhaps the highest visibility features have been the doctrine of contextualism and the heuristic of the triangle.

What does the process school add to other interpretive schools, such as Mintzberg and the cultural school? It provides a novel concern for the operation of organizational politics and of power relations in shaping decisions (Pettigrew 1973). The hard-edged words 'power' and 'ideology' explicitly appear (Pettigrew 1987; Butler 2003). Whereas many writers had previously concentrated on conflictual industrial relations between employers and workers, this perspective distinctively suggested that bargaining and contest could emerge between different functions or subunits within the firm itself, with factional attempts to control important power sources such as the flow of information (Pettigrew 1973).

The process school is interested in the study of large scale of field-wide organizational change (Reay and Hinings 2005, 2009) rather than incremental or local forms of change. One conceptualization of such changes is as 'a political learning process, a long term conditioning and influencing process' (Pettigrew 1987, p. 689). It includes a cognitive and 'sensemaking' element, although critics might argue this is not that well developed. Investigating the linkage between the micro-context of the particular organization and its macro-context (notably including shifts in the political economy) is a major theme in a number of empirical studies (Ferlie et al. 1996). It connects to the organizational studies literature, in particular institutionalist analysis of shifts inside the professionalized organization (Cooper et al. 1996).

The process school is thus a strongly 'upwards looking' and politically aware perspective. It suited the 1980s and 1990s which can be seen as a period of large-scale shifts in the political economy in various countries with the rise of the New Right, globalization, and liberalization. Private corporations faced major shifts away from traditional and protected markets (Pettigrew 1985; Pettigrew and Whipp 1991), deregulation, hyper competition, mergers and acquisitions, and more financially driven and short-termist shareholder behaviour. Contextualism and multi-level analysis were important in moving beyond a purely micro-level perspective which was not enough to understand the impact of these 'macro shocks' on even large and well-established firms (Pettigrew 1985). Public sector agencies – such as the UK NHS (Pettigrew et al. 1992; Ferlie et al. 1996) – were by the late 1980s similarly facing major top-down policy pushes. The strong analytic connection to shifts in the political economy with the rise of the New Right led to a useful and distinctive appreciation of the energizing role of political ideology and associated reform doctrines (such as privatization and outsourcing), empirically evident in specific public agency settings such as an ideologically zealous UK Local Authority Housing Department (Butler 2003).

What are the main criticisms made of the process school? A conventional and predictable one (Sminia and de Rond 2012) has been the lack of external or statistical generalizability available from a small number of cases. Compared to much qualitative research, however, there is a use of large-scale comparative case study research designs, indeed the empirical scale of Pettigrew et al. 1992 was commented on by Marinetto (2012) as unusual in UK health care organizational research. Some process studies have been extended/replicated by the same authors (e.g. Reay and Hinings 2005, 2009) or by colleagues working in the same tradition (Pettigrew et al. 1992; Butler 2003; also a contribution from an author of this book, namely Ongaro 2006, is a piece of research dealing with the dynamics of devolution processes in a different institutional setting than the high-NPM ones – namely a 'Napoleonic administration,' legalistic setting – which is firmly rooted in this tradition of inquiry, albeit employing a single, rather than multiple, case study research design) which build up a wider corpus of work, potentially available for overview work (which is indeed needed). The search for generalizability in qualitative research may not take the form of empirical data, of course, but in developing models or concepts which could then be investigated in other settings and developed further (such as the model of Receptive and Non Receptive Contexts for Change, Pettigrew et al. 1992; Butler 2003). It is theoretical, rather than statistical, generalizations that are aimed at (Yin 2009; see also Van Thiel 2013).

There has been a developing critique of the process school from some strategy as practice texts, as we have discussed in Chapter 3. Johnson et al. (2003, 2007, pp. 10–11) acknowledge the positive role of the process school in getting inside 'the black box of the organization' and as being open to the influence of organizational politics, especially in early work done in the 1980s and early 1990s. But they argue that more recent work (they cite the example of Chakravarthy and White's 2006 more formalistic and systems-based analysis) and other texts on strategic decision making has moved away from this tradition and back towards cross-sectional studies. This is not a major objection in principle, as it is possible to revive the old finely grained process method (as in Ferlie et al. 2013). They also make the argument that some strategy-as-process research took a highly individualist, sense making, and cognitive view (Hodgkinson and Sparrow 2002) which underplayed the role of teams, groups, and networks in strategy making. Yet many core texts reviewed here were clearly broader, included politically based as well as cognitive forms of analysis.

How might process scholars react to this position of high pluralism in the strategy-as-practice school? This response needs to be informed by the position one takes in descriptive (rather than normative) analysis on the distribution of societal power within the advanced capitalist societies typically being studied. Process studies are open to studying the role of non-managerial actors, notably politicians and senior professionals (Reay and Hinings 2005, 2009), but often assume a position of bounded pluralism. Essentially, there appears to be a cast drawn from an 'iron triangle' of senior managers, elected politicians, and senior professionals apparent in many of the process studies reviewed. For example, there is greater interest in the health care studies in studying the behaviour of the (few) senior clinicians than the (many) health care assistants who do not appear widely in these accounts (although Reay and Hinings 2005 do consider the reactions of nursing and other professionals as well as doctors to the politically sponsored reform projects as to a greater extent they might gain from field restructuring).

A final area for questioning lies in the interest in and definition of 'performance' apparent in the process studies reviewed. The school does have a clear interest in performance: which organizations are doing 'well' in terms of strategic change capability and why. Some of the studies, however, use an intermediate and indeed contested notion of 'performance,' such as the local ability to implement national health policies (Pettigrew et al. 1992). Thus, a health care organization that was able to close a mental hospital and reallocate provision of local services on a community basis in line with national policy is here defined as a 'fast mover'; yet critics would claim that community care was a flawed policy. The definition of 'performance' needs careful thought and is not simple, given these are pluralist and contested policy arenas; we return to this debate about the relationship between strategy and performance in Chapter 8.

6.5 Process research in public services organizations: a future research agenda

Where might strategy process research be best developed in public services organizations over the next years? Given a distinctive feature of the school is its connection to an analysis of the political economy and associated political and ideological perspectives, work has sought to characterize high-level UK public services reform narratives of the New Public Management under Thatcherite governments (Ferlie et al. 1996) and Network Governance under New Labour (Ferlie et al. 2013).

In the UK case, for example, what does the 'levelling up' agenda of the present government imply for public agencies in the field which may now be charged with extra and more interventionist tasks especially in the field of economic development? Is the impact of the COVID-19 epidemic resulting in a re-expansion of the field of government? Are there underlying models of public management which are informing these potentially major transitions? There may even be some early signs of a move back to a Weberian command and control, as in certain proposals in the early 2020s to restrict the operational independence of NHS England and increase direct ministerial control.

It would also be interesting to track in the future the impact of Brexit on UK public agencies and whether this change reduces the influence of European and EU-based models of public management and increases that of non-European models. There are networks inter-linking European Union and Associate Member States, like the European Union Public Administration Network (EUPAN), which facilitates exchange of practices and reform ideas in public administration: the radical decoupling of the UK from this and other networks may possibly lead to some form of drifting away from European debates. Whether this results also in more intense involvement of the UK in non-European debates about public sector reform (for example, India has been held up as a country of special interest in post-Brexit diplomatic policy) is, however, to be seen, and far from unproblematic, given the UK public sector – with its large welfare, national health service, and so forth – is in many ways patterned on European models of public administration and public services governance and management (Ferlie and Ongaro, forthcoming).

Theoretically, basic ideas around punctuated equilibrium models and of occasional archetype change remain important. If we take the view that at least in some jurisdictions, there was an archetype shift from the Weberian bureaucracy towards the NPM in the 1980s, the next question is whether there has been a further transition to a post-NPM archetype (Benington and Moore 2011a; Christensen and Laegreid 2007; Osborne 2010b; note that a review of post-NPM narratives is carried out in Chapter 6) or whether the NPM has remained embedded, even if dysfunctionally so. Some empirical research in NHS London suggests fewer signs of NPM deinstitutionalization so far than one might think (Trenholm and Ferlie 2013), but this important question needs more exploration.

An enduring theme in some process studies (e.g. Reay and Hinings 2005, 2009) has been that traditional professional and rising political/managerial elements both have roughly equal power resources and therefore that some form of enduring accommodation may be reached between them. One question is whether this picture continues or whether there have been more recent shifts which tip the power balance one way or another. Has there been a process of deprofessionalization and loss of traditional dominance? There is a need here to connect with the wider literature on the public services professions and how they are evolving. On the other hand, has there been a loss of activism and confidence on the political side, with the ageing of the New Right movement from the 1980s? Any retreat back into transactional forms of government might allow professional elements to reassert dominance. Retrospective studies from such jurisdictions as the UK, Canada, New Zealand, or Sweden at the turn of the 2010s, all with Conservative or Conservative-led governments at that time, would be interesting for the purposes of addressing such questions comparatively.

Some early process studies focused on strategic change within large and vertically integrated organizations (e.g. Pettigrew 1985, on ICI). With the rise of strategic alliances, joint ventures and networks, this single organization-based perspective now appears rather old fashioned. It reinforces the case from bringing in whole systems and complexity modes of thinking (Denis et al. 2001; Butler and Allen 2008; Trenholm and Ferlie 2013) to study how whole organizational systems reconfigure and evolve, perhaps in unexpected or even perverse ways.

In conclusion, the strategy as process perspective has been an important addition to the strategic management literature. It is interested in public organizations as well as private firms. Its use of qualitative and historical methods and its openness to concepts of organizational culture and politics added significantly to the field. Its emphasis on context and contextual influences is also a contribution of major significance for the field of strategic management (we develop this topic in the next chapter). Historically, it fitted well with the high-change decades of the 1980s and 1990s when there were major external shocks affecting public agencies: the question is how to renew this interesting and important tradition by building a forward-looking research agenda for the next decades.

7   Framing the context

Managing strategically public services organizations in different politico-administrative 'Houses'

Public services organizations operate in many, and remarkably diverse, 'houses.' Shaped by the still nowadays very visible frontiers of the 'old' nation states or by less visible borders drawn by history, geography, demography, affluence, culture, language, and religion, diverse 'contexts' host and provide the frame in which public organizations act. The cultural, politico-institutional and administrative 'context' in which public services organizations operate is a remarkably significant feature – indeed, certain authors argue that context, far from being an 'inert' backdrop against which to situate action, animates action, making things 'thinkable . . ., possible, relevant, desirable and necessary' (Clarke 2013, p. 24). Yet very little is said in the literature about how context affects strategy in public services organizations: many texts on strategic management in the public sector appear to be very thin in their treatment of context, if not outright 'context-free,' as if managing strategically one public organization in one political, administrative, cultural, geographic, historical context (e.g. a school in the London area in the 1980s) were the same as managing it in another one (e.g. a school in the Rio de Janeiro area in the 2010s). It is the goal of this chapter to review and analyze how contextual influences shape the very premises of strategy making in public services organizations.

7.1 Context and strategy

The first step lies in the awareness of the significance of context and contextual influences. Sometimes context and contextual influences are simply overlooked. Other times and specifically, it is argued that there is long-term global convergence on NPM reforms as a master narrative. The convergence argument comes in less and more sophisticated versions. The less sophisticated (and in our view highly unconvincing) argument suggests that NPM reforms are the 'one best way' and that all countries will naturally converge on them. The more sophisticated and academic argument, however, comes from an institutionalist perspective. It examines patterns in the diffusion of management knowledge internationally and suggests that there are powerful 'knowledge carriers' at work, who may be effective in exporting NPM reforms globally.

The observation is made that private sector-based general management knowledge – which often underpins NPM reforms – has grown explosively over the last 30 years (Thrift 2005), and it is now diffusing strongly internationally out from its base in the USA to other countries and also from private firms into public services and not-for-profit settings. This 'cultural circuit of capitalism' (Engwall 2010; Jung and Keiser 2010; Thrift 2005) produces a linked constellation of MBAs, major business school

DOI: 10.4324/9781003054917-7

faculty, management gurus, consulting firms, business media, journals and presses, inspirational conferences, and 'blockbusting' texts. Engwall (2010, p. 372) writes of the symbiosis of business school academic writing and consulting. Thrift (2005, p. 85) suggests this circuit has 'autopoietic' status, given powerful interlocking institutions, self-referential insulation, and an ability to acquire ever more resources. Theoretically, Sahlin-Andersson and Engwall (2002a, 2002b) explore how general management knowledge expands both geographically and intersectorally into the public sector (so NPM reforms may be spread by global diffusion agents such as the Organisation for Economic Co-operation and Development, management consulting firms, or authors in leading business schools). NPM reforms may indeed be imposed by global donors as conditions associated with structural adjustment packages in countries in the developing world.

The 'comparative argument' in public management counters that such a convergence conception (even in its more sophisticated formulation) is badly flawed. The comparative argument, to make a long story short, is that 'context does matter' in the functioning, performance, continuity, and change of public services organizations (Pollitt 2013; Pollitt and Bouckaert 2017), as it has been widely recognized more recently by international organizations such as the Organisation for Economic Co-operation and Development and the World Bank. The comparative argument is also 'embedded' in certain approaches to strategic management (though not in others): as we have remarked before, the process school of strategy also accords an important role to context in shaping strategic process and outcomes. So, does context matter not just generally in public management but also when the object of analysis is strategy formation in public services organizations? Our argument is that it does and that the issue of how best to characterize and understand 'context' in strategically managing public organizations is extraordinarily important and requires careful examination.

There is an obvious, yet not trivial, objection to this argument: it is that 'context' is simply another word to mean 'the environment' in strategy analysis – in fact, the most radical critique to the comparative argument can be summed up in the following question: does the notion of 'context' make sense at all when grappling with the issue of how best to understand strategic management, or is it the case that conceptually strategic management treats the same phenomenon through the very notion of environment (making it superfluous, perhaps even tautological, to introduce the notion of context)? According to such critique, what matters is the 'immediate environment' (policy sector, key stakeholders, authorizing environment, key funders, level of affluence of the territory, demography of the users of public services, and the like), which is *the* influencing factor on strategy (in different ways and with different emphasis according to the school of thought employed as reference); the 'broader context' – the critique goes on – is simply the backdrop from which the specific environmental circumstances that matter for the specific strategy process are drawn.

Whilst we promptly recognize that the terms 'context' and 'environment' may in many respects be interchangeable, our argument is that to the extent that the terminological issue is settled by referring to 'environment' as the more 'immediate' context (here-and-now) and context is adopted to refer to 'the broader and deeper' context ('context denotes an object of undetermined extension,' as aptly noticed by Rugge 2013), then context so defined does matter. It matters because any understanding of organizational behaviour (or any other effect that a social scientific research work aims to understand, for that matter) can never get rid of 'the broader fabric' (the word 'context' derives from the Latin *contextere*, 'to weave together') in which action takes place – indeed, at least under certain epistemological assumptions, context enables action, and human agency always takes place 'contextualised,' woven in a broader fabric.

In this respect, it makes sense to consider the environment (the 'here and now,' or more 'immediate' context) and the context as part of the same broad picture, as authors like Tony Bovaird seem to suggest: Bovaird (by employing complexity theory to the study of public management) argues that any clear-cut distinction between those parts of the picture that constitute the 'interesting relationships' for management purposes, on the one hand, and all the other parts composing 'the rest of the picture' and relegated to an off-screen role, on the other hand, is as a minimum highly suspect (Bovaird 2013). In line with Bovaird's suggestion, we would argue that any such distinction can be useful instrumentally for purposes of analysis, but it is ultimately inadequate and should be overcome to achieve a more comprehensive stance in accordance with the perspective that strategic action and organizational behaviour unfold in an irreducibly broader context.

More specifically, context affects what we label '*the strategic space*' of a public services organization, constituted by:

- The autonomy that a public services organization enjoys (a precondition for strategy to form, the alternative being the absence of any strategy for the organization as such, perhaps partly filled by mere tactical behaviours, utility maximizing behaviours of individuals, or bureaucratic politics); and
- The political-societal expectations towards a public services organization (what is expected of a public services organization, hence of its strategy, as a key source of legitimacy for the organization); and the corresponding obligations and accountability bases under which a public services organization operates (what public managers as 'strategists' are accountable for, to whom, and how).

Context, in this perspective, shapes these very basic premises for organizational and administrative action that are the organizational autonomy as well as the societal expectations towards the organizations and its connected obligations and accountability bases.

Context also furnishes the basic elements that constitute the set of factors shaping strategy according to the models that are used for explaining strategy making, that is the schools of thought in strategic management reviewed in the previous chapters. In sum, we basically argue for a conception of strategic management in the public sector as context-sensitive and context-dependent, in stark contrast to views of strategic management as being generic, universalistic, tantamount, all alike in their basic patterns, throughout history, polities, and cultures. While some schools of thought in strategic management get closer to being context-sensitive than others (for example the strategy as process school is very sensitive to contextual issues), we would argue that context needs to be taken into account for explaining strategy making *tout court*, in its entirety for understanding strategy making in public services organizations through all the schools of thought being used: the analysis of context integrates with the individual schools of thought of strategy, often to be used in combination, to explain strategy making in public services organizations.

To 'treat context seriously,' in the remainder of this chapter, we propose and elaborate a frame for the analysis of contextual influences. In the frame that we employ for treating context in strategic analysis, context is constituted by both the 'politico-administrative' context, that is the relatively stable feature of a politico-administrative system, and the transformative effects of administrative reforms occurring in a given jurisdiction, the more dynamic part of context, subject to more rapid change, especially in periods of intense reforms of the public sector.

In the next section (7.2), we examine the politico-administrative context by resorting in a complementary fashion to three theoretical frameworks which do address this important problem: the Pollitt and Bouckaert model for the analysis of contextual influences on public management reform (Pollitt and Bouckaert 2017), the 'administrative tradition' approach and its repertoire of notions and concepts purveyed by Painter and Peters (2010), and an analysis of culture in public management (Bouckaert 2007; Schedler and Pröller 2007).

In the subsequent section 7.3, we then turn to the analysis of the transformative effects of administrative and public management reforms (in terms of processual, structural, and cultural transformative impacts); we will take the move from the 'traditional' Weberian bureaucracy, to then consider reforms inspired by the New Public Management, by the 'new public governance' discourse and doctrines, including network theory, to eventually, in a sense, go back to Weber by considering the Neo-Weberian model. When discussing the 'effects' of administrative reforms, we make reference to different levels at which such effects may be considered (Pollitt 2002; Pollitt and Bouckaert 2017). At the level of discourse and the rhetoric of 'modern public administration,' administrative reforms may affect the ideational context, that is the 'climate of thought,' the ideas that in a certain period have more currency in one jurisdiction. At the level of the formal binding decisions – embodied in statutes, laws, or regulations – administrative reforms shape the rules and conventions that, in a given jurisdiction, regulate aspects like the formal structure and division of labour in the public sector, personnel management, audit, performance measurement and evaluation, budgeting and accounting, and so on. At the level of the 'actual' implementation of reform and the practices in use, administrative reforms shape the 'actual functioning' of public sector organizations as well as the operational results (what users of public services get, and at what levels of efficiency, effectiveness, equity, and impartiality). These 'results' may in turn have long-lasting transformative effects on the public sector and public services as a whole and may operate to transform the public landscape in some 'fundamental' and 'long-term' ways.

The last section of the chapter (7.4) pulls all the threads together and sums up on the influence of context on the way in which the strategic management of public services organizations may unfold in different jurisdictions (different 'houses,' to go back to the metaphor employed in the title of this chapter).

Before turning to the analysis of context, we deem it useful to spend a few more words on what we mean by 'context,' and on the complexity of dealing with such an issue in public management and strategic management (as well as more generally in management or political science). The reader less interested in methodological (and epistemological) issues may well skip the remainder of this section and go directly to section 7.2.

A note – and a caveat – on the complexity of treating context in public management

We are helped in this necessarily brief tour into some of the subtleties of grappling with the questions about 'what is context (in the social sciences)?' and 'how does it matter (if it does)?' by two major contributions that have tackled such a fascinating yet highly complex theme: they are Pollitt (2013) and Goodin and Tilly (2006). We will here refer mainly to Pollitt's contribution, which is geared to the specifics of public management.

First, it should be noticed that there is not one context, rather multiple and intersecting contexts. The context 'within' which strategy forms in one organization (the organization being in itself a layer of the 'context') is cultural (for example, the national culture, or the 'Western culture'), ideological (for example, during the 1990s, the NPM became a dominant, or quasi-dominant ideology about how to run public sector organizations, shaping a certain climate of thought which is part and parcel of the context in which strategists gave shape to strategy-making processes in that period), political (what are the main traits of politics in the country?), economic (for example, did the case of strategy formation under consideration occur before or after the 2008 financial, economic, and fiscal crises? Or before or after the burst of the COVID-19 pandemic?), and so on. Along each of the previously mentioned dimensions, it should also be considered that context is both temporal (Pollitt 2008; Pollitt and Bouckaert 2009) and spatial (Pollitt 2011) – indeed in a certain sense the broadest context is determined by both space and time: the same place a decade later is a different context where the strategy of an organization takes place; similarly, locality and locale do make a difference, so that two public services organizations, for example two hospitals, in the same country and health system in the same given year are indeed in a certain fundamental sense operating in a different 'context.' Pollitt (Pollitt 2008, 2011; Pollitt and Bouckaert 2009) has widely elaborated on this issue, and we refer the reader to his works for guidance about how to navigate time ('timeship') and place (government as placemaker, and navigating space) in order to interpret context and contextual influences on public services organizations. 'Context' should be conceived of in the plural, as 'contexts.'

Second, contexts are both factual and conceptual. Factual contexts refer to 'entities or dimensions of social reality: place (where?), time (when?), actors (who?), and substances (what?). The factual context is the context of public administration, public administration as part of social reality.' The conceptual context of knowledge creation 'refers to interests, motivations, paradigmatic views and methodological preferences of the subject of knowledge, that is the person researching or the author' (Virtanen 2013, pp. 9–10). We referred in the first chapter to this issue when we grounded our basic argument about why strategic management matters for public services organizations in both 'factual' changes in the configuration of public sectors across the world (due to administrative reforms, changes in societal needs and expectations, and the like) *and* to changes in the theories and concepts enabling to study, analyze, and understand the strategic management of public services organizations. Thus, context refers to the contexts of action but also to the context of the theories from which we draw and through which managerial action is interpreted and made sense of, as well as to the context in which those who analyze strategic management produce their contribution (which leads us as far as the field of the so-called sociology of knowledge) – for example, the context of Britain and the British university system where both authors of this book live and work.

A third point deserves discussion. We earlier referred to the metaphor of context as 'backdrop,' and we briefly hinted to the issue that interpreting context as a backdrop – the scenery against which action takes place – is highly questionable. Scholars in the social sciences interpret context – more often as we have seen in the plural as 'contexts' – as constitutive of action rather than just a mere backdrop: action simply 'is in context,' or it is not (though the ontological implications of this statement require discussion, which is beyond what can be contained in this brief note). Clarke even argues (following Michel Foucault's work) that

> I think it is preferable to treat agency as something that always takes particular forms: there is no agency in general. Instead, I think it worth considering what it might mean to think about agents and forms of agency contextually. Contexts make possible particular types of agent (for example, the school inspector) and particular types of agency (school inspections as one form of governing at a distance). Inspections are actions and forms of agency that are animated by the combination of multiple contexts: political, governmental, educational, organizational – in different national settings . . . agents are always empowered to do something in particular. This represents a radical – and I think irrecoverable – break with sociological notions of agency as a property of human beings.
>
> (Clarke 2013, pp. 26 and 32)

Even if one does not travel that far in terms of conceiving of human agency as making sense only in terms of contextualized types of agents and specific forms of agency, it is possible to delineate theoretical approaches that, while leaving more room for human agency, still place centre stage the significance of conceiving it in relation to the context within which concrete individual decisions and actions occur. This approach, in our view, also resonates with the theory of structuration worked out by Giddens (1979, 1984), which makes a major attempt to combine individual agency and structural influences, seeing them as mutually interacting: social structures hold causal power over social phenomena and shape the conditions under which individuals' choices take place, and yet the free will of individuals is central stage in shaping social phenomena: for analytical purposes, it is possible to distinguish the causal power of social structures on one hand and the individual persons on the other, but they should be seen in an integrated way (this topic is more widely discussed in a book by one of the authors of this volume, dedicated to addressing the philosophical issues in public governance, management, and administration, see Ongaro 2020a, Chapter 4, pp. 133–138 in particular; it may further be noticed that the philosopher Maurice Merleau-Ponty also stressed, from the perspective of the existentialist philosophy, how human decisions are always 'concrete' and embodied into specific situations, into and from which they gain sense).

A fourth crucial point is that any thorough understanding of context must encompass an analysis of the mechanisms and processes (causal chains) that – to use Pollitt's phrasing – 'animate' contexts and enable them to have 'effects' (Pollitt 2013, p. 415). Indeed, the very notion of causality – from 'probabilistic causality' of the kind that is predicated as constituting the basic logic of inference of both quantitative and qualitative research designs in certain 'positivistic' strands of social science research (see King et al. 1994), to more 'traditional' approaches searching for 'necessary and sufficient conditions,' to approaches upholding multiple and conjunctural causation (that is multiple intersecting conditions linking features of context and process to certain outcomes) as the main logic to resort to in contextual analysis (Abbott 1992; Ragin 1987) – should be brought to the fore in theorizing about contextual influences (see Ongaro 2013b).

The purpose of this brief foray into the fascinating issue of how to treat context in public management is to make the reader aware of the subtleties of a tremendously complex topic – and yet in our view a decisive one for furthering the understanding of strategic management in public services organizations. We now go 'back on track' to discuss the 'macro' context intended as the politico-administrative and cultural context of a given polity or jurisdiction. The next section provides an introduction to the state of the art of the knowledge on how to interpret contextual influences in public management and specifically for strategic management.

7.2 Theoretical frames for the analysis of contextual influences on strategic management: the Pollitt and Bouckaert model, administrative traditions, and culture

How, then, to analyze contextual influences? This is of course a long-standing issue and a number of studies in public administration and management have dealt with it (e.g.: Heady 1966; Kickert 1997a; Lynn 2006; Lynn et al. 2001; Peters 2018; Pierre 1995; Riggs 1962; for an overview, Pollitt 2011). Dedicated handbooks of public administration and management (Ongaro and van Thiel 2018a) take context systematically into account, notably by focusing a specific context (in the case, Europe) and discussing the nature of knowledge in public administration and management (i.e. the extent to which it is contextualized or universalistic in thrust – Ongaro and van Thiel 2018b).

A prominent contribution is provided by Pollitt and Bouckaert's highly cited work *Public Management reform: A comparative analysis* (Pollitt and Bouckaert 2017, 4rd edition). Interestingly, in their work, the authors cover all the main 'components' of public management (organization, personnel management, financial management, performance measurement, and management) but strategic management, for which a broad comparative picture seems so far to be absent from the literature; of course, this book covers another terrain than theirs – its focus is the strategic management of public services organizations *per se*, not managerial reforms, but it is interesting to notice that in this respect, the two works may complement each other.

7.2.1 Prominent theoretical contributions for understanding context: the Pollitt and Bouckaert model and the administrative traditions approach

Pollitt and Bouckaert present a framework for the analysis of contextual influences that singles out five dimensions of context as especially significant in terms of the influence they may have on the dynamics of public management reforms. We will pick three of them that we deem to be the most significant for our purpose, that is explaining the broad 'conditions' under which the strategic management of public services organizations unfolds in different houses. They are (in the order in which they will be discussed): the dominant administrative culture ('the beliefs and expectations held by the staff about what is normal and acceptable in that administration'); the configuration of the relationships between executive politicians and senior public servants; and the nature of executive government. We will use the Pollitt and Bouckaert model in combination with another framework: the approach of the administrative traditions as developed by Painter and Peters (2010), and the specific categories of the Pollitt and Bouckaert model will be introduced and discussed after the illustration of the administrative traditions approach.

Before moving on to introduce the second theoretical framework from which we draw, we should briefly recall some of the criticisms of the Pollitt and Bouckaert approach. We made a summary of them in one work (Ongaro 2013a) that also furnishes an integration to the Pollitt and Bouckaert model by resorting to the notion of 'compound polities,' which applies the model to the case of a supranational polity like the European Union; the notion may also be usefully employed for interpreting contextual influences on strategic management in the frame of public services organizations operating at the supranational or international level, like the EU about which we propose a number of case studies of strategy formation in this book. We here report some of those critiques:

> One [criticism] is that the model [of Pollitt and Bouckaert] overlooks a number of important factors (at least for some countries/polities): the modalities of involvement of stakeholders in policy processes (corporatism vs. pluralism, etc.); the effects of political clientelism and more broadly the differential scope of illicit governance in different countries; the influence of the stock of social capital; and others – or that it does not go far enough into the details of each main factor. The obvious reply to this kind of criticisms is that detailing goes to the detriment of parsimony, and especially large scope comparative studies are in desperate need of parsimony. Another line of criticism is that the model is eminently descriptive and the causal texture leading from factors to process dynamics of management reforms are not outlined (see e.g. Barzelay and Gallego 2006). The authors counter, inter alia, that the main purpose of their work is indeed descriptive (Pollitt and Bouckaert 2011), to provide a picture hitherto not depicted of public management reform in the 'Western world', and that the model is a first-approximation model: researchers may well take the model as a starting point and elaborate more sophisticated analyses (on specific countries, under specific circumstances, of specific reform policy episodes).
>
> (Ongaro 2013a, pp. 348–349)

We consider the Pollitt and Bouckaert model to be a valuable starting point for the analysis of contextual influences, which may usefully be complemented by resorting to the other model we have mentioned, which is appealing also for its ambition to reach out beyond the 'Western World,' whilst systematically including it as well. The idea of 'administrative tradition' developed by Painter and Peters (2010) is a way of interpreting and making sense of the commonalities – and the persistency of such commonalities over time – in certain basic traits that characterize the public administration of clusters of countries, countries that to this regard may be reckoned to form a 'family,' as regards the basic features of their administrative system.

A definition of *administrative tradition* is 'a historically based set of values, structures, and relationships with other institutions that defines the nature of appropriate public administration within society' (Peters 2008). Thus, for example, countries that have inherited the French-derived 'Napoleonic' administrative system – a list which includes those in the European South: alongside France, the cluster encompasses Greece, Italy, Portugal, and Spain, though the influence of the Napoleonic model may be found also elsewhere in Africa and Latin America – still display relatively similar traits in their administrative systems, notwithstanding the many differences that the respective histories have engendered (Ongaro 2009, Chapter 7, and 2010). Painter and Peters identify a number of such clusters, intended as major families or groups, based on a range of geographical, historical, and cultural considerations that combine diverse criteria (Painter and Peters 2010, pp. 13–14). The clusters or administrative traditions thus identified are:

- Anglo-American;
- Napoleonic;
- Germanic;
- Scandinavian;
- Latin American;
- Post-colonial South Asian and African;
- Confucian (East Asian);
- Soviet/Post-Soviet; and
- Islamic.

Hybrids and transplants – like the cases of the administrative systems of the Netherlands, Hong Kong, or Japan (where the Meiji Revolution brought into an East Asian system certain basic traits of both the Napoleonic and the Germanic administrative traditions) – are also part of the picture.

More refined and nuanced classifications may be elaborated. The clustering of national administrative systems according to different traditions can be done deductively or inductively, or through an iterative process combining both. The fascinating point of Painter and Peters' approach lies in that it opens up the possibility to treat context at the macro-level on a global scale, whilst limiting the range of features considered to a manageable number, thus providing a conceptual toolkit for making sense of macro-level analysis of contextual influences:

> The ability to hold some variables constant and to highlight significant differences based on a rigorous classification of different traditions provides a key entry point to comparative analysis of a variety of phenomena, such as administrative reform and policy capacity. To some extent traditions fulfil the same function as a model such as Weber's model of bureaucracy. We can compare real world cases against the model of the tradition, e.g. is the United States really an Anglo-American system, or something quite distinctive? On the other hand, we can attempt to collect as much information as we can about the individual systems and attempt to develop the models of the traditions from that empirical data.
>
> (Painter and Peters 2010)

This approach is obviously not immune to critiques: the very underlying rationale – that is, the possibility of clustering nations on a permanent basis – is questionable. According to this line of radical criticism of the traditions argument, countries can only be clustered on a variable basis, as a variable function of the specific aspects under investigation, rather than on a permanent basis. To this critique, we would counter that for certain purposes – one of them being the investigation of certain basic context influences on the conditions under which strategic management unfolds in different parts of the world – some form of permanent clustering may well make sense, at least as a useful starting point for the analysis.

Four basic dimensions, or 'variables,' are introduced for analyzing administrative traditions (Painter and Peters 2010, pp. 7–8 in particular). First, the conception of the state and its fundamental relation to society. The main (dichotomous) distinction is here between contractarian and organic conceptions of the state. In the words of Peters:

> [I]n the organic conception the State is assumed to be linked from its inception with society, and the two entities have little meaning apart from each other. This almost metaphysical conception of the State and its role in governance can be contrasted with a contractarian notion in which the State arose from a conscious contract, expressed through a constitution or other constitutive arrangements, between the members of the society and the institutions that will govern them. . . . In the contractarian conception the State is not a natural entity but rather is a human construct and thus also malleable, and capable of being changed by the parties to the contract.
>
> (Peters 2008, p. 121)

Moving 'downhill' from the heights of the political-philosophical level of the fundamental conception of the state to the more mundane profiles of the ways in which the relationships between the state on one hand and the social actors on the other hand unfold at the policy sector level, a second sub-dimension is defined by the role entrusted to societal actors in public policy making. This role may range from 'natural' in some traditions, for example the Scandinavian states, where the active participation of societal actors to public policy making is seen as a healthy contribution to the process, to being depicted almost as an 'intrusion' in the sphere of competence of public authorities in other traditions, like the Napoleonic one.

The second key dimension qualifying administrative traditions is the relationship of the bureaucracy with political institutions. Such dimension includes a range of profiles, from the politicization of careers within the bureaucracy (i.e. the extent to which appointments within the bureaucracy are politicized) to the extent to which the bureaucracy itself becomes a general-purpose elite for the State (i.e., it furnishes an important part of its ranks also in elective positions, as is the case for France where many elected officials – MPs, ministers, and the like – have historically come from the ranks of the bureaucracy), to the extent to which careers in the civil service are distinct from both political careers and private sector careers, or vice versa they are interconnected.

The third dimension is the relative importance attached to law vs management. We leave the floor to Painter and Peters:

> One dominant strand of thinking has been that the public administrator is in essence a legal figure, perhaps little different from a judge. The task of

the public administrator within an administrative tradition of this sort is to identify the legal foundations of public action and to implement that law. Obviously then, legal education is the foundation for recruitment of public servants. . . . An emphasis on management is the most marked contrast to that legalistic tradition in administration. In this conception of the role of the administrator the principal task is to make programs function, and to make them function as efficiently and effectively as possible. Of course, this management must be carried out within a legal framework, but the first question that the administrator will ask is not about the law but about organizing and managing the program for effectiveness. For the civil servant as manager, lawyers are 'on tap, not on top.'

(Painter and Peters 2010, pp. 7–8)

The fourth dimension is the nature of accountability in the public sector. The main alternative lies in either relying upon the law or upon political actors, especially parliaments, as the primary mechanism.

Powers are delegated to bureaucracies in all political systems, and consequently accountability mechanisms must constrain and monitor the exercise of that discretion. All political systems, even autocratic ones, have a conception of accountability for their public bureaucracies. Conceptions of accountability differ significantly: 'One major option for accountability is to depend upon law as the primary mechanism for controlling bureaucracy. Such an option places much of the action in accountability within the public bureaucracy itself, or in special administrative courts, and involves political actors relatively little in the process. . . . The primary alternative to the legalistic form of accountability is reliance on political actors, especially parliaments, as the primary mechanism' (Painter and Peters 2010).

Besides the actors of accountability, however, also the contents are central in defining a tradition. One main option is to rely, as the principal elements for control, on legal instrumentalities, such as the *Conseil d'Etat* and its analogues, and on legal procedures, which usually involve that controls are exercised *ex ante*, so that administrators often must gain approval prior to making decisions, rather than acting decisively and then be held accountable later (Peters 2008). The primary alternative is relying on forms of accountability on results.

(Ongaro 2009, pp. 251–252)

The model elaborated by Pollitt and Bouckaert and the one wrought out by Painter and Peters partly overlap, since they map the same terrain, although they have a different analytical focus. Pollitt and Bouckaert select the country politico-administrative system as the unit of analysis in their work; Painter and Peters focus on the main traits of bureaucratic systems. Politics at country level is the main differentiating category between the two models. In the remainder of this chapter, we employ the two frames in an integrated way for drawing implications about contextual influences on certain very basic premises of managing strategically a public services organization in a given polity (for an application to public agencies in certain European countries, Ferlie and Parrado 2018).

Combining the Pollitt and Bouckaert model and administrative tradition
approach to analyze contextual influences on the strategic management of public
services organizations

The first dimension we consider – *the conception of the state and culture of governance* – combines the notion of 'administrative culture' or 'culture of governance,' used as almost interchangeable terms by Pollitt and Bouckaert, with the conception of the state and of state-society relationships as employed by Painter and Peters. Pollitt and Bouckaert adopt the distinction between a *Rechtsstaat* culture of governance (the term Rechtsstaat is usually translated with 'state of law,' though the German word contains a more nuanced range of meanings) and a *public interest* culture of governance (in their distinction they draw on previous works, notably Pierre 1995).

> From the Rechtsstaat perspective, the state is a central integrating force within society, and its focal concerns are with the preparation, promulgation and enforcement of laws. . . . In such a culture, the instinctive bureaucratic stance will tend to be one of rule-following and precedent, and the actions of both individual public servant and individual citizen will be set in this context of correctness and control.
>
> (Pollitt and Bouckaert 2011, p. 62)

Administrative law plays a central role in this culture of governance and its inherent logic tends to pervasively permeate administrative action (up to the point that legalism, under certain circumstances, may become a cultural paradigm, as it has been argued to have historically been the case of Italy, see Capano 2003; a discussion and implications are developed in Ongaro 2006, 2011). By contrast, the public interest model

> [a]ccords the state a less extensive or dominant role within society . . . the law . . . is usually in the background rather than the foreground, and many senior civil servants have no special training in its mysteries . . . the process of government is seen as one of obtaining the public's consent for (or at least acquiescence in) measures devised in the public (general, national) interest . . . with pragmatism and flexibility as qualities which may be prized above technical expertise (or even above strict legality).
>
> (Pollitt and Bouckaert 2011, p. 62)

Though not identical, there are many points of overlapping between Rechtsstaat cultures of governance and organic conceptions of the state, on the one hand, and public interest cultures of governance and contractarian conceptions of the state, on the other hand. The two pairs tend to go hand in hand, both notionally and in terms of their territorial diffusion. They also tend to correlate with the relative importance attached to law (higher in Rechtsstaat, organic cultures) vs the importance attached to management (higher in public interest, contractarian cultures).

The basic implication for strategy concerns the very relationship with the legitimacy of public services organizations. There are two options here: one is that performance, and hence strategy as a driver of performance, is a legitimating criterion in the foreground for a public services organization: 'does university X or public agency

Y produce value for money and ultimately serve the public interest?' is the question that is fundamentally asked in public interest cultures of governance. The other one is that legitimacy lies elsewhere, in the very fact that 'university X or agency Y are the embodiment of the state in that place,' and that suffices – provided such entities comply with the prescriptions of the law – in a Rechtsstaat conception of the state, which leads to the consequence that the strategic management (and management in general) of such public organizations is vested an ultimately ancillary position. This regards what is ultimately expected of a public services organization and shapes the very premises, the underlying rationale for making strategy in a public services organization. We may draw the broader implication that making strategy in different houses is not tantamount: the form strategy takes may be similar (e.g. through multi-annual plans, like in the planning school), but the ultimate meaning of it may be different (the plan may be conceived as first and foremost a management tool – in a public interest context – or as first and foremost a legal requirement and authorizing tool – in a Rechtsstaat context). This is not to say that strategic management is impeded in Rechtsstaat contexts, nor that administrative law should only be read as an impediment or antithetical to management (see Ziller 2003, for an argument about the contribution administrative law may provide to enabling certain developments of public management); but the meaning that strategic management takes in different contexts is different, and such difference cannot be overlooked.

Context also affects the autonomy of public services organizations, which is a condition for strategy to form. To the extent that the core concerns of a public organization lie in the preparation, promulgation, and enforcement of laws (as in a Rechtsstaat context), autonomy may be – *ceteris paribus* – lower than in contexts where 'pragmatism and flexibility [are] qualities which may be prized . . . even above strict legality,' as in a public interest context (Pollitt and Bouckaert 2011, p. 62). Moreover, the role societal actors are entrusted in public policy making, which as we noticed earlier is assumed as 'natural' in some traditions (e.g. the Scandinavian states) and depicted almost as an 'intrusion' in other traditions (e.g. the Napoleonic one) also has implications for strategy making in public services organizations, notably for the acceptability and the leeway that network-based and collaborative models of strategy may be given in different contexts. Even hybrid organizations and public–private partnerships may find the very premises of action very different under the two types of regimes – to the extent that action configures itself as 'administrative action regulated by administrative law' in one context, as opposed to delineating simply a mode of delivery orientated to the pursuit of 'public interest' in the other context. There seems to be a big chasm separating the two worlds, and public services organizations operate and form their strategy under either of these regimes, each with its distinctive internal logic and consistency.

Thus, for example the head teacher/headmaster of a school in England in the 2010s finds herself or himself operating as a full-fledged manager of resources, able to hire or dismiss the school staff, and redesign its organization and set of relations with stakeholders. Across The Channel in France or Italy – the same period – the homologue of our English head teacher will have to operate in accordance with strict procedures, will not have any possibility to hire or dismiss staff (recruitment occurs through public competitions occurring on a national basis, and the ranking in the reserve list entitles teachers to express their preference about which school to go to – the employer is the state, not the individual school, and the head teacher is usually not even consulted in this process), restructures will have to be authorized centrally somewhere in the provincial or regional capital (indeed will often be the results of decisions taken centrally likely without consulting the head teacher), and relations with stakeholders may at most be managed informally, with much caution as any formal(istic) breach in procedures will bring with itself a big dose of administrative risks for our head teacher and may ultimately be detrimental to her career prospects. Whilst a reform a decade earlier in Italy had partly increased the managerial autonomy of head teachers, it has not in this case had any transformative effect in the terms of substantially changing the strategic space of schools in this country. Would-be strategists in the education sector face very different premises depending on which country and jurisdiction they happen to operate.

The second basic feature of context we consider is the *relationship of the bureaucracy to political institutions*, and the way in which the relationships between executive politicians (and more broadly elected officials) and senior public servants (tenured officials, though some of them in some countries have lost the 'tenure' as an effect of administrative reforms since the 1980s) are structured. Their career paths may be closely interconnected and entwisted (as in the Napoleonic tradition, see Peters 2008, although differences on a national basis are apparent, see Ongaro 2009 Chapter 7 and 2010; see also Ongaro 2018) or relatively distinct. Post-holding may be highly politicized (and this may occur not only at the top but also at the bottom of the administrative pyramid, see Soutiropoulos 2004 and Spanou 2008 about politicized recruitment of operational staff in southern European countries), or 'merit' or other 'objective' criteria like seniority may determine the conditions for accession to the top posts. The bureaucracy may be (also) the purveyors of a general purpose elite for the state (as is the case of the French bureaucracy, whose exponents fill many elective posts), or rather be confined to its stricter borders of exerting authority delegated from political institutions (like the British bureaucracy). The civil service may represent a relatively isolated social group (like in Germany), or porosity with commercial sector careers may be high and frequent interchanges the norm (like in the USA).

Such profiles may tend to change more rapidly than the basic conception of the state and culture of governance, perhaps as an effect of administrative reforms, yet these features tend to be relatively stable properties of a country or a cluster of countries. The role of civil servants and the basic features of the civil service may also be combined with considerations about accountability: are public officials accountable to the elected representative – like in the UK – or 'to the law' (and to a system of courts ensuring compliance with the law) – like in France or Germany? The role assigned to the civil service and the modalities and underlying logic whereby civil servants are held to account have, we would argue, profound implications for the question 'who is the strategist?' and for the way in which strategy processes unfold.

The third basic feature is the *nature of executive government*, that is the working habits and conventions shaping governing processes. This trait is dependent on the nature of the political system (hence differences are driven by the political form of the state). The style and conventions of governing range between majoritarian/adversarial conventions – more often associated with single-party or minimal winning coalitions, that occur where one party only, or two or more parties, hold more than 50% of the seats in the legislature – to consensual-orientated/less adversarial conventions – more often associated with minority cabinets, that occur when the parties in government hold less than 50% of the legislative seats, or grand coalitions, where additional parties are included in the executive beyond the number required for a minimal winning coalition (see Pollitt and Bouckaert 2011, pp. 54–55, drawing on Lijphart 1984, 1999).

The nature of executive government may powerfully shape who the strategist is, notably in carving out different roles for elected officials in the assemblies *vis à vis* politicians in executive positions in government. Importantly, there may be profound differences across levels of government in the same country, which may lead to different countries having different, even reversed, styles and conventions of governing at different levels. For example, at the national level, governing conventions in the UK are majoritarian/adversarial, whilst in Italy they tend to be more consensual, with grand coalitions often necessitated to furnish government to the country; yet at the local government level since a reform in 1993, conventions of governing are majoritarian in Italy (where the mayor is directly elected and the associated electoral lists get the majority in the local council), whilst in the UK, more consensual elements are part of the governing conventions in local authorities.

The nature of executive government as a contextual feature is especially significant for those parts of the public sector that are more directly connected to the elected officials (be they at national, regional, or local level): a ministerial administration hierarchically dependent upon and reporting to the minister (e.g. the department for transportation of a country) is more affected by the conventions of government than a relatively autonomous agency executing a relatively specific, technical task and placed at some distance from elected officials (e.g. an agency issuing driving licences). To this regard, it has been argued that the public sector is 'more than elective governments,' indeed that it is *more and more* 'more than elective government,' due to some trends that have been depicted, with iconic efficacy, as 'the rise of the unelected' (Vibert 2007), whereby organizations relatively detached from 'the core government' – non-departmental public bodies, executive agencies, independent administrative authorities, etc. (to use a UK yet internationally known terminology for classification of public bodies) – are becoming more and more important in the provision of public services. The point has been effectively expressed by the title of a major study on public agencies: '*Public agencies: How governments do things through semi-autonomous organisations*' (Pollitt et al. 2004), and this observation formed an important part of the argument we put forward in the introductory chapter about why strategic management may be more significant nowadays than it was in the past for public services organizations. Yet elective governments do retain a crucial role in public services, and the working habits and conventions in executive government are an important contextual factor affecting the strategy processes taking place yonder.

7.2.2 Expanding the analysis of contextual influences to encompass culture

Thus far, the bulk of the contribution has been provided by the two theoretical perspectives of the Pollitt and Bouckaert model and the administrative traditions approach of Painter and Peters. We may now further expand on the cultural dimension of context. The picture provided so far about contextual influences has already included a cultural component: the culture of governance, or administrative culture. The cultural lens can be further enlarged to encompass the societal culture broadly intended, in view of identifying the ways in which it has an influence on public management in general and strategic management in particular (Schedler and Pröller 2007).

Bouckaert (2007) provides a thorough analysis about how to study 'culture' in relation to public management research and practice. He first reviews the manifold definitions of culture; we will here cull three. First, an anthropological one whereby culture can be defined as 'the relationship of a society to the primordial nature or law of the earth' (Lawlor 1992, p. 2). Second, a 'fundamental questions-orientated' definition whereby culture is defined by the answers to five questions: what is the relationship of individual to others (relational orientation)?; what is the temporal focus of human activity (time orientation)?; what is the modality of human action (activity orientation)?; what is a human being's relation to nature (human–nature orientation)?; and what is the character of innate human nature (human nature orientation)? (Trompenaars and Hampden-Turner 1993). Third, a notion of culture as

> patterns, explicit and implicit, of and for behaviour acquired and transmitted by symbols, constituting the distinctive achievement of human groups . . . the essential core of culture consists of traditional (i.e. historically derived and selected) ideas and especially their attached values: culture systems may, on the one hand, be considered as products of action, on the other hand as conditioning elements of future action.
>
> (Kroeber and Kluckhohn in Adler 1993)

Relying especially on the third definition, Bouckaert then identifies four levels at which culture may be significant for public management, and three models to determine the mutual relationships of culture and public management. We now analyze these in turn.

Levels of culture

In terms of levels of culture, culture may be interpreted at macro, meso, micro, and nano levels. The macro level concerns culture in relation to time, in relation to space and human geography, to language, and to religion (religion is 'beyond culture, but it also has important cultural aspects,' Bouckaert 2007), and in relation to structures like the nation state or the policy field and the functioning of structures within institutional settings.

As an illustrative example of the significance of the cultural context at the macro-level for strategic management, we will consider culture in relation to time. Following Bouckaert (2007), we can observe that a first aspect is the time horizon: the most obvious distinction here is the one between long-term vs short-term horizon cultures. Long-term-orientated cultures have a different tolerance and inclination to accept postponement of results manifesting themselves in the short run 'in exchange for' confirmations that things are proceeding in the 'right' direction: from a Western viewpoint, Bouckaert (2007) notices that the

> Chinese have a long term perspective in their administrative attitudes and behaviours. Contracting out Macau or Hong Kong for about 500 years is not problematic, just as Taiwan is ultimately moving back into the 'one country, different systems' model [while] In the West we have an increasingly myopic point of view of reform which is institutionalised in our political election cycles and

administrative mandated terms which are shortened from a life-long career to contracts limited in time.

Cultural differences concerning basic conceptions of time exert a profound influence on management and administration: the influence of the basic conception of time for strategy making can hardly be exaggerated: the way in which a strategic plan is formulated and implemented (planning school) or the ways in which learning processes are expected to occur and produce benefits that may be reaped (emergent approach to strategy, learning school) have a higher-order dependence on the basic time conception characterizing the context in which organizational strategy unfolds. The last part of the commentary by Bouckaert also points out the interesting aspect that administrative conventions and reforms, whilst they probably cannot modify the fundamental time-horizon of a culture, can however tilt the balance more towards one or the other pole (short-term vs long-term), albeit within the basic traits of a culture, which is and remains fundamentally orientated towards the short-term or towards the long-term (the basic time horizon of a culture is itself changeable only over long time spans).

A second element in the cultural conceptions of time concerns the interrelatedness between past, present, and future. This may range from 'absence of interrelatedness between the three dimensions of time' (Russia) to 'temporal integration' (Japan) to the touching of past with present and of present with future but no overlapping (India) (see Bouckaert 2007, based on Cottle in Trompenaar and Hampden-Turner 1993, p. 127). Time orientation 'has an impact on management issues. Elements of strategy, goals, objectives, risk assessment and planning are obvious elements that are subject to time orientation' (Bouckaert 2007). Cultural and political elements may combine in determining the time horizon in which policy entrepreneurs and public services organization strategists have to operate (Mele and Ongaro 2014).

The meso level in interpreting culture and its influence on public management concerns the administrative and the professional culture, both of which have already been dealt with. Administrative cultures have been examined earlier, applying such notions as that of the distinction between Rechtsstaat and public interest cultures of governance. As regards professional cultures, they are associated with professions present and highly influential in public services organizations – doctors and clinicians, teachers, policemen, military and homeland security agents, social workers, auditors, magistrates, firemen, and the like – and the interconnections between professionals and strategic management have been thoroughly examined throughout Chapters 2 to 6; they will be further discussed later in relation to reform narratives and the role of 'managers' in public organizations.

The micro culture basically overlaps with the organizational culture, and it has been discussed elsewhere, especially in relation to the cultural school in strategic management (Chapter 2). It is, however, important to notice that embedded within organizations, there may be nano-cultures of specific professional groups within the organization itself. For example inspectors within a ministry of finance may have a specific and distinctive culture. Moreover, even within the same broad profession, field offices and officers operating in diverse territories throughout the country may over the time form their own nano-culture, perhaps imbued with the local culture of the location where they operate, and local cultures may differ profoundly even across the same country.

Models to determine the mutual relationships of culture and public management

We can now turn to the second part of the framework proposed by Bouckaert: the analysis of the ways in which the mutual influence between culture and management can be modelled. Bouckaert proposes an analysis based on a sequence of four concepts: culture, values, attitudes, and behaviour (drawing also from Adler 1993). First, culture determines values ('that which is explicitly or implicitly desirable to an individual or group, and which influences the selection from available models, means and ends to action'). Values in turn determine attitudes (an attitude 'is a construct that expresses values and disposes a person to act or react in a certain way towards something'). Attitudes determine behaviour (intended as 'any form of human action'). Through this causal chain, culture ultimately affects behaviours, of individuals and organizations, hence it constitutes a fundamental dimension in public management (and strategic management as a component of it).

There are three models whereby the mutual relationships between these four concepts may be analyzed: in model one ('management by culture,' or 'idealistic') culture and values determine attitudes and behaviour. In model two ('culture by management,' or 'materialistic'), attitudes and behaviour (that to some extent in an organization can be shaped by 'management' and managers) determine culture. In model three 'culture and management have something *sui generis*, sufficient to keep some autonomy and independence; however, there is also an overlap which guarantees mutual adjustment: culture by management and management by culture' (Bouckaert 2007); model three is about mutual relationships without one direction of causal influence prevailing over the other (different from model one, where culture is the cause and attitudes and behaviour the ensuing effect, or model two, in which attitudes and behaviours are the cause and culture an effect).

Bouckaert's favour (like ours) leans towards the third model: culture and management are to some extent distinct, and they interact, often in complicated ways, 'on an equal footing.' Another and probably more popular way of putting the question of the relationship between culture and behaviour is to refer to culture as the 'chicken-and-egg' of public management: culture may be either a driver or an obstacle (or both) for public management (depending on how they reciprocally interact); culture may be a given, something which is simply 'there' in a given location in place and time, or it may be a target of management interventions ('the ultimate goal of the intervention is to change the culture of the NHS,' as one of the authors of this book happened to hear during a Parliamentary audition at the House of Commons broadcast live whilst he was writing, in the first edition of the book, this section).

It should further be noticed that for analytical purposes, causality may be examined in one direction only (especially depending on the time scale considered): if the analytical focus is the impact of a strategic approach to the appreciation of the distinctive resources of a public organization of a given country (say, an agency operating in the field of national security, or the military air force of the country), then causality may be investigated in the direction from national and organizational culture towards management. If, as in the case of a British NHS reform that was being discussed in the year 2013, the goal of the reform is 'changing the culture' of NHS Trusts, then causality should be investigated in the direction from management (the contents of the reform) towards culture (what changes such reform can realistically bring about in the organizational culture of the NHS?).

A key issue in the study of strategic management is the extent to which societal culture affects organizational culture[1]; in the terminology we have adopted, the question is: how dominant macro culture is for meso and micro culture, and notably (considering the main unit of analysis of this book is the individual public services organization) how dominant are macro and meso culture for micro (i.e. organizational-level) culture? As Bouckaert phrases it, a key issue is: 'to what extent can an organisational culture be specific and divergent from a broader organisational environment?' Ripostes to this question and its implications for management may ultimately be boiled down to three basic options. The first option is one we could label as 'generic management': in a more generic point of view, the broader culture percolates onto organizational culture, and such leaching is pervasive and ultimately decisive: 'contrary to the currently popular notion of organizational culture, we claim that the existence of local organizational cultures that are distinct from more generally shared background cultures occurs relatively infrequently at the level of the whole organization' (Wilkins and Ouchi 1983, p. 468 – cited in Bouckaert 2007). The opposite position is one which we may label 'contingency management' whereby organizational cultures interact with macro and meso cultures but are ultimately distinctive and entirely irreducible to them: organizational cultures are distinctive and distinct from the larger background cultures in which they are immersed (although a number of public services professions may have distinctive cultures which are international more than national, like medicine or engineering). The third position is an intermediate one; mixed points of view lie in-between: '[w]hile organizational culture might be expected to reflect national cultures, it may also have its own distinct characteristics' (Morris et al. 1994, pp. 65–66 cited in Bouckaert 2007).

The debate in the scientific literature about the extent to which societal culture affects organizational culture has so far developed mainly in relation to private sector organizations, and it is a field in many respects yet to be ploughed in the public sector. We should notice, however, that here may be grounding to formulate the tentative statement that in the public sector, *ceteris paribus*, the organizational culture is more exposed to the broader country's administrative (meso) and societal (macro) culture than the private sector (in other words, the macro and meso levels may have a higher impact on organizational cultures). The rationale for such (tentative) statement lies in the consideration that public organizations are institutionally embedded into the nation's core structures and are territorially linked to the communities, at the national and local levels, they serve (see Borgonovi 1984; Bouckaert 2007; Capano 2003; Ongaro 2004, 2011). We are not here suggesting that position one (generic management approach, whereby the influence of the macro and meso cultures is pervasive over organizational culture) is necessarily to be opted for over the other approach; indeed our broad stance is tilted towards position three whereby organizational cultures partly reflect national and professional cultures and partly are distinctive; however, the influence of the broader country's administrative (meso) and societal (macro) cultures is likely to be influential, or at least more influential than in the private sector.

The notable exceptions here are supranational (like the EU) and international (like the UN and UN-related agencies and programmes and funds) organizations, whose nature of compound institutional systems (Ongaro 2013a) may have implications also for the interactions between macro and micro cultures.

If public sector organizations are more permeable to the national macro culture, that is the generic management point of view (whereby the broader culture percolates onto organizational culture), as opposed to the contingent point of view (whereby organizational cultures are ultimately distinctive and irreducible) tends to prevail, then implications are notable (though we should remind the reader that this is a big 'if,' as such hypothesis may only be conjectured or tentatively hypothesized but requires testing through yet-to-be-done research work). This is especially the case where the cultural school of thought in strategic management is brought to the fore. If culture is a higher-order factor affecting strategy, and consistency between culture and the 'other' organizational variables is ultimately the key to performance (these are the key tenets of the cultural school), then it makes a big difference that public services organizations tend to be relatively homogeneous within national or country-cluster borders: if such is the case, a relative homogeneity – the reasoning proceeds – would then characterize organizational strategy within the entirety of the public services organizations belonging to a cultural cluster (every other thing being equal, that is, controlling for the policy sector, the tier of government, and the like).

7.2.3 Summing up on the influences of the relatively stable dimensions of context on strategic management

Summing up on this long journey towards the exploration of the significance of context for strategy in public services organizations, we have identified a number of contextual dimensions that can affect the strategic management of public services organizations and outlined certain possible 'lines of influence.' In this section, we have been discussing the relatively stable features of the context and, for the sake of the simplicity of the analysis, we have so far treated them, and their implications for strategic management, to some extent as if they were fixed conditions – as if they were immutable and permanent traits that characterize the different houses that public services organizations inhabit (albeit, as we have highlighted since the beginning, this doesn't mean that they are unchangeable).

Moreover, given most public services organizations are intrinsically linked to a territory, since they are established to represent and to serve a specific territory (be it a local community or a national one), the whole picture so far portrayed could sound a bit deterministic, as if immutable contextual features exerted a dooming influence over the strategy process of public services organizations in different jurisdictions. Such a picture would partly contradict the argument we have put forward in the introductory chapter: that there have been changes, not just in the way in which strategic management is conceived and theorized, thanks to the broadening of the schools in strategic management, but in 'the real world out there' of public services, because of the transformative effects of reforms of the public sector. Changes in the political economy, sectoral public policies and the public management policy have partly recast the configuration of the public sector, opening up new and diverse ways of considering the strategic management of public services organizations (Chapter 1).

We then now need to turn to complete the depiction of the 'context' in which the strategy processes of public services organizations unfold by examining the other key set of factors moulding the context, in an especially intense way over the decades since the 1980s: public management reforms.

We are interested in exploring the claimed 'transformative' effects of reforms of the public services (Ferlie et al. 1996). In terms of Pollitt and Bouckaert (2017)'s discussion, we are especially interested in process changes (changes to the processes whereby the public sector 'functions'), the changes to the structure of the public sector, and even the cultural changes (the changes in certain profiles of culture brought about by changes originating in public management, see earlier discussion), because our analytical focus here is the transformative impact of reforms of public management in a given polity on the context in which strategy processes unfold in public organizations. The next section reviews such reforms and their transformative effects.

7.3 The transformative effects of administrative reforms and strategic management

This section explores the relationship between various narratives of public management reform apparent in different countries and implications for preferred approaches to strategic management. By 'reform narrative' is meant an integrated and high-level account which mixes theoretical constructs, empirical observations, and normative argumentation in a story about why major reforms are needed. Such narratives seek to produce practical reform doctrines and to be persuasive and actionable in the policy and political domains. As an example, Ferlie et al. (2009) characterize and use three narratives – New Public Management, Network Governance and Democratic Revitalization – as alternative prisms through which to analyze higher education reform patterns across a number of European countries.

We introduce and briefly illustrate three such reform narratives: the New Public Management (NPM), the Neo-Weberian model, and the 'governance turn' in public management, notably the so-called New Public Governance. Implications for strategic management of the transformative effects of each of these narratives are discussed; they will be more systematically wrapped up in the subsequent and final section of the chapter.

7.3.1 NPM cluster and doctrines

There is a significant cluster of countries where the New Public Management (NPM) has had a deep impact, including many Anglo-Saxon jurisdictions (Pollitt and Bouckaert 2017) and certainly including the UK (Hood 1995; Ferlie et al. 1996). NPM reforms represent an interlinked package of interventions which substantially increase the applicability of some strategic management models to restructured public services organizations.

The revamp and downsizing of the large public sectors inherited from the social democratic era of the 'big welfare' was a core element of the wider neo-liberal project of the 1980s. The simplest policy response was straightforward privatization or the moving of functions from the public to the private sectors (e.g. the utilities in the UK), sometimes under new regulatory regimes. Yet elements of the 'core' public sector (e.g. health, education, criminal justice) proved more complex and resistant to straightforward privatization: instead, they were to be reformed on market-like lines while remaining in the public sector. Starting with small-scale experiments, reform ambitions in relation to the remaining public sector quickly became more synoptic.

In an important article, Hood (1991) described and analyzed the key features of the emergent New Public Management form which could be seen as a distinct archetype (Dunleavy and Hood 1994) quite distinct from old public administration, that was summarized in the formula: 'specialization' plus 'marketization' plus 'incentivization.' While NPM reforms contained multiple strands, they had a common logic which moved the public sector 'downgroup' (Dunleavy and Hood 1994), making it less distinctive and increasing the blurring with private firms.

So, during the 1980s and 1990s, the combination of embedded NPM reforms, which move the public sector downgroup and make it less distinctive from private firms and more open to conventional private sector-based forms of strategy, together with the growth of models of strategy rooted in the social sciences other than industrial economics have implied that the space for applying strategic management approaches to contemporary public sector organizations expanded. In particular, the autonomization of large service delivery units was a key shift which increased the scope for their strategic behaviour: strong quasi markets produce 'quasi firms' on the supply side.

Hood's (1991) early analysis of the key 'signs and symptoms' of NPM highlighted major shifts which made these restructured public agencies more 'firm-like' or, to use an expression we favour over firm-like, we observe that 'processes of corporatization of public service organisations paved the way to a more widespread recourse to models of strategy,' most of which had previously been developed and experimented on private sector organizations. A first such shift was the development of 'hands on management' (Hood 1991) as opposed to the facilitative administrators of the old public bureaucracies (Mintzberg 1983). Public sector managers were now supposed to manage actively and to act as a countervailing force against strong public sector trade unions and professions. An example would be the introduction of general management in the UK National Health Service (NHS) in the mid-1980s (after Griffiths 1983). Key managers were imported from the private sector (although in this NHS example, they tended not to stay long) and young public sector managers put on MBA or leadership development programmes. While their salary levels increased, these managers were now tasked with meeting centrally specified key performance objectives and their job security decreased. Reforms to UK public sector corporate governance systems (Ferlie et al. 1996) brought in senior private sector personnel from outside as non-executives on strengthened public sector boards, based on a conventional private sector model. These boards were increasingly tasked with making strategy and ensuring good corporate governance (mirroring corporate governance reforms in the private sector); there was therefore an upgrading of management capacity, including at this strategic level.

A second major trend was towards the set-up of new markets (through privatization) but also of quasi markets designed to mimic the effects of markets in those services that remained in public hands. The old vertically integrated hierarchies were broken up and replaced by distinct sets of purchasers and providers who now related through contracts rather than hierarchies. A good example would be the first UK NHS internal market period (1990–1997), in which two novel forms of purchasing organization were introduced (District Health Authorities as macro purchasers and General Practitioner Fund holders as micro purchasers) and providers were given more operational autonomy as NHS Trusts. The espoused policy was also that purchasers could place contracts with alternative non-NHS providers, but in practice there was at this stage little market entry or exit (because of central and political fears of system instability).

The disintegration of the NHS was an example of a third major trend (Hood 1991) towards disaggregation and unbundling (partly seen also elsewhere, see Bouckaert et al. 2010) whereby previously large public sector organizations were broken up into more manageable and corporatized subunits. Another good case example is the spinning out of executive agencies (such as the UK Borders Agency) and the downsizing of central ministries. This is far from being a British or Anglophone countries trend (an overview of the trend towards agencification throughout Europe is reported in Verhoest et al. 2012; cases from across the world can be found in Pollitt and Talbot 2004). These agencies (Pollitt et al. 2004) were designed to concentrate on a small range of operational tasks with high volume (e.g. the UK Identity and Passports Service, an executive agency of the Home Office responsible for issuing passports), and liberated to search for greater operational efficiencies internally. Sometimes new senior management was brought into these agencies from outside to strengthen its grip.

A fourth key shift (Hood 1991) was towards more explicit performance measurement and management systems, with the elaboration of Key Performance Indicators (KPIs) made transparent (e.g. waiting times to get a hospital appointment; the educational performance of pupils as measured by tests; and the like). The measurement and understanding of 'performance' became a key domain in public management scholarship (Boyne et al. 2007). These KPIs were used to construct publicly available league tables, thereby putting visible pressure on lowly ranked 'low performers' to improve. If there were no timely improvements in measured performance, these public sector providers could face the prospect of being merged on unfavourable terms with a higher performer, a top-down clear out of the top management team, losing their jurisdiction to a private provider or even going bankrupt as their income flows dried up. Though the form and extent to which performance is 'managed' needs to be put in the proper contextual and temporal frame (Bouckaert and Hallighan 2008; Van Dooren and Van de Walle 2011), and the sanctioning systems associated with poor scores in the indicators may be a contextually sensitive feature and work only in certain countries and contexts, the trend was remarkable and left a mark on the contemporary public sector across the globe (Bouckaert and Hallighan 2008).

The influence that management reforms may have in producing endurable transformations in the public sector (Ferlie et al. 1996) has manifested itself also, and notably, in the direction of legitimating a new function and a new social group (that of professional managers, in charge of making the strategy at the corporate level in the public organization) partly to the effect of displacing 'content professionals' that have traditionally wielded a dominant role in public services (doctors, lawyers, teachers, firemen, and the like). The practice and the language of 'performance' and long-term trends towards higher-level usages of performance information (from performance administration to the management of performance to performance management to performance governance, to use Bouckaert and Hallighan's frame, 2008) may also be interpreted as redefining the border between the management professionals (managers, consultants, auditors) and the content professionals, by tilting the balance in favour of the former group. In this picture, one implication is that the management professionals will also bring with them and diffuse in the public sector a rhetoric of strategic management, more likely packaged in the formats of the more 'prescriptive' schools in strategic management, like the design, planning, positioning, and the Public Value school (whether this rhetoric ultimately enhances 'actual' performance of public services organization is another question, see Chapter 8).

A fifth shift is the one from process to output controls (Hood 1991). The doctrine in the NPM was that public agencies should be assessed more on their results and less on compliance with process ('less procedures and more results' was a favourite slogan of would-be reformers in many countries). There is debate about the extent to which such a shift ever took place: entrenched bureaucracy seemed difficult to dislodge, and some of the new control technologies such as audit (Power 1997) soon seemed to take on an expansionist life of their own. However, it is possible that in the long term, the shift from hierarchy to new forms of regulation in a number of sectors (e.g. utilities) did lead to a lightening of process controls and gave utility providers more scope to act strategically by entering the market (including foreign firms, such as EDF that massively entered the UK electricity and power distribution sector), to make acquisitions and to diversify.

We can now develop further these key signs of NPM-based organizational forms (Hood 1991). A further legacy in our view is an increased blurring between the private and public sectors as part of the moving 'downgroup' process that we have already mentioned. There are more hybrid organizational forms within a mixed economy of financing and ownership. Some public organizations are now generating substantial flows of private income. This phenomenon may be illustrated with an example (see Box 7.1).

Box 7.1   Royal Marsden NHS Foundation Trust

UK NHS Trusts, for example, are able by law to generate flows of private patient income to supplement public funding, although a cap has to be agreed with the sector regulator (NHS Monitor). At the time this edition of the book goes to press, the cap is generally set at a low level, although that may change in the future. A current outlier is the well-known Royal Marsden NHS Trust which is an internationally leading cancer hospital in London. Its private patients' income cap was agreed originally with NHS Monitor at 31% of total income. Its board immediately agreed a target to increase its private patients' income to £100 million per annum (described as a 50% to 60% per increase in the text) over the shortest possible lapse (out of a 2011–2012 income of £311.5m per annum), taking it up to the top of its cap. Clearly, this is a substantial shift in the funding mix and might well be expected to lead to a need to grow internal core competences in such areas as marketing, contracting, and quality assurance. The language used in the Annual Report available on their website contains 'firm like' references to the Marsden 'brand' and the need for a portfolio analysis.

Source: Trust website (Royal Marsden NHS Foundation Trust 2012)

There may be progressive privatization of 'spun out' executive agencies, such as in the Defence sector, which slowly migrate from the public to the private sector. A good UK example is QinetiQ which is an internationally leading internal security and defence technology firm. It was originally spun out of the old Defence Evaluation and Research Agency and any remaining Ministry of Defence equity was later sold off. However, the Ministry of Defence retained a 'special share' which enables it to block any hostile takeover attempts.

Finally, it should be observed that there typically is a lessening of the scope of direct democratic control through NPM-led reorganizations. In particular, UK local governments have progressively lost direct control of manifold key services which have passed to various non-elected bodies. These include independent corporations like the new group of 'post 1992 Universities' that were previously under local government control and became independent organizations; new autonomous and self-managed schools (e.g. the Free Schools or Academies); or growing not-for-profit or private providers (e.g. social housing; social care). An implication for strategic management is that models such as Democratic Public Administration (DeLeon 2005) or the public value perspective (Moore 1995; Moore and Benington 2011) may be increasingly difficult to apply in what are 'post democratic' settings.

While NPM reforms varied in their impact internationally (Hood 1995) and there are certainly jurisdictions on which this reform narrative had a much lower impact (such as France or China – see Boxes 2.3 and 7.2 reporting on cases of strategic management in these countries), nevertheless the global impact of the NPM wave was considerable. International diffusion agents such as OECD, the World Bank (where NPM-inspired reforms were often a condition for financial aid for developing countries, as they were seen by donors as improving transparency and good government), management consultants, academics, and 'blockbuster texts' (Osborne and Gaebler 1992) all contributed to spread these ideas globally. These dynamics changed during the second decade of the 2000s, but the long-term impact of the promotion of NPM doctrines has left a 'layer' of NPM tools and logics in many jurisdictions across the globe. The range of jurisdictions in which NPM ideas became common or relatively common currency included some surprises, like Nordic European countries such as Denmark, Finland, or Sweden (though for these countries the way in which NPM 'menus' were adapted to the local palates situates them well outside of the 'core' NPM jurisdictions, even if in terms of managerial instruments they seem to have adopted a number of the NPM 'dishes' – see Pollitt and Bouckaert 2017, Chapters 1 and 4).

There is some evidence that reformed NPM-style organizations are more open to adopting a set of conventional strategic management tools (see Hansen 2011, on Danish schools), like SWOT analyses, long-term financial planning, or the analysis of internal competences (see Chapters 2 and 3). NPM reforms introduce more market- and firm-like conditions both at the level of a sector/industry and at the level of a public agency/corporatized public organization. They also tend to autonomize service delivery agencies in particular (e.g. 'executive agencies'), reduce the scope of direct political oversight, and increase managerial autonomy, possibly also with the intent to elicit innovation (Wynen et al. 2014), though the overall picture of the autonomy of public agencies and their steering and control by the parent administrations is multifarious and cannot be boiled down to being a product of extensive application of NPM recipes only (see Laegreid and Verhoest 2010; Verhoest et al. 2012). Such reforms create more hybrid forms, hybrid governance organizations which mix public and private agencies or traits of public and private governance arrangements and are often based on mixed streams of finance, partly from the public purse, partly from market operations. Taken together, these shifts increase the applicability of

Porterian and RBV models (Rosenberg Hansen and Ferlie 2016 – see Chapters 2 and 3), especially if strong quasi markets emerge and consolidate.

It may also be considered that, quite often, in NPM jurisdictions (and beyond) the adoption of a strategic plan is a formal requirement for many public sector organizations. These 'strategic plans' adopted for reasons of compliance may well be referred to as dormant documents, a task to which organizations have to comply either because administrative reforms have made the strategic plan a compulsory document to adopt, or as a remnant of the past, the inheritance of rational planning models that historically dominated public administration in the 1960s and 1970s, and have proven to be resilient in practice (see Ferlie 2002, p. 280). A distinction has to be drawn between the public strategy of an organization (which is usually only a portion of the overall strategy) and a merely 'publicly authenticated' strategic plan, a document for external communication purposes only (that may be adopted also in the absence of any strategy, in a formalistic way). But the very presence of these dormant documents can make a difference: the preparation of a strategic plan may over the time become an institutionalized practice that can at a later stage, under different circumstances, be converted to new uses (on the mechanism of conversion, Streeck and Thelen 2005). In other words, even formalistic, dormant strategic plans may over the time act as seeds for longer-term transformative effects of managerial reforms

One final reflection on the dynamics of reform in 'NPM countries' and their relations to strategic management. Authoritative beholders of public sector transformation in such countries (Andrews et al. 2012) have observed something which at first sight might sound striking: they notice, in fact, that 'reforms are sometimes associated with hindering the development of organisational strategies.' Their argument is that frequent and radical reforms, forcing both continued and radical changes in business processes and organizational structures (e.g. mergers and splits of public organizations), may thwart the deployment of full-fledged strategies, be they in deliberate or emergent fashion. Associating public management reforms to the hindering of the development of organizational strategy may sound strange to the ears of public administrators in continental European countries or elsewhere in many public administration systems throughout Asia, Africa, or Latin America: in these systems, it is rather the pervasiveness of regulation to frustrate attempts by public managers to steer strategically the organization they are responsible for; the law is often perceived as an impediment, and public management reform may be the way forward to create the conditions for the deployment of strategic thinking in public services organizations (by both 'making managers manage' and by 'letting managers manage'). Yet the point is very interesting and leads us to consider, alongside the contents of administrative reforms, also their dynamics: too frequent and radical reforms – the kind of menu that has been served in great abundance in many 'NPM-countries' – may disrupt business processes and simply wipe off the organizations that were forming their strategy: it is not only the content of reforms that matters, also their differential dynamics across countries are relevant in creating the strategic space enabling public organizations to form their strategy.

7.3.2 The Neo-Weberian State

In their comparative analysis of public management reforms in 12 countries, Pollitt and Bouckaert (2017) outline a trajectory of what they term 'Neo Weberian State'

(NWS) reforming apparent in some major continental European states (e.g. France and Germany) which are distinct from the 'high on NPM' Anglo-Saxon cluster. They suggest that they should not be dismissed as NPM 'laggards' but that they are on a separate trajectory, which does not include the standard NPM recipes of disaggregation, incentives, or quasi markets. This narrative considers the state to act to protect a European ideal of the social market economy from a globalizing neo-liberal wave apparent in high NPM countries.

The continuing Weberian elements (after the famous German sociologist Max Weber, who also contributed to the pioneering study of modern public administration) in this configuration include (i) a reaffirmation of the central steering role of the positive State in response to public policy problems; (ii) a reaffirmation of the legitimating function of representative government; (iii) a reaffirmation of the role of (modernized) administrative law as ensuring a constitutional state which protects citizens; and (iv) the preservation of a distinct and distinctive public service (see Pollitt and Bouckaert 2011, pp. 118–119).

At the same time, Pollitt and Bouckaert (2011) suggest that 'neo' elements of modernization are emerging which include (i) a shift from internal rule following to an external orientation meeting citizens' needs and wishes, based not so much on market mechanisms but the promotion of a professional culture of quality and service; (ii) supplementation of representative democracy with a range of devices to consult with citizens; (iii) a modernization of administrative law to focus more on results than process, involving some performance management; and (iv) a professionalization of public service with some move away from a predominant and almost exclusive legal training and thinking towards a more managerial set of skills and competences.

The Neo-Weberian model may also be appreciated 'by contrast' with the NPM. If we assume (though this is not unproblematic) that the NPM is a theory of governing that challenges previous theories of governing (like Weberianism), then the NPM represents a radical restructuring of the organization of the public sector involving different bases of accountability (Ferlie et al. 1996). In other words, if it is assumed that the NPM is not simply about adding 'a layer of managerial tools' above the foundation of another theory of governing that remains unaltered and continues to represent the bedrock of 'legitimate government' in that polity, but the NPM was and is more than that as it aims to furnish a comprehensive model of governing, then, against this backdrop, the NWS may be interpreted as a conscious reaction by (continental) European administrative elites to the NPM by resorting to a model that considers the 'traditional' lines of accountability to still be at the core of the functioning of the public sector. According to the NWS perspective, such lines of accountability may be integrated (to make government both more competent and more responsive to society), but not supplanted: they still are the backbone of the functioning of the public sector. The NWS may thus be interpreted also as a political response – a state-centred response – by the elites of continental European countries to the pressures of global capitalism to recast the state-society border (Pollitt 2008) – and possibly more globally a reaction to the excessive power of 'impersonal forces' (like those at work in global financial capitalism, Roberts 2010), a riposte in which resurgent democracy is the dominant note (Lynn 2008).

Along another profile of analysis, it may be observed that the NWS is a 'territorially localised' paradigm, that is it concerns a defined set of countries (continental European), at least in the sense that it presupposes a number of features to be in place (like a separate branch of law, the administrative law, or a distinctive public service) for the NWS trajectory to be undertaken, whilst the NPM is a territorially de-localized paradigm, that is it may be intended as a global recipe applicable in principle if not in fact anywhere in the world. It has thus been critically discussed the extent to which the NWS has expanded in countries where the legitimation of the state and its ultimate societal acceptance – some pre-requisites for the NWS – are deemed to have been lower than in Germany or France, like in southern European countries like Greece, Italy, Portugal, or Spain (Ongaro 2009, Chapter 7). The conclusion, in short, is that the NWS model is applicable to these countries as well, though with very important qualifications. Finally, the Neo-Weberian model has also been employed to interpret the trajectory of reform of the European Commission (Ongaro 2015b).

The basic argument put forward by Pollitt and Bouckaert is that the NWS is an instance of path dependency (pp. 119–120), a logic whereby institutions, once formed, shape the range of possibilities and have a continuing and largely determinate influence over the choices that will be made at all levels and phases of the policy cycle (Peters 1999, Chapter 4). Hence, it reinforces certain traits (the traditional Weberian lines of accountability) whilst integrating other traits (managerial logics) into it. What is interesting for the purposes of the present book is that these 'new,' managerial elements would appear to open up more space for certain aspects of strategic management, even in the continued presence of a bureaucracy with mostly Weberian traits. An interesting theoretical perspective to interpret how this may occur seems to be that of the 'management of meaning' (where the notion is used in a way that combines both Pettigrew 1987, and Bouckaert 2007): management as a rhetoric of control (and distribution of authority) in organizations is somehow legitimized within this reform narrative as part and parcel of the running of public services organizations by public servants – provided it 'fits' an undergirding and pre-existing logic (the traditional Weberian chain of allocation of authority and accountability), to which it ought to comply for overall consistency to be kept. Provided compatibility is kept, the conceptual paraphernalia and the techniques of a number of schools in strategic management may be employed (for an example of strategic management tools in the Belgian public sector, allegedly a Neo-Weberian one, see Bernard et al. 2009; Drumaux and Goethals 2007). The most immediate examples include such schools like the planning school or the design school, with their emphasis on the managerial cadres or organizational apex to take on a strategic role (the list may be enlarged to encompass others: the case of the European Aviation Safety Authority illustrated in Box 2.4 falls squarely into the Neo-Weberian model), or the resource-based view and its manifold applications, whose focus on building and renewing distinctive resources appears quite in line with the emphasis on the building and renewing of administrative capacities at the core of the 'neo' elements of the NWS (see Chapter 3).

Albeit arisen in an altogether different environment (the American schools of government and public policy), the Public Value school (Chapter 3) in its emphasis on public managers as 'entrepreneurs' that ought to operate well beyond the confines prescribed to 'traditional' public bureaucrats may also be interpreted as compatible with a Neo-Weberian narrative – however queer the coupling of the two models (the Public Value school and the Neo-Weberian model) might seem to some purists on both camps. An example of a strategic approach that encompasses important traits of the Public Value school in what could be considered a Neo-Weberian context is reported in Box 7.2, accounting on strategic management in the Swiss canton of Argovia.

Box 7.2   Government on track of its strategy: outcome-based management in the Canton of Argovia, Switzerland

By *Isabella Pröller*

'*Government is on track*' was the headline of a newspaper article in one of the regional newspapers in the canton of Argovia in March 2010 (see Fricktal24, 27 March 2010).[2] The lead text of the article continues that 'regarding 90 percent of the goals spelled out in the cantonal Development Plan relevant decisions and conceptions have already been passed. . . . The evaluation confirms the high conformity to strategy of the government during its first year in office.' (Fricktal24, 27 March 2010). Such a headline is noteworthy and not common-place in the context of government: not so much for its message of eventual success, but rather for its line of argument and terminology of 'conformity to strategy.' It signals that the government of Argovia publicly committed to a strategy and aimed to act strategically.

The canton of Argovia is located in the northern part of Switzerland between the economic centres of Zürich and Basel. With roughly 630,000 inhabitants, it is the fourth-biggest of the 26 Swiss cantons. The politico-administrative system is characterized by Swiss direct democracy, for example parliamentarians, but also members of the executive government are elected directly, and people vote in referenda on new legislation and relevant new financial expenses. With regard to the members of government, the vote is rather a vote on persons than for parties, for example composition of government in many cases does not reflect majorities in parliament. In Argovia, the government consists of five ministers which, taking as example the legislative period 2013–2016, belonged to five different parties, while in parliament the parties are represented unevenly. Each minister heads one of the departments (ministries), and the government as a whole is supported by the state chancellery in its duties.

Government in the canton of Argovia has committed to run its office, ministries, and activities more strategically. For that purpose, it has introduced a new management system called 'Outcome Oriented Management' (WOV is the German acronym used in Argovia) in 2005 (for details, see www.ag.ch/de/rr/strategie_rr/strategie.jsp). With WOV, processes and instruments were designed and implemented by which the executive level of government, for example the cabinet and the ministers and their administration, have more systematic means to deliberately and proactively steer for strategically relevant issues. The state chancellery acts as an active strategic support unit for government and acts as facilitator and coordinator of the process. As a result, government in Argovia is more proactive and systematic in addressing upcoming strategic issues for the canton, has suitable mechanisms to set priorities and manage them 'through.' Evaluation has shown that also parliament now sees more possibilities for mid-term planning and that the link of managing finances on the one side and tasks on the other side has been considerably increased.

What are the key features and mechanisms in the Argovian strategic management approach? In the beginning of a legislative term, the Argovian government develops and publishes a so-called Development Leitbild, which represents the strategic planning tool for government and provides guidelines for the governmental work. In this Development Leitbild, political directions and priorities are spelled out based on a time horizon of ten years. It is a rather slim document, and the version for the period 2013–2020 comprised about 30 pages specifying nine policy priorities. For each of those priorities, the central challenges, the strategic-political relevance for the canton, and finally the long-term objective of government are described. The ten-year time frame is not linked to or predefined by another mechanism in the Swiss politico-administrative system but has been set up for managerial reasons to explicitly set a time frame beyond legislative cycles which otherwise often dominate political discourse and thinking. So, the ten-year planning period should only encourage and enable to spell out long-term thinking and objectives by political actors in government. However, even though set up for ten years, the Leitbild document is updated for every new government coming into office, and therefore is renewed and republished at least every four years.

The strategic and political priorities spelled out in the Development Leitbild are then implemented by another instrumental innovation, the four-year tasks and financial planning. The tasks and financial planning are consolidated and managed as a mid-term planning, which includes the current and the three upcoming years, but is yearly updated, for example each year a new four-year planning is drafted, extended by one year. It is structured in 44 task areas and 150 services groups and presents the financial planning (e.g. the budget) as part of the tasks planning (e.g. objectives, performance indicators).

On top of those planning tools and processes, the canton of Argovia has developed a strategic environment monitoring. For this, about 150 sources (research, think tanks, associations, national and international authorities, etc.) are systematically monitored: those sources are defined, and responsibilities and tasks in monitoring each of those are assigned. The results of the monitoring are presented in a regular meeting, further analyzed, and ultimately also prioritized on which issues to pursue. The monitoring analyses are reported to government and on selected key issues individual strategic reports are prepared and published. As a consequence, the strategic management system developed in Argovia not only relied on planning but also included an 'early warning system' which in the past had already led to changes and implications for the long- and mid-term planning of the canton.

Being aware of the complexity and comprehensiveness of a strategic approach to public management, of course, the efforts and innovations in the canton of Argovia continued to further improve the system. So, the system of strategic management goes far beyond a mere 'planning school' approach and the instrumental innovations just outlined earlier; it also includes other issues like outcome evaluations, leadership competences, controlling and reporting processes, but also structural changes. As an example of a structural effect, the restructuring of the state chancellery can be mentioned. The state chancellery defines its mission among other things but first as 'effectively supporting government in coping with current and future challenges' (www.ag.ch/de/sk/sk.jsp accessed on 1 May 2014). It acts as strategic management support unit for government. To align with its mission, the staff of the state chancellery, however, did not increase but on the contrary was dramatically reduced at the beginning of the WOV process. This reduction mainly resulted from a concentration of tasks on management support and staff functions, and the restructuring of all non-staff/support functions within line ministries. As a consequence, the chancellery was enabled to concentrate on its management support mission and to free (and to also built up again additional) capacities for strategic management tasks. As of today, the state chancellery's structure includes 'strategy and external relations' as one of its three main departments and has built up capacities to perform its strategic support function more professionally as before.

As it could be appraised in the year 2014, the canton of Argovia disposed of a set of established instruments and routines which enabled the administration and government to identify and address strategic questions and decision. Of course, in this case as well, there are drawbacks and remaining potentials. Besides criticism with regard to user friendliness of instruments, an evaluation of the project stated that the culture of strategic, outcome-oriented control had not (yet) been institutionalized throughout administration. Further, it was critically observed and discussed that – on the contrary to government – parliament hardly uses the array of new control mechanisms implemented for the parliamentary level. While parliament acknowledges that it had better control means than before, it was not yet actually using the newly created control means of outcome-oriented control which would enable it to steer not only the finances but also tasks directly, by setting or changing objectives and indicators [Evaluation der Wirkungsorientierten Verwaltungsführung (WOV) – Schlussbericht, Kanton Aargau: Büro des Grossen Rats, p. 100].

At first sight, the case of WOV in canton of Argovia seems to strongly correspond and rely on the planning school approach of strategic management. The vast design of newly created planning instruments and processes, the clear structuring of the planning and control process are such planning school features. However, WOV in canton of Argovia puts a strong focus on evaluation, feedback, and adaptation not only with regard to implementation of public policy, but also with regard to learn and improve the system itself. In that regard, also learning and emergent school approaches are reflected. Last but not least, WOV in canton of Argovia sees the 'strategists' in its politico-administrative system not only at the parliamentarian and government level. Rather it is designed around a notion of administration – the chancellery, but also departments and offices – as crucial strategists. This notion is more commonly to be found in the Public Value school than classical planning school. To understand WOV in Argovia as a planning school approach to public sector strategic management would misinterpret and ignore very important features of the system as a whole: rather it combines and integrates important features of various schools.

7.3.3 Governance and networks

Since the end of the 1990s, there seems to have been a shift in the emphasis in the public management community, away from the NPM and towards 'governance approaches'; the term 'governance' has taken root and become immensely popular. Governance is an English word quite difficult to translate into other languages (Ongaro and van Thiel 2018c), and used in a variety of ways, across many disciplines and the practice of politics and policy making (Rhodes 1997, provided a review of the notions of governance that proved highly influential on subsequent debates and treatments of the notion; for a standard governance text, see Pierre and Peters 2000; for an adherents', yet critical and interesting, view on the 'governance turn' in public management, see Bovaird and Loeffler 2009). These trends have been explored in an earlier chapter and we here draw out some implications for the analysis of the strategic management of public governance-style reforms.

Broadly speaking, advocates of 'public governance' approaches put emphasis on the steering of society through networks and partnerships between government organizations and 'private' organizations – both businesses and civic society associations, although in certain strands the accent is put especially on the latter, that is on mobilizing the voluntary sector – as the key to providing effective and sustainable solutions to public problems. There is also a strong emphasis in such approaches on networks as the privileged mode of governing transactions, over both hierarchies (associated with the traditional, Weberian bureaucracy) and markets (connected to the NPM). Indeed, the 'public governance' movement in the public administration literature has entwined with the huge literature on 'networks' as a dominant form in modern society (Castells 2010). The guiding idea that public problems cannot be tackled by organizations in isolation, rather it is networks that can provide the most apt solutions, has been translated into a set of ideas about how to analyze and run public services by taking networks, rather than individual public services organizations, as the focus of the analysis (Agranoff 2007; Kickert et al. 1997; O'Toole 1997). We have widely reviewed the literature on networks and collaborations in Chapter 4, delineating its significance for strategic management.

It should be noticed that, whilst the overall shift in emphasis may have represented a novelty and in a number of respects a breakthrough from the previously dominant NPM discourse and practice, the notions of network, partnership, engagement of societal actors in tackling complex public problems, and the like, are far from being a novelty in administrative studies and the social sciences in general. Moreover, the upsurge in the scholarship on governance and networks has been impetuous, but also far from internally consistent, and a variety of definitions, theories, and doctrinal claims are made within such huge strand of literature. It may further be noticed that some strands in this literature display connections and take roots in long-standing strands of literature, like those on intergovernmental relation, multi-level governance, and others (for an overview of some of the interconnections between network theories and the two frames of, respectively, the more 'American' stream of intergovernmental relations literature and the more 'European' – and more recent – strand of the multi-level governance literature, see Ongaro 2010, 2015a; for a critical review of certain profiles of multi-level governance, Ongaro 2015a).

What can be the implications for strategic management? Such reform narrative(s) may be at odds with certain schools of thought in strategic management, like the planning and the positioning schools, with their emphasis on the *individual* public sector organization rather than networks, and with their reliance on the possibility to concentrate all relevant information in one (the design school) or a few (the planning school) minds, capable of processing all the necessary information (a task somehow 'outsourced' to external analysts in the positioning school, in which the analysis of the industry structure guides the identification of the limited set of strategies from which to select the most adequate one for the focal organization to employ). However, it is contended that strategic planning may have adapted to the 'governance revolution' and be nowadays much more receptive to 'incorporating' into strategic planning both the need to operate in inter-organizational settings and the need to empower the organizations staff to be adaptive and responsive, rather than mere executor of higher-level objectives that get cascade upon them (Klijn and Koppenjan 2020). Perhaps the same shortfalls would apply to the resource-based view, with its emphasis on the 'competitive advantage' of the individual organization. More nuanced and articulated is the relationship between the governance narrative and the Public Value school; its founding fathers seem to argue for a peaceful coexistence and complementarity between the two (at least this is our reading of Benington and Moore 2011b, pp. 261–263 in particular), though authors rooted in a public governance/network management perspective might perhaps contend that the governance narrative and the Public Value school are underpinned by radically different (and incompatible?) premises.

However, the repertoire of schools of thought from which to draw for explaining the process and contents of strategy has much expanded. We have encountered in Chapter 3 and widely developed in Chapter 4 the network-based and collaborative models of strategy, a strand of literature focused on private sector organizations whose development somehow mirrors that of network theory in the field of public management. Such models of strategy making are akin to network management approaches, and governance reform narratives may be deemed to create conditions facilitating the application of such models.

Another evident and explicit connection lies in the emphasis that public governance approaches put on the engagement of third-sector and civil society organizations in public services: the analysis of the strategy process of third-sector organizations, notably social enterprises (developed in Chapter 5), is a useful addition to the literature on partnerships (public–private partnerships) and societal organizations engagement in public service delivery. Literature on networks and partnerships may benefit from a more thorough understanding of the strategy process in third-sector organizations, and the latter may borrow from network analysis to expand its reach beyond the (porous) borders of the individual third-sector organization.

Within governance approaches, Osborne's 'New Public Governance' is one of the most management centric accounts (Osborne 2010a). One key idea – beside the emphasis on networks, participatory approaches and partnerships that we have already encountered (and that Osborne sums up around the idea of 'plurality': '[The New Public Governance] posits both a *plural* state, where multiple interdependent actors contribute to the delivery of public services, and a *pluralist* state, where multiple processes inform the policymaking system,' Osborne 2010b, p. 9 – italics in original) – is the idea of the shift from a manufacturer to a service paradigm: the critique made by Osborne, in a series of works, to both 'old' public administration and 'new' public management is that they both share a manufacturer's view of public services, a 'fordist' conception that is (and it was in the past) unfit to the public sector, which is concerned with the delivery of services rather than products. One implication is that strategic management approaches developed for the commercial sector focused on service delivery organizations may represent a more apt source of conceptual tools for the study of public services organizations than models elaborated mainly by studying manufacturers (models that, according to Osborne, have permeated previous models of management adopted in the public sector).

Another set of implications that governance reform narratives bring about concerns the fundamental question 'who is the strategist?' (a question which we revisit and discuss in the final chapter). The direct answer in a public governance narrative is this: politicians rather than career officials. Indeed, both the setting up and the steering of complex networks is more the task of politicians – democratically legitimated – than of tenured officials. One claim of governance narratives is that politics is brought back to the centre of the stage, where it ought to stay (the reasoning goes on), a place whence, by contrast, NPM narratives removed it, by confining politicians to the role of 'defining the targets,' whose attainment was then entrusted to the 'public managers' (useless to say, this is a very stylized representation of the story).

A network perspective seems to have interconnections with a *strategizing approach*, whereby the practice of strategy as a socially situated activity spans beyond the formal borders of one organization (see Chapter 3). Although it may come as a surprise, to relate an approach to strategy that emphasizes the micro, day-to-day activities that 'make up' strategy with an approach that transcends the individual organization at the other side of the spectrum and somehow dissolves the organization into broader networks as the focal unit of analysis, interpretations of strategizing that encompass different levels of praxis (defined as 'the flow of activity in which strategy is accomplished,' Jarzabkowski and Spee 2009) and put emphasis on the macro level of strategy practices (that is, on practices that have an influence at the sector or policy level), may complement the strand of literature on policy networks analysis by bringing human agency more centre stage into the picture.

In conclusion of this section, we should mention that the doctrinal debate on the organization of the public sector is wider than the necessarily abridged account that for reasons of space we could provide here, and beside the narratives of the NPM, the 'governance approaches' and the Neo-Weberian model, others may be added like, *inter alia*, democratic governance (March and Olsen 1996) or the so-called post-NPM perspective (whose proponents argue about a layering of NPM and post-NPM elements, see Christensen and Laegreid 2007 and Box 7.3). We will content ourselves with this synthesis to make the case that the transformative impacts of reform narratives do matter in shaping the context affecting the strategic management of public services organizations.

In the next section, we pull some of the threads together and attempt to sketch a framework for interpreting what we dub 'the strategic space' of a public services organization: the conditions under which strategy may form and be deployed in public services organization.

Two cases from very different countries – both in term of contextual differences and for the reform trajectories undertaken, conclude this section (Box 7.3 and 7.4).

Box 7.3 Strategic management in the Norwegian welfare administration

By *Tom Christensen and Per Lægreid*

The largest reform ever in the public sector in Norway was the reform of the welfare administration in 2005, with a reorganization of the reform in 2008. The main aims of the reform were to get more people from benefits and into the workforce, to increase efficiency and to improve user-friendliness, especially making a more holistic service for the multi-service users. The main structural changes were the merger of the agencies for pension and employment service into a new welfare agency, and the establishment of local welfare offices (one-stop shops) in every municipality as a partnership between the new agency and the locally based social services. Internally, the new organization used a system of performance management and a split centrally between a purchasing and providing units, the latter mostly ICT services, was set up. The reorganization of the reform in 2008 moved more resources up to the regional level, to back-offices. It also was a re-specialization, bringing specialization by purpose back in by establishing pension units.

The background for the reform was a fragmented service structure and the initiative came from the Parliament, in something that could be seen as a post-NPM move. The Parliament's demand was a fully integrated service on all levels. The government at the time, a Conservative-Centre government, backed by the bureaucracy tried to resist the reform, but finally gave in. The minister finally bringing the reform through, acting as an entrepreneur and leading a ministry that has gathered all the three welfare services of relevance, struck a compromise implying only a partial merger, not including the social service in the new organization, but making a partnership. The latter reflected what was politically feasible at the time. The main actor behind the reorganization, also an entrepreneur, was the director of the new welfare agency.

The politico-administrative context surrounding the reform was characterized by a minority coalition government, making reaching a compromise necessary, and a fragmented service delivery structure in the relevant policy sector, increasing the pressure for a more coordinated delivery of welfare services. Even though Norway very much attended (and attends) to values of local self-government, the central government is rather strong and can impose important restructures of public services, as is reflected also in this reform. Even though the local offices are a partnership between the central and local level, it is the central level that has the upper hand and is providing most of the resources.

So, what kind of preconditions is this reform narrative, and the politico-administrative context outlined, giving for strategic management in the welfare administration, and how can we understand strategic management in the welfare administration based on the schools outlined? First, there are obvious elements from the design and strategic planning schools in the reform and reorganization. The main strategy behind the reform is structurally holistic, meaning that the main aims of the reform are believed to be fulfilled through structural merger and partnership, that is this is a structural and not a policy content reform. But the reform approach was divided. On the one hand, it reflected post-NPM structural thoughts concerning the effects of structural mergers. On the other hand, it catered to NPM through a purchaser-provider split and the use of performance management and performance indicators. The preconditions after the structural reform for strategic management was challenging, because the one-stop shops did not actually function in accordance with the stated aims, with too much pressure on the resources, competence, and quality of work, so it was decided through the reorganization to make a differentiation to make the structure work better. The local offices should have the face-to-face contact with the users and furnish them information but send the actual case-handling up to the regional level for decisions and payment of benefits, before the local level again took over concerning helping people to get a job. All this seems to have improved the competence, quality, and rights of users. Concerning the public-provider split, it did not function either, and it was eventually reorganized and removed. But the main performance management system has prevailed, even though it has been criticized for being too detailed.

Is the welfare administration a learning organization like stressed in much of Mintzberg's approach to strategic management? Is it adjusting along the way, in an incremental way? For a long time, learning did not feed back into decision processes, because it had been obvious over a long period that the fragmented service delivery did not function well for the users. Eventually, change occurred through a radical reform, which was certainly not incremental. The reform of this administration was not a case of incremental learning, but the subsequent reorganization of the reform can be understood by resorting to this school. When the management of the new organization after the reform did not function, at different levels, the structure was adjusted learning from the problems encountered in the initial period; likewise, it was found to be appropriate to revise the purchaser-provider split centrally, and that occurred a few years later.

The entrepreneurial school has also something to say about the strategic management in the reform and reorganization process, but not much in the daily life of the welfare organization thereafter. The minister in charge for the decision on the reform, really showed entrepreneurship, because he understood the political dynamics in full. It was impossible not to cater to the Parliament's wish for some integrated services, as it was impossible to define all service as belonging to the central state, which made the compromise feasible. This reflected a screwed political entrepreneur's work: it was a case of political entrepreneurship more than of public entrepreneur in the strategic management sense more widely elaborated in this book. When the reform was decided on, the power of the new agency increased and its leader acted as a strategic entrepreneur in leading the reorganization of the reform that turned out to be necessary, at the organizational and service delivery level. The preconditions for this was that the manifest malfunctioning of the structure designed by the original reform, and the fact the political and administrative high flyers in the ministry were reluctant to accept the new structure, so a reorganization partly turning the clock back was feasible.

A crucial part of the reform and reorganization is to get three former groups of people with different cultures and competences to work together – the pension employees coming from a Weberian judicial culture, the employment people from a more modernized culture, and social service employees with local knowledge and discretion as major assets. According to a cultural school perspective, strategic management in such a mixed and composite culture could be challenging. What happened in the welfare administration was that because of cultural resistance there was not any agreement on a new type of education for people working in the welfare administration, but organizational innovations like teamwork and shoulder-to-shoulder learning did occur, which facilitated the development of a common culture along the way, melding earlier subcultures.

The corporate governance school has also something to say about the use of strategic management in the Norwegian welfare administration, because the performance management system was built on this. Even if this is a rather 'soft' sector, performance management and indicators have been used rather substantially as instruments of control. However, it should be noticed that the welfare agency, because of its political salience, did not enjoy much autonomy, as other more typical NPM-oriented agencies in Norway.

Lastly, the network and collaborative models of strategy can be of relevance. The one-stop shops are a form of collaboration and in themselves a network between two hierarchies, the central and local ones, which makes strategic management at the local level rather challenging. And in a public governance sense, the welfare administration is depending on a good collaboration with the employers concerning getting work opportunities for users. The strategic triangle model (Moore 1995) has also some relevance to understand this case. Specification of the overall mission of purposes of the new organization was important, support and legitimacy for the decisions in the broader political environment was crucial, and how to organize the tasks and implement the decisions was a core issue. In this case, the administrative executives were not neutral instruments in the hands of political executives but had an independent influence on the process and outcome.

Box 7.4 Strategic management in the Chinese health administration

By *Tom Christensen*

The Chinese health services and administration has been through several phases of reform but has struggled to deliver good quality services to affordable prices for most of the population. The march towards the market started in 1978 when hospitals were required to attend to economic measures; later private medical practice was allowed, as a supplement to and relieving of burdens for public hospitals. Fees for patients were also allowed to be charged and hospitals and doctors granted permission to earn extra money, for example on selling medicines (at high prices), so market mechanisms were emerging. The reform efforts were complex and the direction and priorities ambiguous (Li and Chen 2012).

The breakthrough of marketization in the Chinese health services occurred in 1992. Under the pressure from growing demand for health care in the big cities, the government decided to make a distinction between non-profit and for-profit hospitals, meaning a privatization of many hospitals, increasing social inequalities. The hospitals that remained public struggled with reduced public funding and had to seek other sources for financing themselves. On the other hand, the government faced a lot of critique for non-affordable health care services and tried to improve the health coverage both for urban and especially rural areas (Cao and Chen 2011). The period after the turn of the millennium has seen more of a returning to the public nature of health care, improving the health coverage of people, and trying to curb the prices of drugs, through more coordinated efforts among the diverse units in the health administrative system.

The contexts of the Chinese health administration/services and its reforms is rather complex. In a traditional one-party state with a planned economy, eventually called 'socialist market economy,' the central state basically decides all the major health reforms and policies. In that endeavour, the state displays a very complicated structure, at the time this book is being written) as many as 16 ministries involved with related subordinate levels and organizations, which makes coordination challenging (Dong 2009). On the other hand, the central government is also dependent on the local levels – provinces, prefectures, counties, and townships – for provision of services since these levels hold most of the resources for implementing health measures. This brings with it potential problems of implementation but also allows for local experiments, with new health care solutions that eventually would become central policies (Xu 2010).

So what kind of preconditions is the Chinese reform narrative, and the politico-administrative context outlined, giving for strategic management in the health administration, and how can we understand those based on the approaches, or schools, outlined? For the first two periods, the reform narrative was imbued with the NPM focus on transforming a system from monopoly to a partly privatized health care system, with structural and procedural changes and connected focus on performance management and indicators, de-emphasizing social equality norms and values. The performance management system also produced a lot of 'gaming' and tampering with data, reporting from lower levels on reaching all the main goals of health service. The last period showed a marked emphasis on rebalancing the system, reflecting more of a post-NPM attitude, with more emphasis on centralization and coordination, collective public solutions, and more control of health service, in particular private ones, etc. Solutions that give less leeway to the local levels in steering health services.

The corporate governance school has something to say about the use of strategic management in the health administration in China. Performance management has been used rather substantially as instrument of control. The problem has been that in such a vast country, with such a complex politico-administrative system, it is not easy to ascertain whether the results reported through the health indicators have been real or tampering and manipulation have extensively occurred. Chinese media have over the years been replete with stories of the gaming in the system, the massive use of 'creative statistics,' pretty loosely coupled to reality.

Is the health service administration in China a learning organization, in the way theorized in Mintzberg's approach? One problem with learning in the Chinese health care system was that it focused on particular aspects and aimed at vicarious learning from experiences of very different countries and contexts, like the USA. The eventual radical change in the system attended mostly to hospitals in the big cities and proposed privatization and market principles, instead of broadening the coverage of primary health care, in particular in the country-side, where the largest problems lay. This widened the social gaps in the system. The reforms in the last decades reveal more of a genuine learning organization, where compensatory solutions for broader health coverage are implemented to prevent more social inequalities. The entrepreneurial school has something to say about the strategic management in the reform process, in the way that entrepreneurs on the lower levels, through many and diverse experiments of new health care solutions and policies, strove to transform the system from the bottom, at the level of individual public services organizations, which also led to more learning at the central level.

There is definitely a vertical and horizontal dimension in considering the reform of health care in China. The horizontal one is very challenging, since most of the 16 different ministries involved have different roles and tasks to work with, reflected in the development of different administrative subcultures. There are for example large differences in the stance towards the health administration between the Ministry of Finance, controlling the funding, the Ministry of Civil Affairs, focusing on health care for the needy, and the State Food and Drug Administration, focusing on drug supervision. And vertically, there are large differences between a central health administrative culture and the diverse local cultures, where health services have to be balanced towards other regional and local concerns and tasks.

Lastly, the network and collaborative model of strategy can be relevant. Regional and local experimentation with new health care systems and policies has been most effective when there has been a close cooperation between different levels.

7.4 Pulling the threads together: context, autonomy, strategic space, and strategic management

A key underlying issue recurring throughout this book regards why and under what conditions public services organizations can make a strategy. The analysis of the politico-administrative context and the transformative effects of public management reform narratives provides part of the answer. One way of modelling contextual influences is in terms of considering their effects on what we could label 'the strategic space' of a public services organization. In this perspective, the extent to which strategy – at least organizational-level strategy – can develop is a function of its strategic space. In turn, such strategic space is a function of the organization's autonomy, of its 'endogenous' orientation to strategy making, and of the political-societal expectations towards it and the corresponding obligations towards the political community it serves and the accountability bases under which it operates. Such expectations and obligations are only partly embodied in the statute or mandate of the organization (which for the state as a whole is the written or unwritten constitution). In more formal terms, we suggest that for a public services organization:

Strategy formation = function (strategic space)

Where

Strategic space = function (organizational autonomy; political - societal expectations and obligations)

where

- Organizational autonomy is the extent to which the organization can decide on its own goals and/or resources without external approval/authorization, function = (politico-administration and cultural context, reform narratives);
- Political-societal expectations towards the public services organization and the obligations of the agency = function (politico-administrative and cultural context, reform narratives, and economic and societal needs of the communities the public services organization serves).

The way in which such factors co-evolve over time, and hence the way the strategic space of a public services organization changes, is non-linear (i.e. factors interact in complex ways and are not necessarily simply additive). We now turn to discuss the main dimensions shaping such strategic space in turn.

Organizational autonomy

There are two reasons why the organizational autonomy is crucial. On the one hand, it is a precondition for strategic management: without some extent of autonomy, the unfolding of any organizational strategy process may be clamped. On the other hand, the search for more autonomy might be an end in itself for the organization, a substantive content of its strategy. A clear example is provided by Carpenter (2001), whose careful investigation of the forming of the American federal administration shows and explains why in the first decades of the twentieth century, certain US federal agencies were capable of acquiring considerable autonomy from their political 'masters' in the Congress, whilst others were not (cases of the former are the US Department of Agriculture and the Post Office, a case of the latter is the Interior Department).

Key ingredients in this autonomizing process of these agencies were the building of reputation for the agency (convincing key stakeholders that the agency delivers something uniquely valuable), the setting up of supporting networks, and ensuring continuity in the organizational leadership. These three factors helped an agency acquire a high level of organizational capacity. This capability-building exercise may well be interpreted as a process of formulation and implementation of an organizational strategy, even more so if we consider that such a high level of autonomy was not determined by the initial design: in the words of the author (and considering the very different terminology employed by Carpenter from the conventional terminology in the strategic management literature that we have adopted throughout this book), 'Bureaucratic capacity is first and foremost a function of organizational evolution. Neither formal authority nor spending suffices to create an organizational ability to discover and solve problems' (Carpenter 2001, p. 28).

How can such 'autonomy' be defined? This topic has already been widely explored in the public management literature, notably in the strand of literature investigating public agencies. Studies on the 'public agency' phenomenon have introduced the notions of managerial and policy autonomy (Laegreid and Verhoest 2010; Verhoest et al. 2004a, 2004b, 2012). The former concerns the extent to which the organization may decide on resources (acquisition and employment of financial and human resources, that is, capital and labour, intended as the main 'production factors') without the authorization/approval of the 'parent' administrations to which the agency is accountable (for example a fiscal agency will usually be accountable to the finance ministry). The latter may be defined as the extent to which the organization may decide on the targets of the policy and/or the instruments to pursue such targets.

Agencies are just a subset of public services organizations: the extent of autonomy agencies enjoy is located in an intermediate area between, on the one hand, 'independence' and, on the other hand, very limited if not outright absence of autonomy. Independence is the 'realistic' maximum of autonomy which characterizes authorities like a Central Bank, that usually has both policy autonomy (it decides on the targets of the monetary policy and the instruments to better pursue them, only based on a given mandate) and managerial autonomy (it decides on the acquisition of capital and human resources without external constraints set or overseen by 'parent administrations,' ultimately responding only to the provisions of the statutory act establishing it). Limited autonomy is for example the case of a directorate or department hierarchically embedded into a larger organization, like a ministry, or also a nominally distinct entity that is de facto entirely hetero-directed by external decision makers: these organizational units may have some leeway but are simply not allowed to form their own strategy. Elective governments, generally speaking, enjoy higher levels of policy autonomy (though extensively depending on the system of intergovernmental relations in the given polity), whilst managerial autonomy may vary widely across the different kinds of public services organizations depending on the features of the governmental system.

Vining (2011) argues that autonomy is for public sector organizations the functional equivalent of 'competitiveness and profitability' for business sector enterprises. He argues that

> [E]xternal forces constrain public agency autonomy in the public sector in the same way that external forces constrain enterprise 'margin' or profit in the

private sector . . . the degree of competitiveness and profitability is of interest to business executives because a key to an effective strategy is 'a defendable position against the five competitive forces' [and similarly] in the public sector autonomy provides a 'defendable position' vis-à-vis external forces.

(Vining 2011, p. 68)

The key passage in the work of Vining (whose contribution we have already discussed in Chapter 2) for the discussion reviewed in this section is the statement that 'autonomy is a functional equivalent to what profitability is for the commercial sector, because it is a condition of the long-term survival and economic sustainability of a public organisation.' Organizational autonomy is thus of crucial significance for strategic management. Vining further argues that both policy autonomy and managerial autonomy are a goal of public agencies (according to a line of argumentation whereby bureaucrats are assumed to want more control of discretionary resources), and he stresses that autonomy is a condition for strategy to occur ('Given the importance of both policy autonomy and fiscal autonomy in prescribing the strategic degrees of freedom available to managers, the combination of both is called the degree of strategic autonomy,' Vining 2011, p. 69). In other words, the basic argument of Vining is that autonomy is both a precondition for strategy making and a goal of strategy.

It is important to recognize that this assertion about organizational autonomy as both a precondition and a goal of the organizational strategy is far from being a novel proposition: in various national scholarly communities, the centrality of autonomy for public management is amply recognized and widely debated (to mention one scholarly community of public management of which one author of this book has first-hand knowledge, this theme has been debated in Italy since the first half of the twentieth century: for an overview of this debate, see Borgonovi 1984 and Zangrandi 1994). The very notion of 'sustainability' as a key dimension of performance ascribes a central significance to an organization's autonomy: it makes sense to speak of an organization attaining long-term sustainability only if this same organization enjoys a certain extent of autonomy (see Pollitt and Bouckaert 2017).

As a precondition for strategy, the argument is that without any actual autonomy in deciding on resources and/or on policy goals, any possibility of developing a strategy for the organization is hollowed out (we stress 'actual' autonomy, as enjoyed by decision makers, rather than *de jure* discretion, as afforded by the regulatory frame, since the two may significantly differ, see Yesilkagit and van Thiel 2008, and it is the latter to matter for the strategy formation process). If in fact external decision makers (it may be noticed that autonomy is an inherently relational concept: autonomy 'from' external decision makers) or other more impersonal forces are able to entirely shape the behaviour of the organization in its relations with the environment, then the very premises for conceiving of an organization's strategy as distinct from environmental pressures disappear.

As a goal of strategy, the basic argument that an overarching goal of public managers is increasing their organization's autonomy may be accepted because autonomy is to some extent instrumental to pursuing any other set of objectives and values.

The case of the privatization of the railways in Japan is also illustrative of an inner dynamic: the regaining of 'sufficient' autonomy to pursue its strategy by an otherwise over-constrained public corporation (Box 7.5).

Box 7.5 The privatization of the Japanese National Railways as a politician-led solution to the problem of a baffled public corporation

By *Hiroko Kudo*

Introduction

The Japanese National Railways (JNR) was privatized on 1 April 1987 as part of the political reform realized by the Prime Minister Yasuhiro Nakasone (Prime Minister 1982–1987). The dominating Liberal Democratic Party (LDP) of Japan had promoted political as well as administrative reforms since the beginning of the 1980s as a response to the problem of a soaring public debt. The reform included two other major privatizations: *Nippon Telegraph and Telephone Public Corporation* and *Japan Tobacco* and *Salt Public Corporation,* and a series of deregulation interventions, especially in the field of trade and industry.

The privatized Japan Railways (JR) consisted of six regional railway companies, Japan Freight Railway Company, Railway Telecommunication Company (later Softbank Telecom Corp.), Railway Information Systems Co. Ltd., Institute for Shinkansen (bullet train), Railway Technical Research Institute, and the JNR Settlement Corporation. Regional railway companies still operate (at the time this book goes to press) in their almost original structures, while Institute for Shinkansen and JNR Settlement Corporation were dissolved in 2003 into a governmental agency, an independent administrative institution called Japan Railway Construction, Transport and Technology Agency.

Japanese privatization had been considered a success case and had become a model to Sweden in 1988 and later to Germany, the Netherlands, and the UK – though in appraising the 'success' of the privatized companies, some distinctive features of the Japanese case should be considered, including the share of train transportation (which is in Japan much higher than most other counterparts) and the capabilities and technological standard of JNR (which were much higher than those of its homologues elsewhere, see Wolmer 2002), factors which made it difficult to replicate the original success in other countries.

One aspect of the Japanese railways case is of special interest for our discussion of the relation between strategy and autonomy, the fact that JNR was so restrained in its operational autonomy up to the point to be incapacitated to act autonomously: managers were unable to form an organizational strategy. Privatization was a solution contrived mainly by politicians in government to overcome conditions which hindered the operations of this public corporation – alongside reaching eminently 'political' goals, notably reducing the excessive (at least from their standpoint) influence of certain trade unions.

The moral of this story is *not* that privatization in itself is necessarily a solution to efficiency problem – rather this story highlights that autonomy is a precondition for public services organizations – be they public or private in statutory terms – to form a strategy, which in turn is generally conducive to higher performance (see Chapter 7).

The main traits of the privatization of the Japanese railways

Several significant features qualify the Japanese railways privatization (University of Tokyo, Faculty of Law Library 2004; Unyusho Ministry of Transport 1986). First, differently from European counterparts that introduced a separation between government or some public body managing the infrastructure and private companies managing passenger services, the Japanese approach to privatization did not operate such 'unbundling.' Second, the Japanese government opted for the split of JNR into regional companies, rather than adopting an open system approach.

Another important characteristic was the overstaffing of JNR, due to a historical reason. JNR, from its very institution, was forced to hire the former employees of the railway companies established by the Japanese government in China before the Second World War. JNR operated as a welfare institution part and parcel of the labour policy targeting these personnel, a fact which turned out to be a major issue in the privatization process (Sumiya 2003). This is why the leading figure in the reform process, Professor Mikio Sumiya, a labour economy expert who served as the chairman of the Committee for Supervision on Restructure of JNR, had as major task to discuss the dismissal strategies with the labour unions, chairing as many as 159 meetings between June 1983 and March 1987 (University of Tokyo, 2004).

A number of politicians, historians, and political scientists have put forward the interpretation that crushing the influence of the major labour union in the industry (the National Railway Workers' Union, or NRU) was a driver of privatization. Former Prime Minister Nakanose declared that '(we) wanted to crash the General Council of Trade Unions of Japan. We were aware that the collapse of NRU would lead to the collapse of General Council of Trade Unions of Japan and we did it' (interview to the former Prime Minister Nakasone, published on *AERA*, 30 December 1986 – AERA 1986). This 'power school' interpretation of the events may contain some degree of truth; however, it does not explain the whole picture. A careful revision of the materials of the Committee for Supervision on Restructure of JNR (re-edited by the reference room of the Faculty of Economics, University of Tokyo) reveals that the labour unions of JNR, which included other unions like the National Railway Motive Power Union (NRMU), were not monolithic and their position changed in the course of the negotiations (University of Tokyo, 2004, Sumiya 2003). The agreement with the unions provided for privatizing approximately 70% of the JNR, let the new companies continue to hire about 220,000 employees, and charging the government and JNR with the debt (JNR was then dissolved in March 1987).

Background of privatization

Historical and systemic issues of Japanese government

After the Second World War, Japan started its astonishing climb that led it to become the world's 'economic miracle' (Clesse et al. 1997). One of the most popular views to explain this development was that power in Japan was central-ized in the hands of 'Japan Inc.' – a ruling triad, consisting of the elite of the bureaucracy, the ruling political party (LDP), and big business (Hayao 1993; Mishima 1998). According to this view, bureaucracy was the key actor of the three, helped by its long tradition, prestige, and expertise. The significance of the 'Japan Inc.' view in creating this 'iron triangle' of administrative, political, and economic elites has been emphasized both to explain the 'economic miracle' of the 1960s–1970s and to account for the extant difficulties Japan faces in conduct-ing systemic reform (Kerbo and McKinstry 1995; McVeigh 1998; Price 1997).

A cogent interpretation of this view is provided by Curtis (1999), who focuses particularly on the '1955 regime' (Stockwin 1997a, 1997b). Curtis suggests that the system was maintained by four mutually supportive pillars: (i) a broad pub-lic consensus to make Japan a leading economic global force; (ii) the presence of large interest groups with close links to political parties; (iii) total one-party dominance; and (iv) a prestigious and powerful bureaucracy (Curtis 1999).

As the country moved from an industrial to a post-industrial economy, the interests of business, farmers, and labour became more diverse and their alli-ance of interests attenuated (Curtis 1999). Special interests were represented by their political representatives called *zoku*, which literally means 'tribe.' *Zoku* were members of the Japanese parliament, usually of the dominant LDP, who specialized in a particular policy area and had close personal contacts with public servants in their corresponding ministries or bureaus. Hence, the 'iron triangle' relations underpinning the 'Japan Inc.' development model were reinforced at the level of these policy communities or sub-governments (Hayao 1993; Callon 1995).

Despite being a major player in these 'iron triangles,' the bureaucracy was still perceived as a beacon of competency and integrity, safeguarding the Japanese national public interest against the short-sighted behaviour of politicians (Koh 1989; Curtis 1999). This reputation, however, was significantly eroded by a num-ber of widely criticized policy failures and high-profile scandals involving public servants. Scandals and concerns about political corruption are certainly not new to Japan (Curtis 1999). The important difference between most recent scandals and those in previous decades is that these scandals now appear far more fre-quently and have more visibly involved bureaucrats (Stockwin 1997a, 1997b). One of the most prominent scandals in post-war Japan was the 1988 'Recruit scandal,' which involved insider stock deals. The scandal claimed many top poli-ticians as its victims; however, what was even more shocking to the public was the revelation that senior public servants were also implicated in the scandal. This is exactly the same period of the privatization of three major public corporations, which was decided not only on economic but also on political ground.

One of the objectives of administrative reforms had been to reduce the size of government, in terms of both public expenditure and staff. This history of downsizing intervention has nowadays produced one of the slenderest public sectors at the national level among industrialized democracies. In the 1960s and again in the 1980s, the reforms stemming from the works of the Provisional Commission for Administrative Reform (PCAR) led to significant cutbacks and the parcelling out of public competencies to local governments or public corporations (in the 1960s) and to massive privatizations in the 1980s. The Second PCAR, well known as *Dokou Rincho* (PCAR) after the name of its chairman, was indeed the major driver of the privatization of JNR.

Economic, managerial, and political issues

JNR had been instituted in 1949 as a national public corporation but ran into troubles since 1964 (In 1964, JNR registered the first loss and after 1980, the annual loss amounted more than 1 trillion yen), partially due to the construction of Shinkansen or the bullet train but also because of rapid motorization of the country and high labour cost. On the other hand, the government continued to invest in construction of local lines, supported by the 'Plan for Remodelling the Japanese Archipelago' promoted by the Prime Minister Kakuei Tanaka. In 1986, when the discussion for its privatization initiated, JNR had serious financial trouble, accumulating 15,500 billion yen of net operating loss carry forwards.

JNR lost almost two-thirds of its share in passenger and freight transportation between 1950 and 1985. Since the beginning of 1970s, car became the most important transportation means. JNR had around 400,000 employees under one national and unified contract, making it difficult to manage the human resources efficiently; all investment and human resource management plans were subject to national regulation. JNR was incapacitated to act autonomously: managers were unable to form an autonomous strategy. The solution for the Japanese government, made explicit in a 1982 report, lay in privatization and the splitting up of JNR into various regional operators. The Committee for Supervision on Restructure of JNR was subsequently established, based on the law of 13 May 1983.

To accomplish the privatization process, the Japanese government had to set up a wide range of alliances: it closely collaborated with Transportation *zoku* of LDP, which initially strongly opposed privatization but later adopted a collaborative stance; it developed strong ties with the NRMU, which became a counterpart of the Committee already in 1982, leaving the mainstream NRU alone in the negotiation process; it more broadly worked out solutions that might accommodate as much as possible to manifold interests at stake. Various figures in the executive government, the Committee Chairman, JNR managers (one of the key managers was Yoshiyuki Kasai, personnel manager of JNR and current president – at the time this book goes to press – of the Central Japan Railway Company), and labour union leaders all performed a central role in the process.

Context – both the cultural and politico-administrative context and the reform narratives – affects the autonomy of public services organizations. The very institutional design of the public sector – of local governments, public agencies, health care providers, schools, universities, and so on – in a given jurisdiction affects all dimensions of agency autonomy. Administrative and managerial reforms also affect autonomy: rules and routines in the areas of personnel administration exert an influence on the managerial autonomy of all the organizations in the jurisdiction; financial and audit rules and routines affect the financial autonomy of public services organizations in the jurisdiction; procurement rules influence the autonomy public agencies have in acquiring and employing the inputs of their production processes, and so on (Barzelay 2001, 2003). Rules and routines in areas such as labour regulation, procurement, audit, financial administration and accounting, etc. – which we summarize as 'input controls' – exert an influence especially on managerial autonomy.

It is not only input controls in place to have an influence on autonomy, however; also outcome-oriented controls, like those introduced by public management reforms in certain countries, especially Anglophone ones, affect strategic space (Stewart 2004). Outcome controls may constrain an organization: externally set targets that get defined outside the interaction with the agency and are mainly imposed over it by the minister powerfully limit the organization's autonomy, notably its policy autonomy. Such scenarios may lead the agency to 'have little alternative but to resort to tactics of control – leading, at the extreme, to a bureaucracy that survives by keeping its Minister in the dark, and its clients under its thumb' (Stewart 2004, p. 19), which poses an issue: the smaller the strategic space, the more other forms of bureaucratic politics may emerge.

Summing up on this point, reform narratives exert a profound influence on the conditions in which public agencies operate; hence, they affect their autonomy, alongside affecting the political-societal expectations towards the public services organization. Reform narratives are powerful shapers of the strategic space of public services organizations.

Political-societal expectations towards the public services organization and its accountability bases

Political-societal expectations towards a public services organization and its accountable bases – what it is expected of it – also shape the very premises of strategy. What an organization is for, what is expected of it by the society in which it is established and operates, gives shape to the very premises of what strategy is for – an argument much in line with the idea of the 'ecology of public administration' à la John Gaus: that it is impossible to understand public administration if not within the society where it is established and operates.

The starting point in understanding the expectations that a society (individuals, communities, economic agents for and not-for-profit forming and formed by the broad societal contexts) vests in public services organizations is informed by the cultural and politico-administrative contexts in a given jurisdiction. Therefore, context shapes what is expected of a public services organization and therefore shapes the very premises of its strategy.

Political-societal expectations are contextual yet far from being immutable; indeed, certain societal expectations may change relatively fast. For example, new technologies and the development of e-commerce affect expectations towards governments about modes of delivery to be reproduced also by public services organizations (Pollitt 2012). The effects of technological developments as both enablers of new modes of service delivery and shapers of novel expectations may inform and transform societal expectations towards the modalities of delivery of public services, a process that may often later be reflected into a diverse set of statutorily prescribed obligations for the public services organization. On the other hand, certain features like statutory obligations for certain public organizations may remain unaltered over long time periods, providing a more stable foundations for what is expected of a public organization. Either way, context is a key shaper of what is expected of the strategy of a public services organization, hence it moulds the very premises on which strategy can be formed.

Absence of strategy

A final reflection, after having examined how context shapes the strategic space of its organization – namely, its autonomy and its obligations/accountability bases – concerns the meaning of 'absence' of strategy: what does it mean to say that an organization is not making any strategy at all?

The question is not confined to public sector organizations: Inkpen and Choudhury (1995) discuss conditions under which strategy may be absent in any organization (though their empirical evidence is mainly about private organizations). Absence of strategy may occur under conditions of major change in which 'direction is lost' and the organization fluctuates and is pulled in different directions by external forces (in many respects, this is the position of an entire strand of work in strategic management: the environmental school of thought assigns the environment a decisive role and the borders of the organization are interpreted as 'collapsing' under the pressure of such external forces – see Mintzberg et al. 2009).

Absence of strategy may also be the outcome of a deliberate decision. This latter option may be especially significant for public sector organizations: awaiting inputs from the political masters and passively adapting and complying with regulatory pressures may be a stance – indeed in itself strategic – deliberately pursued and adopted, as the best way to satisfy the 'main stakeholders' – political masters, and citizens whose collective will is compounded in representative democracy and produces collective choices through laws and regulations. In public services organizations, action is mandated rather than being based on individual will as in the private sector sphere (Lynn 2006): regulation and political principals may dictate what 'proper behaviour' is (its 'administrative duty,' see Johanson 2009), and such inputs may be deemed to suffice. Indeed, a passive stance may well help agencies adapt to ever-mutable circumstances and to the fickle pronouncements of political masters.

Yet by itself, the administrative mandate is not enough to determine (nor predict) the actual behaviour of an organization. Public services organizations do make strategies (indeed the absence of strategy is in itself a strategic stance), hence we need to comprehend it to understand the organizational behaviour of public services organizations, and ultimately their impact on public policy making, and how they meet political-societal expectations. Moreover, as argued later (see Chapter 8), absence of strategy may be detrimental to performance (Andrews et al. 2012).

7.5 Concluding remarks: revisiting the 'schools of strategy' approach

The previous discussion of contextual influences does not provide any deterministic approach to strategy: neither the possession of some autonomy, nor changes in societal expectations towards the agency, nor reform narratives spurring public managers to engage strategically with their organization do by themselves determine strategy.

It is necessary to resort to the schools of thought of strategy delineated and discussed in the previous chapters to identify the active drivers of strategy making for a public services organization.

The schools that we have reviewed and the case studies provided as examples throughout this book suggest the drivers for strategy formation are varied: from the strategizing by multiple actors in one case (e.g. the case of the European Training Foundation, illustrated in Box 3.1), to the strong leadership of a public entrepreneur providing vision and energizing a newly established agency in another case (e.g. the case of the European Aviation Safety Agency, see Box 2.4), to the functional and structural conditions enabling the dynamic renewal of the key capabilities in yet another case (the Calgary Health Region discussed in section 3.1), and so on.

However, the societal and political expectations about the public services organization – the taken for granted premises rooted in a specific administrative tradition – and the varied degree of autonomy enjoyed by a public services organization do make a difference in how strategy forms. Organizational strategies unfold in different politico-administrative 'houses,' and such contextual influences can never be ignored. This proposition warns against any naïve endorsement of any alleged 'global recipe' for the strategic management of public services organizations, valid always and anywhere. Such recipes may be fashionable (at least for a short time) but are unlikely to have universalistic validity and law-like generalizability, and may indeed be dangerous if adopted in ways insensitive to the basic and enduring contextual differences (Pollitt 2013) discussed in this chapter.

Notes

1 A problem which is at the core of another theoretical framework that Pollitt and Bouckaert have also applied to the comparative analysis of the public sector: Hofstede's famous framework for the analysis of organizational cultures (see Hofstede 2001).
2 Fricktal24, 27 March 2010, Regierungsrat ist auf Kurs, www.fricktal24.ch/Aargau.244* M5dcbbe39a7d.0.html accessed on 28 April 2014 [translated by author].

8   Strategy and performance

One question has been looming throughout the previous chapters, a question whose answer is vital for the very rationale of any book on strategic management in public services organizations: what is the impact of strategically managing a public services organization on its performance? Does performance change for the better (i.e. improves) because of the 'strategic choices' that are made in a public services organization, as contrasted to the situation in the absence of strategy? In other words, does strategic management make a difference? And if so, how and to what extent?

It is the main task of this chapter to address such questions. Leading authors on this theme notice that 'The idea that public organizations perform better if they adopt the 'right' strategy is prevalent in generic management theory, public management literature, policy debates, governmental reforms and popular culture' (Andrews et al. 2012, p. 149) and these authors have made, through their work, a major contribution to demonstrating that the widely held idea that strategic management does make a positive difference to performance is grounded, though they also warn about the complexity of the causal chains linking different strategies to diverse dimensions of performance in public services organizations (Andrews et al. 2012, see especially pp. 146–148 and 158–162). A meta-analysis of 87 correlations from 31 empirical studies conducted by George et al. (2019) suggests that, specifically, strategic planning improves organizational performance:

> A random-effects meta-analysis reveals that strategic planning has a positive, moderate, and significant impact on organizational performance. Meta-regression analysis suggests that the positive impact of strategic planning on organizational performance is strongest when performance is measured as effectiveness and when strategic planning is measured as formal strategic planning. This impact holds across sectors (private and public) and countries (U.S. and non-U.S. contexts).
>
> (George et al. 2019, p. 810)

As Bryson (2021, p. 13) argues:

> [T]he study suggests that strategic planning should be part of the standard managerial repertoire – in marked contradiction to many of the critiques of strategic planning. Further, and again in contrast to critiques, the formality of the strategic processes (i.e., the extent to which strategic planning includes internal and

DOI: 10.4324/9781003054917-8

external analyses and the formulation of goals, strategies, and plans) is important to enhancing organizational performance.

Finally, Bryson observes that strategic planning is 'particularly potent in enhancing organizational effectiveness (i.e., whether organizations successfully achieve their goals), but it should not necessarily be undertaken in the hope of achieving efficiency gains' (George et al. 2019, p. 810), thereby suggesting that the relationship between strategic management and performance is composite: different models of strategy, used in combination, may lead to performance improvement along certain dimensions of performance (in the case discussed by Bryson of combining strategic planning with the strategizing approach, this may lead to enhanced organizational effectiveness, but not, or not necessarily, to more efficiency).

In the previous chapter, we have discussed the argument that autonomy and permanence may be the overarching goal of public organizations (Vining 2011). Yet it is dubious that the public to which public services organizations are accountable may be satisfied to know that public organizations are effective in pursuing the inward-facing goal of ensuring their own survival. This is the reason why the relationship between the forming of strategy and (enhanced) performance is a crucial issue. The positive contribution of strategy to performance is part of the very rationale for interest in the strategic management of public services organizations, as we discuss in Chapter 1. More broadly, we argue throughout this chapter that the adoption of a 'schools of thought' approach to strategic management in the public sector (paralleling and hopefully matching the contribution made by Mintzberg and colleagues to the study of strategy in the private/commercial sector) may further our understanding of 'how strategy matters' for public services performance levels.

In the unfolding of this chapter, we at first dwell on the notion of 'performance' and its relationship with public management (section 8.2), before delving into the issue of whether and how strategy may make a difference to the performance of public services organizations (sections 8.3 and 8.4).

8.1 Defining performance and linking it to organizational strategy

Performance measurement and management have become increasingly important in many public services settings, but this domain is far from uncontested and raises a number of important issues. Jenny Lewis's case on research performance management systems in Australian universities (see Box 8.1) highlights their connection with national-level NPM-style reforms. The (re)design of successive metrics within this system reflected changes of political control and also extensive bargaining within the academic system about choice of appropriate methods to be used (e.g. metrics vs peer review; quantitative vs qualitative assessment). There was recurrent contest, for example, as to which scientific journals were ranked in official lists as top class ('A star' journals) and why.

This national performance management system in turn intensified performance management within individual higher education institutions, with the danger that crude quantity-based measures could be overemployed. The implications of the more elaborate performance management regime – and the resulting judgements arrived at – for the career of the individual academics could be considerable.

Box 8.1   Research performance management in Australia: from quantity to quality?

By Jenny M. Lewis

National research policy determines how funding for university research will be allocated, and this in turn informs the strategic choices that individual universities make in organizing their internal structures and how managers (department heads) communicate with academics. Concerns about the accountability of institutions and individuals receiving public funding for research moved to centre stage in the 1980s. The foundations for this are the familiar and well-rehearsed set of socio-economic challenges and the growing acceptance of a set of organizing ideas focused on frugality and efficiency, often labelled New Public Management. The concurrent expansion of the university sector increased the need to find a rational mechanism for distributing limited funds. As a consequence, Australia introduced a performance-based research assessment system in 1995. This has had a significant impact on strategic management within universities, with a number of important consequences for academics in regard to their research activity.

Australia has, in effect, a dual funding model for research. The Australian Research Council and National Health and Medical Research Council provide the bulk of competitive research grant funding. Basic research capacity in universities is funded by research block grants and administered by the Federal Department responsible for research and tertiary education. The various grant schemes use a mix of inputs to calculate funding allocations, with the combinations varying depending on the scheme. The inputs used include:

- Research student total load;
- Research student total completions;
- Research income;
- Research publications; and
- Previous programme payments.

Unlike the research assessment in the UK (called 'Research Assessment Exercise (RAE) – and since 2014 Research Excellence Framework (REF)), the initial Australian system did not include peer review panels but was presumed to incorporate peer review through the fact that there are elements of this in the marking of theses (research student completions), the assessment of competitive grant applications (research income), and the refereeing of research publications. Most inputs were composed of several measures, some of which incorporate weightings and other differentiation metrics. There was an annual calculation of funding for each university, based on a formula that includes quantities of publications, research income, research degree completions, and research degree enrolments (the research quantum). Not surprisingly, this led university managers to encourage academics to publish in greater quantities, and there was an increase in publication numbers as well as a proliferation of new journals to publish the growing number of articles being produced by academics.

In 2005, the incumbent (conservative) Australian government released its plans for moving to a new system called the Research Quality Framework (RQF). This looked much more like the UK's RAE with assessment of quality by peer review panels and a five-year time frame instead of annual reporting. The RQF also included an assessment of research impact based on things such as reports to government and industry, patents and licenses, expert advice to governments, influence on policy, and media presence.

A change to a Labor government in 2007 saw the demise of this idea and the introduction of a new system called Excellence in Research for Australia (ERA), which was first implemented in 2010. This was also clearly influenced by the RAE, with the unit of assessment shifting from the institution to a discipline base, and a greater emphasis on active peer review using discipline panels within eight clusters, which review a 20% sample of research outputs for the relevant discipline. Each cluster uses different technical approaches to evaluation to fit with the different types of research being assessed. The inclusion of an (external) impact score, proposed in the RQF documents, was not part of the ERA (although this found its way into the REF in the UK, first fully implemented in 2014).

In essence, the most important shift in the ERA was away from the heavily quantitative approach to measuring publications (the 'more is better' message associated with the previous system), to a stronger emphasis on quality, with journal and publisher rankings in place to differentiate publications on quality and impact grounds, the inclusion of bibliometrics in some cases, and the introduction of panels. This shift was fuelled by evidence that the composite index had resulted in an increase in the quantity of research publications but that there had been a simultaneous decrease in quality as indicated in research impact factor data.

The earlier system did not provide rankings (just a quantum). The new ERA scale ranked disciplines within universities as follows:

5 – outstanding performance well above world standard
4 – performance above world standard
3 – average performance at world standard
2 – performance below world standard
1 – performance well below world standard
n/a – not assessed due to low volume of research outputs.

A controversial aspect of the ERA system was the associated quality ranking of journals in each discipline into four ranked categories – A* (one of the best journals in the field), A (very high quality), B (high quality), and C (quality), with all other journals designated as 'unranked.' This ranking process was contentious for many reasons, including that a consultation process about the ranking of journals opened up an extended round of bargaining, and a non-transparent process of disciplinary associations and individual journals mounting arguments about why they should be ranked A* or A. As a result, it was unclear how particular journals had been allocated to certain disciplines and how they had been allocated to a specific tier. This ranking was abandoned for the second round of the ERA, conducted in 2012. Otherwise, the ERA was largely unchanged from 2010, and it was being conducted again in 2014 (see Lewis 2013 for a more complete discussion).

A positive evaluation of this shift to the ERA casts it as a move from quantity to quality as the focus of research performance measurement. In terms of strategy, it recognizes that more is not necessarily better. Yet an adherence by both individual staff and university management to a focus on quantity has continued. While department heads now have performance review conversations with academics that go beyond the number of publications produced each year, this remains an important undercurrent in these conversations, even if the new strategy is directed at being published in highly ranked journals. In effect, academics are now being asked to deliver both quantity and quality in their publication efforts, because an informal benchmark based on a quantity approach has been established by the previous system. This, combined with the national assessment process occurring every second year, directs attention to the need to be constantly publishing, rather than taking a longer-term view about producing quality research.

But what is performance and how can it be defined? There appear to be different lenses through which to gauge, or at least to intend and interpret, 'performance.' Focusing the dimension to which Rainey refers to as the 'competence' of the public organization, the most immediate frame of reference is based on the commonly assumed criteria of the economy, efficiency, effectiveness, and sustainability as baselines for assessing the performance of a public organization. In simple terms, a public services organization (or a public programme) is modelled as a system transforming inputs (resources) into outputs, which in turn produce a modification, allegedly an improvement, in the needs of the users of such outputs, to which we refer as outcomes. The model assumes that public institutions are set up to address socio-economic needs: in the pursuit of such needs, public organizations establish objectives concerned with such needs and acquire and employ resources to ultimately address such needs and have an impact on them, which is the expected and/or actual outcome (see Pollitt and Bouckaert 2011, p. 134; also Borgonovi 1984; Borgonovi et al. 2008). The acquisition of resources at the most convenient conditions is named *economy*; the ratio of inputs used to produce the outputs delivered by the organization is defined as *efficiency*; the adequacy of the outputs to engender a certain modification in the needs of the recipients of the outputs, that is the outcomes, is the *effectiveness*; and *sustainability* refers to the long-term relationship between the needs or problems to be tackled and the resources on which the organization may physiologically rely to address such needs (e.g. in relation to a 'reasonable' level of taxation that is acceptable to the community in the long term), on the one hand, and the outcomes of its action (the actual impact the organization has on addressing the needs), on the other hand (see Bouckaert and Hallighan 2008; Van Dooren et al. 2010).

This is only part of what constitutes performance for a public services organization, as the dimensions of fairness, equity and equality, neutrality, openness and transparency, and accountability are all part and parcel of 'good performance' for it (Rainey 2010). These dimensions are at times placed under the category of accountability, and if we adopt this terminology, the performance of a public organization is provided by its competence plus its accountability. We can well say that the efficacy of the definition proposed by Fried (1976) of performance of a public services organization as 'the achievement of collective goals by due process' is probably still unmatched, at least for its capacity of synthesis.

This chapter tackles the question of how strategy relates to performance. In other words, how and to what extent is strategy (the forming of strategy in a public services organization) a determinant of performance?

Addressing such question is made even more challenging both by the consideration that performance is a multidimensional concept (there are multiple dimensions of performance) and by the composite nature of management (what the function of managing an organization is), and of strategic management as part of it. A number of prominent scholars, including George Boyne, Kenneth Meier, Laurence O'Toole, and Hal Rainey and colleagues (for some summative and 'research agenda setting' works, see Boyne 2004; Boyne et al. 2006; Meier and O'Toole 2010; O'Toole and Meier 2011; Walker 2010; Walker et al. 2010) have set up a research agenda explicitly addressing the key issue of what is the influence of managers and the managerial function ('independent variable or cause') on the performance of public services organizations ('dependent variable or effect') controlling for other explanatory factors ('controlling variables'). This research agenda aims at investigating how different dimensions of 'management' (organizational configuration, leadership, management of innovation, etc. – a list in which 'strategy' figures prominently) make a difference to performance.

Within this research mainstream, Andrews, Boyne, Law, Walker, and colleagues have addressed the question of what specifically the influence of strategic management is on the performance of public services organizations, controlling for a range of other factors. These authors have developed a substantial research agenda addressing the question of whether and how the contents and process (formulation and implementation) of strategy affect organizational performance in public sector organizations (most of these findings are recapitulated in Andrews et al. 2012; see also Snow 2012). We revisit their research work to tackle the crucial question of the impact of strategy on performance.

Preliminarily, the reader should be made aware of certain limitations in their study. One point of attention is that in their research work, they gauge performance mainly in terms of effectiveness and service delivery quality, thus possibly overlooking other dimensions of performance, from efficiency to equality of treatment and due process. Another potential limitation concerns the practical usage for managers of such knowledge, an issue which is more problematic than it may appear at first sight: in fact, even if knowledge indicates a certain strategic approach may lead to higher performance, how then to put it into effect in the specific circumstances in which one organization operates? We return to these concerns in the next chapter (dealing with the research of 'best practices' in public management: what practices work under specific circumstances to improve performance) and in the subsequent and final chapter (discussing the nature of strategy and its broader societal significance: strategy as art, science, and profession).

One further point of attention in appraising the scope of the studies carried out by Andrews and colleagues is that their empirical unit of analysis are mainly service departments within local authorities. Whilst this methodological choice enables the authors to enlarge the number of observations (there are many departments within each local authority they studied), it may be questioned whether service departments enjoy enough autonomy to fully deploy a strategy of their own (see Chapter 7).

Other distinctions are also important to keep in mind. Performance may be considered at the level of the individual public organization (organizational performance), or at the higher level of the so-called performance regimes. Performance regimes are composed of the broader frame encompassing the institutional context of performance (who is endowed with the formal rights and other instruments with which to steer public organizations and programmes: the powers assigned to elective organs, bureaucratic organs, and supervisory and judiciary organs that entitle them to intervene on the conditions in which public agencies operate) and the actual performance interventions (what actions these various institutional actors actually take, individually and collectively, to try to influence the performance of public organizations and programmes, see Talbot 2010, p. 81 and Chapters 4 and 5). Performance regimes are obviously influential on performance (as we have seen in Box 8.1), but in this chapter, we mainly restrain our analysis to organizational performance.

Organizational performance should also be distinguished from the performance of individuals: whilst the contribution of staff, and stakeholders at large, is usually crucial to the performance of an organization (and is part and parcel of any organizational strategy), it is on organizational performance and on strategy as a correlate of organizational performance that we centre our attention in this chapter.

There are multiple levels of analysis at which performance and strategy relate. Bouckaert and Hallighan (2008) distinguish between (i) performance administration and measurement; (ii) performance management; and (iii) performance governance (the latter intended more as a guiding idea for a research agenda than as an actual practice in public management). Strategic management links instrumentally to (i) and substantively to (ii). It links instrumentally to (i) because if you can't measure performance at all, it is impossible to test whether strategic management makes a difference to performance; it links substantively to (ii) because strategy is also an approach to managing performance, and performance management at the organizational level may also be interpreted as a component of the strategy process, especially in the planning school (see Poister 2010; Poister et al. 2010); indeed, certain approaches to performance management, especially those more akin to rational planning approaches partly overlap with strategy making in a strategic planning mode. Finally, and at perhaps more abstract a level, approaches like strategy-as-practice and strategizing provide a linkage to the inter-organizational-level and the system-level, and hence may connect strategic management approaches to performance governance as well.

It has opportunely been noticed that also performance management approaches suffer from incomplete (if at all) empirical assessment of their impact on performance: the linkage between the adoption of a performance management system and organizational performance is often posited, yet receives only lacklustre support (Hendrik 2003) in the literature and confined to certain areas of performance (Boyne and Chen 2007; Boyne and Gould-Williams 2003; for an overview of these studies, see Andrews et al. 2012, pp. 72–73). Indeed, performance management is itself often appraised as a component of managerial effectiveness: the very fact of adopting a performance management system becomes a measure of effectiveness, hence of performance (a measure which is often included in these studies, e.g. Yang and Hseih 2007). This is a point of interest for strategic management as well, as also in this field too often the very fact of developing a strategy is sometimes appraised as a 'result' or 'success': a view we would certainly not content ourselves with.

Finally, performance has at times been linked to the theme of 'public value' (see the Public Value school in Chapter 3) and to 'public values': the distinction has been made between value 'in the singular' (how to run the valuing process, and encompassing whom in such process) and values 'in the plural' (value systems in the public sector, see Bozeman 2007, and Frederickson 1997; Jorgensen and Bozeman 2007 produce a detailed inventory of values in the public sector). Van Wart (1998) highlights certain properties of values systems in the public sector: they are especially complex; they derive from multiple sources – individual, professional, organizational, legal, public interest; they serve also as instruments to accommodate multiple interests; they change over time; and they are subject to competition and contested. The multiple and sometimes competing objectives of public organizations may make it very hard to track the impact of strategy on performance. Yet the effort is worth its while, as the question of how strategy affects performance is a major component in the study of strategic management in public services organizations. The Public Value school is indeed centred on the notion of public value as a possible synthetic measure of performance and a way to gauge whether strategy has made a 'positive' contribution to organizational performance or not: in the perspective of the Public Value school, if strategy has led to the creation of public value, then strategy has positively contributed to performance.

The rest of the chapter tackles these fundamental questions of whether and how strategic management makes a difference to performance.

8.2 Why strategic management makes a difference to performance

Having queried what 'performance' is, we may now turn to address key questions surrounding the issue of the relationship between strategy and performance in public services organizations. A first and crucial question is whether strategy makes any difference: does strategic management positively contribute to performance? Arguing that strategy does contribute to performance – not any strategy, but an 'adequate' strategy – is the very rationale for this chapter (and this book): if strategy were irrelevant to the performance of public services organizations, then understanding the strategy process would be almost pointless.

The argument requires important qualifications and underpinnings. One claim we make is that strategic processes can and do develop in public services organizations. Whilst strategy may be absent in a number of instances (absence of strategy being in itself a strategic option, that may be adopted in both deliberate and emergent fashion), public services organizations *can* (are capacitated to) form a strategy, and indeed they do so in many concrete instances (as the cases we have presented in this book and countless cases that can be found in literature clearly show). Although it has been argued that strategic discretion is more limited in the public sector than it is in private sector organizations (Borgonovi 1984; Boyne 2002; Perry and Rainey 1988; Ring and Perry 1985) due to a range of factors spanning from the limits imposed by legal, political, and regulatory constraints to the territorial ties that link most public services organizations to the territory they are expected to serve, thus bounding at least geographically its remit, public services organizations can have a strategy and often actually do have it. In the previous chapter, we have amply argued why such is the case, identifying as a crucial condition that a certain degree of autonomy is granted to the public organization under consideration.

The second claim underpinning our argument is that strategies are differentiated across public organizations, that is, that strategic management actually varies across public organisations, or, to rephrase it in the negative form of the statement, that not all public organizations adopt the same strategy. This claim is predicated on the condition that public organizations enjoy a certain extent of autonomy, and on the consideration that different factors (from the kind of leadership to the learning dynamics, to the environmental pressures, and so on) are at work in a differential manner in the manifold and varied circumstances where public services organizations operate, combining in very diverse ways in shaping the strategy process. The consideration that strategies actually vary across public organizations brings us back to the starting point: that an 'adequate' strategy developed by a public services organization can make the difference in terms of performance.

Finally, it is important to emphasize that what matters are the 'ultimate' effects of strategic management on performance: as observed by Andrews et al. (2012, p. 105),

> many of the previous studies [reporting the findings of research on the strategy process] measured success as the implementation of the strategy rather than an improvement in service performance. The causal chains connecting strategy and performance in public services organisations are complex, conditional, mediated as well as moderated, and the ultimate 'impact' of strategic management on performance may be hard to detect – yet it is an impact of crucial significance, because strategic management is intended to improve the performance of public services.

Why does strategy make a difference on performance? The first part of the argument lies in demonstrating that the organizational environment, however influential, is not the sole determinant of organizational performance (otherwise strategy would be uninfluential). Andrews et al. provide a book-length contribution making this case, by both systematically reviewing the literature and testing this claim on their own empirical evidence (Andrews et al. 2012).

In examining the influence the environment has on performance, and to rule out it is the sole determinant of differential performance, they examine both what they characterize as the 'technical environment' and what they dub the 'institutional environment.' The technical environment is characterized along the dimensions of the munificence (the 'scarcity or abundance of critical resources for operational activities' available in the territory/community served by the public organization), the complexity (the basic profile of the needs of the people served by the public organization, and the way in which they combine), and the dynamism (the pace with which the profile of people's needs change – instability – as well as the foreseeability of the change – predictability, whereby the dynamism of the environment is determined by the non-linear relations between instability and unpredictability). The institutional environment comprises the constraints imposed on the organization by key external stakeholders, that is the set of institutions providing legitimacy and resources to the organization whilst simultaneously constraining its leeway, substantively and procedurally, albeit the authors eventually focus on 'regulatory pressures in the form of inspections' only, and query the conditions under which they may ameliorate or deteriorate performance. In their test of the effect of strategy contents and process on the performance of local governments departments in Wales, they control for the effect of the two crucial variables of (i) the level of service expenditure and (ii) past performance. The level of public expenditure may be a determinant of performance: 'a prosperous service in one authority may be able to buy success while a poor one in another area can afford only mediocrity' (Andrews et al. 2012, p. 41). The other crucial control variable is past performance: 'Public organisations are best understood as autoregressive systems which change incrementally over time' (Andrews et al. 2012, p. 41). Their results provide support for strategic management (managing strategically a public services organization) as having an effect on the performance of public services organizations also when controlling for a range of factors. Such an effect may be deployed directly or moderated by other factors (what the statistical language would qualify as independent or dependent effect), but it is such that it cannot be subsumed under other factors.

After having ruled out that the environment is the sole determinant of performance, the second part of the argument making the case for strategic management in public services organizations to be capable of producing better performance is predicated on the existence of causal mechanisms linking strategy and performance. Such causal mechanisms have been amply, albeit partly in only an implicit way, examined throughout the earlier chapters devoted to the analysis of the schools of thought of strategy. We now make these links connecting strategy and performance more explicit. Strategy can produce better results because it can drive the organization to position itself properly in the environment and along the value chain as seen in the positioning school; strategy can build support (financial, political) for administrative action to deploy more effectively (an aspect especially emphasized in network-based and collaborative models of strategy); strategy is a source of learning (especially in emergent approaches to strategy), which by itself may be a cause of improved performance; strategy may be based upon and develop distinctive (valuable, rare, inimitable, and non-substitutable) resources of a public services organization, something which may ultimately lead (especially in knowledge-intensive public services organizations, as argued in Chapter 3) to sustained levels of effective delivery (although on this final point it should be noticed that the relationship between an organization owning and developing valuable, rare, inimitable, non-substitutable resources and the level of performance measured in 'absolute terms,' rather than in the relative terms of outperforming competitors, can be problematic: the resource-based view of an organization was originally developed to explain what drives an organization to outmatch its competitors, rather than to explore the determinants of 'absolute increments' in the levels of performance). These are all ways in which strategy may be proved to, at least potentially, have a positive effect on performance.

The work of Andrews et al. (2012 and previous publications) represents an important effort to tackle the issue of the link between strategy and performance, as well as representing a very effective summative work of the debate on the topic. The authors take as starting point the strategy model developed by Miles and Snow (1978), a model centred on the idea of 'fit' between the internal configuration and the external circumstances and placing emphasis on the content of strategy (intended as the basic strategic stance that the organization adopts). Miles and Snow identify four types of strategic stances: Prospectors, which are firms that continually develop new products, services, technologies, and markets; Defenders, which are firms with stable product or service lines that leverage their competence in developing process efficiencies; Analyzers, which are firms that use their applied engineering and manufacturing skills to make a new product better and cheaper and their marketing resources to improve product sales; and Reactors, which are organizations lacking a consistent and stable strategy. This is a categorical approach that Andrews and colleague revisit by treating strategy content as a continuous variable (Andrews et al. 2012, Chapter 3; a previous full analysis is reported in Walker 2010). Such a review of the model has implications not only at the operational but also at the conceptual level: conceptualizing organizations as adopting mixed strategies rather than fitting squarely into a type of this fourfold typology also entails narrowing down to three the logical categories: Prospectors (continuously scanning the external environment and innovating) and Defenders (focusing on the core services, consolidating their existent position, and adopting innovation only when already tried and tested elsewhere) are placed on a continuum (and the intermediate category of the Analyzers may then be dropped), and the third residual type, Reactors (awaiting instructions from the external environment), in many respects embodies the option 'absence of strategy' (that is, outside of the continuum between innovators and consolidators).

The starting point and the core focus of the approach employed by Andrews and colleagues lies in strategy content, qualified at a very abstract/general level as either the orientation to innovate (continuously scanning the environment to be the first mover, a leader in the field, perhaps invading the 'policy space' of other public agencies; such organizations are often in the public sector the winners of some 'innovation award'), or the orientation to improve the core processes (concentrating on the operations to improve the quality of the services delivered and the efficiency, concentrating on retaining existing activities and protecting the share of public budget). In other words, strategy content is identified with the basic strategic stance, rather than more detailed profiles of strategic 'positioning' (e.g., when a portfolio analysis is carefully developed, see e.g. Rebora and Meneguzzo 1990).

What Andrews and colleagues ultimately test is a specific model of contingency theory applied to strategy conceived of as the basic stance of an organization, combined with strategy formulation and implementation styles (controlling for the moderating effect of both the 'internal' organizational structure, modelled along the dimensions of the degree of centralization/decentralization of decision authority and the extent of participation by the staff to the strategy process, and the 'external' environment, modelled along the dimensions previously outlined). They make an impressive effort to test the joint effects of the technical and institutional environment and strategy content and formulation and implementation styles on the performance of public services organizations. A major caveat in gauging the results of their analysis – as already noticed – lies in that it is focused mainly on the dimension of effectiveness (seen as the adequacy of the outputs to determine 'desirable' outcomes) and the related dimension of service quality; thus, their findings may perhaps underestimate the impact of strategy on the efficiency of public services organizations, as well as profiles such as the long-term sustainability of administrative action, or the dimension of 'due process' – fairness, equality of access to public services and treatment of individuals, transparency and accountability, compliance with the law, and the like.

The empirical tests they conducted led to partial disconfirmation of the propositions, especially when controlling for environmental variables. The authors acknowledge that most of the hypotheses they formulated based on the Miles and Snow model as tailored to the contingencies of public sector organizations either did not receive support or for an important part ran counter to the expectations (when controlled for the moderating effect of the environment, see Andrews et al. 2012, Chapter 7). However, the main finding of the Andrews et al. research work is that in most instances, the presence of a strategy – be it prospecting or reacting in stance and/or incremental or rational in the formulation and/or the implementation style – determines a higher level of performance than the absence of it – a finding which corroborates the core argument put forward in this book (and in Andrews et al.'s book too): that strategy does matter in improving performance.

The limited explanatory power of employing the Miles and Snow model to detect the specific effects of specific strategies on performance does not undermine the broader rationale for exploring the effects of different contents, processes, and overall approaches to strategy on the performance in public services organizations; rather, it urges to employ other models beyond the Miles and Snow model. Disentangling the relations linking strategy and performance is an undertaking that may be developed by employing systematically the array of schools of thought in strategic management identified and reviewed throughout Chapters 2 to 6. George et al. (2019) make a step in this direction by detecting a positive correlation between specifically strategic planning (the planning school) and performance.

Thus, if the empirical knowledge to date about the effect of strategy on performance is limited – albeit one important finding is that strategy *does* matter – it is important to explore how knowledge can be expanded, at least at the conceptual level and in mainly a speculative fashion, in this way also guiding further future empirical research work on the multiple and complex linkages between strategy and performance. Exploring the contribution that the schools of thought approach to strategic management may bring to the study of the nexus between strategy and performance is the task undertaken in the next section.

8.3 The relation between strategy and performance in the different schools

Taking (in a selective way) the schools in turn, we at first consider the design school (Chapter 2). The design school is ostensibly the main framework of reference underpinning the research work by Andrews, Boyne, Law, Walker, and colleagues delving into manifold usages of the Miles and Snow model to appraise the impact of strategy on performance in local governments and other public services organizations. The Miles and Snow model is framed around certain key notions (namely that of 'fit') and theoretical perspectives (especially contingency theory) that are at the heart of the design school. It is important, however, to notice that the Miles and Snow model is at the same time more specific (a specific 'model' rather than a broad school of thought) and more abstract in terms of level of analysis than the design school (it is about basic strategic stances rather than detailed techniques to analyze the environment and the fit between the organization and its environment, like the PESTEL or SWOT tools illustrated in Chapter 2).

There seems to be, however, a common basic underlying logic, lying in the idea that seeking to achieve a strategic fit between a particular organization and its environment is the key to 'organisational success.' In this sense, the research run by Andrews and colleagues is a major attempt – to our knowledge the most systematic and in-depth effort so far undertaken – to test the impact on performance of design school approaches to strategic management in public sector organizations.

Turning to the planning school, Andrews et al. also probe into the effects of different styles of strategy formulation and implementation. Notably, they contrast rational planning and logical incrementalism as two basic alternative logics in the process of strategy forming – admittedly a stylized way of characterizing the strategy process (for a more nuanced view of the strategy process in public organizations, see e.g. Barzelay and Campbell 2003, who examine the case of the US Air Force during the 1990s developing a systematic process of preparing for the future and 'visioning'). The research work of Andrews and colleagues is an attempt to appraise how and to what extent an eminently process-orientated approach to strategy, that is the planning school (widely discussed in Chapter 2), can affect performance. Andrews et al.'s work represents a systematic attempt to appraise the impact on performance provided by a rational-planning approach and to test it by contrast with the alternative approach of logical incrementalism (seen as the basic alternative approach when severe limits to rational analytic planning are taken into account: see Quinn 1980, whose work is inspired also by Lindblom's famous commendation of the virtues of 'muddling through,' see Lindblom 1959, 1979).

Their systematic review of literature and associated statistical analysis aims at uncovering both the independent effect on performance of the strategy style (rational planning vs logical incrementalism) and its effect as moderated by the basic strategic stance, the internal organizational configuration, and environmental factors. Whilst their specific hypotheses find only lacklustre support (for the full details, see Andrews et al. 2012, Chapters 3 to 7), their findings further corroborate the proposition that public organizations adopting either strategy style, that is developing an 'autonomous' strategy almost irrespective of its content and style of formulation and implementation (i.e. irrespective of whether it is rational planning or logical-incremental), outperform public organizations that do not adopt any strategy, a datum that arises as possibly the main finding of their overall research effort.

Shifting to other schools of strategy, certain strands of the positioning school relate directly to the issue of linking strategy and performance: the value chain analysis (discussed in Chapter 2) is in itself an instrument to measure a profile of performance, namely, the value the organization's activities and processes contribute to create. Originally conceptualized by Porter, the VCA has found applications in public services in certain countries and sectors (e.g. in the UK NHS; see also Rebora and Meneguzzo 1990, for interesting applications in various policy sectors in the Italian public sector). However, one problematic aspect is the extent to which the analysis of the added value contributed by each activity (primary and support) of the value chain may actually be translated into a full-fledged strategy that guides and permeates organizational behaviour, and hence ultimately lead to sustainable improved performance. In sum, one problematic aspect of the value chain analysis is the extent to which it is an overall approach to strategic management or only a supporting tool. The ways in which VCA is at times implemented by consultancies or taught in business schools may suffer from a mechanistic approach and put a misplaced optimism in the virtues of re-engineering techniques, oblivious of the broader organizational and political context. In other words, a tool of analysis is not by itself sufficient to deploy a full-fledged strategy: organizational culture, leadership, learning, and the like are higher-order factors, likely to matter in a more fundamental way in the strategy process (as scholars analyzing strategy from the viewpoint of other schools would promptly contend).

Another school that, for the purposes of the present discussion of the strategy-performance nexus, displays certain similarities with the VCA is the Public Value school (Benington and Moore 2011a; Moore 1995). Such an approach, explicitly public sector management-orientated rather than derived from the literature of the private firm, represents a school of thought in strategic management in its own right, and as such it has been systematically reviewed in Chapter 3 (to which we refer for a commentary). However, it too like the VCA approach is centred on the measurement of public value – a key synthesis of multiple dimensions of performance – as a key driver for redefining the strategic direction of a public services organization, and, in this sense, it too embeds a tight nexus between strategic decision making and performance. This school also shares certain important ideas with the resource-based view: these include the idea that public organizations might have distinctive competences wider than their current use and that agency flexibility and adaptability may help unleash the potential of such distinctive resources, hence ultimately 'making a better use of the available resources,' which is akin to 'improving performance,' at least along the dimensions of efficiency and effectiveness. Both schools may in this sense be seen as providing a direct link to performance.

There are, however, two problematic issues in the relationship between performance and strategy in the Public Value school which require discussion. One such issue is measurement: how to measure the creation of public value? Talbot (2010, Chapter 6, and 2011) offers interesting perspectives to grapple with such an elusive issue. First, he warns that the 'price' that citizens are willing to pay in exchange of public value should be included in the equation and carefully gauged; this is a point which is also clearly present in the initial definition proposed by Moore 1995, when he states that public value should be obtained 'on the cheap,' that is contrasted with alternative, private uses of the same resources, but it appears to have been partly overlooked in subsequent debates on public value. In the words of a British Cabinet Office Strategy unit paper:

> For something to be of value it is not enough for citizens to say that it is desirable. It is only of value if citizens – either individually or collectively – are willing to give something up in return for it. Sacrifices are not only made in monetary terms (i.e. paying taxes/charges). They can also involve granting coercive powers to the state (e.g. in return for security), disclosing private information (e.g. in return for security), giving time (e.g. as a school governor or a member of the territorial army) or other personal resources (e.g. blood).
> (Kelly et al. 2004, *Creating Public Value – An Analytical Framework for Public Service Reform*, Cabinet Office Strategy Unit, London, cited in Talbot 2010).

The second issue is that, if the notion of public value encompasses multiple values, it is necessary to disentangle them. The contribution provided by Talbot is pertinent: he provides a discussion of Moore's perspective by applying in a combined way the notions of private interest, public interest, and procedural interest (Talbot 2011). He takes the move from philosophical considerations about human nature whereby, going beyond uni-dimensional conceptions of the human being (as *either* individual- istic *or* altruistic), individuals are considered to be *both* selfish *and* altruistic, *both* self- regarding *and* other-regarding. Moreover, 'beyond selfishness and altruism . . . people value and derive pleasure from participation in fair and transparent processes, what- ever the outcome' (Talbot 2011, p. 29), a consideration that leads to including proce- dural fairness, or procedural interest, alongside private and public interest as a third constitutive dimension of public value (something which is present in Moore's origi- nal conception of public value when public value is defined roughly as the impact on public needs *collectively identified and selected through democratic means*).

Institutional and cultural factors explain different balances struck in different cul- tural and politico-administrative contexts amongst the three sets of interest – private interest, public interest, and procedural interest – and over the time (Chapter 7), yet all three need to be somehow included in the equation (and if the balance gets tilted towards one to the detriment of the others, countervailing institutional and cultural forces will tend to offset it, or as a minimum 'It is tempting to suggest that any strong movement towards privileging one set of interests could be met with countervailing pressures towards the other two,' Talbot 2011, p. 30). Talbot then goes on to suggest using a 'balanced scorecard approach' to identify five foci along which to map the impact on the three sets of interests that a given intervention will bring about, as a way forward in the attempt to measure the impact on interests – hence on public value – of a public intervention. The balanced scorecard is a template for assessing different dimensions of organizational performance – notably financial performance, inter- nal business processes, orientation to the customer, and longer-term organizational development – that is intended to provide guidance to the strategic planning process (Kaplan and Norton 1996, 2004). In terms of schools, such approach fits squarely into the planning school. The balanced scorecard approach has proved popular, and it is often taught also in management schools having a public sector focus (Lega and Cristofoli 2009). Whether applied in versions closer to the original formulation by Kaplan and Norton or conjugated for special application to the public sector, the main strength of the balanced scorecard approach is that it provides measures of performance which may be subsequently used for appraisal of the impact on per- formance of the strategy that stems from the adoption of the balanced scorecard. It may, at least in principle, represent one way forward for gauging the results of strategy, formed in accordance with the tenets of the strategic planning school and/ or the Public Value school. A criticism to using this approach to connect strategy and performance lies in the chasm between what is in the end an assessment instrument (the balanced scorecard) and a full-fledged strategy process; in other words, very different 'real' strategies might be made to fit the same balanced scorecard (in the words of Talbot 2011, p. 32 'it is a template into which any strategic content – includ- ing diametrically opposite ones – can be poured'), thus making it hard to 'test' what the impact of strategy ultimately was, because of the indeterminateness of the very strategy that is purportedly tested.

In continuing our discussion of the strategy-performance nexus, the 'emergent' perspective on strategy advocated by Mintzberg (see Chapter 2) leads us to the dia- metrically opposite pole of the conundrum: the approaches that focus on the *process* of strategy formation, like the learning school or – it goes without saying – the process school, amply examined throughout Chapter 6. These approaches encounter the opposite problem in linking strategy to performance than the one met by the more prescriptive schools centred on the strategy contents (design, planning and positioning school, and the tool-based approaches to strategy like the value chain analysis or the balanced scorecard). Schools emphasizing the content of strategy, in fact, are more directly amenable to being appraised in terms of performance, partly because the very content of the strategy provides the terrain – the measures – on which performance may be gauged, and partly because it is easier to collect a relatively ample sample of instances of application of one or the other strategy and empirically test the impact on performance (at least to the extent that the declared strategy is actually implemented: it is on this terrain that Mintzberg challenged the previously dominant mindset for conceiving of strategy, by introducing the notion of emergent strategy and analytically distinguishing the realized from the intended strategy).

Conversely, process-orientated schools provide powerful analytical tools for detecting how strategy actually forms in organizations, yet their emphasis is on differentiation and nuances that tend to make each individual case different and in some sense 'unique,' making it difficult to test the impact on actual performance, and even to identify the profiles on which to detect and measure performance. Indeed, in certain extreme versions, the 'contextualist' approaches to strategic management might even lead to reducing the 'performance' of public services organizations and the 'numbers' with which it is measured to 'stories,' more or less plausible depending on both the transmitting and the receiving end of the story that is being communicated. We would join Bouckaert in countering these forms of radical social constructivism, noticing that '[T]o reduce public administration and its numbers to stories which construct realities is to ignore tangible bottom lines of policy problems such as poverty, health issues or security' (Bouckaert 2013, p. 85); the strategy of a health care organization may make an important difference to how health problems of individuals are addressed and treated, and the actual impact on health needs of thousands of people cannot be boiled down to a story with no anchorage in objective performance measures. However, the problem remains that linking strategy to performance in process-orientated approaches is a tall order task.

To this already complex picture, the strategy-as-practice (strategizing) school adds the further complication that the focus is partly shifted away from the organizational level-performance and expanded to encompass both the micro level of the immediate surroundings where the would-be strategists operate and interact (like an individual public bureau/office, an organizational process, a critical juncture between providers involved in the delivery of a certain public service) and the macro level of the policy or industrial sector. Organizational-level strategic outcomes are, in the narrative of Jarzabkowski and colleagues (see Jarzabkowski and Spee 2009), but one of the three levels of praxis (defined as 'the flow of activity in which strategy is accomplished').

Finally, in this review of the link between schools of thought of strategic management and performance, the corporate governance school places emphasis on the role of the board, the organ which in private firms is entrusted the right and duty to formulate the company's strategy: from a legal and governance perspective, in most jurisdictions, the responsibility for making strategy formally lies with the board. As widely discussed in Chapter 3, the transfer of important public functions from elective to appointed institutions and organizations has led to a proliferation of 'agencies,' 'trusts,' 'foundations,' and the like, throughout the OECD world and beyond;

these bodies feature a wide variety of configurations but – often – there is a board at the top which is explicitly or implicitly entrusted the task of providing the strategy for the body (generally in conjunction with other tasks and responsibilities). Research on public agencies (Pollitt and Talbot 2004; Verhoest et al. 2012) has focused prevalently on issues such as how the board affects the autonomy of the organization, or on the ways in which it partakes in the process of steering and control of the agency by the parent administration, or more broadly on the ways in which the board contributes to configuring the relationships between the agency and the parent administration in either the terms of a principal-agent relationship or in the terms of a trustee, or stewardship, relationship. What has been lacking to date is a systematic enquiry into the ways in which different configurations of the board (in terms of its composition, the role of non-executive members, and the broader style of operation of the board, see Ferlie et al. 1996, discussed in Chapter 3), by affecting strategy, have an impact on organizational performance. This is a promising venue for research which may help better understand the strategy-performance nexus in an important set of public services organizations.

Summing up, the linkage between strategy – as unfolding along the lines of the various schools – and organizational performance is a terrain yet to be ploughed fully, although important research work has been undertaken in this area. We hope the articulation of the framework of the schools of thought in strategic management for public services organizations worked out in this book may provide a valuable framework for much-needed research work that may shed further light on the linkage between strategy and organizational performance.

9 Strategic management, the quest for excellence, and the 'Best Practices' research in public management[1]

One final topic deserves inclusion in a book on strategy in public services organizations before we turn to some concluding reflections in the final chapter: the search for 'best practices' in strategic management – possibly one of the main concerns of practitioners (and the consultancy industry). Osborne and Gaebler (1992) wrote a highly cited bestseller (*Reinventing Government; How the Entrepreneurial Spirit Is Transforming the Public Sector*) that provided a set of 'tenets' or principles for good government that later came to be placed under the umbrella of the doctrinal paraphernalia of the NPM (see Chapter 7). Their argument is not so much 'ideological'; rather, it relies heavily on the logic of the 'best practices': they claim to have found throughout the US highly innovative organizations – permeated by the 'entrepreneurial spirit,' as the subtitle of their work suggests – that represent models or patterns for the rest of the public sector, in the US and elsewhere: these organizations are claimed to operate according to certain 'best practices.' Some key questions therefore arise: are those cases – or any other cases which are deemed to represent a 'best practice' – really cases of 'best' performance? And even admitting they embody the 'best' performance levels available given the technology of the time, what can be extrapolated from those cases that would work also elsewhere?

These are important questions of wider implications. Whilst many have questioned the extent to which the specific cases to which Osborne and Gaebler make reference were actually cases of best performance, and even more sharply it has been questioned whether the doctrines they have drawn from those cases are actually helpful 'always and under all circumstances' to improve the public sector, the key underlying issue remains. Strategic management – and management more broadly – is for an important part concerned with the search for cases of 'excellence' – the 'best' practices – and their replication elsewhere. What can be learnt from a case of 'excellence' (Peters and Waterman 1982) or 'success' (however gauged) to be applied to other organizations, in other circumstances, with the purpose of replicating the successful outcome? We will address this question from the point of view of the more general theme of the 'best practices research in public management': a strand of research addressing the question of how to identify and extrapolate a 'best practice' from one case ('source site') and make it work elsewhere ('target site') to reproduce its outcome – a strand of research of which the practices for managing strategically public services organizations is one important domain of application.

Preliminarily, we note that the extrapolation of practices also relates to two other issues of central importance discussed throughout this book: first, the issue of contextual differences and how they affect the way in which public organizations

DOI: 10.4324/9781003054917-9

are managed; and, second, the very conception of strategic management as both 'science' and 'art and profession.' As regards the issue of contextual influences on the way an organization forms its strategy, in Chapter 7, our discussion remained somewhat at the meso and the macro levels. However, as approaches like strategy-as-practice suggest, strategy also forms at the micro level in the 'specific' circumstances in which an organization operates: '[T]ime and place are the fundamental elements of contextualization' (Pollitt 2012, p. 192) and strategy in a certain sense always takes place in the specific '*hic et nunc*,' the here and now (spatially and temporally determined) in which decisions are made – a given 'situation.' Thus, the extrapolation process is another aspect of the broader issue of contextual influences that we have analyzed in Chapter 7. Extrapolation also concerns the practical problem of how to replicate a desired state of affairs from one set of circumstances to another one: this problem concerns the very nature of public management, and strategic management as part and parcel of it, as an art and a profession aimed at solving practical problems, a theme we examine in the next chapter.

The 'best practices research' explores the issue of whether and how analysts in public management can address the problem of improving the performance of public sector organizations in one situation (target site) by employing experience acquired elsewhere (source site), a strand of research typified by Osborne and Gaebler's best-seller. A lively debate on 'best practices research' (Bardach 2004 and Barzelay 2007) has raised the issue of whether current research conventions in public management are effective as regards the identification and supple elaboration of 'best' practices. Learning from second-hand experience (the extrapolation problem) is more complex than simply ascertaining whether a given practice is effective in the source site (the evaluation of performance problem which has been addressed in the previous chapter). Extrapolation is the process of learning from vicarious experience and designing practices fitting the (new and diverse) circumstances to which the practices are to be applied.

Researching 'best' practices involves at least two crucial problems: the identification of cases that contain a best practice; and the extrapolation of the practice, that is the way by which experience acquired elsewhere can be employed in the target site. The problem of the best practices research may then be deconstructed into two problems:

- The search of excellence problem (how to find what is truly 'best'); and
- The extrapolation problem (how to replicate experience acquired in another site for the target site).

They are examined in turn.

9.1 The search of excellence problem

The first problem concerns how to find 'where excellence lies,' how to identify cases that contain practices of excellence (i.e. at the highest possible level of performance, given the state of the art of management knowledge). A major contribution to addressing this problem is proposed by Bretschneider et al. (2005). The authors define the two joint necessary and sufficient conditions for finding a 'best' practice (or better: for finding a case that contains a best practice to be extrapolated): the completeness of cases considered; and the comparability of cases. If both conditions are met (admittedly a big 'if,' as it generally requires surveying large populations and defining performance in such a way that the level of performance across cases can be compared), then the relevant population where the best practice lies is identified.

The subsequent step in the approach proposed by Bretschneider and colleagues consists in the elaboration of a general framework for selecting the proper technical option available to researchers for estimating relationships of inputs to outputs capable of focusing on extreme behaviours, to find the best performing case, that is for finding the unit where the transformation of inputs into outputs – the production function – is performed at the best level.

The focus on the production function is also, in our view, the main limitation in the approach suggested by Bretschneider and colleagues. The general framework proposed is undergirded by the theory of production drawn from economics – which leads the authors to recognize that, in their words, 'a 'best practice' is essentially about comparing how organizational units transform inputs (resources) into output(s)' (Bretschneider et al. 2005, p. 313). While productivity or efficiency of service delivery is clearly a central dimension of performance, there are in public services other categories of situations, like the management of complex change processes, where performance cannot generally be expressed in the terms of a production function. As a pertinent example, it may be considered the formulation of strategic visioning in the US Air Force accounted by Michael Barzelay and Colin Campbell (2003), in which the performance of the process was

> [e]xpanding the horizons for strategic planning to encompass visioning, and to do it in such ways to, first, enable the US Air Force to focus on issues other than the development of technical system – [issues] like human knowledge and skills, managerial systems, and norms and values – and, second, to question issues previously regarded as settled matters concerning whether the core technological capability should continue to be the application of military force by land-based fixed wing aircraft flown by Air Force pilots.
>
> (Barzelay and Campbell 2003, pp. 2–3)

From this definition, it follows that the kind of 'performance' pursued by this important public services organization – the US Air Force – cannot be formulated or expressed in the terms of a production function. To put it differently, the kind of practices that are of interest for public managers, and notably 'strategists' in public services organizations, are partly about performance in terms of efficiency (the dimension considered by Bretschneider and colleagues), but they are also about effectiveness and long-term sustainability (usually in themselves multidimensional and composite), about flexibility and adaptability to mutable circumstances (the core capabilities to win the wars of the future, to cite again the US Air Force example), as well as about accountability and responsiveness, and equity and fairness in the treatment of individuals – dimensions that are not considered in the study conducted by Bretschneider and colleagues.

The case of the US Air Force, for which it is strictly speaking difficult to find directly comparable cases (the second condition in Bretschneider et al. 2005, for the identification of 'best' cases), leads us to another consideration: how to employ a case for generating useful knowledge (as is done, in our view, in the account by Barzelay and

Campbell) even if it is not possible to demonstrate that the case under investigation is the best case, since surveying the overall population is simply not possible (for example because other military air forces in other countries might not grant access to their sites for comparative scholarly enquiry), or because significant constraints to conducting large-scale research through systematic comparison are present. These constraints make it sensible, in our view, to proceed in the search for practices also with single case studies, or research designs that investigate in-depth a limited number of cases, even if in these studies it is not possible to claim to have surveyed an entire population.

A single case study may provide material enough for extrapolating practices about complex change processes, provided that the causal reconstruction of the events of the experience under investigation is carried out. What we argue is that also specimens of 'good' or 'smart' practices (as Bardach calls them, see Bardach 1998) derived from single or small-N case study research designs may be valuable for practitioners, provided a theory-driven and process analysis of the causal texture of the dynamics of change is developed in the case study: the account of the causal texture of the experience and how the practice intervenes on the system may be sufficient source of ideas for practitioners to solve the design problem they face. The case investigated is here interpreted as a design exemplar (Barzelay 2007), that is, a concrete solution to a design problem that is somewhat similar to the one that actors aim to solve. Under extrapolation-based design, actors would narrow down the design problem they face to devising contrivances fitting their specific circumstances that would activate a causal process like the one evident in the functioning of the design exemplar, to produce similar effects. The extrapolation of practices from a single case may well be enough for practitioners – indeed, a number of contributions to the research on practices in public management (like Bardach 1998; Barzelay and Campbell 2003; Barzelay and Thompson 2003) focus exclusively on the extrapolation phase, in most cases from single case study research designs. This leads us to tackling the second problem, that is the extrapolation problem.

9.2 The extrapolation problem

How can 'a practice that works' be extracted from one case (source site) and applied elsewhere (target site) to generate similarly successful outcomes? This is the core question of the extrapolation problem. As a preliminary step, we will consider the criticisms addressed to current research conventions concerning the way extrapolation is conducted in the field of public management (and possibly also beyond that), and what may be tentative ripostes to improve the extrapolation process.

At the dawn of the NPM, in the 1980s and early 1990s, a strand of literature had emerged, in particular from US public policy schools, which put emphasis on transformative, even 'revolutionary,' practices that could be employed by public managers to achieve excellence. Such works included, alongside Osborne and Gaebler's *Reinventing Government*, Behn's *Leadership Counts* (1991) and Barzelay's *Breaking Through Bureaucracy* (1992), among the others. Barzelay's is a study of the radical changes – qualified as a change of paradigm – that occurred in the Minnesota government during the 1980s. Such works raised a host of criticisms (see Lynn 1996). The criticisms raised were basically concerned with the lack of theorized knowledge found in this strand of scholarship, which, according to the critics, undermined the way the extrapolation process was conducted.

In proposing the 'smart practices' approach, Bardach (1998) makes his own criticisms to these approaches to extrapolation-oriented research. Bardach's first criticism shares with Lynn's a common concern about the fact that best practice research proceeds without sufficient methodological rigour (Bardach 1994, p. 260, referring also to the work of Overman and Boyd 1994). A second criticism is about the method employed by best practice research approaches for the identification of 'solutions' to problems. A flaw, according to Bardach, lies in the way the question is posed:

> What works? . . . the rhetoric standard solution-seeking question is not well posed; it seeks too big an answer at once . . . it would be better to decompose it into two questions, one nested into the other.
>
> (Bardach 1994, p. 263)

The point is that, in the research for practices 'that work,' a first step lies in understanding how the system operates at all, before questioning how specifically the practice intervenes onto the system to make it function at a higher level of performance. In this way, an insight can be gained about the sources of high performance as well as about the modes of failure. Such sources are interpreted as 'opportunities' of which the practice purportedly tries to make advantage: only once features of the opportunities of which the practice tries to make advantage have been analyzed (these are based on gaining knowledge of how the system operates), the second question: 'how can we make the system work better?' can be fruitfully addressed.

In this approach, a practice can be conceived as a means to exploit opportunities, a method of interacting with a situation that is intended to produce results. To better figure the way the smart practices research operates, an analogy can be drawn with the process of reverse engineering that (Bardach 1998, p. 41):

> [I]n its simplest form finds an amazing gizmo, takes it apart, and tries to figure out the clever trick that makes it work so well. . . . It may be noted that such a process, far from being simple and immediate, can involve a complex process of theoretical reasoning. Furthermore, the analogy must not be 'stretched' too far: differently from the ordinary work of engineers, smart practice analysis lacks the capacity to thoroughly break down and reconstitute the gizmo, . . .[n]or does it have access to the body of scientific and technical knowledge that permits engineers to arrive at a realistic understanding. Furthermore . . . for an engineer to generalize beyond the specimen at hand is often straightforward.

The starting point of the smart practices approach is thus the breakdown of the 'practice that works' in the source site: it is the analysis of the practice that is conducive to the identification of the proper body of theorized knowledge that enables to understand how the practice interacts effectively with the system. Such approach may also address the criticism about the method employed for the identification of solutions to problems. As noted previously, this approach is construed and operationalized to systematically relate the candidate practice to the nature of the opportunities it seeks to exploit.

Ultimately, grounded on the analysis of the different ways in which a practice interacts with a situation and can produce differentiated results (success as well as failures), categories of contingent solutions can be identified. The problem is how to conduct the analysis on the source site in such ways that the practice may be extrapolated and thus made applicable in a range of potential target sites. The analysis carried out by Bardach – whilst in our view thorough in outlining the substantive elements required for a research agenda on practices – seems to be shorter in proposing a protocol of analysis for conducting the extrapolation process.

A development of the smart practices approach in this direction is proposed by Barzelay (2007, see also Barzelay and Campbell 2003). An operationalization for conducting smart practices analysis on change processes is elaborated by identifying for each activity the related 'design features' and 'context factors,' and analyzing the respective relations, that is the way context factors – or contextual features affect the functioning of the system – affect the properties, or design features, of the practice. The analysis of the context factors allows the identification of the 'domain of applicability' of the practices: practices are generalizable (in the sense that they apply beyond the specific case from which they are extracted to a wider range of situations), but at the same time they work under specified conditions, which are qualified by the context factors.

How can such context factors be identified and qualified? The direct answer is that it is the theory-based knowledge of how the system on which the practice intervenes works that guides the identification of context factors. Combined with the methodological innovation of distinguishing design features from context factors in addressing the question 'how the practice intervenes on the system,' this approach may guide the identification of the 'good practices,' following a reverse engineering protocol of analysis.

9.3 A Protocol for the analysis of 'Practices' in public management

These previous methodological contributions (Bardach 1994, 1998, Barzelay 2007; Barzelay and Campbell 2003) have been here discussed and summarized also for paving the ground for outlining a protocol of analysis about how to conduct the extrapolation process. The protocol is illustrated in this section and schematized in Table 9.1, which makes reference to an exemplar case and illustrates a concrete application of the protocol by extrapolating practices for the management of devolution processes, which are processes of reallocation of public competences and resources across levels of government.

The protocol has been developed based on a study of a devolution process done by one of the authors of this book (Ongaro 2006). This protocol is especially geared to practices utilizable for enabling complex change processes to occur, rather than for practices addressed at improving productivity ratios or other efficiency-related dimensions for performance (like the ones focused by Bretschneider et al. 2005). Complex change processes are in fact at the heart of strategic change, which is the core area of interest for this book (see also and specifically Chapter 5).

Devolution of competences from the regional to the local tier of government in the Italian region of Lombardy was a process of high strategic significance for the incumbent government of those days (1998–2002), whose political and policy priority was centred on repositioning the regional government from a delivery organization to a 'steering' organization, setting out the policy objectives while the local governments were in charge of service delivery. The new 'vision' that the regional government was striving to implement was that of Lombardy as 'the region of subsidiarity' (a political-ideological tenet that was extremely dear to the leading political figure of the time in the Lombard political system, the then regional President Roberto Formigoni).

The process of devolution of competences from the regional to local governments started in the policy field of agriculture, and in that sector, it ran very smoothly: the designed devolution programme reallocating public functions and tasks from the regional government to the local governments was successfully implemented over a very short time frame. This was a puzzling outcome when appraised against the backdrop of a broad picture of contemporaneous interventions of devolution elsewhere in Italy mostly failing to be implemented: so, what drove the 'success' of this process of devolution? It appears that a set of practices were set in motion that made the devolution process unfold smoothly. The protocol for extrapolating the practices that enabled the devolution policy to be implemented, notwithstanding certain unfavourable conditions, is presented for illustrative purposes (Figure 9.1 and Table 9.1), to show how the extrapolation protocol may be utilized. This specific application was based on a general protocol, which we now illustrate.

The extrapolation protocol

The proposed protocol for the extrapolation of 'practices' in a source site for application elsewhere in a target site with the ultimate purpose of enabling complex change processes is composed of five steps, which may be summarized as follows:

1   Identify the function to be performed: what is the function that the practice has made it possible to achieve? (example: mobilize constituencies for supporting change);
2   Define what specifically the practice is about;
3   Describe the practice, by answering the following two questions:

  • How does the system operate?
  • How does the practice try to take advantage of the way the system operates?

4   Identify all the effects of the practice:

  • Main effects of the practice (main results);
  • Variations of the practice (what accounts for unusually satisfactory performances, what accounts for possible breakdowns?);
  • Possible side effects of the practice.

5   Define the key 'context factors': under what conditions does the practice work?

  • The causal mechanisms that have made it possible for the practice to work in that specific context must be identified so that the practice may be geared to the recipient context.

The extrapolation protocol is discussed in further detail in the remainder of this section, using the case of devolution in the Italian region of Lombardy for illustrative purposes.

The first step concerns the identification of the functions to be performed for the change process to take place: functions are here defined as sub-processes of the overall change process that needs to be performed if the desired goal (the achievement of which the practices are instrumental) is to be attained (see also Barzelay and Camp-bell 2003, Chapter 5). In the specific case used as exemplar, the functions leading to such changes can be characterized as in Figure 9.1. In the case of devolution, complex change processes unfolding over a long a period require: (i) momentum of the devolution process to be gained (function F1) and (ii) sustained over time (F2); it also requires (iii) reallocating programmatic activities, that is the tasks devolved to local governments (F3) and eventually (iv) institutionalizing the new state of affairs (F4).

Looking in closer detail at the sub-functions composing these higher-order functions, we may notice that having social groups that could resist change to instead commit to the progress of the devolution process (or at least not to hinder it) affects the overall advancement of the process (F1–1 and F1–2). The social (causal) mechanisms of attribution of opportunity and attribution of threat (McAdam et al. 2001, pp. 16–18 and pp. 315–317 in particular) by the different social groups to the new envisaged devolved institutional setting, and notably the ways in which attribution of opportunity may be exploited and attribution of threat be counteracted by properly employed practices to maximize the support for the change process, is crucial to understand the practices that made performing such functions possible. Sustaining momentum over a long period also requires keeping the cohesion within the top management in the organization leading the devolution process (F2). Performing the new programmatic activities requires both the reallocation of personnel (F3–1) and the adaptation of structure and routines in the public sector organizations that have changed their programmatic tasks (F3–2). Finally, once the new situation has been achieved, the new organizational configuration has to be consolidated (institutionalization, F4).

Though tailored to the specific case of implementing devolution (i.e. the goal is setting up a devolved institutional setting across tiers of government), the functions outlined in Figure 9.1 are quite general and represent a quite conventional way of describing complex change processes. Change is schematized according to the very conventional model of the change process as a three-phase process: the unfreezing of a previously stable situation (F1), change (trajectory from the initial to the end 'state' – F2 and F3), and then consolidation ('freezing') of the new end state (F4). This conventional model applies only in the case of the 'episodic change,' that is change occurring when organizations are moving away from a given equilibrium situation (Weick and Quinn 1999). This form of change is labelled episodic because it tends to occur in distinct periods during which shifts are precipitated by events, internal or external, that sometimes may be labelled as characterizing a 'crisis' situation. It is anyway a very important category of change processes. For other types of change, other templates of the key functions may be required.

The Lombardy case provides evidence of a number of distinct social groups affected by devolution. For at least three groups, the costs engendered by devolution exceeded the benefits: tenured officials in the staff of local governments, managers at the regional level in associations of agricultural businesses, and the personnel to be reallocated (the underlying reasons are widely discussed in Ongaro 2006). All these three categories of people could have provided sources of resistance to change, but this did not occur. Why? The practices that were employed counteracted these sources of resistance, whilst at the same time, other practices prompted the backing by those other categories of actors that were instead

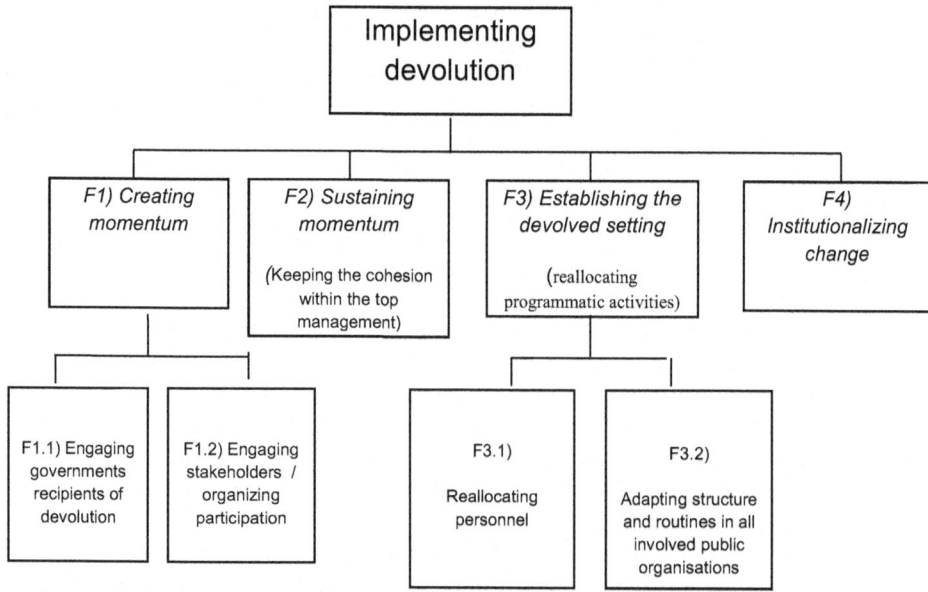

Figure 9.1 Functions in implementing an intervention of devolution

potentially discontent with the extant state of affairs and could reap benefits from the new situation ('triggering the discontents' of the status quo to support change, as Kelman 2005, puts it).

The second step in the protocol is to define what exactly the practice is about. The description of the practice – third step – is based on answering two interconnected questions: (i) how does the system operate? and (ii) how does the practice try to take advantage of the way the system operates? In fact, as we have seen, it is first necessary to have an understanding of how the system works; in the case in point, that devolution is not a 'neutral' process, but it is a process that objectively affects a number of categories of actors, and for certain of them in such terms that costs by far exceed benefits, which may lead to these categories of people perceiving change as a threat and resisting it: attitudes of resistance which may be impossible to overcome if the actors are endowed with enough means to stop the process. Only once it is understood that this is 'the way the system operates' in devolution dynamics, the question about how the practice works can more properly be addressed in terms of 'how the practice tries to take advantage of the way the system operates' (to counteract some unfavourable effects and determine favourable others). In the case, the practice worked by appropriating a mobilizing structure to make the change be interpreted as an opportunity and not as a threat, as well as by facilitating the development of inter-organizational teams and other structures and routines for the supplier inter-organizational coordination of transactions. The practice can be seen as a means to trigger social mechanisms (Elster 1989; Hedstrom and Swedberg 1998; Granovetter 1978; Stinchcombe 1991) and concatenations thereof (Gambetta 1998) enabling certain process dynamics to occur.

Moreover, and this leads us to step 4, it is not only the main effect(s) of the practice that must be identified, but also side effects. Thus, for example the exclusion of some categories of actors from the inter-institutional coordination venues may lead those categories to perceive the envisaged devolution as a threat. For the underlying practice to work effectively, it is thus important that such 'inter-institutional venues for coordination' are as inclusive as possible.

Last, but definitely not least, practices are assumed to work under specific conditions – only very seldom practices may be considered as operating 'free of context,' and such practices are very likely to have already been discovered and extensively applied. The fifth step in the protocol is therefore the definition of the context factors under which the practice works. This is a crucial component of the transferability of the practice: practices work only in 'similar' conditions; or, to put it in another way, practices have to be adapted, and combined in different ways, to fit partly different context factors (i.e. to produce similar effects as they did in the original case), and in the absence of functionally similar context factors, practices are very likely not to work, or to produce unintended consequences. For example (see Practice 4 related to the implementation of F3–1 in Table 9.1), the 'social status' and the economic treatment of public servants at different levels of government is a country-specific factor that powerfully affects the extent to which relocation across levels of government is a gain or a net loss for the personnel being relocated (which is more often the case when relocation occurs from upper to lower levels of government), and hence it affects the effectiveness of the measures that may be taken to soothe the resistance to change by the staff affected.

Table 9.1 illustrates the set of practices that may be extrapolated from the Lombardy experience for implementing a reform programme of devolution of competences from upper to lower tiers of government in a given polity. The logical structure of the proposed protocol of analysis for the extrapolation of practices is as follows. First (column 1), each practice must be related to the function it performs. In general, the practice employs one or more social or other causal mechanisms to counteract mechanisms that would 'naturally' inhibit or sap the unfolding of the process (referred to as 'the problem addressed').

The content of the practice must then be described (column 2). The way the practice works has to be described by addressing the two distinct though interrelated questions of, first, how the system operates, and second, how the practice tries to take advantage of the way the system operates (how it exploits opportunities lying in the system) (column 3). Theory-based understanding of how the system works is the basis for characterizing the practice and the way it works.

Effect or 'result' of the practice is the way in which the outcome of running the practice enables performing the function. The sensitivity of the effects of the practice to possible variations in running it must be described (point 2 in column 4). In particular, the questions about what accounts for unusually satisfactory performance or, at the opposite, what accounts for possible breakdown determined by the practice must be examined. Finally, and complementarily, possible side effects of running the practice, an aspect that may be too often overlooked in the management literature, have to be investigated (point 3 in column 4).

Context factors of the change process are considered in column 5. Context factors determine the 'domain of applicability' of the practice (they also create the conditions that the practice exploits to attain a certain level of performance). It is the

Table 9.1 Practices extrapolated from the Lombardy experience of devolution

(1) Function (in brackets the problem addressed by the practice)	(2) Practice	(3) Description 1. How does the system operate? 2. How does the practice try to take advantage of the way the system operates (design and innovation dynamics)?	(4) Effects 1. Main effects of the practice (Results) 2. Variations of the practice (what accounts for unusually satisfactory performances, what accounts for possible breakdowns?) 3. Possible side effects	(5) Key context factors
F1–1 ('Attribution of threat' by civil servants in the recipients authorities concerning the new responsibility and risks)	**P1** Setting to work *loci* for empowering communication channels and joint decision making among public sector organizations (in the Lombardy case, the inter-institutional table of agriculture)	1. The system Attribution of threat or opportunity to the new situation. The replacement of intra-organizational, hierarchy-based mechanisms of governing the transactions with inter-organizational settings and network-based transactions mechanisms. 2. How the practice takes advantage of the way the system operates By appropriating a mobilizing structure to make the change be interpreted as an opportunity and not as a threat By facilitating the development of inter-organizational teams and other structures and routines for inter-organizational coordination of transactions	1. Main effects Momentum of the devolution process is initiated (and sustained). Network-based mechanisms of governing the transactions are set to work. 2. Variations of the practice Training programmes attended jointly by personnel of the different levels of government and other procedures may further facilitate the development of the implementation network. 3. Possible side effects Exclusion of some actors may amplify attribution of threat	Nature of the division of labour across levels of government and asymmetry in powers and expertise (facilitating the appropriation of mobilizing structures by the upper level of government) Collaborative dynamics of the political system, especially regarding the relations between upper (devolving) and lower (recipient) levels of government.

(Continued)

Table 9.1 (Continued)

(1) Function (in brackets the problem addressed by the practice)	(2) Practice	(3) Description 1. How does the system operate? 2. How does the practice try to take advantage of the way the system operates (design and innovation dynamics)?	(4) Effects 1. Main effects of the practice (Results) 2. Variations of the practice (what accounts for unusually satisfactory performances, what accounts for possible breakdowns?) 3. Possible side effects	(5) Key context factors
F1–2 (Attribution of threat by relevant constituencies to the new situation)	**P2** Setting to work *loci* for empowering communication channels between public sector organizations and stakeholders (in the case, the 'agricultural table') and incentives for prompting stakeholders to back the devolution intervention (in the case, the Centres for Agricultural Assistance that were contracted out important public administrative tasks)	1. The system The reshaping of electoral and non-electoral constituencies determined by the reallocation of decision powers and administrative tasks implied by devolution affects attribution of opportunity and threat by relevant stakeholders 2. How the practice takes advantage of the way the system operates By making the change be interpreted as an opportunity By linking stakeholders' (in the case, farmers') representatives agenda to the devolution agenda performed by the regional government (brokerage mechanism)	1. Main effects Momentum of the devolution process is initiated (and sustained) by enhancing stakeholders' consensus towards devolution. 2. Variations of the practice Linking the decentralization agenda with other cross-sectoral, highly political *loci* for communication and joint decision making may strengthen the effects (in the Lombardy case, the 'pact for the development table' for consulting stakeholders in all the main economic fields). 3. Possible side effects Exclusion of some actors may amplify attribution of threat	Nature of the relations between the government and the stakeholders in the policy sectorFeatures of stakeholders' internal organization

F2 (in complex change processes, some interventions tend to lose the recognition by key actors of their significance for the progression of the devolution agenda	**P3** Interconnecting the individual interventions required for implementing devolution by having top managers to take part in all or most of the project's teams	1. The system Complex processes tend to split into a variety of distinct, though interdependent, adaptation efforts ('projects'). Actor certification/de-certification of the devolution interventions affects key actors' commitment. 2. How the practice takes advantage of the way the system operates By having the key actors to take part in all or most of the working groups, validation is maintained over time and interdependencies in the change process are governed	1. Main effects The variety of adaptation efforts are recognized and strongly interconnected, thus sustaining momentum and increasing coordination 2. Possible side effects Exclusion of some actors may amplify attribution of threat	Stability and continuity of the governing coalition Nature of the interdependencies of the different adaptation efforts
F3–1 (Problem: being reallocated is a net loss for personnel)	**P4** Combination of: inducing a belief of inevitability by properly manipulating the organizational designcareful selection of personnel monetary incentives	1. The system The move to another level of government affects the social as well as the material labour contract between the organization and its labor force: as a result, an unbalance between contribution and reward in the staff to be transferred is produced. Threshold-based behaviours about whether to accept or resist transfer may be operating 2. How the practice takes advantage of the way the system operates By explicitly reducing the unbalance by providing a compensation By constraining available decisional alternatives through the formation of a belief of inevitability By triggering rational imitation (specifically threshold-based behaviour) at the individual level	1. Main effects Attenuation of resistance to transfer by the personnel. 2. Variations of the practiceThe block transfer of personnel may either reinforce the process or hamper it. The gradual transfer of personnel over the time period of devolution may facilitate the activation of persistent patron–client networks, in turn leading to some of the personnel avoiding transfer. 3. Possible side effects Attribution of threat connected with the perception of being superseded on the side of staff already in the payroll of the lower level of government.	'Social status' and labour contract of personnel at different levels of government (a country-specific factor) Organizational culture and preferences structure of personnel

(Continued)

Table 9.1 (Continued)

(1) Function (in brackets the problem addressed by the practice)	(2) Practice	(3) Description 1. How does the system operate? 2. How does the practice try to take advantage of the way the system operates (design and innovation dynamics)?	(4) Effects 1. Main effects of the practice (Results) 2. Variations of the practice (what accounts for unusually satisfactory performances, what accounts for possible breakdowns? 3. Possible side effects	(5) Key context factors
F3–2 (The new institutional division of labour may enhance room for opportunistic behaviours. Adaptation of structure and routines to the new tasks performed is required)	**P5** Developing a 'professional bureaucracy' organizational model for the public sector entity that devolves tasks, and establishing specialized bodies Setting to work routines for processing information on performances and tasks execution across the policy subsystem (in the case, the new inter-organizational computerized information system)	1. The system New tasks are to be executed at the different levels of government, hence different organizational configurations are required. Fragmentation of tasks increases the scope for opportunistic behaviours. 2. How the practice takes advantage of the way the system operates By providing top executives with the organizational instruments for keeping the grasp over the overall policy process By empowering middle management and staff by enriching their job By sharing information and thus reducing the scope for opportunistic behaviours	1. Main effects Enabling the regional government to focus on its new core activities and keeping the grasp over the entire agriculture policy formulation and delivery process Improving working relationships between levels of government; providing 'platforms' for improving service delivery2. Side effects Integrated information system: risks of breakdowns when the hierarchical logic overextends and/or when information is used only according to a 'negotiation' logic	Contents of the reform policy package (what is re-allocated)Collaborative dynamics of the political system, especially regarding the relations between upper (devolving) and lower (recipient) levels of governmentDivision of labour across levels of government; nature of interdependencies among the tasks

careful consideration of these 'operating conditions' of the practice that allows avoiding unwarranted generalizations. The identification of context factors, though mainly a craftsman work that cannot be done according to pre-codified, automatic procedures, is guided by the theorized knowledge acquired about the way the system works, produced by the extrapolation-oriented case analysis based on the two questions in column 3. Distinguishing the two questions (Bardach 1994) about 1. how the system works, and 2. how the practice intervenes on the system for exploiting opportunities for improving performance, provide the bases for the identification and the proper qualification of the context factors.

9.4 Co-creating practices that work

So far in this chapter, we have only considered the pattern whereby a practice first somehow is contrived in one given site to tackle a contingent problem (practitioners in a certain situation 'invented' and elaborated on a way to tackle an extant problem), and only at this point its success 'makes the practice to be spotted': its existence gets detected, the practice is somehow discovered, typically by a consultant or an academic searching for 'excellent practices,' or because the practitioners who originally contrived it have showcased the practice at some forum or venue where consultants, academics, or others involved in the job of 'transferring practices' have noticed it. It is then that the practice is analyzed and 'reverse-engineered' in such a way as to make it possible to replicate the practice elsewhere, that is for the practice to be transferred from the source site where it originated to potentially multiple target sites, where replication of the practice is expected to improve organizational performance.

But what about adopting the opposite approach: inventing the 'practice that works' on the site (rather than importing it replicated from elsewhere), by bringing together the practitioners with the academics/consultants studying and theorizing the practice? This different approach lies in *co-creating* practices on the spot, rather than detecting them *ex post*. It is to this approach that we now turn our attention. Prominent scholars Eva Sørensen and Jacob Torfing have, over the years, investigated the dynamics of processes of co-creation of solutions to extant public problems, and they have experimented with practitioners novel ways to develop co-creation. Some of these ideas are illustrated by Sørensen and Torfing in the following Box 9.1.

Box 9.1   Strategic transition to co-created political leadership: a co-production between engaged researchers and public leaders?

By *Eva Sørensen and Jacob Torfing*

Strategic leadership aiming to transform public organizations can be exercised top-down, bottom-up, or any combination of the two. It may also involve collaboration with external stakeholders, consultancy firms, or public administration researchers. What follows is a brief account of how we as researchers worked closely with public leaders to promote co-creation at all levels in the municipality of Gentofte in Denmark, with a special focus on facilitating interactive political leadership (Sørensen 2020; Sørensen and Torfing 2019).

In Denmark, politicians increasingly complain that they leave policy development to the administration, spend most of their time in specialized committees discussing implementation issues, and have little interaction with the local citizens. To reverse this trend, we collaborated with elected politicians and public managers in designing a new platform for interactive political leadership that links representative democracy with participatory and deliberative democracy. The process took the form of a protracted design experiment based on iterative cycles of design intervention, practical testing, evaluation, and redesign.

It all began back in 2014, when we were invited to speak to the city council about how to strengthen the exercise of political leadership. We argued that political leadership involves (i) setting the agenda by defining problems and challenges that call for public action; (ii) giving direction to problem-solving and contributing to the development of new ideas; and (iii) mobilizing support for the most promising solution; and (iv) overseeing its practical implementation. We also claimed that interaction with citizens and local stakeholders would help the elected councillors to better understand the problems at hand, create new and promising solutions, and muster support for their implementation. Finally, we sketched out some new ideas about how the traditional political committees could be scaled back and supplemented with some new arenas for collaborative interaction between a group of councillors and a group of relevant and affected citizens. To avoid the new participatory and deliberative arenas undermining the institutions of representative democracy, we suggested that the city council should play a proactive role in forming the new arenas and endorsing the policy proposals that they were fostering.

A year late, we were approached by the conservative mayor Hans Toft who told us that: 'Now we have done what you suggested. Could you help us to evaluate the experiment and suggest how to further improve the model?' We gladly accepted the challenge as the new model was very close to our ideas about interactive political leadership.

The new platform that came to be known as the 'Gentofte Model' was pretty simple. Every year, the city council would form a number of so-called Task Committees in which typically five politicians and ten citizens are working together, assisted by three administrative facilitators, to solve a pressing problem confronting the local community. The city council would craft a written mandate for the Task Committee specifying the task to be solved and the expected delivery. The city council also appointed the participating politicians and drew up the competence profiles of the citizen participants that were found through public advertisement and careful mapping of the interested citizens and the competence profiles. This procedure helped to prevent participation bias and ensure diversity. The Task Committees would typically work for three to six months, having fortnightly meetings that were completely self-regulated and often used tools drawn from design thinking. Some of them used their relative autonomy to form working groups with external participation of experts and citizens. Last but importantly, the work in the traditional political committees was cut back by 66% and changed so that it was more focused on strategic oversight than administrative case processing.

We carefully evaluated the first round of Task Committees based on document studies, participant observation, interviews, and mini-surveys. Our evaluation report documents how the new Task Committees strengthen the political leadership of the elected councillors and helped foster new innovative solutions that would not have emerged without the Task Committees. The majority of the politicians, administrative facilitators, and participating citizens were satisfied with the new way of co-creating policy solutions.

Our evaluation report also pointed out a series of problems and came up with a number of alternative solutions to each problem. The report was presented for and discussed with the city council and debated in a series of meetings with the mayor, the CEO and the Head of Development. The discussions led to a number of institutional design changes in the next rounds of Task Committees.

Between the start of this process and 2021, there have been 40 Task Committees that have not only helped foster more creative and effective governance solutions, but also strengthened the role of the elected councillors in policy development, provided them with input from relevant and affected actors, and created a new channel for democratic participation and influence that has been used by more than 1,600 citizens representing different local constituencies.

The 'Gentofte Model' was a huge success, and many local politicians and public managers see it as the largest achievement of the conservative mayor who led the city council for 28 years. The municipality has received countless delegations from other municipalities in Denmark, Sweden, and Norway that wants to hear about the new model for interactive political leadership. The model has been exported to several Norwegian municipalities, and we have tested the model's robustness and viability in the Norwegian municipality of Svelvik, where it achieved equally positive results despite less than optimal conditions. The results from Svelvik were compared with the results from Gentofte's as part of the POLECO project financed by the Norwegian Research Council.

To continue to follow the Task Committees in Gentofte, we started a PhD project that was co-financed by the municipality and Roskilde University. The project explores how public leaders manage dilemmas and cope with paradoxes emerging in co-creation processes initiated by either politicians (Task Committees), public managers, or citizens. Insights from the project feeds into the internal group of administrative co-creation facilitators who are continually enhancing the skills and competences. Another PhD project was started to explore the diffusion of the 'Gentofte Model' to the general housing sector, led by local elected housing councils, which were experiencing problems similar to those of the city councils.

At the time this book goes to press, we are conducting a design experiment with a new Task Committee that is aimed to find a new model for turning public libraries into cultural hubs. The focus is here on how co-creation processes can be arranged in ways that enhance the willingness to pursue innovative solutions. The design experiment is conducted as a part of the EU-financed COGOV project, and the ultimate ambition is to turn Gentofte Municipality into a European beacon for co-created policy making.

None of all this had happened if not for the trust-based collaboration between highly competent, agile, and risk-willing public leaders and public administrators who are committed to an interactive research strategy that aims to develop and test new research-based ideas in practice. The joint effort to promote co-creation through a co-created strategic leadership owes its success to three factors. First, the municipality is rich and well-managed and had the courage to innovate its political institutions and administrative tasks and procedures. Second, there has been a common goal and a close dialogue between public leaders and researchers all the way through. Finally, we found a way of combining representative democracy with participatory and deliberative democracy so that the new model was not accused of undermining the established forms of liberal democracy but praised for its expansion of democratic forms of co-created political leadership.

9.5 Concluding remarks

In this chapter, we have outlined approaches for the extrapolation or the co-creation of practices that may guide public managers in learning from experiences that occurred elsewhere or in creating innovative solutions. We have confined ourselves to the level of the method for setting in operations 'practices that work,' as there is no available, off-the-shelf 'general menu of good practices' for the management of public services organizations, and notably for the strategic management of them.

Such an achievement, such as the construction or the co-creation of a menu of practices (properly analyzed in accordance with protocols like the one we have illustrated in this chapter) would require the joint efforts of (i) institutions engaged in organizing major exercises for the identification of good practices or the invention of them through co-creation, (ii) researchers engaged in a research programme on different categories of good practices, and (iii) practitioners willing to provide full accessibility to their experience (including the least attractive downsides, the negative aspects of their experiences) and to critically re-examine them together with researchers. Such a joint effort would provide a major contribution to public management and strategic management.

It would also epitomize the nature of public management as both a 'science' and an 'art and profession' and contribute to the development of it. We dwell on these foundational issues about the nature of public administration and management, and of the strategic management of public services organizations as a key component of it, more at length in the next and final chapter.

Note

1 The considerations developed in this section originate from an elaboration of the paper 'A protocol for the extrapolation of "Best" Practices: How to draw lessons from one experience to improve public management in another situation' presented by one of the authors of this book, Edoardo Ongaro, on occasion of the 2009 ceremony of awarding of the European Public Sector Award (EPSA) for excellence in public management (Maastricht, European Institute of Public Administration, 4–6 November 2009).

10 Conclusion

Strategic management in the public sector as both 'Science' and 'Art and Profession'

The nature of public administration and public management has been widely debated. Two 'giants' in the field, Herbert Simon and Dwight Waldo, have famously duelled on this issue in a series of rejoinders (Simon 1946, 1947/1997, 1952; Waldo 1948, 1952a, 1952b). The main object of contention is whether public administration is first and foremost 'science,' and notably in the sense attributed to the word by the logical positivist movement (Carnap 1937), or whether public administration is primarily a profession, and the practice of it is an 'art,' requiring experience, wisdom, judgement, and creativity. According to the former perspective, led by Simon, 'acquisition of knowledge about public administration should be based *in fact*: empirically derived, measured, and verified. Values, he claimed, had no place in the study of public administration phenomena. He urged scholars to take as their primary unit of analysis the decisions that administrators made. Decisions could be studied scientifically in terms of their effects as well as the processes for making them. Such enquiry, in his view, could be value free and morally neutral, uncorrupted by the normative preferences of the people involved' (we here report the very effective synthesis made by Riccucci 2010, p. 9).

According to the latter perspective, championed by Waldo, while conceding that some administrative matters 'may lend themselves to "treatment in the mode of natural science, . . . administration is generally suffused with questions of value." . . . An administrative problem is characteristically a problem of 'what should be done?' Administrative study, as any social science, is concerned primarily with *human beings*, a type of beings characterized by *thinking* and *valuing*' (Waldo 1984, p. 171). Waldo conceived of the practice of public administration as essentially imbued with values (due to its being inherently political), and he questioned the adoption of efficiency as an allegedly value-neutral criterion. For Waldo, public administration as practised is primarily an art, requiring intuition, experience, 'artful' insight, and wisdom (see Riccucci 2010). In such perspective, the *practice* of public administration and management is an irreducible source of understanding of what public administration is, that cannot be replaced by 'neutral' observation of administrative phenomena by allegedly external beholders (the social scientists). Knowledge in public administration is knowledge to act and to solve pressing extant problems (in this similar to such disciplines like engineering and medicine, which embody a form of 'knowledge for action,' for solving pressing problems, and to the cognate fields of public administration and management, that is, policy analysis, education, criminology, and the like). Complementarily, due to its being inherently value-laden (and in this differently from engineering and, in a certain sense, from medicine, but once again similarly

DOI: 10.4324/9781003054917-10

to the cognate fields of public policy, education, criminology, and so on) and to its being concerned with persons (public administration is practised by human beings for human beings), public administration finds in the reason and reasoning a chief source of knowledge (i.e., including deductive reasoning and also beyond knowledge that derives from empirics).

Our own position (in line with an important strand of thought among public administrationists: for a convincing elaboration of the argument, see Riccucci 2010) is that public administration is *both* 'science' and 'art and profession' (a composite nature of public administration which we discuss further in Ongaro 2020a, Chapter 1, and, in relation to the teaching of public administration in educational programmes, in Ongaro 2019). As Frederickson (1997, pp. 51–52) put it:

> the analytical tools of social sciences help us *know* how organizations operate and how public managers function. But to know public organizations and public managers is not to *understand* them. Understanding requires perspective, experience, judgement, and the capacity to imagine. These qualities have less to do with analytical skills and more to do with philosophy, language, art and reason.

What we further argue in this book is that *strategic management contributes both to public administration as science and to public administration as art and profession* – indeed we claim that the strategic management of public services organizations has become a very significant component of both the social scientific knowledge of public administration (*to know* public organizations and public managers) and the art and profession of public administration (*to understand* public organizations and public managers); and as a growing field of research and practice, it surely has the potential to further develop its contribution to both.

In this chapter, we first discuss how and in what sense strategic management contributes to public administration and public management as a social science (we undertake this task in a rather long section: see 10.2). We further delve into certain epistemological premises in studying strategy processes in public services organizations (section 10.3). We then turn to the examination of the contribution of strategic management to public management as practical knowledge and profession (section 10.4), also aided by reflections elaborated by John Bryson on this theme (Box 10.2). A review of the main findings on one key question – who is the strategist in public services organizations? – that cross-cuts much of what we examined throughout this book (section 10.5) and a summative discussion (section 10.6) conclude our journey into the wilds of strategic management in public services organizations.

10.1 Strategic management as science

Our first claim is that strategic management as applied to public services organizations can be properly conceptualized as a social science – albeit a kind of science that progresses through multiple, more complementary than competing, paradigms, rather than science dominated by one paradigm at a time (Kuhn 1962). Yet multiplicity of paradigms does not prevent accumulation of knowledge (albeit in a partial and patchy rather than a comprehensive way), nor does it preclude complementarity among the elements of knowledge accumulated, and that such elements may be combined and used in a supplementary way (Moynihan 2009): the very idea of the schools of thought in strategic management put forward by Mintzberg and colleagues – that we elaborate for public services organizations in this book – is, we would argue, grounded in this premise.

Such perspective allows discussing the significance and contribution that strategic management can make for a better understanding of the organizational behaviour of public services organizations. This section discusses the question: 'Does strategic management provide a distinctive contribution to furthering our understanding of how decisions are made in organisations?' that is a contribution which is substantive, significant, and ultimately irreducible to the findings of other disciplinary fields. In addressing the question, we contrast explanations of the behaviour of public services organizations stemming from a strategic management viewpoint with alternative explanations rooted in disciplines that have historically dealt with decision processes in public administrations, notably political science, public policy, economics, and organization science (our analysis should in principle be enlarged to encompass other disciplines such as sociology, social psychology, anthropology, political philosophy, and moral philosophy: constraints to the size of this book alongside the humble recognition by the authors of this work of them being – very – limitedly equipped for traversing terrains as diverse as these will hopefully suffice to the reader as the reason why we confine our discussion to a brief excursus on the terrain of the four disciplines mentioned before opening these brackets).

Political science

The terrain of strategic management has in the public sector traditionally been covered by a discipline like political science that is specifically devoted to the social scientific study of political (hence 'public') institutions and organizations. Students of public administration from a political science perspective might formulate the critique that strategic management provides at most 'residual' explanations, on aspects of the behaviour of public organizations at the interstices between what is not addressed by political science studies and what is not directly investigated by other 'major' disciplines for the study of public administration like law or public economics.

Some preliminary observations are in order, to be able to fruitfully discuss this critique and highlight the distinctive contribution strategic management can furnish. Students of the public sector from a strategic management perspective may indeed get the impression they have come to a different charting of the same terrain already ploughed by political science from an altogether different perspective. The critical spirits amongst them – especially those knowledgeable of both political science and strategic management – will probably observe a tendency since the 1980s–1990s, especially in the grey literature on strategic management in the public sector (stemming mainly from the consultancy industry), to treat with the language of strategic management complex topics traditionally investigated by political science, and to do so in ways that often do not do justice to the complexity of the issues at stake. In other words, there is in this grey literature – and at times also in certain academic literature – a tendency to boil down to a strategic management perspective all that can be observed about the 'behaviour' of public services organizations, ignoring the complexities of political systems, complexities of which political scientists are acutely aware. We would argue that such literature may ultimately be detrimental to the cause of making the case for the usefulness of strategic management as a social scientific approach to the study of public administration. (As an example on this point, one of the authors of this book happened to read in the official syllabus of a master-level module of strategic management that 'strategic management binds together politics and policy' – a statement that is at least questionable.)

Political scientists, over the course of decades of research work and scientific enquiry, have delved into aspects of bureaucratic theory that cover much of the same terrain as strategic management applied to public sector organizations. An exemplar is 'the politics of bureaucracy' as developed by Guy Peters: it is a theoretical perspective to interpreting and explaining bureaucratic influence on policy making. One central idea of what is nowadays a classic of public administration (the book being in its seventh edition as the time this volume goes to press) is the analogy with how a political party may influence policy (Peters 2010, p. 197 and following in particular): starting from a set of criteria that a political party must fulfil if it is to provide government after it has been elected (and modifying the components that apply strictly to political parties), Peters identifies a set of criteria that any group attempting to govern ('the root word for government implying control and steering') a society has to fulfil (Peters 2010, p. 197). These are as follows: (i) the group must formulate policy intentions for enactment in office – in other words, it must have its own well-developed idea about what government should do (applied to bureaucracy, this has been labelled 'agency ideology'); (ii) these intentions must be supported by the availability of 'not unworkable means' to reach the ends; (iii) there should be some competition over the allocation of resources; (iv) the group should be in sufficient numerical strength in the most important positions in the regime; (v) those given office in such positions must have the skills necessary for running a large bureaucratic organization; and (vi) high priority must be given to the implementation of goals.

Peters then discusses the extent to which bureaucracies and bureaucrats fulfil such criteria. He concludes that bureaucracies encounter many limitations in fulfilling such criteria (Peters 2010, pp. 197–210 in particular), and, of course, ultimately they can only provide 'non-consensual directions,' legitimacy by the public ultimately missing to bureaucracies as providers of government: although operational legitimacy as the appropriate collective allocators of values may under certain conditions be gained by bureaucracies, formal legitimacy remains the missing element (Peters 2010, p. 228), and popular control remains a highly problematic issue. However, the basic idea is confirmed that, although only sector by sector and without any unifying philosophy of government (as could be provided by party government), bureaucratic government may occur: the bureaucracy may supply government to a society. In a plurality or even in all the policy sectors in a given political system, bureaucratic elites – with differentiated ideas usually on a sector-by-sector basis and thus steering in diverse directions – may provide government in the form of 'non-consensual directions' and act as a sort of cartel of elites for society. The author then discusses at some length the resources that bureaucracies may deploy to influence public policy (Peters 2010, pp. 211–213), as well as the resources that political institutions may mobilize as a counteracting force (Peters 2010, pp. 213–214), and the dynamic games between bureaucrats and politicians that unfold through a variety of ploys, including affecting the budgetary process, holding sway over the planning process, and accrediting the bureaucratic office/agency as a venue where policy making occurs, for example because of it statutorily gaining an advisory role.

This theoretical perspective enlightens important aspects of bureaucratic behaviour – but the question is: does it by itself suffice to explain the dynamics of how public organizations behave? Recent empirical work (partly published in Ongaro and Ferlie 2019 and 2020) has applied this theoretical perspective to the study of a category of public organizations, namely, the agencies of the European Union, to interpret the behaviour of such agencies and discuss whether and to what extent these agencies operate in such ways to be influential actors in the European public policy process. The main conclusion is that the politics of bureaucracy perspective is important but can provide only a partial explanation for agency behaviour, and it is not apt to explaining other important aspects of the organizational behaviour of these agencies: from the search for enhanced autonomy to their organizational growth, from their striving to achieve a recognized, legitimate, and central position in the European and global landscape to developing innovation in the services they deliver – these dynamics can more fully be explained only when incorporating a strategic management perspective into the explanatory framework. 'Traditional' bureaucratic theory, on one hand, and strategic management applied to the study of public sector organizations, on the other hand, seem to provide supplementary explanations, complementing, rather than displacing, each other.

Summing up, we fully recognize – and indeed most welcome – the contributions from a political science perspective to the study of the organizational behaviour of public services organizations, while at the same time arguing that there are significant profiles of the behaviour of public services organizations on which strategic management may shed light. We also hope that this book will contribute to bridge two worlds that seem so far to have proceeded in mutual isolation, namely, political scientists approaching public administration and experts in strategic management studying public services organizations. As a minimum, we hope to contribute to avoid incommunicability between scholars (and practitioners) who implicitly or explicitly consider that any 'true' understanding of public administration can come only from political science (indeed, that public administration *is* part and parcel of political science) and dismiss the contribution that an 'applied' and 'practice-orientated' discipline like strategic management can provide, on one hand, and scholars and practitioners who consider that political science may provide at most a kind of background knowledge about the institutional backdrop and broader context where the action of public sector organizations take place, but that it is of limited use when 'how to' questions have to be addressed: 'how to lead a public organisation?', 'how to improve value for the citizens?' – these are questions on which political science is short of answers, the critique from the strategic management camp goes on. Indeed 'how to' questions represent a crucial set of questions in public administration/public management and definitely one of central concern of all university students attending masters of public administration, masters of public policy, or masters of business administration with a public management track. In this chapter, we aim to provide at least some bricks for building up a much-needed bridge between these two strands of research and discourse, which have so far not been in other than sporadic communication. Our basic argument is that strategic management is *supplementary and complementary* to the explanations so far developed by political science to address both questions about 'what explains the ways in which public administrations work' and questions of 'how to get public organisations to work (in some sense) better.' These are constitutive questions for the very field of public administration and public management, and strategic management in public services organizations is part and parcel of any social scientific attempt to address such questions, though its actual application to this intellectual endeavour is, historically speaking, a more recent development than the contributions stemming from a political science perspective. Strategic management may bring a novel and fresh perspective to the study of public administration and public management, not just to address 'how to' questions but also as regards 'what explains' questions. We hope this book may represent a way forward beyond incommunicability between these two positions and towards further advancements of public administration and public management (in themselves two different mappings of the same terrain) as an inherently multidisciplinary endeavour. Such endeavour is based on the absence of one dominant paradigm, an absence which should not prevent forms of accumulation of knowledge and fruitful exchanges among different disciplinary approaches investigating the same phenomena.

Public policy: a 'strategy–public policy' continuum?

The second theoretical perspective that we examine in this (admittedly very succinct) discussion of the terrain covered by, respectively, strategic management and other disciplines that have historically contributed to the interdisciplinary study of public administration is public policy. An argument is at times put forward that the overall frame and perspective of strategic management applies and is mainly confined to 'public agencies' (for a critical discussion, see Johanson 2009). By public agencies, or similar denominations (non-departmental public bodies, semi-autonomous public entities, etc.), it is meant 'mandated, task-specific public organisations' more or less autonomous in making their decisions about the acquisition and employment of resources and about how best to execute the tasks and achieve the goals assigned by 'political,' elective governments. When turning to the 'core,' the elective government – the argument goes on – it is to public policy analysis that we need to turn: core governments produce policies, agencies implement them, in more or less 'strategically managed' ways.

Is it so? We would argue that this frame is too narrow. In a study of decision processes in the British central government in 2004–2005, Joyce (2012) interprets the Cabinet approach to core public policies during the difficult coexistence in government between Tony Blair and Gordon Brown (as Prime Minister and Chancellor of the Exchequer – Minister for the Economy – respectively) as a case of strategically managing the core government: strategy process analysis, more than public policy analysis, explains the approach to policies by the prime minister Cabinet (notably, in the case considered, welfare-related policies). Under certain conditions, the argument wrought out by Joyce continues, frameworks in strategic management do provide explanations for decisions taken in the core government, and not just in public agencies (in the case discussed, such conditions were identified first and foremost in the thrust towards regaining control of certain key policies by a besieged Cabinet, a Cabinet in which the prime minister and his followers, the Blairites, were beleaguered by the 'Brownites' – those more in line with the views of the then Treasury Minister Gordon Brown and scattered throughout the government – and their room for manoeuvre was severely constrained by the fact of being at rows with the Treasury, the powerful institution, especially so in the British governmental system, holding the strings of the purse).

In further elaborating on the interplay between individual organizations' strategy and policy making, and notably between elective government and public agencies, some authors have minted the notion of 'policy strategy,' to refer to 'what government wants to change – its agenda, and the ways in which the agency will move to help it achieve this agenda,' or, with a different wording, 'policy strategy refers to the ongoing relationships Ministers and agencies use in developing and deploying policy' (Stewart 2004, p. 19). 'Making strategy' means for public agencies to affect public policies, throughout the whole cycle, though this influence may sometimes be more pronounced on certain phases (e.g.: policy implementation) and less on others (e.g. agenda setting).

Another way of framing the question is by asking whether strategy includes 'political' decision making or not. This issue relates to the question about who is the strategist in the public sector: are strategists always tenured officials, or also elected officials (politicians) are 'strategists' in the fullest sense of the term and in their own right? The topic is discussed later (section 10.5), but we here pinpoint that if the strategist is an elected official, the question pops up again, and unavoidably: how does 'strategic' decisions differ from 'political' decisions (and strategy making differs from policy making)? Disentangling strategy from policy making remains an arduous task. The case of the redesign of the Catalan Health Sector – see Box 10.1 – provides a clear illustration of an analysis rooted in the disciplinary field of public policy of a change process that may be read also through the lenses of strategic management: it shows that the two disciplines cover partly the same terrain and may turn out to be complementary for an improved understanding of the dynamics of public sector organizations.

Box 10.1   Institutional-organizational change in the Catalan health sector: a public management policy analysis perspective[1]

By *Raquel Gallego*, *Nicolás Barbieri*, and *Sheila González*

This case illustrates a significant organizational change that occurred to the public sector of Catalonia around the year 2007 and shows how this administrative phenomenon can be conceptualized alternatively through the lens of strategic management analysis or through the lens of public policy analysis, and notably according to the latter perspective as a case of shift in the public management policy. It is this latter perspective which is developed in this case study.

The shift occurred in the Catalan health sector over the first decade of the 2000s, and a particular focus is given to a 2007 legislative decision that changed the management model of public provision – namely, from administrative body to public enterprise. Over almost three decades, the Catalan political and managerial elite in the health sector had explicitly considered such a change as not worth pursuing, because it was too difficult from both a political and a juridical point of view. The reasons, they argued, derived from structural features of the

Catalan health policy sector. So, *why were these factors not an obstacle to the passage of the 2007 Law?*

Institutional and policy change outcomes may be partly explained by policy sector-specific variables (Radaelli et al. 2012), which in the health sector may include the relative weight of private and public provision, the number and characteristics of pressure groups, and their relationship with the political elite. However, analytically significant policy-sector features are, by definition, structural variables with a considerable degree of stability. Thus, explaining change may require observing the role of other, perhaps external, but more dynamic factors, such as developments in the political arena, and understand how they interact with policy-sector, more stable factors.

Policy-sector specific variables

The trajectory of the health policy in Catalonia since the onset of devolution in the early 1980s has been widely analyzed (Gallego 2000, 2001, 2003). The public providers transferred by the Spanish government to the Catalan government in 1981 amounted to over 90% of primary care providers in Catalonia, but only to a third of the hospital beds at that time – thus, contracts with external providers could play a prominent role. The public providers transferred by the Spanish government were units of a single organization, the Catalan Health Institute (ICS), which became the health authority within the Catalan government. The ICS performed the roles of both provider and purchaser, as it also contracted with the existing network of non-ICS providers. Since then, the contracted network was substantially expanded and strengthened as an explicit political option by the Catalan government to develop an extensive indirect provision model. By contrast, ICS did not experience formal changes in its legal nature, but the transformative effect of the introduction of NPM doctrines and logic in the system changed the ICS's situation in the health system, confining it outside the prevailing rules of the game. The evolution of the ICS fitted the Mahoney and Thelen's (2010) category of *drift*, as small changes were mainly caused as a result of 'non-decisions' by policy makers.

The 1990 Law of Organization of Health in Catalonia (LLOSC) further weakened the ICS's role: the ICS lost its authority to contract with other complementary providers and was left only with its provider functions, while the purchasing/contracting functions were assigned to a newly created health authority body that would act under private management regulations – the Catalan Health Service (SCS). The LLOSC also formulated an ambiguous mandate that the ICS should disaggregate into its provider units, which would each contract with the SCS. However, whereas the SCS was quickly set up, the ICS was not extinguished but was left with its inherited legal nature of a Social Security management body, acting fully under an administrative law management framework. Thus, the ICS remained as an isolated exemplar of direct, public provision model in the Catalan health system: a large provider of health services, with a single legal personality, and which itself was the largest firm in Catalonia – over 35,000 workers, most of whom civil servants.

Overall, the reform approach of strengthening a management model different and parallel to the ICS model could be interpreted as *layering*, in Mahoney and Thelen's (2010) terms. The Catalan health system's design had relied on the support of major pressure groups: the Catalan Union of Hospitals (representing managerial interests from contracted providers) and the Hospital Consortium of Catalonia (representing the interests of those local governments that had management responsibilities in contracted health providers). The ICS lost its purchasing functions after the LLOSC, which mitigated those pressure groups' mistrust for it being both purchaser and provider. But the ICS still kept its differentiated public regulation in general and civil service and labour relations regulations in particular, with different financing mechanisms, and therefore was still seen as an opaque isle of obsolete privilege.

The Catalan political and managerial elite in the health sector had persistently criticized the ICS's management model as deeply inefficient. Some top officials would have preferred a radical change towards a private management framework – namely, a *displacement* in terms of Mahoney and Thelen's (2010) typology. According to numerous political and executive officials interviewed, several previous ICS's directors-managers had tried to address this issue with or without changes to the legal bases, but over two decades, they had not found political support to achieve it. A common interpretation of this lack of support is that the governing coalition (Catalan nationalist, centre-right *Convergència i Unió*) identified ICS as an instance of Spanish centralist politics, on one hand, and of bureaucratic and obsolete management model, on the other. Those interviewees argue that CiU was not only convinced of the impossibility to modernize or reform ICS into an efficient organization, but would have no interest in trying, just in case a public provision model could prove manageable effectively and efficiently – which would contradict the assumptions in CiU's discourse.

Although the reformulation of the ICS's legal nature and the need to modernize its management tools had been permanent issues in the political and professional discourse, published research also highlight that these same actors considered that changes had not been addressed over those years because of high veto possibilities by external and internal actors; from a legal point of view, it was very difficult to change regulations from a Social Security management body form to a Publicly-Owned Enterprise or to Autonomous Body forms. Specifically, the Ministry of Economy and Finance of the Catalan government, and particularly its Intervention Unit, due to the institutional bias derived from its control role, opposed a management model that might involve ex post economic and financial control; and the unions would probably mobilize a strong professional opposition if that proposal involved a change in labour relations. Some arguments also pointed out that a legal redefinition of the ICS required an injection of economic resources (to balance budgets) that the budget of the Catalan government could not afford. Also, successive ICS's director-managers had perceived a high degree of discretion for improving management by low-visibility changes in tools and organizational practices, without a need to make formal authoritative changes. Considering that these arguments are based on factors that could be expected to remain stable over time, because they refer to institution-biased roles, the question is: why were these factors not an obstacle to the passage of the 2007 ICS Law?

Political context and policy change

The Catalan regional elections of November 2003 brought the first ideological turnover in the Catalan government since the Spanish democratic transition of the late 1970s. The nationalist, centre-right party federation *Convergència i Unió* (CiU) had ruled the Catalan government over 23 consecutive years, since the first regional election in 1980, and with an absolute majority between 1984 and 1995. As a result of the 2003 Catalan elections, a post-electoral centre-left coalition formed to add-up to an absolute majority in parliament and took office. The coalition included the Party of the Socialists of Catalonia (PSC), the independentist Republican Left of Catalonia (ERC), and the eco-socialist coalition Initiative of Catalonia-Green (ICV-Verds), each of them representing different intensities of Catalan nationalist and leftist leanings.

The government ideology shift helped activate the mechanism of *attribution of opportunity* on several fronts, leading numerous actors to believe that efforts might eventuate in policy changes. The impact of that mechanism was strongly reinforced by several factors. First, a *focusing event* in the political stream – namely, the victory of the PSC 'brother-party' PSOE at the central government level – created positive expectations on Spain-Catalonia relationships. Second, a sensible increase in the regional budget had *spillover effects* on many policy domains, including health policy. That budget increase had resulted from a change in the macro-economic policy domain, with the approval of the 2001 new territorial financing system, and the upward economic cycle. As a leftist leader of the 'municipalist' movement, and with a prospective generous budget, Catalan Health Minister Marina Geli's priorities may be interpreted under the *logic of appropriateness*: she should promote the modernization and sustainability of public health care, but she should do it through enhancing the political role of local governments in health policy making and management. She explicitly defined non-contentious policy aims at the outset of her mandate: consolidating the structural features of the Catalan provision system, promoting public health better regulation, promoting service quality, and modernizing ICS's management, all under the general umbrella of territorialization.

The tripartite government promoted a different *issue image* of the challenges facing ICS. The Minister for Health of the Catalan government made her intention explicit to address the ICS's modernization through a change in its legal nature and the improvement of its management tools and autonomy, with an aim to make it closer to the way of operating of the contracted providers, all with an aim to ensure its sustainability as a central piece of the health system. She pursued a strategy for *lowering other actors' veto possibilities*. She took action for promoting cooperation and building trust on the *level of compliance* of spending and financial management rules – for example, through regular control and report meetings between top officials of Health and Economy, including an agreement to gradually clear the health budget debt. This agreement was facilitated by the positive *interference effect* derived from the increase in the regional budget. She also *weakened veto possibilities* coming from top officials within the ICS by appointing director-managers with a favourable profile: they were committed to the sustainability of the public sector through the development of quality, efficiency, and management modernization strategies, and were sensitive to the interests of local governments in the health sector and the need to corporatize management strategies. This stance also helped *weaken veto possibilities* coming both from local governments and from the contracted providers' network. Unions' *veto possibilities* were managed by ensuring the preservation of the *acquis* for those health professionals who were civil servants.

Understanding policy change

The 2007 ICS Law formally sought both an institutional change and a policy change: it transformed the ICS from an administrative body into a public enterprise with the corresponding change in the public management model. At first sight, it could be argued that this change amounted to *displacement* and that it derived from the external shock or critical juncture created by the ideology shift in the Catalan government. Over the previous decades, the strong veto possibilities from a multiplicity of actors had converged on a lock-in situation combining *drift* and *layering*, which had involved low-visibility adaptations but which had not been enough to provide the ICS with the tools necessary for its modernization. The 2003 government ideological shift boosted a new context of low veto possibilities where ICS internal actors, both executive and unions and professionals, could develop opportunist behaviours.

However, deeper analysis of the content and enforcement of the ICS Law places this institutional and policy change closer to *conversion*. In principle, shifting from administrative body to public enterprise involves a higher degree of discretion in rule interpretation and enforcement, which was in line with what challengers of the status quo defended. However, the existence of numerous veto players and the need of parliamentary consensus as a veto point made it difficult for decision makers and executive officials to force *displacement*. At the same time, defenders of the status quo, despite having the power to press for the preservation of existing rules, were unable to prevent the introduction of small modifications.

The negotiations centred on four issues: ICS's legal personality, its degree of financial autonomy, the (non-)civil service status of its health professionals, and the degree of disaggregation into provider units. Each issue had its own veto players and veto points: the Ministry of Economy and Finance of the Catalan government, the trade unions, and the Department of Interior (responsible for civil service regulation). The issue of organizational unity or disaggregation of the future ICS confronted several alternatives: disaggregating the ICS into different public companies; creating a public holding company (organizations with different legal statuses); or maintaining the existing legal unity. The alternative chosen was transforming the ICS into a unitary public company, its provider units (hospitals and primary care centres) would not have independent legal personality, and the use of the ICS's premises and services for private health care would be prohibited.

Most actors in the field believed the law had a limited impact on the specific management of ICS's activity. It was seen more as a formalization of pressures for specific management improvement practices that came from the ICS itself but which did not aim to revamp it. The alternative chosen of a *sui generis* public company legal personality and a single unitary structure gathered consensus on the bases of providing legal exceptions: avoiding links to central government legislation, avoiding a potentially controversial debate on privatization, and protecting workers' civil-service status. The mechanism activated here was *attribution of opportunity* by all actors involved: some interpreted this design as the protection and consolidation of the ICS's strength within the Catalan health system, and others considered this effort as a first step to further, deeper changes in the direction of private management.

Finally, yet another way of framing this problem can be developed if we take the perspective of security studies: in this field, 'strategy' is in most regards synonymous with (security) policy (see e.g. Baylis et al. 2010), and it is often used with a meaning not dissimilar to the one taken by Joyce, to refer to the 'grand strategy' which defines the overarching framework of the security policy as a whole and shapes the specific policy decisions that are taken within it.

Summing up, the argument we put forward is that strategic management may be a theoretical source with explanatory power, under certain conditions, also for core elective governments. More broadly, we argue that the oft-employed way of drawing a distinction between strategic management and politics, or at least between strategic planning and policy making (Joyce 2000, p. 4), by ascribing strategy to the dimension of the individual organization, whilst policy making, almost by definition, is ascribed to the level of the whole policy domain in which the policy cycles unfold, does not hold. Whilst it is sensible to argue that it is at the organizational level that strategy mainly makes sense (as strategy is the system for integrating decisions and actions and ensuring consistency in organizational behaviour) and it is almost by definition that policy analysis – being concerned with the analysis of the whole of the policy cycle – cuts across the organizational boundaries (policies usually cross-cut a plurality of organizations), such repartition is too narrow: it may be an acceptable starting point, yet qualifications are required. First, because the two dimensions are obviously interrelated and mutually influential: organizational strategies affect and shape the policy cycle, and policies constrain individual organizations' strategies. Moreover, as we have seen (Chapter 3), certain perspective in strategic management like the strategy-as-practice approach argue for 'strategizing' to apply at multiple levels, including the macro level of the policy or industry sector (Jarzabkowski and Spee 2009). Second, because, under certain conditions, perspectives rooted in strategic management carry explanatory power also for interpreting decision processes in the core government, in elective institutions (or in key areas of it, as is the case of the so-called strategic studies in the field of security studies), and 'strategic' and 'political' decision making tend to overlap and are hard to disentangle (if that is at all possible).

Economics (public choice)

Public economics and notably the public choice literature – a strand of economic theory applied to the study of collective, rather than individual, decision-making processes – is another potentially important theoretical source for explaining bureaucratic behaviour. An exemplar is the bureau-shaping model elaborated by Patrick Dunleavy (1991), based on a systematic review (and critique) of previous literature and especially of Downs's *Inside Bureaucracy* (1967) and Niskanen's theory on budget-maximization in public bureaus (Niskanen 1971, 1973).

Drawing mainly from economic theory, Patrick Dunleavy proposes a highly sophisticated model for explaining the shape of public bureaus. Dunleavy (1991, p. 226) also suggested this model – called *bureau*-shaping – has the potential to explain the UK 'Next Steps' reform, a major reform occurred in 1988 which disaggregated many newly established executive agencies from the core government and contributed to trigger the 'fashion' for parcelling out executive agencies from the core governments in many countries all over the world. This suggestion has been picked up by Oliver James in his systematic application of the model to study the reform that radically reshaped the British central government at the end of the 1980s, by establishing 'executive' agencies and 'unbundling' ministerial administrations, breaking them down into leaner core governments surrounded by satellite agencies.

James (2003) further elaborates on the bureau-shaping model for the application of this framework to the study of the Next Steps agencies and proposes what he labels 'the bureau-shaping perspective,' deriving from the blending of Dunleavy's bureau-shaping model and Niskanen's budget-maximizing perspective. According to this model, collective strategies for bureau-shaping (where bureau-shaping is more than 'simply' maximizing the budget of their own office, as assumed in the model originally proposed by Niskanen) are carried out by bureaucrats designed to bring their agency into line with an ideal configuration which confers to the agency both high status and agreeable work tasks and the highest possible level of budget associated with producing outputs by the department (i.e., the core budget spent by an agency on its own activities, excluding the share of the budget that is passed to others to spend), within the constraints set by political masters contingent on the existing and potential shape of the agency's activities. In qualitative terms, characteristics of an agency which are positively valued by senior officials (bureaucrats) include (Dunleavy 1991, p. 202):

- Staff functions allowing for innovative work, longer-time horizons, broad scope of concerns, high level of managerial discretion, and low levels of public visibility (as opposed to line functions including routine work, short-time horizons, narrow scope of concerns, low level of managerial discretion, and high levels of public visibility);
- A collegial work atmosphere, attainable in small-sized work units, restricted hierarchy and predominance of elite personnel (highly qualified staff), and cooperative work patterns (as opposed to what Dunleavy labels 'a corporate atmosphere,' characterized by large-sized work units, extended hierarchy and predominance

of non-elite personnel, work patterns characterized by coercion and resistance, and conflictual personal relations); and

- A central location, meaning it is proximate to the political power centres, metropolitan (capital city location), and conferring high-status social contacts (as opposed to a peripheral location, remote from political contacts, in a provincial location, and remote from high-status contacts).

On the budgetary side, the core budget and the bureau budget (the one which may be directly spent on the agency's delivered outputs) are what senior officials would prefer to have as high as possible, differently from other public choice models that emphasize total budget maximization (e.g. Niskanen 1971; other variants may put emphasis also on 'power' maximization – e.g. measured as the range of competences or tasks assigned to the agency – and on effort minimization – translating into a formal model of bureaucratic behaviour the oft-heard and widely abused rhetoric of 'bureaucrats as laggards').

The 'bureau-shaping perspective' (James 2003) blends Dunleavy's perspective with Niskanen's in that it opens the possibility to consider other components of the budget alongside the core budget in the utility function (thus determining utility functions that are different but of similar shape, hence reflecting a broadly similar pattern of behaviour). In formal terms, following James (2003, pp. 154–155), the utility function may be expressed as:

$$U = X^{\wedge}(1/2) + Y^{\wedge}(1/2)$$

Where U is the level of utility, X is the budget per senior official, and Y is an indicator of high status and agreeable tasks (in the model elaborated by James, this is the proportion of policy work in total time work; however, broader weighed or un-weighed combinations of factors determining 'high status' may be employed to get closer to the wider Dunleavy's formulation of 'status').

The constraint on the official imposed by politicians is:

$$Y = 1 - aX$$

Where 1 is the limited work time available to the senior official, a is the proportion of management time in total work time which politicians insist an official must spend supervising each unit of budget per official and $0<a<1$. At the interior optimum, the slopes of the constraint and indifference curve are equal (assuming independence of the marginal utilities of X and Y, entailing that policy work time and budget per senior official affect utility only by the sum of their separate contributions).

Dunleavy developed the bureau-shaping model as a general model to explain a range of administrative situations. It is mainly a design theory, a perspective for explaining administrative reforms: what kind of contents of the reform package bureaucrats will prefer to consider and which ones they will tend to discard, given the desires of their political masters as well as the level of attention politicians will deploy over the detailed design of the reform package. A limitation of this model is thus that it is about explaining the shape of agencies, not (directly) their organizational behaviour. However, it may also be interpreted as a theory (indeed one of the most sophisticated and elaborated in studies of the bureaucracy) that aims at predicting the kind of form that agencies will tend to have over a given period of time, through successive adjustments under the steering of the senior officials, given the constraints set by politicians and by exploiting the opportunities that will present themselves as a result of the dynamics in the political system. In this respect, the bureau-shaping perspective may tentatively be applied for explaining organizational shape-related profiles of the 'strategy' of a public agency.

Is the bureau-shaping perspective a thorough and comprehensive predictor of the behaviour of bureaucratic organizations, up to the point that other explanations like those rooted in strategic management are made redundant? Empirical work on three public agencies at the EU level (also partly published in Ongaro and Ferlie 2019, 2020) has tested this assertion, to conclude negatively: 'innate strategies' based on predetermined utility functions like those predicated of bureaucrats by the bureau-shaping perspective require being complemented by alternative perspectives that explain strategy formation, ranging from the entrepreneurial school of thought in strategic management to perspectives putting learning processes centre stage. For example, an account of the way in which a European agency developed and throve during its first ten years of activity (the European Aviation Safety Agency, EASA, see Box 2.4 and Ongaro and Ferlie 2020) shows the limits of interpreting organizational behaviour (only) according to this model. At the core of the bureau-shaping perspective, there is the idea of a set of deliberate attempts along the direction of upgrading the organization towards the execution of 'high-level' tasks, which in the case considered could be modelled in the form of acquiring policy advice tasks whilst remaining small in size. Whilst the function of drafting technical regulations (a form of policy advisory task) was a task that the agency actively pursued and developed, there seems to have been no consistent set of deliberate attempts in the direction of 'getting rid' of operational activities: on the contrary, executives of the agency actively engaged to make EASA a large 'delivery organisation.' Organisational growth is indeed a goal in the entrepreneurial school of thought in strategic management ('Let's face it. . . . We're empire builders. The tremendous compulsion and obsession is not to make money, but to build an empire,' from *Fortune*, 1956, cited in Mintzberg et al. 2009), rather than in the bureau-shaping perspective.

The EASA case also shows a pattern of behaviour by its first director during his decade-long term of office deeply inspired by the ethos and conceptions of the *service public à la française*, entailing a strong sense of the pre-eminence of the public service and an authoritative way in which solutions are administered to the community recipient of a public service. Such worldview did mark the behaviour and the set of consistent decisions that were made over the time: bureaucrats are simply *not* (as a minimum: not always, or not only) utility maximizers. Their previous social identity is a crucial explanatory factor: the personal and professional life of the bureaucrat is a crucial 'predictor' of managerial behaviour.

Taking another case – the story of the European Research Council and its Executive Agency (ERCEA) over the first five years after its establishment (Ongaro and Ferlie 2019) – it is a story showing that conditions for bureau-shaping behaviour were largely absent in the ERCEA case, due to the prominent role of professionals, the scientists in the scientific council, whose utility (if the utility maximization perspective makes sense at all for explaining that case) lay in expanding their own research time rather than the policy advisory or other status-related tasks for the agency. In the case, the perspective of the design school in strategic management, properly reformulated to account for a collective rather than an individual strategist (constellation of actors jointly providing leadership to strategic change), provided important explanations of the agency's organizational behaviour.

Summing up, it may be stated that strategic management approaches have an explanatory power of their own in enabling the analysis and interpretation of certain profiles of the behaviour of public organizations. Approaches rooted in bureau-shaping (and, as extension of the argument, in other public economics frameworks) and perspectives of analysis stemming from strategic management shed light on different profiles, and they complement, rather than supplant, each other in explaining the organizational behaviour of public services organizations.

Organization science

Since the thrust of this section is the analysis of decision-making processes in organizations, a 'natural' source from which to draw analytical tools is organization science. Several strands of literature in organization science are engaged in the task of explaining how decisions happen in organizations as their central research question. We very briefly recall some of the major theoretical achievements in organization science to then address the pertinent question for this section: whether such achievements are in themselves sufficient to explain decision processes and organizational behaviour, de facto subsuming into organization science the explanations that may be provided by models and theories developed in strategic management.

Preliminarily, we should notice that strategic management (especially schools of thought orientated to explaining 'how' the strategy process unfolds, rather than 'what' substantive contents should inform strategy) heavily relies on organization science. Hence, the question may more properly be formulated as whether strategic management schools substantively add to organization science, by enabling more comprehensive explanations of the behaviour of public sector organizations, or conversely whether the conceptual tools of organization science suffice, and strategic management simply adds a layer that may be broken down to its composing elements (hence, the criterion of parsimony would suggest to simply remove that additional layer: to resort directly to organization science rather than strategic management to explain the behaviour of public services organizations).

It is commonly held (perhaps even fashionable) that there are two main logics of action (March 1999; March and Simon 1958/1993): the logic of consequences and the logic of appropriateness. The former depicts actions as being chosen by evaluating their probable consequences for the preferences of the actor; the logic of consequences is linked to conceptions of anticipation, analysis, and calculation. The latter is based on the matching of situations (recognized by the actor on the basis of previous classification) to a set of rules; in the perspective of the logic of appropriateness, decision makers have a conception of their personal, professional, and officials identities and evoke particular identities in particular situations: through matching, decision makers do what they see as appropriate to their identity in the situation in which they find themselves (see March 1999, pp. 21–22). Organizations can be seen as assemblages of rules by which appropriate behaviour is paired with recognized situations: some of these assemblages are imported into an organization by employing professionals, other assemblages are developed in an organization through collective experience and stored in the organizational memory as standard procedures.

Interestingly, rules are maintained even despite turnover in personnel and without necessary comprehension of their bases, which is why the processes for generating, changing, evoking, and forgetting rules become essential in analyzing organizations (March and Simon 1958/1993).

The notion of the logics of action in organizations is a crucial, basic concept. Yet by itself, it represents only a tool for the analysis, rather than a comprehensive interpretation of how direction forms in organizations and how consistency may be achieved over the time and when the organization traverses varied circumstances. The ways in which the influence of the designer (design school), or of the entrepreneur, or of planners, unfold on the organization and affect organizational behaviour may be interpreted according to either logic depending on the circumstances, or more often by resorting to both, combined in different ways. Yet the design school, the entrepreneurial school, or the planning school have more to say about how strategy forms than just the appraisal of which logic may explain the decision pattern of the designer, or the entrepreneur, or the planners. Let alone the explanations that may be provided by the cultural or the resource-based view, to mention other schools of thought illustrated throughout this book, which take the move from other dimensions than individual decision making.

Indeed, an important stream in organization science investigates decision-making ecologies: decisions and actions must not be observed in isolation, but in their intermingling: 'many of the features of decision making are due less to the intentions or identities of individual actors than to the systemic properties of their interactions' (March 1999, p. 28). Organization science thus once again furnishes a fundamental raw material to strategic management, notably to those schools emphasizing aspects different than individual decision making as central to strategy formation. Yet the two disciplines are partly distinguished for their substantive focus, and strategic management is more concerned with incorporating such findings in broader patterns whereby the overall direction and consistency of decisions over time are achieved in organizations, while organization science is more concerned analyzing the specific features of interactions in decision making (which is instead the core concern of organization science).

Learning processes (Levitt and March 1988; Dunlop and Radaelli 2018) are another central area of enquiry for organization scientists. It is possible to distinguish between direct and vicarious learning. Direct learning is about learning from direct experience; organizations may be seen as learning by encoding inferences from history into routines that guide behaviour. Organizational memory is central to this process: recording, conservation, and retrieval of experience is crucial, and memory loss may be a major challenge to learning from experience (regarding public sector organizations, it has been argued that post-bureaucratic 'New Public Management' organizations may have less memory than 'traditional' bureaucratic organizations, see Pollitt 2008). There are, however, important limits to learning from direct experience, ranging from the limits of experience to the problematic nature of interpreting experience (the past may be as uncertain and ambiguous as the future is). Suggested remedies to these shortcomings include experiencing history richly, or from simulating experience. Yet these may not suffice, and the fundamental alternative is vicarious learning: learning from the experience of others, a topic that we have already discussed in Chapter 9 in examining the 'best practices' literature and the problem of how to extrapolate from a given set of circumstances a 'practice that works' and apply it elsewhere. In strategic management, learning is obviously central to the learning school of thought, and ubiquitous across all the other schools. However, learning studies as such (as developed in organization science) furnish the 'raw materials' that strategic management studies pick up to explain strategy formation; here too some division of labour seems to account for the complementary contributions that the two disciplines make.

In conclusion, organization science provides crucial conceptual and analytical tools for the analysis of decisions in organizations and of organizational behaviour, yet explanations in strategic management (incorporating contributions from other disciplines as well) provide full-fledged patterns of how the overall process of providing direction to an organization forms – patterns that are not, or not entirely, by themselves explained by organization science. Thus, we may claim that strategic management ultimately provide a distinctive contribution to the understanding of decisions in public services organizations.

10.2 Reflections on certain epistemological (and ontological) premises of studying strategy processes

We have argued in the previous section that strategic management provides explanations of the dynamics of public services organizations that are *supplementary and complementary* to the explanations offered by other disciplines studying these organizations. It should at this point be made explicit the assumption implicit in the statement that different disciplines are reciprocally supplementary and complementary: what we mean is that the ultimate aim of the study of a phenomenon is to achieve a unifying theory capable of providing a 'robust enough' explanation of the phenomenon (though such theory remains always subject to what the philosopher Karl Popper defined as 'falsification': each theory is always 'provisionally accepted,' and it has to undergo further empirical testing that might later prove the theory was dependent on specific previously unspecified conditions, which requires the theory to be amended, or mean that it was plain wrong, see Popper 2002, original edition in German 1935).

What was also implicit in our argument is a critique of the 'juxtaposition approaches': a perspective according to which the contributions of different disciplines to the study of social phenomena are ultimately irreconcilable and what research in the social sciences may aim at is only 'fragments of knowledge'; in this perspective, what research may aspire to at most is a fragmented mosaic of incommensurable contributions based on irreducibly inconsistent assumptions, a kind of knowledge which is irremediably impossible to generalize beyond very narrow boundaries. In other words, according to this perspective, researchers should forego any attempt to comprehensive explanations. To the contrary, we side with scholars like Riccucci who argue that in public administration and public management (and more broadly in the social sciences), there are indeed multiple paradigms providing complementary contributions, yet this does not prevent the search for unifying explanations (Riccucci 2010) and the pursuit of the goal of the ultimate consistency among the findings of different disciplines applied to the study of administrative phenomena. According to this perspective, assumptions made by one discipline (e.g., economics, about a certain pattern of behaviour of individuals) cannot contradict the results of other disciplines (e.g., anthropology or social psychology about the manifold drivers of human behaviour and the ultimate irreducibility of these to linear models of human behaviour), and researchers cannot and should not content themselves with contradictory, inconsistent findings.

These considerations lead to the rejection of simplistic assumptions about human nature, beyond either depictions of the human being as a 'rational utility maximiser' (economicistic explanations that ignore human-cultural evolution and the findings of behavioural genetics and social psychology – and more fundamentally of philosophical enquiry – about altruistic, other-regarding behaviour as a constitutive dimension of the human being) or interpretations of the human being as a blank slate on which almost anything can be written, ultimately resulting in hetero-determined human behaviour (consider, e.g. approaches close especially to certain versions of normative or sociological new institutionalism, whereby, in a logic of appropriateness and a perspective of isomorphism, appropriate behaviour is dictated upon individuals by institutions or institutional fields – approaches that we criticize on the grounds that they are oblivious of the impossibility to reduce the behaviour of all individuals, always and under any circumstances, to conformity). Indeed, the fundamental openness to a plurality of coexisting dimensions in human behaviour (Ongaro 2020a, Chapter 4) is one more reason why the approach of the multiple schools of thought in strategic management appears convincing to the authors of this book.

A number of 'epistemological' traditions may be detected in public administration and management (these are discussed from a philosophical standpoint in Ongaro 2020a, Chapter 6). A common classification identifies at first a 'positivist tradition,' also known as empiricism, whose roots may be traced back to the neopositivism philosophical movement. In such perspective, reality is 'out there,' not in the subject investigating it, and there is in such tradition a strong reductionist thrust and an emphasis on quantitative methods (a thrust that may be perhaps be captured by the maxim 'only what is measurable is knowable'), perhaps deriving from an underlying conception whereby the social sciences are broadly likened to the natural sciences, and they can progress only to the extent they become tantamount to the natural sciences in their methods and logic. Indeed, in such tradition, the natural sciences provide the pattern, and according to such perspective, little is left beyond what is measurable. It may further be argued – though this is contestable – that the inductive method is the preferred, if not the only, logic of inference, and little room is left for deduction and broadly the role of the subject in the process of knowing.[2]

Partly as a reaction to the positivist tradition, the constructionist tradition (usually known through terms like constructionism, or social constructionism – also terms like postmodernism or relativism are at times employed for referring to broadly the same tradition) puts an (over?)emphasis on the subject and on considering that 'reality' can only be understood subjectively (observations and categorizations being ultimately culturally specific claims). It may be claimed that in countries like the UK, over the last decades, such perspective has gained terrain and at times has become dominant.[3]

We feel uncomfortable with such dichotomy. First, the range of epistemological options is larger than what this perspective affords (see Riccucci 2010). Second, we side with scholars like Talbot (2005, 2010) in arguing that an intermediate position – indeed a third, distinct position – is available (Talbot 2010): the realist tradition. Such tradition broadly attempts to reconcile these irreconcilable positions (namely positivism and constructionism). Ontologically it accepts that there is indeed a real reality 'out there,' independent of our observation of it. To that extent, it agrees with positivist assumptions. However, in relation especially to human organizations, it also sees that there are major epistemological problems in understanding how we can know this reality that are not resolved by the reductionist and quantitative methods of positivism. . . . Realists generally advocate 'mixed methods' as a solution.

(Talbot 2010, p. 57)

A major advocate of a realist approach is Pawson (2002, 2013; Pawson and Tilley 1997).

What are philosophical – ontological and epistemological – foundational issues of the realist tradition? This is obviously a topic that goes well beyond what may be developed in these concluding pages of this volume. Yet after having enticed the curiosity of the reader, we feel obliged to provide a few additional notes on our own reflections on this question (for an effective argument on the significance of questions of ontology for the study and practice of public administration, see Stout 2012; for a systematic treatment of ontological questions in relation to the field of public administration and public management, see Ongaro 2020a, Chapter 4 in particular). As preliminary definitions, ontology refers to the nature of being,[4] or the nature of reality; epistemology concerns how humans can know about reality, the conditions, and nature of human knowledge. We share the conceptual and terminological definitions that 'methodology' is a term that should be used for the whole bundle of ontology, epistemology, and the research methods employed in empirical investigation (Talbot 2010, p. 55), rather than as synonym for 'methods of research.'

One possible foundation of the realist tradition lies in *realist phenomenology* (Ongaro 2020a, Chapter 6) – which requires introducing two more notions: 'nous,' which concerns the things in themselves, the thing as it 'really' is, a pure object of intellection; and 'phenomenon,' which regards the manifesting of things and their becoming apparent to the senses. In such philosophy, things transcend the subject, but the subject is necessary for the manifest*ing* of things to occur. In the other mainstream within phenomenology, namely *idealist* phenomenology (Husserl 1980; for an overview, Kenny 2010, pp. 879–880 and Reale and Antiseri 1988, pp. 427–444), the 'metaphysical status' of the essences that are known to the subject is left unresolved, that is it is unclear whether they are existent beyond the subject to whom they manifest themselves, or not; in the latter case, things exist only in the process of revealing themselves – a perspective which could perhaps provide a foundation for constructionist positions (which is why we side with realist – rather than idealist – phenomenology). Epistemologically, the subject is capable of knowing through the process of 'epoché' (ἐποχή), or the suspension of judgement to 'enable' things to manifest themselves. In a realist phenomenology, 'things as they are' are revealed to the subject, but they 'precede' it, they come before the subject. However, in realist phenomenology, the subject plays a crucial role in allowing things to manifest themselves: citing Leibniz's famous 'motto,' *'nihil est in intellectu quod prius non fuerit in sensu, excipe: nisi ipse intellectu,'* which we may translate as follows: nothing is in the intellect that was not in the senses (that did not pass through sensorial perception) beforehand, with one (major) exception: the intellect itself[5] (see also Reale and Antiseri 1988, pp. 354–355 for an appreciation of the background to it, notably in Aristotle's metaphysics).

The other crucial foundational assertion of phenomenology is that phenomena are not the limits of knowledge, the only domain that is knowledgeable to humans (to the self-conscious subject); rather, they are the door through which the nous, the things in themselves may get to be known. In such perspective, the phenomenon is conceived of as an 'open door,' the gate through which human knowledge, albeit always limited,[6] may get access to things in themselves (which are referred to as 'essences,' the 'substance' or with a Latin word *quidditas* – notice that 'essence' is a word generally repudiated by the neo-positivist tradition). This is in contrast to Kantian formalism (Reale and Antiseri 1988, pp. 653–678; Kenny 2010, pp. 576–582) whereby things get knowable only due to the way they are structured by the human mind (only the phenomenon is knowable, and the categories of knowledge reside in the human mind that enables phenomena to be known, by having them to be structured by the human mind).

Critiques have been moved to the phenomenological approach, pointing the finger to this approach as adding a 'morass,' notably with its distinction between nous and phenomenon, and about the function of 'reason' and *a priori* reasoning (i.e. before empirics). Yet ontological issues are inescapable, and no epistemological approach can avoid confronting itself with such issues (exactly as no explanation in the social sciences can claim to be theory-free, yet theories in turn require an underpinning in more fundamental ontological-epistemological foundations). The realist tradition grounded in realist phenomenology makes a major attempt to grapple with foundational issues in the investigation of social systems, allowing for both the 'knowing' and the 'understanding' of them (where understanding is intended as the organizing and making sense of what is known, also for practical usages).

10.3 The contribution of strategic management to public management as practical knowledge and profession

At the outset of this chapter, we introduced the 'dichotomy' between public administration as 'science' and public administration as 'art and profession,' arguing that public administration (and public management) is both.[7] Notably – given the purposes of this book – we argue that strategic management contributes to both the social scientific enquiry of public administration and to the practice of administering and the profession of the public administrators. Section 10.2 has then elaborated on the distinctive contribution furnished by strategic management to the field of public administration as science. In this section, we elaborate on the contribution of strategic management to public administration as practical knowledge: as a profession and an art.

Public administration as art refers to a set of skills that are practised and that may be learnt – or at least developed starting from certain original, innate predispositions – and transmitted from generation to generation, for the administering of public institutions and services to actually take place. Yet such skills can only partly be codified, hence they are not (or not entirely) amenable to forms of 'scientific' treatments for the 'scientific organisation of labour' (Taylor 1911). One can think of the debate on the skills for leadership (the extent to which these are innate or can be learnt, and crucially the inherent limitations to the extent these skills may be codified and treated by means of 'scientific observation' in the sense adopted by Taylor). Leadership is a theme which is inherently part of strategic management (or at least of some approaches to strategic management like strategizing, which was considered in-depth in Box 3.2: 'Strategizing is a feature of leadership,' Bryson 2021, p. 15), indeed it is from strategic management that an important part of the copious literature on leadership stems, although the scholarly study of leadership, and within it public leadership, has its own distinctive scope and foci of enquiry (Crosby and Bryson 2005; Hartley et al. 2015).

Public administration and management is a profession (for a discussion, see Lynn 1996; on the systems of professions in contemporary society, Abbott 1988; on the implications for the teaching of public administration, Ongaro forthcoming), with its well-codified professional associations, 'epistemic community' and learned societies, status in the academia, institutions and procedures for the training of its members (institutions include notably national schools of administration in many countries).

Parallels may be drawn with strategic management as a profession (Jarzabkowski 2005). Indeed, the teaching of strategic management is seen by many as a constitutive component of the rucksack of the public manager. The procedures for the training of public administrators/public managers include notably the 'Masters of Public Administration,' the 'Masters of Public Management' (or tracks thereof in Masters of Business Administration), and masters or executive courses of government and public policy, and related. Indeed, this book has the ambition to make the case for the systematic study of strategic management in Masters of Public Administration and Masters of Public Management and Policy, Masters in Government or Public Policy, as well as in the public management tracks of Masters in Business Administration (MBAs). Strategic management of public services organizations – properly conceived through the idea of the multiple schools of thought, and attentive to contextual issues and influence – should be part and parcel of these programmes and the training of public administrators and public managers.

A few words should be said in the conclusion of this section about the problem of the division of the intellectual labour between researchers and practitioners, that is between public administrationists (scholars) and public administrators (practitioners), concerning especially the topic of 'usable knowledge' and the related issue of what practices can be applied by practitioners (a problem we have targeted in Chapter 9). Designing practices apt to solving extant problems is the daily concern of practitioners and of the practice of public administration. Although also direct learning (i.e. based on lived experiences) is a powerful source for designing solutions to problems, the width of direct experience is inescapably narrow (March, Sproull and Tamuz 1991). Practitioners must thus rely on vicarious learning, that is on the works of researchers producing accounts of 'significant' experiences. In turn, such 'experiences' have been begotten by practitioners acting to solve problems, and it is based on their recounts that scholars may work out their own accounts. Researchers' accounts – which are theory-intensive, that is provide explanations and compare alternative explanations for the observed 'practice that works' – are the basis for extrapolation processes and the application of the acquired knowledge to other cases (the application of what can be extrapolated from one source site to the target sites, as we discussed throughout Chapter 9). At the core of this process lies a division of the intellectual labour between scholars and practitioners, and – like for any form of division of labour – both sides need the output of the other part for the 'final' and usable outputs to be made available.

Before turning to the conclusion of this book, there remains one question that cuts across much of what we have been examining throughout the book, and on which the reader may perhaps find it useful to dwell upon: *who* is the strategist in public services organizations? We discuss this question, by way of wrapping up on what we have discussed about this issue throughout Chapters from 2 to 5, in the next section.

10.4 Who is the strategist?

A crucial question for strategic management as profession – next to the analytical significance for strategic management as science investigating decisions and patterns of decision and behaviour – concerns 'who' the strategist is in public sector organizations (Joyce 2000, 2008).

The answer is different according to the different schools. In the design or planning school, distribution of authority within organization and 'formal involvement in decision options' are attributed an important part of the answer and the chief executive of the organization is *the* strategist in the design school, flanked by the planners working in staff offices supporting the organizational apex in the planning school. This may, however, be seen as an outdated perspective, notably when schools like the strategy-as-practice or the public value are brought into the picture: whoever *does* strategy (strategizing approach, see section 3.5 and specifically Box 3.2) or entrepreneurially creates public value (Public Value school) is the strategist. And the strategist may well be a collective rather than an individual actor.

Furthermore, a cross-cutting issue arises when the politics-administration dichotomy is brought into the picture. There seems to be an important stream in the literature on strategic management in the public sector for which the answer seems to be that the career bureaucrats in top executive positions are the strategists. This answer seems to be quite explicit in certain works of authors like Paul Joyce, who conceives of strategy as 'the bridge between political processes and the recurrent episodes of changes in budgets and activities' (Joyce 2000, p. 135), that is between politics/policy making on one hand, and organizational/business processes on the other hand, and who conceive of strategists as those who mesh together the priorities and objectives of the politicians, on one hand, and the bottom-up interests and commitment of managers and employees in public sector organizations, on the other hand (it is noticed that in another contribution, Joyce revisits this question and adds a different perspective, arguing that politicians, notably the very prime minister in charge, may be the strategist – Joyce 2012). Such a picture seems to be broadly aligned with the perspective of 'the rise of the unelected' (Vibert 2007) that is allegedly a feature of government in the epoch of 'global capitalism' (Roberts 2010).

Yet this perspective raises different questions and issues. First, questions about how they are appointed and confirmed in top executive positions, and what is their previous identity before getting to such top executive positions, with the related implications for the interpretation of their role. Second, there is the issue of 'how remote' politicians are: Joyce (2000) notices that in certain public organizations, like hospitals, elected officials may be quite remote from top executives, whilst in others, like local governments, elected officials and those executives who make the strategy (like the city manager) are very close to each other.

In the public value perspective, 'strategist' is whoever engages in a conduct capable of creating public value (Moore 1995, preface); thus, such school seems to simply move beyond any politician-bureaucrat dichotomy regarding the question of who the strategist is. However, a key function in managing strategically is obtaining the necessary political support, which seems to point to the consideration that strategists tend to reside in a camp which is not that of politics (although individual politicians may act as strategists). Also, Osborne and Gaebler, in their well-known 1992 book, seem to make a similar statement about the need to gain some form of support from politicians for the running of the organization according to 'rational' strategic planning to be feasible. Following the line of reasoning of these authors, gaining political support may also be interpreted as a function that has to be performed for inter-posing a filter between the (alleged) 'rationality' of strategic planning and the allegedly fickle (read: 'irrational') short-termism of (democratic) politics.

That bureaucrats, not politicians, are the strategists may however be not the general case, but simply the most frequent one. In a work based on a comparative analysis of the US General Performance and Results Act (GPRA) started in 1993 under Vice-President Al Gore and run until 2004 and 2005, well within the Bush II presidency, with the UK Blair's governments, with special reference to the strategic plans of 2004 and 2005, Joyce (2012) has introduced the distinction between politician-oversight approach to strategic planning and the politician-led approach to strategic planning. Politician-oversight approaches are all those approaches in which tenured officials, 'bureaucrats' are the strategist, and politicians are confined to an oversight role, indispensable for ensuring democratic accountability to the process, and for the feasibility of it. In politician-led approaches, instead, it is the elected official to be the primary strategist, as was the case for British Prime Minister Tony Blair especially during the 2004 and 2005 when he and his Cabinet led the process that conducted the development of strategic plans for the respective years. Whilst politician-oversight approach seems to be by far the most prevalent form, it is argued that politician-led approaches to strategic management may occur too, although under relatively more specific circumstances. Also 'governance' or network-based and collaborative models of strategy (Chapter 4) put an emphasis on politicians, especially operating as boundary-spanners, adding a further emphasis on collective decision makers (e.g. Conteh et al. 2014).

The question 'who is the strategist?' therefore has a composite answer, varying according to the circumstances. The strategist may be top executives (design and planning school, partly the entrepreneurial school), but also whoever (within or outside the organization) learns and engages in strategizing (strategy-as-practice, strategy-as-process); the strategist may be a tenured official (and this is perhaps more often the case), as well as an elected official; also, and crucially, the strategist may be an individual or – probably more often – a plurality of persons interacting in manifold ways and dynamically forming a collective strategist.

10.5 Concluding remarks: the 'Schools Approach' to strategic management in public services and paths of development of the discipline

This book provides a general framework for the strategic management of public services organizations. We try to parallel the contribution made by Mintzberg and colleagues to the strategic management of (mainly) private or commercial sector organizations (Mintzberg et al. 2009) by introducing and systematically reviewing the schools approach to strategic management in the field of public services.

In making the argument for such approach, we pointed out the significant transformations which have occurred, on one hand, at the level of the ideas and theories made available for the understanding of strategy and the strategy process by the progress of the discipline, and, on the other hand, the changes on the public policy side in the terms of the long-term transformative effects of public sector reforms that have swept many countries and jurisdictions over the past decades. The broadening of the schools of thought in strategic management has provided the conceptual tools for a more comprehensive and nuanced understanding of the strategy process (see Chapters 2 to 6). The transformative effects of public management reforms have created the conditions for the wider usage of strategic management models in public services organizations (by expanding what we have labelled 'the strategic space of public services organizations,' see Chapter 7).

At the core of our argument also lies an understanding of strategic management as context-sensitive, rather than context-free. The politico-administrative and cultural contexts shape some of the very basic premises for the management of public services organizations, hence of the strategy process of them, as we have widely argued in a chapter dedicated to this fundamental issue (Chapter 7).

Finally, we side with prominent authors like Rhys Andrews, George Boyne, Kenneth Meier, Laurence O'Toole, Hal Rainey, and colleagues in arguing that strategic management does have an influence on the performance of public services, and we suggest some ways forward for understanding how and under what conditions such influence unfolds and may be understood and deployed for purposes of bettering performance in public services settings (Chapters 8 and 9).

Managing strategically public services organizations may be of utmost importance for all citizens and individual beneficiaries of public services, yet a more in-depth understanding of 'strategy' and the strategic process is required than what is usually assumed: there are manifold models of strategy, and contextual influences are key to understanding the dynamics of the strategy process. Both the social scientific understanding of strategic management and the practice of it – the profession of public strategist in public services settings – involves a complexity that goes well beyond simple models of strategic management (too often still nowadays narrowed down to 'adopting a strategic plan,' or simply re-labelling with the terminology of the strategic management language formal job titles and names of units in the organization chart). Recognizing such complexity is a step towards better understanding and better practice. We hope this book may contribute, if not a cornerstone, at least a useful and valuable brick to the edifice of the field of the strategic management of public services organizations.

Notes

1 This case is based on Gallego, R.; Barbieri, N.; González, S. 2013 "Explaining cross-regional policy variation in decentralized states: integrating public management policy-making in new institutionalist analysis." Paper presented at the First International Conference on Public Policy, Grenoble, 26–28 June.
2 This statement requires important qualifications: an important part of modern physics (often considered the 'queen' of all sciences – though this statement too is obviously questionable)

grants the subject a fundamental role. An exemplar is the principle of indeterminacy of Heisenberg ('A principle in quantum mechanics holding that increasing the accuracy of measurement of one observable quantity increases the uncertainty with which another conjugate quantity may be known,' from the American Heritage Dictionary of the English Language, Fourth Edition, copyright ©2000 by Houghton Mifflin Company, updated in 2009, published by Houghton Mifflin Company): in short, the perturbation introduced by the subject who measures properties of particles in quantum mechanics determines a situation whereby the more precisely the position (as an example of a property) of the particle is known, the less precisely the speed vector (direction and speed of movement, as an example of a conjugate quantity) of the particle is knowable. The Schrödinger equation (the integral of the distribution of the probability of presence of the particle applied to the whole universe) leaves us with only one 'certainty': that the particle is somewhere in the universe(!) (the integral, in fact, equals 1).

3 Lister and colleagues, for example argue that in the field of media studies, the dispute over the extent to which new technologies have a determinate influence on the cultural and social outcomes of the new media, or rather it is the way in which new technologies come to be socially constructed to ultimately matter, it is the latter to have won and be the dominant approach in the field, at least in the context of British cultural and media studies (Lister et al. 2008). Yet as Kember and Zilinska argue, this may turn out to be a pyrrhic victory, as one-sided explanations fall short of explaining change that is engendered by basic properties of technologies and the way in which they interact with human biology: an approach aiming at a more comprehensive understanding arises as the most appropriate for furthering the knowledge of the impact of new media on people's life (Kember and Zilinska 2012).

4 The order of being in itself (ontology), as distinct from the order of entities (ontic as distinct from ontological).

5 Philosophers like Immanuel Kant and St Anselm of Canterbury (also known as Saint Anselm of Aosta, his birthplace in nowadays northwestern Italy) argue – from different premises – for one, major exception: God's knowledge, which is immediate, not mediated, and God as subject, rather than being the condition for things to manifest themselves, is the condition for them being kept into existence. A distinction is here introduced between being and existence, perhaps better expressed in languages like Latin, in which 'esse' refers to being (without connoting any 'transformational' dynamics perhaps suggested by the suffix 'ing' forming the participle: on key terminological issues about the usage of the terms 'being' in philosophical enquiries conducted in English language, see Kenny 2010, p. 160), and 'existere' ('ex' meaning 'outside of' and 'sistere' is the root for 'stay': staying outside of itself) suggests that entities 'are' because the being – outside of them – lets them stay into existence ('why the being rather than nothingness?' in the formulation of the fundamental metaphysical question according to Saint Thomas Aquinas – or, 'why does Being let entities be?' in Heidegger's formulation).

6 It should be added that there is always a limit to the extension of the phenomena that can be observed by human beings, hence opening up to the possibility that knowledge based on a limited number of 'observations' may be rejected when further observations are added.

7 Barzelay 2019 distinguishes terminologically between public administration as a science, on one hand, and public management specifically as a profession, which more specifically could be re-conceptualised as a 'design oriented professional discipline,' on the other.

References

Abbott, A. (1988) *The System of Professions*. Chicago, IL: University of Chicago Press.

Abbott, A. (1992) "From Causes to Events: Notes on Narrative Positivism." *Sociological Methods and Research* 20 (4): 428–455.

Abbott, S., R. Smith, S. Procter, and N. Iacovou (2008). "Primary Care Trusts: What Is the Role of Boards?" *Public Policy and Administration* 23 (1): 43–59.

Abrahamson, E. (1991) "Managerial Fads and Fashions." *Academy of Management Review* 16 (3): 586–612.

Abrahamson, E. (1996) "Management Fashion." *Academy of Management Review* 17 (6): 254–285.

Ackermann, F., and C. Eden (2011) *Making Strategy: Mapping Out Strategic Success*. Thousand Oaks, CA: SAGE.

Adler, N. (1993) "Do Cultures Vary?" In *Societal Culture and Management*, edited by T. D. Weinschall, 23–46. New York: Walter de Gruyter.

AERA (1986) *Issue of 30 December 1986, Asahi Shimbun Shuppan*. Tokyo: Asahi Shimbun Publications Inc.

Agranoff, R. (2007) *Managing within Networks: Adding Value to Public Organizations*. Washington, DC: Georgetown University Press.

Aguilar Villanueva, L. F. (2006) *Gobernanza y Gestión Pública*. México: FCE.

Ahmad, R., N. J. Zhu, A. J. Leather, A. Holmes, and E. Ferlie (2019) "Strengthening Strategic Management Approaches to Address Antimicrobial Resistance in Global Human Health: A Scoping Review." *BMJ Global Health* 4 (5): e001730.

Aiken, M. (2010) "Social Enterprises – Challenges from the Field." In *Hybrid Organizations and the Third Sector*, edited by D. Billis, 153–174. Basingstoke: Palgrave Macmillan.

Alford, R. (2008) "The Limits to Traditional Public Administration or Rescuing Public Value from Misrepresentation." *Australian Journal of Public Administration* 38 (2): 130–148.

Allen, P., J. Keen, J. Wright, P. Dempster, J. Townsend, A. Hutchings, A. Street, and R. Verzulli (2012) "Investigating the Governance of Autonomous Public Hospitals in England: Multi Site Case Studies of NHS Foundation Trusts." *Journal of Health Services Research and Policy* 17 (2): 95–100.

Allison, G. T. (1983) "Public and Private Management: Are They Fundamentally Alike in All Unimportant Respects?" *Policy* 1 (2): 14–29.

Allix, M., and S. Van Thiel (2005) "Mapping the Field of Quasi-Autonomous Organizations in France and Italy." *International Public Management Journal* 8 (1): 39–55.

Amin, A. (ed.) (1994) *Post Fordism: A Reader*. Oxford: Blackwell.

Andrews, K. (1971) *The Concept of Corporate Strategy*. New York: Dow Jones-Irwin.

Andrews, R., G. A. Boyne, J. Law, and R. M. Walker (2012) *Strategic Management and Public Service Performance*. Basingstoke: Palgrave Macmillan.

Andrews, R., G. A. Boyne, and R. Walker (2006) "Strategy Content and Organizational Performance: An Empirical Analysis." *Public Administration Review* 66 (1): 52–63.

Anheier, H. (2005) *Non Profit Organizations: Theory, Management, Policy*. London: Routledge.

Ansell, C. (2011) *Pragmatist Democracy*. New York: Oxford University Press.

Ansell, C., and J. Torfing (2021) "Co Creation – The New Kid on the Block." *Policy and Politics* 49 (2): 211–230.

Ansoff, H. (1965) *Corporate Strategy*. Homewood, IL: Dow Jones-Irwin.

Arellano Gault, D. (2004) *Gestión estratégica para el sector público*. México: FCE.

Arellano Gault, D., W. Lepore, E. Zamudio, and F. Blanco (2012) *Sistemas de evaluación del desempeño para organizaciones públicas: ¿Cómo construirlos efectivamente?* México: CIDE.

Aucoin, P. (1990) "Administrative Reform in Public Management: Paradigms, Principles, Paradoxes and Pendulums." *Governance: An international Journal of Policy, Administration, and Institutions* 3 (2): 115–137.

Baker, K. (2015) "Meta-governance, Risk and Nuclear Power in Britain." In *Multi-Level Governance: The Missing Linkages*, edited by E. Ongaro, 247–270. Bingley: Emerald.

Ballesteros, M. F., and A. L. Moreno (2021) "Pemex, en las antípodas de la transición energética." *México Evalúa*. www.mexicoevalua.org/pemex-en-las-antipodas-de-la-transicion-energetica/

Barbieri, D., and E. Ongaro (2008) "EU Agencies: What Is Common and What Is Distinctive Compared with National-Level Public Agencies." *International Review of Administrative Sciences* 74 (3): 395–420.

Barbieri, D., F. Paolo, G. Davide, and E. Ongaro (2010) "Determinants of Result-based Control in Italian Agencies." In *Autonomy and Control of Public Agencies in Europe*, edited by P. Laegreid and K. Verhoest, 133–156. Basingstoke: Palgrave Macmillan.

Barbieri, D., F. Paolo, G. Davide, and E. Ongaro (2013) "Drivers of Autonomy of Public Agencies in Italy." *Financial Accountability and Management* 29 (1): 26–49.

Bardach, E. (1994) "Comment: The Problem of 'Best Practice' Research." *Journal of Policy Analysis and Management* 13 (2): 260–268.

Bardach, E. (1998) *Getting Agencies to Work Together: The Practice and Theory of Managerial Craftsmanship*. Washington, DC: Brooking Institutions Press.

Bardach, E. (2004) "Presidential Address – The Extrapolation Problem: How Can We Learn From the Experience of Others." *Journal of Policy Analysis Research and Management* 23 (2): 205–220.

Barney, J. (1991) "Firm Resources and Sustained Competitive Advantage." *Journal of Management* 17 (1): 99–120.

Barney, J., and D. Clark (2007) *Resource based Theory: Creating and Sustaining Competitive Advantage*. Oxford: Oxford University Press.

Barzelay, M. (1992) *Breaking through Bureaucracy: A New Vision for Managing in Government*. Berkeley, CA: University of California Press.

Barzelay, M. (2001) *The New Public Management: Improving Research and Policy Dialogue*. Berkeley, CA: University of California Press.

Barzelay, M. (2003) "Introduction: The Process Dynamics of Public Management Policymaking." *The International Public Management Journal* 6 (3): 251–282.

Barzelay, M. (2007) "Learning from Second-Hand Experience: Methodology for Extrapolation-Oriented Research." *Governance* 20 (3): 521–543.

Barzelay, M. (2019) *Public Management as a Design-Oriented Professional Discipline*. Northampton, MA: Edward Elgar.

Barzelay, M., and C. Campbell (2003) *Preparing for the Future: Strategic Management in Government*. Washington, DC: The Brookings Institution.

Barzelay, M., and R. Gallego (2006) "From 'New Institutionalism' to 'Institutional Processualism': Advancing Knowledge About Public Management Policy Change." *Governance* 19 (4): 531–557.

Barzelay, M., and F. Thompson (2003) *Efficiency Counts: Developing the Capacity to Manage Costs at the Air Force Materiel Command*. Washington, DC: IBM Center for the Business of Government.

Bate, P., G. Robert, and H. Bevan (2004) "The Next Phase of Healthcare Improvement: What Can We Learn from Social Movements?" *Quality and Safety in Health Care* 13 (1): 62–66.

Baylis, J., J. J. Wirtz, and C. S. Gray (2010) *Strategy in the Contemporary World.* Oxford and New York: Oxford University Press.

Behn, R. (1991) *Leadership Counts.* Cambridge, MA: Harvard University Press.

Bellone, C. J., and G. F. Goerl (1992) "Reconciling Public Entrepreneurship and Democracy." *Public Administration Review* 52 (2): 130–134.

Benington, J. (2011 [2010]) "From Private Choice to Public Value?" In *Public Value: Theory and Practice,* edited by J. Benington and M. Moore, 31–51. Basingstoke: Palgrave Macmillan.

Benington, J., and M. Moore (2011a) "Public Value in Complex and Changing Times." In *Public Value: Theory and Practice,* edited by J. Benington and M. Moore, 1–30. Basingstoke: Palgrave Macmillan.

Benington, J., and M. Moore (2011b) *Public Value: Theory and Practice.* Basingstoke: Palgrave Macmillan.

Bennett, C., and E. Ferlie (1994) *Managing Crisis and Change in Health Care: The Organizational Response to HIV/Aids.* Buckingham: Open University Press.

Berle, A., and G. Means (1932) *The Modern Corporation and Private Property.* New York: Macmillan.

Bernard, B., A. Drumaux, and J. Mattijs (2009) "Foresight: A Link between Policy Intents and Management Reforms." Paper presented at the 7th ASPA-EGPA Trans-Atlantic Dialogue on Strategic Management of Public Organizations, Newark, NJ, 23–25 June 2011.

Berry, F. S. (1994) "Innovation in Public Management: The Adoption of Strategic Planning." *Public Administration Review* 54 (4): 322–330.

Bezes, P. (2009) *Réinventer l'État: Les Réformes de l'Administration Française (1962–2008).* Paris: Presses Universitaires de France.

Bierly, P. E., F. Damanpour, and M. D. Santoro (2009) "The Application of External Knowledge: Organizational Conditions for Exploration and Exploitation." *Journal of Management Studies* 46 (3): 481–509.

Billis, D. (2010) "From Welfare Bureaucracies to Welfare Hybrids." In *Hybrid Organizations and the Third Sector,* edited by D. Billis, 3–24. Basingstoke: Palgrave Macmillan.

Birn, A. E., and E. Fee (2013) "The Rockefeller Foundation and the International Health Agenda." *The Lancet* 381 (9878): 1618–1619.

Bishop, M., and M. Green (2008) *Philanthrocapitalism: How Giving Can Save the World.* London: A&C Black.

Bloom, G. (2006) "The Social Entrepreneurship Laboratory: A University Incubator for a Rising Generation of Social Entrepreneurs." In *Social Entrepreneurship,* edited by A. Nicholls, 270–305. Oxford: Oxford University Press.

Bogason, P. (2005) "Post Modern Public Administration." In Ferlie et al., op cit, Chapter 10, 234–256.

Boltanski, L., and E. Chiapello (2005) *The New Spirit of Capitalism.* London: Verso.

Borgonovi, E. (1984) *Introduzione all'economia delle Aziende e delle Amministrazioni Pubbliche.* Varese: Giuffré.

Borgonovi, E., G. Fattore, and F. Longo (2008) *Management delle Istitutioni Pubbliche.* Milan: EGEA.

Boston, J., J. Martin, J. Pallot, and P. Walsh (1996) *Public Management: The New Zealand Model.* Auckland: Oxford University Press.

Bouckaert, G. (2007) "Cultural Characteristics from Public Management Reforms Worldwide." In *Cultural Aspects of Public Management Reform,* edited by K. Scheduler and I. Pröller, 29–64. Oxford: Amsterdam; San Diego, CA: Elsevier.

Bouckaert, G. (2013) "Numbers in Context: Applying Frege's Principles to Public Administration." In *Context in Public Policy and Management: The Missing Link?,* edited by C. Pollitt, 74–87. Cheltenham and Northampton, MA: Edward Elgar.

Bouckaert, G., B. Guy Peters, and K. Verhoest (2010) *The Coordination of Public Sector Organizations: Shifting Patterns of Public Management.* Basingstoke: Palgrave Macmillan.

Bouckaert, G., and J. Hallighan (2008) *Managing Performance: International Comparisons*. Abingdon: Routledge.

Bovaird, T. (2013) "Context in Public Policy: Implications of Complexity Theory." In *Context in Public Policy and Management: The Missing Link?*, edited by C. Pollitt, 157–177. Cheltenham and Northampton, MA: Edward Elgar.

Bovaird, T., and E. Loeffler (eds) (2009) *Public Management and Governance*. Abingdon: Routledge.

Boyne, G. A. (2002) "Public and Private Management: What's the Difference?" *Journal of Management Studies* 39 (1): 97–122.

Boyne, G. A. (2004) "Explaining Public Service Performance: Does Management Matter?" *Public Policy and Administration* 19 (4): 100–117.

Boyne, G. A. (2006) "Strategies for Public Services Turnaround: Lessons from the Private Sector. *Administration and Society* 38 (3): 365–388.

Boyne, G. A., and A. Chen (2007) "Performance Targets and Public Service Improvement." *Journal of Public Administration Research and Theory* 17 (3): 455–77.

Boyne, G. A., and J. S. Gould-Williams (2003) "Strategic Planning and the Performance of Public Organizations: An Empirical Analysis." *Public Management Review* 5 (2): 115–132.

Boyne, G. A., K. J. Meier, L. J. O'Toole Jr, and R. M. Walker (2006) *Public Service Performance: Perspectives on Measurement and Management*. Cambridge and New York: Cambridge University Press.

Boyne, G. A, K. J. Meier, L. J. O'Toole, and R. M. Walker (2007) *Public Services Performance: Perspectives on Measurement and Management*. Cambridge: Cambridge University Press.

Bozeman, B. (2007) *Public Values and Public Interest*. Washington, DC: Georgetown University Press.

Bozeman, B., and J. Straussman (1990) *Public Management Strategies: Guidelines for Managerial Effectiveness*. San Francisco, CA: Jossey Bass.

Breton, M., R. Pineault, J.-F. Levesque, D. Roberge, R. Borgès Da Silva, and A. Prud'homme (2013) "Reforming Healthcare Systems on a Locally Integrated Basis: Is There a Potential for Increasing Collaborations in Primary Healthcare?" *BMC Health Services Research* 13: 262.

Bretschneider, S., F. J. Marc-Aurele Jr., and J. Wu (2005) "Best Practices Research: A Methodological Guide for the Perplexed." *Journal of Public Administration Research and Theory* 15: 307–323.

Brivot, M. (2011) "Controls of Knowledge Production: Sharing and Use in Bureaucratised Professional Services Firms." *Organization Studies* 32 (4): 459–508.

Brown, H. (2007). "Great Expectations." *The British Medical Journal* 334 (7599): 874–876.

Bryson, J. M. (1988) "A Strategic Planning Process for Public and Non Profit Organizations." *Long Range Planning* 21 (1): 73–81.

Bryson, J. M. (2018) *Strategic Planning for Public and Not Profit Organizations* (5th ed.). San Francisco, CA: Jossey Bass.

Bryson, J. M. (2021) "The Future of Strategizing by Public and Nonprofit Organizations." *PS: Political Science and Politics* 54 (1): 9–18.

Bryson, J. M., F. Ackermann, and C. Eden (2007) "Putting the Resource based View of Strategy and Distinctive Competencies to Work in Public Organizations." *Public Administration Review* 67 (4): 702–717.

Bryson, J. M., F. Berry, and K. Yang (2010) "The State of Public Strategic Management Research: A Selective Literature Review and Set of Future Directions." *American Review of Public Administration* 40 (5): 495–521.

Bryson, J. M., and B. George (2020) "Strategic Management in Public Administration." In *Oxford Encyclopedia of Politics*. New York: Oxford University Press.

Buckland, R. (2004) "Universities and Industry: Does the Lambert Code of Governance Meet the Requirements of Good Governance?' *Higher Education Quarterly* 58 (4): 243–257.

Buckland, R. (2009) "Private and Public Sector Models for Strategies in Universities." *British Journal of Management* 20 (4): 524–536.

Buse, K., and G. Walt (2000) "Global Public Private Partnerships: Part 1 – A New Development in Health?" *Bulletin of the World Health Organization* 78: 549–561.

Buse, K., and K. Lee (2005) Business and Global Health Governance, Discussion Paper n.5. Department of Health and Development, World Health Organization.

Butler, M. (2003) "Managing from the Inside Out: Drawing on Receptivity to Explain Variation in Strategy Implementation." *British Journal of Management* 14: 47–60.

Butler, M., and P. Allen (2008) "Understanding Policy Implementation Processes as Self Organising Systems." *Public Management Review* 10 (3): 421–440.

Byrkjeflot, H., P. Du Gay, and C. Greve (2018) "What Is the 'Neo-Weberian State' as a Regime of Public Administration?" In *The Palgrave Handbook of Public Administration and Management in Europe*, edited by E. Ongaro and S. van Thiel, 991–1010. London: Palgrave Macmillan.

Cabrero, E. (1997) *Del Administrador al Gerente Público*. México: INAP.

Cadbury Report (1992) *Committee on the Financial Aspects of Corporate Governance*. London: Moorgate.

Callon, M., J. P. Courtial, W. A. Turner, and S. Bauin (1983) "From Translations to Problematic Networks – An Introduction to Co-Word Analysis." *Social Science Information Sur Les Sciences Sociales* 22 (2): 191–235.

Callon, S. (1995) *Divided Sun – MITI and the Breakdown of Japanese High-Tech Industrial Policy, 1975–1993*. Stanford, CA: Stanford University Press.

Cao, Y., and X. Chen (2011) "Institutional Difficulties of and Policy Recommendations for Bringing Back the Public Nature of Public Hospitals." *Journal of Shandong University Humanities and Social Sciences Edition* (1): 152–156.

Capano, G. (2003) "Administrative Traditions and Policy Change: When Policy Paradigms Matter. The Case of the Italian Administrative Reform During the 1990s." *Public Administration* 81 (4): 781–801.

Carnap, R. (1937) *The Logical Syntax of Language* [original in German 1934]. Abingdon: Kegan Paul.

Carpenter, D. (2001) *The Forging of Bureaucratic Autonomy*. Princeton, NJ: Princeton University Press.

Casebeer, A., T. Reay, J. Dewald, and A. Pablo (2010) "Knowing Through Doing: Unleashing Latent Dynamic Capabilities in the Public Sector." In *From Knowing to Doing: Connecting Knowledge and Performance in Public Services*, edited by K. Walshe, G. Harvey and P. Jas, 251–275. Cambridge: Cambridge University Press.

Castells, M. (2010) *The Rise of the Network Society* (2nd ed.). Chichester: Wiley-Blackwell.

Cejudo, G. (2017) "Policy Analysis in the Mexican Federal Government." In *Policy Analysis in Mexico*, edited by J. L. Méndez and M. I. Dussauge-Laguna, 31–44. Bristol: Policy Press.

Chakravarthy, B., and R. White (2006) "Strategy Process: Forming, Implementing and Changing Strategies." In *Handbook of Strategy and Management*, edited by A. Pettigrew, H. Thomas, and R. Whittington, 182–205. London: SAGE.

Chambers, N. (2012) "Healthcare Board Governance." *Journal of Health Organization and Management* 26 (1): 6–14.

Chambers, N., and C. Cornforth (2010) "The Role of Corporate Governance and Boards in Organisational Performance." In *From Knowing to Doing: Connecting Knowledge and Performance in Public Services*, edited by K. Walshe, G. Harvey and P. Jas, 99–127. Cambridge: Cambridge University Press.

Chambers, N., G. Harvey, R. Mannion, J. Bond, and J. Marshall (2013) "Towards a Framework for Enhancing the Performance of NHS Boards – A Synthesis of the Evidence about Board Governance, Board Effectiveness and Board Development." *Health Services Delivery Research* 1 (6). doi: 10.3310/hsdr1060.

Chandler, A. (1962) *Strategy and Structure*. Cambridge, MA: MIT Press.

Chandra, Y., and R. M. Walker (2019) "How Does a Seminal Article in Public Administration Diffuse and Influence the Field? Bibliometric Methods and the Case of Hood's 'A Public Management for All Seasons?'" *International 'Public Management Journal* 22 (5): 712–742.

Charkham, J. (1986) *Effective Boards*. London: Chartec, The Institute of Chartered Accountants.

Charkham, J. (1994) *Keeping Good Company: A Study of Corporate Governance in Five Countries*. New York: Oxford University Press.

Chávez Presa, J. (2000). *Para recobrar la confianza en el gobierno*. Mexico: FCE.

Child, J., D. Faulkner, and S. Tallman (2005) *Cooperative Strategy: Managing Alliances, Networks and Joint Ventures* (2nd ed.). Oxford: Oxford University Press.

Child, J., D. Faulkner, S. Tallman, and L. Hsieh (2019) *Cooperative Strategy: Managing Alliances and Networks* (3rd ed.). Oxford: Oxford University Press.

Christensen, T., and P. Laegreid (eds) (2007) *Transcending New Public Management the Transformation of Public Sector Reforms*. Aldershot: Ashgate.

Clarke, J. (2013) "Contexts: Forms of Agency and Action." In *Context in Public Policy and Management: The Missing Link?*, edited by C. Pollitt, 22–34. Cheltenham and Northampton, MA: Edward Elgar.

Clesse, A., T. Inoguchi, E. B. Keehm, and J. A. A. Stockwin (1997) *The Vitality of Japan*. New York: Macmillan.

Cohen, J. (2006) "The New World of Global Health." *Science* 311 (5758): 162–167.

Cohen, W., and D. Levindhal (1990) "Absorptive Capacity: A New Perspective on Learning and Innovation." *Administrative Science Quarterly* 35 (1): 128–152.

CONEVAL (2020) Diagnóstico de los objetivos e indicadores de los programas del ámbito social derivados del PND 2019–2024. www.coneval.org.mx/coordinacion/Documents/monitoreo/Sectoriales_19-20/Diagnostico_sectoriales_2020.pdf

Conteh, C., T. J. Greitens, D. K. Jesuit, and I. Roberge (eds) (2014) *Governance and Public Management Strategic Foundations for Volatile Times*. London: Routledge.

Contu, A., and H. Willmott (2003) "Re Embedding Situatedness: The Importance of Power Relations in Learning Theory." *Organization Science* 14 (3): 283–297.

Cooper, D., R. Hinings, R. Greenwood, and J. Brown (1996) "Sedimentation and Transformation in Organizational Change: The Case of Canadian Law Firms." *Organization Studies* 17: 623–747.

Cornforth, C. (2014) "Non Profit Governance Research – The Need for Innovative Perspectives and Approaches." In *Non Profit Governance: Innovative Perspectives and Approaches*, edited by C. Cornforth and W. Brown, 1–14. Abingdon: Routledge.

Cornforth, C., and R. Spear (2010) "The Governance of Hybrid Organizations." In *Hybrid Organizations and the Third Sector*, edited by D. Billis, 70–91. Basingstoke: Palgrave Macmillan.

Crilly, T., A. Jashapara, S. Trenholm, A. Peckham, G. Currie, and E. Ferlie (2013) "Knowledge Mobilisation in Healthcare Organisations: Synthesising Evidence and Theory using Perspectives of Organisational Form, Resource based View of the Firm and Critical Theory. Final Report to National Institute of Health Research Health Services and Delivery Research Programme, Project 09 1002 13. www.nets.nihr.ac.uk/projects/hsdr/09100213

Crolly, H. (2011) "Mannheim ist die Streberin unter den Kommunen." *Die Welt*, July 19. Accessed August 3, 2021. www.welt.de/dieweltbewegen/article13495230/Mannheim-ist-die-Streberin-unter-den-Kommunen.html

Crosby, B., and J. Bryson (2005) *Leadership for the Common Good: Tackling Public Problems in a Shared-Power World*. San Francisco, CA: John Wiley and Sons.

Crosby, B., J. Bryson, and M. Stone (2010) "Leading across Frontiers: How Visionary Leaders Integrate People, Processes, Structures and Resources." In *The New Public Governance*, edited by S. Osborne, 200–222. Abingdon: Routledge.

Crozier, M. (2003) *The Bureaucratic Phenomenon*. New Brunswick, NJ and London: Transaction Books.

Curtis, G. L. (1999) *The Logic of Japanese Politics*. New York: Columbia University Press.

Davies, H., S. Nutley, and I. Walter (2010) "Using Evidence: How Social Research Could Be Used to Improve Public Services Performance." In *From Knowing to Doing: Connecting Knowledge and Performance in Public Services*, edited by K. Walshe, G. Harvey and P. Jas, 226–250. Cambridge: Cambridge University Press.

Davis, G., and M. Useem (2006) "Top Management, Company Directors and Corporate Control." In *Handbook of Strategy and Management*, edited by A. Pettigrew, H. Thomas, and R. Whittington, 232–258. London: SAGE.

Deal, T., and A. Kennedy (1982) *Corporate Cultures: The Rites and Rituals of Organizational Life.* Reading, MA: Addison-Wesley.

Deal, T., and A. Kennedy (1988) *Corporate Cultures: The Rites and Rituals of Organizational Life.* London: Penguin.

DeLeon, L. (2005) "Public Management, Democracy and Politics." In *The Oxford Handbook of Public Management*, edited by E. Ferlie, L. Lynn, and C. Pollitt, 103–132. Oxford: Oxford University Press.

Denis, J. -L., and N. van Gestel (2015) "Leadership and Innovation in Healthcare Governance. Chapter 27, Part IV Concepts and Instruments of Health Policy and Governance." In *The Palgrave International Handbook of Healthcare Policy and Governance*, edited by E. Kuhlmann, R. H. Blank, I. Lynn Bourgeault, and C. Wendt, 425–440. London: Palgrave Macmillan.

Denis, J. -L., H. T. O. Davies, E. Ferlie, L. Fitzgerald with the collaboration of A. McManus (2011) Assessing initiatives to transform healthcare systems: lessons for the Canadian healthcare system. May 2011, CHSRF Series on Healthcare Transformation: Paper 1.

Denis, J. -L., L. Lamothe, and A. Langley (2001) "The Dynamics of Collective Leadership and Strategic Change in Pluralistic Contexts." *Academy of Management Journal* 44: 809–832.

Department of Health of the United Kingdom (2011) *Innovation, Health and Wealth.* London: Department of Health.

Di Maggio, P., and W. Powell (1983) "The Iron Cage Revisited: Institutional Isomorphism and Collective Rationality in Organizational Fields." *American Sociological Review* 48: 147–160.

Diario Oficial de la Federación (2019) Plan Nacional de Desarrollo 2019–2024. www.dof.gob. mx/nota_detalle.php?codigo=5565599&fecha=12/07/2019

Dixon, A., J Storey, and A. Alvarez Rosete (2010) "Accountability of Hospital Trusts in the English NHS: Views of Directors and Governors." *Journal of Health Services Research and Policy* 15 (2): 82–89.

Dodgson, R., K. Lee, and N. Drager (2002) "Global Health Governance – A Conceptual Review." Discussion Paper n.1, Department of Health and Development. Geneva: World Health Organization.

Donaldson, L., and J. Davis (1991) "Stewardship Theory and Agency Theory: CEO Governance and Shareholder Returns." *Australian Journal of Management* 16: 49–64.

Dong, L. (2009) "An Administrative Policy Analysis of Central-Local Relationships in China." In *The Role of Central and Local Administrations in Economic Development in Italy and China*, edited by M. Barbato and L. Hongbo, 139–174. Beijing: China Social Sciences Academic Press.

Downs, A. (1967) *Inside Bureaucracy.* Boston, MA: Little Brown.

Drumaux, A., and C. Goethals (2007) "Strategic Management: A Tool for Public Management? An Overview of the Belgian Federal Experience." *The International Journal of Public Sector Management* 20 (7): 638–654.

Drumaux, A., and P. Joyce (2020) "New Development: Implementing and Evaluating Government Strategic Plans – The Europe 2020 Strategy." *Public Money & Management* 40 (4): 294–298.

Du Gay, P. (2000) *In Praise of Bureaucracy.* London: SAGE.

Dunleavy, P. (1991) *Democracy, Bureaucracy and Public Choice. Economic Explanations in Political Science.* New York: Harvester Wheatsheaf.

Dunleavy, P., and C. Hood (1994) "From Old Public Administration to New Public Management." *Public Money and Management* 14 (3): 9–16.

Dunleavy, P., H. Margetts, S. Bastow, and J. Tinkler (2006a). "New Public Management Is Dead – Long Live Digital-Era Governance." *Journal of Public Administration Research and Theory* 16 (3): 467–494.

Dunleavy, P., H. Margetts, J. Tinkler, and S. Bastow (2006b). *Digital Era Governance: IT Corporations, the State, and e-Government.* Oxford: Oxford University Press.

Dunlop, C., and C. M. Radaelli (2018) "Policy Learning and Organizational Capacity." In *The Palgrave Handbook of Public Administration and Management in Europe*, edited by E. Ongaro and S. van Thiel, 595–620. London: Palgrave Macmillan.

Dussauge-Laguna, M. I. (2008) "Paradoxes of Public Sector Reform: The Mexican Experience (2000–2007)." *International Public Management Review* 9 (1): 56–75.

Dussauge-Laguna, M. I. (2013) *Cross-National Policy Learning and Administrative Reforms: The Making of "Managing for Results" Policies in Chile and México*. PhD Thesis, London School of Economics and Political Science.

Dussauge-Laguna, M. I. (2021) " 'Doublespeak Populism' and Public Administration: The Case of Mexico." In *Democratic Backsliding and Public Administration: How Populists in Government Transform State Bureaucracies*, edited by M. Bauer, G. Peters, J. Pierre, K. Yesilkagit, and S. Becker. Cambridge: Cambridge University Press.

Easterby-Smith, M., and I. M. Prieto (2008) "Dynamic Capabilities and Knowledge Management: An Integrative Role for Learning?." *British Journal of Management* 19 (3): 235–249.

Eck, N. J. V., and L. Waltman (2009) "How to Normalize Cooccurrence Data? An Analysis of Some Well-known Similarity Measures.' *Journal of the American Society for Information Science and Technology* 60 (8): 1635–1651.

Eisenhardt, K. (1989) "Agency Theory – An Assessment and Review." *Academy of Management Review* 14 (1): 57–74.

Eisenhardt, K., and F. Santos (2006) "Knowledge-Based View: A New Theory of Strategy?" In *Handbook of Strategy and Management*, edited by A. Pettigrew, H. Thomas, and R. Whittington, 139–164. London: SAGE.

El Financiero (2019) Plan propuesto por Urzúa parecía hecho por Carstens o Meade: AMLO. www.elfinanciero.com.mx/nacional/plan-nacional-de-desarrollo-propuesto-por-urzua-parecia-hecho-por-carstens-o-meade-amlo/

Elster, J. (1989) *Nuts and Bolts for the Social Sciences*. Cambridge: Cambridge University Press.

Elstub, S. (2006) "Towards an Inclusive Social Policy for the UK: The Need for Democratic Deliberation in Voluntary and Community Associations." *Voluntas* 17 (1): 17–39.

Enderlein, H., S. Wälti, and M. Zurn (eds) (2010) *Handbook on Multi-level Governance*. Cheltenham and Northampton, MA: Elgar.

Engwall, L. (2010) "Business Schools and Consultancies." In *The Oxford Handbook of Management Consulting*, edited by M. Kipping and T. Clark, 364–385. Oxford: Oxford University Press.

Etzkowitz, H. (2003) "Innovation in Innovation: The Triple Helix of University-Industry-Government Relations." *Social Science Information* 42: 293–337. https://doi.org/10.1177/05390184030423002

Etzkowitz, H., and L. Leydesdorff (2000) "The Dynamics of Innovation: From National Systems and "Mode 2" to a Triple Helix of University–Industry–Government Relations." *Research Policy* 29 (2): 109–123.

Fama, E. (1980) "Agency Problems and the Theory of the Firm." *Journal of Political Economy* 88: 288–307.

Fama, E., and M. Jensen (1983) "Separation of Ownership and Control." *Journal of Law and Economics* 26: 301–325.

Färber, G., M. Salm, and C. Schwab. (2014). *Evaluation des Verwaltungsmodernisierungsprozesses "Change²" der Stadt Mannheim*. Speyer: Deutsches Forschungsinstitut für öffentliche Verwaltung Speyer.

Ferlie, E. (2021) "Concluding Discussion: Key Themes in the (Possible) Move to Co-production and Co-creation in Public Management." *Policy and Politics* 49 (2): 305–317.

Ferlie, E., L. Ashburner, and L. FitzGerald (1995) "Corporate Governance and the Public Sector: Some Issues and Evidence From the NHS." *Public Administration* 73 (3): 375–392.

Ferlie, E., L. Ashburner, L. FitzGerald, and A. Pettigrew (1996) *The New Public Management in Action*. Oxford: Oxford University Press.

Ferlie, E., and L. FitzGerald (2002) "The Sustainability of the NPM in the UK." In *New Public Management: Current Trends and Future Prospects*, edited by K. McLaughlin, S. Osborbe, and E. Ferlie, 341–353. London: Routledge.

Ferlie, E., L. Fitzgerald, G. McGivern, S. Dopson, and C. Bennett (2011) "Public Policy Networks and 'Wicked Problems': A Nascent Solution?" *Public Administration* 89 (2): 307–324.

Ferlie, E., L. FitzGerald, G. McGivern, S. Dopson, and C. Bennett (2013) *Making Wicked Problems Governable? The Case of Managed Networks in Health Care*. Oxford: Oxford University Press.

Ferlie, E., C. Musselin, and G. Andresani (2009) "The Governance of Higher Education Systems: A Public Management Perspective?" In *University Governance: Western European Comparative Perspectives*, edited by C. Paradeise, E. Reale, I. Bleiklie, and E. Ferlie, 1–20. Dodrecht: Springer.

Ferlie, E., D. Nicolini, J. Ledger, D. D'Andreta, D. Kravcenko, and J. de Pury (2017) "NHS Top Managers, Knowledge Exchange and Leadership: The Early Development of Academic Health Science Networks a Mixed-Methods Study." *Health Services and Delivery Research* 5 (17).

Ferlie, E., and E. Ongaro (forthcoming) "Introduction to the Europe Section of the Oxford University Press Handbook of Public Administration." In *The Oxford Handbook of Public Administration*, edited by K. Baehler. Oxford: Oxford University Press.

Ferlie, E., and S. Parrado (2018) "Strategic Management in Public Services Organisations: Developing a European Perspective." In *The Palgrave Handbook of Public Administration and Management in Europe*, edited by E. Ongaro and S. Van Thiel, 101–120. Basingstoke and London: Palgrave Macmillan.

Fleishman, J. L. (2007). *The Foundation: A Great American Secret – How Private Wealth Is Changing the World*. Cambridge, MA: Perseus Book Group.

Francis Report (2013) *Report of the Mid Staffs NHS Foundation Trust Public Enquiry – Summary Report*. London: Department of Health.

Frederickson, H. G. (1997) *The Spirit of Public Administration*. San Francisco, CA: Jossey Bass.

Freidson, E. (1970) *Professional Dominance*. New York: Atherton Press.

Fretzel, W., J. Bryson, and J. Crosby (2000) "Strategic Planning in the Military." *Long Range Planning* 33: 402–429.

Fried, R. C. (1976) *Performance in American Bureaucracy*. Boston, MA: Little Brown & Co.

Gaceta Parlamentaria (2019) Plan Nacional de Desarrollo 2019–2024. http://gaceta.diputados.gob.mx/PDF/64/2019/abr/20190430-XVIII-1.pdf

Gaddis, J. L. (2018) *On Grand Strategy*. New York: Penguin.

Gallego, R. (2000) "Introducing Purchaser/Provider Separation in the Catalan Health Administration: A Budget Analysis." *Public Administration* 78 (2): 423–442.

Gallego, R. (2001). "La Política Sanitària Catalana: La Construcció d'un Sistema de Provisió Pluralista." In *Govern i Polítiques Públiques a Catalunya (1980–2000)*, edited by R. Gomà and J. Subirats. Barcelona: Edicions Universitat de Barcelona-Servei de Publicacions Universitat Autònoma de Barcelona.

Gallego, R. (2003) "Las políticas sanitarias de las Comunidades Autónomas." In *Estado de Bienestar y Comunidades Autónomas*, edited by R. Gallego, R. Gomà, and J. Subirats. Madrid: Tecnos-UPF.

Gambetta, D. (1998) "Concatenations of Mechanisms." In *Social Mechanisms: An Analytical Approach to Social Theory*, edited by P. Hedstrom and R. Swedberg. Cambridge: Cambridge University Press.

Garud, R., and A. Van de Ven (2006) "Strategic Change Processes." In *Handbook of Strategy and Management*, edited by A. Pettigrew, H. Thomas, and R. Whittington, 206–231. London: SAGE.

George, B., R. Andrews, and J. Monster (2019) "Does Strategic Planning Improve Organizational Performance? A Meta-Analysis." *Public Administration Review* 79 (6): 810–819.

George, B., A. Drumaux, P. Joyce, and F. Longo (2020) "Editorial: Strategic Planning That Works: Evidence from the European Public Sector." *Public Money & Management* 40 (4): 255, 259.

Giddens, A. (1979) *Central Problems in Social Theory.* London: Macmillan.

Giddens, A. (1984) *The Constitution of Society.* Berkely, CA: University of California Press.

Gioia, D., and K. Chittipeddi (1991) "Sensemaking and Sensegiving in Strategic Change Initiation." *Strategic Management Journal* 12 (6): 433–448.

Gobierno de México (2019) Presidente López Obrador declara formalmente fin del modelo neoliberal y su política económica. www.gob.mx/presidencia/prensa/presidente-lopez-obrador-declara-formalmente-fin-del-modelo-neoliberal-y-su-politica-economica-lo-que-hagamos-sera-inspiracion-para-otros-pueblos

Goodin, R., and C. Tilly (eds) (2006) *The Oxford Handbook of Contextual Political Analysis.* Oxford: Oxford University Press.

Granovetter, M. (1978) "Threshold Models of Collective Behavior." *American Journal of Sociology* 83: 1420–1443.

Grant, R. (1996) "Prospering in Dynamically Competitive Environments: Organizational Capability as Knowledge Integration." *Organization Science* 7 (4): 375–387.

Grant, R. (2008) "Why Teaching Strategy Should be Theory Based." *Journal of Management Inquiry* 17 (4): 274–281.

Grant, R. (2010) *Contemporary Strategy Analysis.* Hoboken, NJ: Wiley & Sons.

Greenwood, R., and C. R. Hinings (1993) "Understanding Strategic Change: The Contribution of Archetypes." *Academy of Management Journal* 36: 1052–1081.

Griffiths, R. (1983) *NHS Management Inquiry.* London: HMSO.

Guo, C., B. Metelsky, and P. Bradshaw (2014) "Out of the Shadows: Non Profit Governance Research from Democratic and Critical Perspectives." In *Non Profit Governance: Innovative Perspectives and Approaches,* edited by C. Cornforth and W. Brown, 47–68. Abingdon: Routledge.

Hall, P., and D. Soskice (2001) *Varieties of Capitalism: The Institutional Foundations of Comparative Advantage.* Oxford: Oxford University Press.

Hammack, D., and H. K. Anheier (2013) *A Versatile American Institution: The Changing Ideals and Realities of Philanthropic Foundations.* Washington, DC: Brookings.

Hammer, M., and J. Champy (1993) *Reengineering the Corporation: A Manifesto for Business Revolution.* New York: Harper Collins.

Hampden-Turner, C. (1990) *Charting the Corporate Mind: From Dilemma to Strategy.* Oxford: Basil Blackwell.

Hansen, J. R. (2011) "Application of Strategic Management Tools after a NPM Inspired Reform: Strategy as Practice in Danish Schools." *Administration and Society* 43 (7): 770–806.

Hansen, J. R., and E. Ferlie (2014) "Applying Strategic Management Theories in Public Sector Organizations: Developing a Typology." Unpublished working paper. London: King's College London, Department of Management.

Hansen, M. T., and N. Nohria (2004) "How to Build Collaborative Advantage." *MIT Sloan Management Review* 46 (1): 22–30.

Harris, M. (2010) "Third Sector Organizations in a Contradictory Policy Environment." In *Hybrid Organizations and the Third Sector,* edited by D. Billis, 25–45. Basingstoke: Palgrave Macmillan.

Hartley, J. (2018) "Ten Propositions about Public Leadership." *International Journal of Public Leadership* 14 (4): 202–217.

Hartley, J., J. Alford, O. Hughes, and S. Yates (2015) "Public Value and Political Astuteness in the Work of Public Managers: The Art of the Possible." *Public Administration* 98 (1): 195–211.

Harvey, G., P. Jas, K. Walshe, and C. Skelcher (2010) "Absorptive Capacity: How Organizations Assimilate and Apply Knowledge to Improve Performance." In *From Knowing to Doing: Connecting Knowledge and Performance in Public Services,* edited by K. Walshe, G. Harvey, and P. Jas, 226–250. Cambridge: Cambridge University Press.

Hatten, M. L. (1982) "Strategic Management in Not for Profit Organizations." *Strategic Management Journal* 3: 89–104.

Hayao, K. (1993) *The Japanese Prime Minister and Public Policy.* Pittsburgh, PA: University of Pittsburgh Press.

Heady, F. (1966 [expanded 2nd edn 1979]) *Public Administration: A Comparative Perspective.* New York: Marcel Dekker.

Hedstrom, P., and R. Swedberg (eds) (1998) *Social Mechanisms: An Analytical Approach to Social Theory.* Cambridge: Cambridge University Press.

Helmig, B., M. Jegers, and I. Lapsley (2004) "Challenges in Managing Non Profit Organizations: A Research Overview." *Voluntas* 15 (2): 101–116.

Hendrik, R. (2003) "Strategic Planning Environment, Process and Performance in Public Agencies: A Comparative Study of Department in Milwaukee." *Journal of Public Administration Research and Theory* 13 (4): 491–519.

Higgs, D. (2003) *Review of the Role and Effectiveness of Non Executive Directors.* London: Department of Trade and Industry/HMSO.

Hinings, C. R., and R. Greenwood (1988) *The Dynamics of Strategic Change.* Oxford: Blackwell.

H.M. Treasury (2005) *Review of UK Health Care Funding: A Report by Sir David Cooksey.* London: HMSO.

Hodgkinson, G., and P. Sparrow (2002) *The Competent Organization.* Buckingham: Open University Press.

Hofstede, G. (2001) *Culture's Consequences: Comparing Values, Behaviors, Institutions, and Organizations across Nations.* Thousand Oaks, CA: SAGE.

Hood, C. (1991) "A Public Management for All Seasons?" *Public Administration* 69 (Spring): 3–19.

Hood, C. (1995) "The NPM in the 1980s: Variations on a Theme." *Accounting, Organizations and Society* 20 (2–3): 93–110.

Hunter, D. (2019) *Health Systems Transformation – Closing The 'Know-Do' Gap.* Briefing for NHS Managers, Newcastle University: Institute of Health and Society, 1–3.

Hunter, D. J., J. Erskine, A. Small, T. McGovern, C. Hicks, P. Whitty, and E. Lugsden (2015) "Doing Transformational Change in the English NHS in the Context of 'Big Bang' Redisorganisation: Findings from the North East Transformation System." *Journal of Health Organization and Management* 29 (1): 10–24.

Husserl, E. (1980) *Ideas Pertaining to a Pure Phenomenology and a Phenomenological Philosophy –* first book trans. F. Kersten (The Hague, Nijhoff, 1982), second book trans. R. Rojcewicz and A. Schuwer (Dordrecht, Kluwer, 1989), third book, trans. T. E. Klein and W. E. Phol (Dprdrecht, Kluwer, 1980).

Huxham, C., and S. Vangen (2000) "Leadership in the Shaping and Implementation of Collaboration Agendas: How Things Happen in a (Not Quite) Joined-up World." *Academy of Management Journal* 43 (6): 1159–1175.

Huxham, C., and S. Vangen (2005) *Managing to Collaborate.* Abingdon: Routledge.

Inkpen, A, and N. Choudhury (1995) "The Seeking of Strategy Where It Is Not – Towards a Theory of Strategy Absence." *Strategic Management Journal* 16 (4): 313–323.

Institute for Health Metrics and Evaluation (IHME) (2012) *Financing Global Health 2010: Development Assistance and Country Spending in Economic Uncertainty.* Seattle, WA: IHME.

James, O. (2003) *The Executive Agency Revolution in Whitehall: Public Interest Versus Bureau-Shaping Perspectives.* Basingstoke: Palgrave.

Jarzabkowski, P. (2005) *Strategy as Practice. An Activity based Approach.* London: SAGE.

Jarzabkowski, P. (2008) "Shaping Strategy as a Structuration Process." *Academy of Management Review* 51 (4): 621–650.

Jarzabkowski, P., J. Balogun, and D. Seidl (2007) "Strategizing: The Challenges of a Practice Perspective." *Human Relations* 60 (1): 5–27.

Jarzabkowski, P., and A. P. Spee (2009) "Strategy-as-Practice: A Review and Future Directions for the Field." *International Journal of Management Review* 11 (1): 69–95.

Jarzabkowski, P., and D. C. Wilson (2002) "Top Teams and Strategy in a UK University." *Journal of Management Studies* 39 (3): 355–381.

Jensen, M., and W. Meckling (1976) "Theory of the Firm: Managerial Behaviour, Agency Costs and Ownership Structure." *Journal of Financial Economics* 3: 305–360.

Jessop, B. (1994) "Post Fordism and the State." In *Post Fordism: A Reader,* edited by A. Amin, 251–279. Oxford: Blackwell.

Johanson, J. -E. (2009) "Strategy Formation in Public Agencies." *Public Administration* 87 (4): 872–891.

Johnson, G. (1987) *Strategic Change and the Management Process.* Oxford: Basil Blackwell.

Johnson, G. (1992) "Managing Strategic Change – Strategy, Culture and Action." *Long Range Planning* 25 (1): 28–36.

Johnson, G., A. Langley, L. Melin, and R. Whittington (2007) *Strategy as Practice: Research Directions and Resources.* Cambridge: Cambridge University Press, 3–26.

Johnson, G., L. Melin, and R. Whittington (2003) "Micro Strategy and Strategizing: Towards an Activity Based View?" *Journal of Management Studies* 40 (1): 3–22.

Johnson, G., R. Whittington, and K. Scholes (2011) *Exploring Strategy: Text and Cases* (9th ed.). Harlow: FT Prentice Hall.

Jorgensen, T. B., and B. Bozeman (2007) "Public Values: An Inventory." *Administration and Society* 39 (3): 354–381.

Joyce, P. (2000) *Strategy in the Public Sector. A Guide to Effective Change Management.* Chichester: Wiley & Sons.

Joyce, P. (2008) "The Strategic and Enabling State: A Case Study in the UK, 1997–2007." *The International Journal of Leadership in Public Services* 4 (3).

Joyce, P. (2012) *Strategic Leadership in the Public Services.* Oxon: Routledge.

Jung, N., and A. Keiser (2010) "Consultants in the Management Fashion Arena." In *The Oxford Handbook of Management Consulting,* edited by M. Kipping and T. Clark, 327–346. Oxford: Oxford University Press.

Kanter, R. M. (1972) *Commitment and Community: Communes and Utopias in Sociological Perspective.* Boston, MA: Harvard University Press.

Kanter, R. M. (1994) "Collaborative Advantage: The Art of Alliances." *Harvard Business Review* 96–104.

Kaplan, R. S., and D. P. Norton (1996) *The Balanced Scorecard.* Boston, MA: Harvard Business Publishing.

Kaplan, R. S., and D. P. Norton (2004) *Strategy Maps.* Boston, MA: Harvard Business Publishing.

Kaplan, R. S., and M. E. Porter (2011) "How to Solve the Cost Crisis in Health Care." *Harvard Business Review* 89 (9): 46–52.

Karreman, D. (2010) "The Power of Knowledge: Learning from 'Learning by Knowledge Intensive Firms." *Journal of Management Studies* 47 (7): 1405–1415.

Kassim, H., and S. Stevens (2010) *Air Transport and the European Union.* Houndsmill: Palgrave Macmillan.

Kellogg, W. K Foundation (2006) *Logic Model Development Guide.* https://www.wkkf.org/resource-directory/resources/2004/01/logic-model-development-guide

Kelman, S. (2005) *Unleashing Change.* Cambridge, MA: Harvard University Press.

Kember, S., and J. Zilinska (2012) *Life after New Media: Mediation as a Vital Process.* Cambridge, MA and London: The MIT Press.

Kenny, A. (2010) *A New History of Western Philosophy.* Oxford: Clarendon Press.

Kerbo, H. R., and J. A. McKinstry (1995) *Who Rules Japan? – The Inner Circles of Economic and Political Power.* Westport, CT: Praeger.

Kessler, M. M. (1963) "Bibliographic Coupling between Scientific Papers." *American Documentation* 14 (1): 10–25.

Khurana, R. (2007) *From Higher Aims to Hired Hands.* Princeton, NJ: Princeton University Press.

Kickert, W. (ed.) (1997a) *Public Management and Administrative Reform in Western Europe.* Cheltenham: Edward Elgar.

Kickert, W. J. (1997b) "Public Governance in the Netherlands: An Alternative to Anglo-American "Managerialism." *Public Administration* 75 (4): 731–752.

Kickert, W., E. H. Klijn, and J. Koppenjan (eds) (1997) *Managing Complex Networks: Strategies for the Public Sector.* London: SAGE.

King, G., R. O. Keohane, and S. Verba (1994) *Designing Social Inquiry. Scientific Inference in Qualitative Research.* Princeton, NJ: Princeton University Press.

Klijn, E. H., and J. Koppenjan (2020) "Debate: Strategic Planning after the Governance Revolution." *Public Money & Management* 40 (4): 260–261. DOI: 10.1080/09540962.2020.1715097.

Koch, S. J. (1976) "Non Democratic Non Planning: The French Experience." *Policy Sciences* 7: 371–385.

Koh, B. C. (1989) *Japan's Administrative Elite.* Berkeley, CA: University of California Press.

Kools, M., and B. George (2020) "Debate: The Learning Organization – A Key Construct Linking Strategic Planning and Strategic Management." *Public Money & Management* 40 (4): 262–264. DOI: 10.1080/09540962.2020.1727112.

Koplan, J. P., T. C. Bond, M. H. Merson, K. S. Reddy, M. H. Rodriguez, N. K. Sewankambo, and J. N. Wasserheit (2009) "Towards a Common Definition of Global Health." *The Lancet* 373: 1993–1995.

Kristol, I. (1995) *Neo Conservatism – Selected Essays.* New York: Free Press.

Kuhn, T. (1962) *The Structure of Scientific Revolutions.* London: University of Chicago Press.

Kumar, S., N. Pandey and A. Haldar (2020) "Twenty Years of Public Management Review (PMR): A Bibliometric Overview." *Public Management Review* 22 (12): 1876–1896.

Laegreid, P., and K. Verhoest (eds) (2010) *Governance of Public Sector Organizations: Proliferation, Autonomy and Performance.* London: Palgrave Macmillan.

Lambert, R. (2003) *Lambert Review of Business/University Collaboration.* London: HM Treasury.

Lane, P., B. Koka, and S. Pathak (2006) "The Reification of Absorptive Capacity: A Critical Review and Rejuvenation of the Concept." *Academy of Management Review* 31 (4): 853–863.

Lawlor, R. (1992) *Voices of the First Day: Awakening in the Aboriginal Dreamtime. Inner Traditions.* Rochester: Vermont.

Lee, K., et al. (2002). *An Introduction to Global Health Policy. Health Policy Making in a Globalizing World.* Cambridge: Cambridge University Press.

Lega, F., and D. Cristofoli (2009) *Strategic Public Management.* Milan: EGEA.

Levitt, B., and J. G. March (1988) "Organizational Learning." *Annual Review of Sociology* 14 (August): 319–338.

Lewis, J. M. (2013) *Academic Governance: Disciplines and Policy.* New York: Routledge.

Li, L., and J. Chen (2012) "A Review of the Progress in Medical Reform: Based on the Historical Perspective and Global Perspective." *Social Security Research* 173 (1): 107–115.

Lijphart, A. (1984) *Democracies: Patterns of Majoritarian and Consensus Government in Twenty-One Countries.* New Haven, CT and London: Yale University Press.

Lijphart, A. (1999) *Patterns of Democracy: Governance Forms and Performance in 36 Countries.* New Haven, CT: Yale University Press.

Lindblom, C. (1959) "The Science of Muddling Through." *Public Administration Review* 19 (3): 79–88.

Lindblom, C. (1979) "Still Muddling, Not Yet Through." *Public Administration Review* 39 (6): 517–526.

Lister, M., J. Dovey, S. Giddings, I. Grant, and K. Kelly (2008) *New Media: A Critical Introduction* (2nd ed.). New York: Routledge.

Llewellyn, S., and E. Tappin (2003) "Strategy in the Public Sector: Management in the Wilderness." *Journal of Management Studies* 40 (4): 955–982.

Lockett, A., R. O'Shea, and M. Wright (2008) "The Development of the Resource based View: Reflections from Birger Wernerfelt." *Organization Studies* 29 (8–9): 1125–1141.

Lodge, M., and D. Gill (2011) "Toward a New Era of Administrative Reform? The Myth of Post-NPM in New Zealand." *Governance* 24 (1): 141–166.

Loftus, B. (2010) "Police Occupational Culture: Classic Themes, Altered Times." *Policing and Society* 20 (1): 1–20.

Lorsch, J. W., and J. McIver (1989) *Pawns or Potentates? The Reality of America's Corporate Boards.* Boston, MA: Harvard Business School Press.

Lusk, S., and N. Birks (2014) *Rethinking Public Strategy.* Basingstoke: Palgrave Macmillan.

Lynn, E. L., Jr. (2008) "What Is a Neo-Weberian State? Reflections on a Concept and Its Implications." Paper presented at the Conference 'Towards the Neo-Weberian State? Europe and Beyond', Tallinn, Tallinn University of Technology, 30 January–1 February.

Lynn, L. (1996) *Public Management as Art, Science and Profession.* Chatham, NJ: Chatham House.

Lynn, L., Jr. (2006) *Public Management: Old and New.* London: Routledge/Taylor and Francis.

Lynn, L., Jr., C. Heirich, and C. Hill (2001) *Improving Governance. A New Logic for Empirical Research.* Washington, DC: Georgetown University Press.

Magaña, F. (2021) El uso de la evaluación del desempeño en México. PhD in Public Policy Thesis. CIDE.

Mahoney, J., and K. Thelen (eds) (2010) *Explaining Institutional Change. Ambiguity, Agency and Power.* New York: Cambridge University Press.

Mannion, R., H. Davies, S. Harrison, S. Konteh, I. Greener, R. McDonald, G. Dowswell, K. Walshe, N. Fulop, R. Walters, R. Jacobs, and P. Hyde (2010) *Changing Managerial Cultures and Organizational Performance in the NHS.* Final Project Report, NIHR SDO 08/1501/94. www. netscc.ac.uk/hsdr/

March, J. G. (1999) *The Pursuit of Organizational Intelligence.* Malden, MA: Blackwell.

March, J. G., and H. Simon (1958) *Organisations.* New York: Wiley. (2nd edition 1993, London: Blackwell).

March, J. J., and J. P. Olsen (1996) *Democratic Governance.* New York: The Free Press.

March, J. G., L. S. Sproull, and M. Tamuz (1991) "Learning from Samples of One or Fewer." *Organization Science* 2 (1): 1–13.

Marinetto, M. (2012) "Case Studies of the Health Policy Process: A Methodological Introduction." In *Shaping Health Policy: Case Study Methods and Analysis*, 21–40. Bristol: Policy Press.

Marsh, D. (2011) "The New Orthodoxy: The Differentiated Polity Model." *Public Administration* 89 (1): 32–48.

Marsh, D., D. Richards, and M. Smith (2003) "Unequal Plurality: Towards an Asymmetric Power Model of British Politics." *Government and Opposition* 38 (3): 306–332.

Marten, R., and J. M. Witte (2008) "Transforming Development? The Role of Philanthropic Foundations in International Development Cooperation." GPPi Research Paper Series n. 10. Berlin: Global Public Policy Institute.

Martin, J., and P. Frost (1996) "The Organizational Culture War Games: A Struggle for Intellectual Dominance." In *Handbook of Organizational Studies*, edited by S. Clegg, C. Hardy, and W. Nord, 599–621. London: SAGE.

Martínez Vilchis, J. (2007) *Nueva Gerencia Pública.* México: UAEM-Miguel Ángel Porrúa.

Martínez Vilchis, J. (2010) *México y sus gobiernos estatales.* México: UAEM-IAPEM-Miguel Ángel Porrúa.

McAdam, D., S. Tarrow, and C. Tilly (2001) *Dynamics of Contention.* Cambridge: Cambridge University Press.

McCain, K. W. (1990) "Mapping Authors in Intellectual Space – A Technical Overview." *Journal of the American Society for Information Science* 41 (6): 433–443.

McGoey, L. (2012) "Philanthrocapitalism and Its Critics." *Poetics* 40 (2): 185–199.

McGrath, R. G. (2006) "Entrepreneurship, Small Firms and Wealth Creation: A Framework Using Real Options Reasoning." In *Handbook of Strategy and Management*, edited by A. Pettigrew, H. Thomas, and R. Whittington, 299–325. London: SAGE.

McKenna, C. (2006) *The World's Newest Profession.* Cambridge: Cambridge University Press.

McNulty, T., and E. Ferlie (2002) *Reengineering Health Care: The Complexities of Organizational Transformation.* Oxford: Oxford University Press.

McNulty, T., and A. Pettigrew (1999) "Strategists on the Board." *Organization Studies* 20: 47–74.

McVeigh, B. J. (1998). *The Nature of the Japanese State. Rationality and Rituality.* London: Routledge.

Meier, K. J., and G. Hill (2005) "Bureaucracy in the Twenty First Century." In *The Oxford Handbook of Public Management*, edited by E. Ferlie, L. E. Lynn, and C. Pollitt, 51–72. Oxford: Oxford University Press.

Meier, K. J., and L. J. O'Toole, Jr (2010) "Managerial Networking, Managing the Environment, and Programme Performance: A Summary of Findings and an Agenda." In *Public Management and Performance: Research Directions*, edited by R. M. Walker, G. A. Boyne and G. A. Brewer, 127–151. Cambridge and New York: Cambridge University Press.

Mele, V., and E. Ongaro (2014) "Public Sector Reform in a Context of Political Instability: Italy 1992–2007." *International Public Management Journal* 17 (1).

Mérindol, V. (2008) "La planification et la prospective au sein des organisations." *Revue Française de Gestion* n° 181.

Miles, R. and C. Snow (1978) *Organizational Strategy, Structure, and Process.* New York: McGraw-Hill.

Millar, R., R. Mannion, T. Freeman, and H. T. Davies (2013) "Hospital Board Oversight of Quality and Patient Safety: A Narrative Review and Synthesis of Recent Empirical Research." *Milbank Quarterly* 91 (4): 738–770.

Miller, D. (1993) "The Architecture of Simplicity." *Academy of Management Review* 18: 116–138.

Miller, D. (1994) "What Happens after Success? The Perils of Excellence." *Journal of Management Studies* 31: 325–358.

Miller, D., and P. Freisen (1984) *Organizations: A Quantum View.* Englewood Cliffs, NJ: Prentice Hall.

Mintzberg, H. (1973) "Strategy Making in Three Modes." *California Management Review* 16 (2): 44–53.

Mintzberg, H. (1983) *Structure in Fives – Designing Effective Organizations.* Englewood Cliffs, NJ: Prentice Hall.

Mintzberg, H. (1994) *The Rise and Fall of Strategic Planning.* New York: Free Press.

Mintzberg, H., B. Ahlstrand, and J. Lampel (2009) *Strategy Safari* (2nd ed.). Harlow: FT Prentice Hall.

Mintzberg, H., and J. A. Walters (1985) "On Strategies: Deliberate and Emergent." *Strategic Management Journal* 6: 257–272.

Mintzberg, H., and J. A. Waters (1982) "Tracking Strategy in an Entrepreneurial Firm." *Academy of Management Journal* 25 (3): 465–499.

Mishima, K. (1998) "The Changing Relationship between Japan's LDP and the Bureaucracy." *Asian Survey* 38 (10): 968–985.

Mizruchi, M. (1996) "What Do Interlocks Do? An Analysis, Critique and Assessment of Research on Interlocking Directorates." *Annual Review of Sociology* 22: 271–298.

Mizruchi, M. (2004) 'Berle and Means Revisited: The Governance and Power of Large US." *Corporations, Theory and Society* 33 (5): 579–617.

Moore, M. H. (1995) *Creating Public Value: Strategic Management in Government.* Cambridge, MA: Harvard University Press.

Moore, M. H. (2000) "Managing for Value: Organizational Strategy in for-Profit, Nonprofit, and Governmental Organizations." *Nonprofit and Voluntary Sector Quarterly* 29 (1): 183–208.

Moore, M. and J. Benington (2011) "Conclusions: Looking Ahead." In *Public Value – Theory and Practice*, edited by J. Benington and M. Moore, Chapter 16, 256–275. Basingstoke: Palgrave Macmillan.

Moran, M. (2011) "Private Foundations and Global Health Partnerships: Philanthropists and 'Partnership Brokerage'." In *Partnerships and Foundations in Global Health Governance*, edited by O. Williams and S. Rushton. London: Palgrave Macmillan.

Morris, M. H., D. L. Davis, and J. W. Allene (1994) "Fostering Corporate Entrepreneurship: Cross-cultural Comparisons of the Importance of Individualism vs. Collectivism." *Journal of International Business Studies* 25 (1): 65–90.

Moynihan, D. (2009) " 'Our Usable Past': A Historical Contextual Approach to Administrative Values." *Public Administration Review* 69 (5): 813–822.

Mulhare, E. M. (1999) "Mindful of the Future: Strategic Planning Ideology and the Culture of Nonprofit Management." *Human Organization* 58 (3): 323–330.

Murray, C. J., B. Anderson, et al. (2011) "Development Assistance for Health: Trends and Prospects." *The Lancet* 378 (9785): 8–10.

Nag, R., D. C. Hambrick, and M.-J. Chen (2007) "What Is Strategic Management, Really? Inductive Derivation of a Consensus Definition of the Field." *Strategic Management Journal* 28 (9): 935–955.

Newman, J. (2001) *Modernising Governance.* London: SAGE.

Newman, J. (2001) *Modernizing Governance: New Labour, Policy and Society.* London: SAGE.

Newman, J. (2005) "Enter the Transformational Leader: Network Governance and the Micro Politics of Modernization." *Sociology* 39 (4): 717–734.

Niskanen, W. A. (1971) *Bureaucracy and Representative Government.* Chicago, IL: Aldine Atherton.

Niskanen, W. A. (1973) *Bureaucracy: Servant or Master?* London: Institute of Economic Affairs.

Niskanen, W. A. (1994) *Bureaucracy and Public Economics.* Cheltenham: Edward Elgar.

Nivón, E. (2020) "Crisis en las políticas públicas de cultura La planeación cultural del gobierno de López Obrador." *Alteridades* 30 (60): 35–49.

Nunes, N. T. S., S. C. Mota, A. C. D. Cabral, and S. M. dos Santos (2020) "The Brazilian Scientific Production on Risk Management in the Public Sector: A Bibliometric Analysis." *Revista Do Servico Publico* 71 (4): 887–920.

Nutt, P. C., and R. W. Backoff (1987) "A Strategic Management Process for Public and Third-Sector Organizations." *Journal of the American Planning Association* 53 (1): 44–57.

Nutt, P. C., and R. W. Backoff (1992) *Strategic Management of Public and Third Sector Organizations: A Handbook for Leaders.* San Francisco, CA: Jossey Bass.

Oakes, L., B. Townley, and D. Cooper (1998) "Business Planning as Pedagogy: Language and Control in a Changing Institutional Field." *Administrative Science Quarterly* 43: 257–292.

Ollila, E. (2005) "Global Health Priorities: Priorities of the Wealthy?" *Globalization and Health* 1 (6).

Ongaro, E. (2004) "Process Management in the Public Sector: The Experience of One-Stop Shops in Italy." *The International Journal of Public Sector Management* 17 (1): 81–107.

Ongaro, E. (2006) "The Dynamics of Devolution Processes in Legalistic Countries: Organisational Change in the Italian Public Sector." *Public Administration* 84 (3): 737–770.

Ongaro, E. (2009) *Public Management Reform and Modernization: Trajectories of Administrative Change in Italy, France, Greece, Portugal, Spain.* Cheltenham and Northampton, MA: Edward Elgar.

Ongaro, E. (2010) "The Napoleonic Administrative Tradition and Public Management Reform in France, Greece, Italy, Portugal, Spain." In *Tradition and Public Administration*, edited by M. Painter and B. G. Peters. Basingstoke: Palgrave Macmillan.

Ongaro, E. (2011) "The Role of Politics and Institutions in the Italian Administrative Reform Trajectory." *Public Administration* 89 (3): 738–755.

Ongaro, E. (2013a) "The Administrative Reform Trajectory of the European Commission in Comparative Perspective: Historical New Institutionalism in Compound Systems." *Public Policy and Administration* 28 (4): 346–363.

Ongaro, E. (2013b) "Explaining Contextual Influences on the Dynamics of Public Management Reforms: Reflections on Some Ways Forward." In *Context in Public Policy and Management; The Missing Link?*, edited by C. Pollitt, 192–207. Cheltenham and Northampton, MA: Edward Elgar.

Ongaro, E. (2015a) *Multi-Level Governance: The Missing Linkages.* Bingley: Emerald.

Ongaro, E. (2015b) "Administrative Reforms in the European Commission and the Neo-Weberian Model." In *The Palgrave Handbook of the European Administrative System*, edited by M. Bauer and J. Trondal, 108–126. Basingstoke and London: Palgrave Macmillan.

Ongaro, E. (2018) "The Napoleonic Tradition in Public Administration." In *Oxford Research Encyclopaedia of Politics.* Oxford: Oxford University Press.

Ongaro, E. (2020a) *Philosophy and Public Administration: An Introduction* (2nd ed.). Cheltenham and Northampton, MA: Edward Elgar. www.elgaronline.com/view/9781839100338.xml

Ongaro, E. (2020b) "Multi-Level Governance and Public Administration." In *Encyclopaedia of Public Administration.* Oxford: Oxford University Press.

Ongaro, E. (forthcoming) "The Fourfold Nature of Public Administration as Science, Art, Profession, and Humanism: Implications for Teaching." In *International Handbook on the Teaching of Public Administration*, edited by K. A. Bottom, J. Diamond, I. Elliott and P. T. Dunning. Cheltenham and Northampton, MA: Elgar.

Ongaro, E., D. Barbieri, N. Bellé, and P. Fedele (2015) "EU Agencies and the European Multi-Level Administrative System." In *Multi-Level Governance: The Missing Linkages*, edited by E. Ongaro, 87–124. Bingley: Emerald.

Ongaro, E., D. Barbieri, P. Fedele, and D. Galli (2012) "EU Agencies." In *Government Agencies. Practices and Lessons from 30 Countries*, edited by K. Verhoest, S. Van Thiel, P. Laegreid, and G. Bouckaert, 400–412. Basingstoke: Palgrave Macmillan.

Ongaro, E., and E. Ferlie (2019) "Exploring Strategy-Making in 'Non-New Public Management Services Settings: The case of European Union Agencies." *Administrative Sciences* 9: 23. www.mdpi.com/2076-3387/9/1/23

Ongaro, E., and E. Ferlie (2020) "Strategic Management in Public Organizations: Profiling the Public Entrepreneur as Strategist." *The American Review of Public Administration* 50: 4–5, 360–374. https://doi.org/10.1177/0275074020909514

Ongaro, E., A. Massey, M. Holzer, and E. Wayenberg (eds) (2010) *Governance and Intergovernmental Relations in the European Union and the United States: Theoretical perspectives.* Cheltenham and Northampton, MA: Edward Elgar.

Ongaro, E., A. Massey, M. Holzer, and E. Wayenberg (eds) (2011) *Policy, Performance and Management in Governance and Intergovernmental Relations: Transatlantic Perspectives.* Cheltenham and Northampton, MA: Edward Elgar.

Ongaro, E., A. Sancino, I. Pluchinotta, H. Williams, E. Ferlie, and M. Kitchener (2021) "Strategic Management as an Enabler of Co-creation in Public Services." *Policy and Politics* 49 (2): 287–304. https://doi.org/10.1332/030557321X16119271520306

Ongaro, E., and S. van Thiel (eds) (2018a) *The Palgrave Handbook of Public Administration and Management in Europe.* Basingstoke and London: Palgrave Macmillan.

Ongaro, E., and S. van Thiel (2018b) "Introduction." In *The Palgrave Handbook of Public Administration and Management in Europe*, edited by E. Ongaro and S. van Thiel, 3–10. London: Palgrave Macmillan.

Ongaro, E., and S. van Thiel (2018c) "Languages and Public Administration in Europe." In *The Palgrave Handbook of Public Administration and Management in Europe*, edited by E. Ongaro and S. van Thiel, 61–98. London: Palgrave Macmillan.

O'Reilly, D. E., and M. Reed (2010) " 'Leaderism': An Evolution of Managerialism in UK Public Service Reform." *Public Administration* 88 (4): 960–978.

Orlikowski, W. (1996) "Improvising Organizational Transformation Over Time: A Situated Change Perspective." *Information Systems Research* 7: 63–92.

Ormrod, S., E. Ferlie, F. Warren, and K. Norton (2007) "The Appropriation of New Organizational Forms within Networks of Practice: Founder Power and Founder Related Ideological Power." *Human Relations* 60 (5): 745–767.

Osborne, D., and T. Gaebler (1992) *Reinventing Government.* Reading, MA: Addison Wesley.

Osborne, S. (ed.) (2010a) *The New Public Governance?* London: Routledge.

Osborne, S. (2010b) "The (New) Public Governance: A Suitable Case for Treatment." In *The New Public Governance*, edited by S. Osborne, 1–16. London: Routledge.

Osborne, S. P., Z. Radnor, and K. Strokosch (2016) "Co-Production and the Co-Creation of Value in Public Services: A Suitable Case for Treatment?" *Public Management Review* 18 (5): 639–653.

Oster, S. (1995) *Strategic Management for Non Profit Organizations.* Oxford: Oxford University Press.

O'Toole, L. (1997) "Treating Networks Seriously: Practical and Research-Based Agendas." *Public Administration Review* 57 (1): 45–52.

O'Toole, L. J., and K. J. Meier (2011) *Public Management: Organizations, Governance and Performance.* Cambridge and New York: Cambridge University Press.

Overman, E. S., and K. J. Boyd (1994) "Best Practice Research and Postbureaucratic Reform." *Journal of Public Administration Research and Theory* 4 (1): 67–83.

Pablo, A., T. Reay, J. Dewald, and A. Casebeer (2007) "Identifying, Enabling and Managing Dynamic Capability in the Public Sector." *Journal of Management Studies* 44 (5): 687–705.

Painter, M., and B. G. Peters (eds) (2010) *Tradition and Public Administration*. Basingstoke: Palgrave Macmillan.

Paradeise, C., E. Reale, I. Bleiklie, and E. Ferlie (eds) (2009) *University Governance: Western European Comparative Perspectives*. Dordrecht: Springer.

Pardo, M. C. (2003) "La modernización administrativa zedillista, ¿más de lo mismo?" *Foro Internacional* 43 (1): 192–214.

Pardo, M. C., and E. Velasco (coords.) (2006) *El proceso de modernización en el Infonavit 2001–2006*. México: El Colegio de México.

Parsons, E., and A. Broadbridge (2004) "Managing Change in Non Profit Organizations: Insights from the UK Charity Retail Insight." *Voluntas* 15 (3): 227–242.

Pascale, R., and A. Athos (1981) *The Art of Japanese Management: Applications for American Executives*. New York: Simon and Schuster.

Pawson, R. (2002) "Evidence-Based Policy: The Promise of 'Realist Synthesis'." *Evaluation* 8 (3): 340–358.

Pawson, R. (2013) *The Science of Evaluation: A Realist Manifesto*. London, Thousand Oaks, CA, and New Delhi: SAGE.

Pawson, R., and N. Tilley (1997) *Realistic Evaluation*. London, Thousand Oaks, CA, and New Delhi: SAGE.

Pearce, J., and S. Zahra (1991) "The Relative Power of CEOs and Boards of Directors: Associations with Corporate Performance." *Strategic Management Journal* 12: 135–153.

Peck, E. (1995) "The Performance of an NHS Trust Board: Actors' Accounts, Minutes and Observation." *British Journal of Management* 6 (2): 135–156.

Penrose, E. (1959). *The Theory of the Growth of the Firm*. New York: John Wiley.

Perry, J., and H. G. Rainey (1988) "The Public-Private Distinction in Organization Theory: A Critique and Research Agenda." *Academy of Management Review* 13 (2): 182–201.

Peters, B. G. (1999) *Institutional Theory in Political Science: The New Institutionalism*. London and New York: Continuum.

Peters, B. G. (2008) "The Napoleonic Tradition." *The International Journal of Public Sector Management* 21 (2): 118–132.

Peters, B. G. (2010) "Meta Governance and Public Management." In *The New Public Governance*, edited by S. Osborne, 36–51. London: Routledge.

Peters, G. B. (2018) *The Politics of Bureaucracy: An Introduction to Comparative Public Administration* (7th ed.). London: Routledge.

Peters, T., and R. Waterman (1982) *In Search of Excellence: Lessons from America's Best Run Companies*. New York: Warner Books.

Pettigrew, A. (1973) *The Politics of Organizational Decision Making*. London: Tavistock.

Pettigrew, A. (1979) "On Studying Organizational Cultures." *Administrative Science Quarterly* 24 (4): 570–581.

Pettigrew, A. (1985) *The Awakening Giant*. Oxford: Basil Blackwell.

Pettigrew, A. (1987) "Context and Action in the Transformation of the Firm." *Journal of Management Studies* 24: 649–670.

Pettigrew, A. (1992) "On Studying Organizational Elites." *Strategic Management Journal* 13: 163–182.

Pettigrew, A. M., E. Ferlie, and L. McKee (1992) *Shaping Strategic Change*. London: SAGE.

Pettigrew, A. M., and T. McNulty (1995) "Power and Influence in and Around the Boardroom." *Human Relations* 48: 845–873.

Pettigrew, A. M., H. Thomas, and R. Whittington (eds) (2002) *Handbook of Strategy and Management*. London: SAGE.

Pettigrew, A. M., H. Thomas, and R. Whittington (eds) (2006) *Handbook of Strategy and Management* (paperback ed.). London: SAGE.

Pettigrew, A. M., and R. Whipp (1991) *Managing Change for Competitive Success*. Oxford: Blackwell.

Pettigrew, A. M., R. Woodman, and K. Cameron (2001) "Studying Organizational Change and Development – Challenges for Future Research." *Academy of Management Journal* 44 (4): 697–713.

Pierre, J. (ed.) (1995) *Bureaucracy in the Modern State: An Introduction to Comparative Public Administration*. Aldershot: Edward Elgar.

Pierre, J., and B. G. Peters (2000) *Governance, Politics and the State*. Basingstoke: Palgrave Macmillan.

Pierre, J., and B. G. Peters (2009) "From a Club to a Bureaucracy: JAA, EASA, and European Aviation Regulation." *Journal of European Public Policy* 16 (3): 337–355.

Pitelis, C. (2009) "Introduction." In *Edith Penrose's "The Theory of the Growth of the Firm" Fifty Years Later*, edited by E. Penrose (4th ed.). Oxford: Oxford University Press.

Pluchinotta, I., H. Williams, E. Ferlie, and M. Kitchener (2020) 'Welsh Water's Water Resilient Project." In *Deliverable number and title: 'Patterns of Strategic Renewals'*, edited by B. Regal and E. Ferlie, 146–160 (Report for the COGOV Project, Deliverable 2.3, Section). London: KCL.

Poister, T. H. (2010) "The Future of Strategic Planning in the Public Sector: Linking Strategic Management and Performance." *Public Administration Review* 70: S246–S254.

Poister, T. H., T. H. Pitts, and L. H. Edwards (2010) "Strategic Management Research in the Public Sector: A Review, Synthesis, and Future Directions." *The American Review of Public Administration* 40 (5): 522–545.

Pollitt, C. (2002) "Clarifying Convergence: Striking Similarities and Durable Differences in Public Management." *Public Management Review* 4 (1): 471–492.

Pollitt, C. (2008) *Time, Policy and Management: Governing with the Past*. Oxford: Oxford University Press.

Pollitt, C. (2011) "Not Odious But Onerous. Comparative Public Administration." *Public Administration* 89 (1): 114–127.

Pollitt, C. (2012) *New Perspectives on Public Services: Place and Technology*. Oxford: Oxford University Press.

Pollitt, C. (ed.) (2013) *Context in Public Policy and Management: The Missing Link?* Cheltenham and Northampton, MA: Edward Elgar.

Pollitt, C., and G. Bouckaert (2009) *Continuity and Change in Public Policy and Management*. Cheltenham and Northampton, MA: Edward Elgar.

Pollitt, C., and G. Bouckaert (2011) *Public Management Reform. A Comparative Analysis: New Public Management, Governance and the Neo-Weberian State* (3rd ed.). Oxford: Oxford University Press.

Pollitt, C., and G. Bouckaert (2017) *Public Management Reform. A Comparative Analysis: Into the Age of Austerity* (4th ed.). Oxford: Oxford University Press.

Pollitt, C., and C. Talbot (eds) (2004) *Unbundled Government: A Critical Analysis of the Global Trend to Agencies, Quangos and Contractualization*. London: Routledge.

Pollitt, C., C. Talbot, J. Caulfield, and A. Smullen (2004) *Agencies: How Governments Do Things through Semi-autonomous Organisations*. New York: Palgrave Macmillan.

Poole, M., and A. Van de Ven (1989) "Using Paradox to Build Organization and Management Theories." *Academy of Management Review* 14 (4): 562–578.

Popper, K. R. (2002) *The Logic of Scientific Discovery* (first edition in German *Logic der Forschung*, 1935, first English edition, 1959). London: Routledge.

Porter, M. (1980) *Competitive Strategy*. New York: Free Press.

Porter, M. (1985) *Competitive Advantage*. New York: Free Press.

Porter, M. (2004) *Competitive Strategy* (Export ed.). New York: Free Press.

Porter, M., and E. O. Teisberg (2006) *Redefining Health Care: Creating Value Based Competition on Results*. Boston, MA: Harvard Business School Press.

Porter, M. E. (2010) "What Is Value in Health Care?" *New England Journal of Medicine* 363 (26): 2477–2481.

Power, M. (1997) *The Audit Society*. Oxford: Oxford University Press.

Price, J. (1997). *Japan Works: Power and Paradox in Postwar Industrial Relations*. Ithaca, NY: ILR Press.

Quinn, J. B. (1980) *Strategies for Change: Logical Incrementalism*. Homewood, IL: Irwin.

Radaelli, C., B. Dente, and S. Dossi (2012) "Recasting Institutionalism: Institutional Analysis and Public Policy." *European Political Science* 11: 537–550.

Ragin, C. C. (1987) *The Comparative Method*. Berkeley, CA and Los Angeles, CA: University of California Press.

Rainey, H. G. (2010) *Understanding and Managing Public Organizations*. San Francisco, CA: Jossey Bass.

Raisch, S., and J. Birkinshaw (2008) "Organizational Ambidexterity: Antecedents, Outcomes and Moderators." *Journal of Management* 34 (3): 375–409.

Ramírez, E., and D. A. Gault (2014) "Estrategias, dilemas y oportunidades de la nueva misión y visión del Infonavit: un estudio de caso." *Gestión y Política Pública* 23 (1): 121–183.

Rathgeb-Smith, S. (2005) "NGOs and Contracting." In *The Oxford Handbook of Public Management*, edited by E. Ferlie, L. Lynn, and C. Pollitt, 591–615. Oxford: Oxford University Press.

Ravishankar, N., P. Gubbins, R. J. Cooley, K. Leach-Kemon, C. M. Michaud, D. T. Jamison, and C. J. Murray (2009) "Financing of Global Health: Tracking Development Assistance for Health from 1990 to 2007." *The Lancet* 213: 2213–2224.

Reagan, P. D. (1999) *Designing a New America*. Amherst, MA: University of Massachusetts Press.

Reale, G., and D. Antiseri (1988) *Il pensiero occidentale dalle origini ad oggi* (9th ed.). Brescia: La Scuola.

Reay, T., and C. R. Hinings (2005) "The Recomposition of an Organizational Field: Health Care in Alberta." *Organizational Studies* 26: 351–383.

Reay, T., and C. R. Hinings (2009) "Managing the Rivalry of Competing Institutional Logics." *Organization Studies* 30: 629–652.

Rebora, G., and M. Meneguzzo (1990) *Strategia delle Amministrazioni Pubbliche*. Torino: UTET.

Rhodes, R. A. W. (1997) *Understanding Governance*. Buckingham: Open University Press.

Rhodes, R. A. W. (2007) "Understanding Governance: Ten Years On." *Organization Studies* 28 (8): 1243–1269.

Rhodes, R. A. W., and J. Wanna (2007) "The Limits to Public Value or Rescuing Responsible Government from the Platonic Guardians." *Australian Journal of Public Administration* 66 (4): 406–421.

Rhodes, R. A. W., and J. Wanna (2008) "Bringing the Politics Back in: Public Value in Westminster Parliamentary Government." *Public Administration* 87 (2): 161–183.

Riccucci, N. (2010) *Public Administration. Traditions of Inquiry and Philosophies of Knowledge*. Washington, DC: Georgetown University Press.

Riggs, F. (1962) "Trends in the Comparative Study of Public Administration." *International Review of Administrative Sciences* XXVIII (1): 9–15.

Ring, P. S., and J. L. Perry (1985) "Strategic Management in Public and Private Organizations: Implications of Distinctive Contexts and Constraints." *Academy of Management Review* 10 (2): 276–286.

Roberts, A. (2010) *The Logic of Discipline: Global Capitalism and the New Architecture of Government*. New York: Oxford University Press.

Roberts, J., T. McNulty, and P. Stiles (2005) "Beyond Agency Conceptions of the Work of Non Executive Directors: Creating Accountability in the Boardroom." *British Journal of Management* 16: S5–S26.

Ropret, M., and A. Aristovnik (2019) "Public Sector Reform from the Post-New Public Management Perspective: Review and Bibliometric Analysis." *Central European Public Administration Review* 17 (2): 89–116.

Rosenberg Hansen, J., and E. Ferlie (2016) "Applying Strategic Management Theories in Public Sector Organizations: Developing a Typology." *Public Management Review* 18 (1): 1–19.

Rosser, C. (2018) "Max Weber's Bequest for European Public Administration." In *The Palgrave Handbook of Public Administration and Management in Europe*, edited by E. Ongaro and S. van Thiel, 1011–1030. London: Palgrave Macmillan.

Royal Marsden NHS Foundation Trust (2012) "Annual Plan for 2012/2013." *NHS Monitor Website*, January 2. Accessed January 2, 2013. www.monitor-nhsft.gov

Rugge, F. (2013) "The Intransigent Context: Glimpses at the History of a Problem." In *Context in Public Policy and Management: The Missing Link?*, edited by C. Pollitt, 44–54. Cheltenham, UK and Northampton, MA: Edward Elgar.

Sahlin-Andersson, K., and L. Engwall (2002a) "Carriers, Flows and Sources of Management Knowledge." In *The Expansion of Management Knowledge*, edited by K. Sahlin-Andersson and L. Engwall, 3–32. Stanford, CA: Stanford Business Books.

Sahlin-Andersson, K., and L. Engwall (2002b) "The Dynamics of Management Knowledge Expansion." In *The Expansion of Management Knowledge*, edited by K. Sahlin-Andersson and L. Engwall, 277–296. Stanford, CA: Stanford Business Books.

Saint Martin, D. (2004) *Building the New Managerialist State: Consultants and the Politics of Public Sector Reform in Comparative Perspective* (2nd ed.). Oxford: Oxford University Press.

Salipante, P., and K. Golden-Biddle (1995) "Managing Traditionality and Strategic Change in Non Profit Organizations." *Non Profit Management and Leadership* 6 (4): 3–20.

Salm, M., and C. Schwab (2016) "Human Resource Management Reforms and Change Management in European City Administrations from a Comparative Perspective." In *Local Public Sector Reforms in Times of Crisis*, edited by S. Kuhlmann and G. Bouckaert, pp. 153–183. London: Palgrave Macmillan.

Sarason, S. (1976) *The Creation of Settings and The Future Societies*. San Francisco, CA: Jossey Press.

Schedler, K., and I. Pröller (2007) *Cultural Aspects of Public Management Reform*. Oxford, Amsterdam, and San Diego, CA: Elsevier.

Schendel, D. (1994) "Introduction to the Summer 1994 Special Issue: Strategy – Search for New Paradigms." *Strategic Management Journal* 15: 1–4.

Scherer, A. G. (1998) "Pluralism and Incommensurability in Strategic Management and Organization Theory – A Problem in Search of a Solution." *Organization* 5 (2): 147–168.

Scott, W. R., M. Ruef, P. J. Mendel, and C. R. Caronna (2000) *Institutional Change and Health Care Organizations: From Professional Dominance to Managed Care*. Chicago, IL: Chicago University Press.

SECODAM (1999) "Metodología de Modernización y reforma al sistema presupuestario en la Administración Pública. Planeación Estratégica", technical guide, October.

Senge, P. M., and J. Suzuki (1994) *The Fifth Discipline: The Art and Practice of the Learning Organization*. New York: Currency Doubleday.

Simon, H. (1946) "Proverbs of Administration." *Public Administration Review* 6 (Winter): 53–67.

Simon, H. (1947/1997) *Administrative Behavior*. New York: MacMillan.

Simon, H. (1952) "Development of Theory of Democratic Administration: Replies and Comments." *American Political Science Review* 46 (June): 494–496.

Skelcher, C. (1998) *The Appointed State: Quasi Governmental Organizations and Democracy*. Buckingham: Open University Press.

Skelcher, C. (2000) "Changing Images of the State: Overloaded, Hollowed Out, Congested." *Public Policy and Administration* 15 (3): 3–19.

Sminia, H. (2009) "Process Research in Strategy Formation: Theory, Methodology and Relevance." *International Journal of Management Reviews* 11 (1): 97–125.

Sminia, H., and M. de Rond (2012) "Context and Action in the Transformation of Strategy Scholarship." *Journal of Management Studies* 49 (7): 1329–1349.

Smircich, L. (1983) "Concepts of Culture in Organizational Analysis." *Administrative Science Quarterly* 28: 328–358.

Smith, R. D. (2010) "The Role of Economic Power in Influencing the Development of Global Health Governance." *Global Health Governance* 3 (2).

Snow, C. C. (2012) "Foreword." In *Strategic Management and Public Service Performance*, edited by R. Andrews, G. A. Boyne, J. Law, and R. M. Walker, pp. viii–x. Basingstoke: Palgrave Macmillan.

Sørensen, E. (2020) *Interactive Political Leadership: The Role of Politicians in the Age of Governance.* Oxford: Oxford University Press.

Sørensen, E., and J. Torfing (2019) "Towards Robust Hybrid Democracy in Scandinavian Municipalities?" *Scandinavian Political Studies* 42 (1): 25–49.

Soutiropoulos, D. (2004) "Southern European Public Bureaucracies in Comparative Perspective." *West European Politics* 27 (3): 405–422.

Spanou, C. (2008) "State Reform in Greece: Responding to Old and New Challenges." *The International Journal of Public Sector Management* (Special Issue on "Public management reform in countries in the Napoleonic administrative tradition: France, Greece, Italy, Portugal, Spain") 21 (2): 150–173.

Stacey, R. (1995) "The Science of Complexity: An Alternative Perspective for Strategic Change Processes." *Strategic Management Journal* 16 (6): 477–495.

Stadt Mannheim (City Council) (2016) *Strategische Haushaltskonsolidierung in Mannheim: Zwischenbericht über die Umsetzung des SHM² Masterplans 2017–2018.* Mannheim City Council: Mannheim.

Steen-Johnsen, K., P. Eynaud, and F. Wijkstrom (2011) "On Civil Society Governance – An Emergent Research Field." *Voluntas* 22: 555–565.

Steiner, R., C. Kaiser, and L. Reichmuth (2018) "Consulting for the Public Sector in Europe." In *The Palgrave Handbook of Public Administration and Management in Europe*, edited by E. Ongaro and S. van Thiel, 475–496. London: Palgrave Macmillan.

Stewart, J. (2004) "The Meaning of Strategy in the Public Sector." *Australian Journal of Public Administration* 63 (4): 16–21.

Stinchcombe, A. (1991) "The Conditions of Fruitfulness of Theorizing about Mechanisms in Social Science." *Philosophy of the Social Sciences* 21 (3): 367–388.

Stockwin, J. A. A. (1997a) "The Need for Reform in Japanese Politics." In *The Vitality of Japan*, edited by A. Clesse, T. Inoguchi, E. B. Keehm, and J. A. A. Stockwin, pp. 91–111. New York: Macmillan.

Stockwin, J. A. A. (1997b) "Reforming Japanese Politics: Highway of Change or Road to Nowhere?" In *Japanese Politics Today*, edited by P. Jain and T. Inoguchi, pp. 75–91. New York: Macmillan.

Stoker, G. (2005) "Public Value Management." *American Review of Public Administration* 36 (1).

Storey, J., and R. Holti (2009) "Sense-Making by Clinical and Non-Clinical Executive Directors Within New Governance Arrangements." *Journal of Health Organization and Management* 23 (2): 149–169.

Stout, M. (2012) "Competing Ontologies: A Primer for Public Administration." *Public Administration Review* 72 (3): 388–398.

Streeck, W., and K. Thelen (2005) "Introduction." In *Institutional Change in Advanced Political Economies*, edited by W. Streeck and K. Thelen, pp. 1–40. Oxford: Oxford University Press.

Sulla, O. (2006) *Philanthropic Foundations: Actual vs Potential Role in International Development Assistance.* Development Economic Prospect Group, International Finance Team, Washington, DC: World Bank.

Sumiya, M. (2003) *Sumiya Mikio Chosakushu Dai Kyu Kan* (in Japanese; Collected Works of Mikio Sumiya Volume 9). Tokyo: Iwanami Shoten.

Sutherland Jason, M., N. Repin, and R. Trafford Crump (2013) *Funding Health and Social Care in Montréal, Québec: A Review of the Methods and the Potential Role of Incentives.* Ottawa: Canadian Foundation for Healthcare Improvement.

Swilling, M. (2011) "Greening Public Value: The Sustainability Challenge." In *Public Value: Theory and Practice*, edited by J. Benington and M. Moore, 89–111. Basingstoke: Palgrave Macmillan.

Talbot, C. (2005) *The Paradoxical Primate.* Exeter, UK and Charlottesville, VA: Academic Imprint.

Talbot, C. (2010) *Theories of Performance – Organizational and Service Improvement in the Public Domain.* Oxford: Oxford University Press.

Talbot, C. (2011) "Paradoxes and Prospects of 'Public Value'." *Public Money & Management* 31 (1): 27–34.

Taylor, F. (1911) *Principles of Scientific Management.* New York: Harper and Brothers.

Teece, D. (2007) "Explicating Dynamic Capabilities: The Nature and (Micro) Foundations of (Sustainable) Enterprise Performance." *Strategic Management Journal* 28: 1319–1350.

Teece, D., G. Pisano, and A. Shuen (1997) "Dynamic Capabilities and Strategic Management." *Strategic Management Journal* 18 (7): 509–534.

The Lancet (2009a) "Who Runs Global Health?" *The Lancet* 373 (9681): 2083.

The Lancet (2009b) "What Has the Gates Foundation Done for Global Health?" *The Lancet* 373 (9675): 1577.

Thrift, N. (2005) *Knowing Capitalism.* London: SAGE.

Torfing, J., and C. Ansell (2017) "Strengthening Political Leadership and Policy Innovation Through the Expansion of Collaborative Forms of Governance." *Public Management Review* 19 (1): 37–54.

Torfing, J., E. Ferlie, T. Jukić, and E. Ongaro (2021) "A Theoretical Framework for Studying the Co-Creation of Innovative Solutions and Public Value." *Policy and Politics* 49 (2): 189–209.

Torfing, J., E. Sørensen, and A. Røiseland (2019) "Transforming the Public Sector into an Arena for Co-Creation: Barriers, Drivers, Benefits, and Ways Forward." *Administration & Society* 51 (5): 795–825.

Trenholm, S., and E. Ferlie (2013) "Using Complexity Theory to Analyse the Organisational Response to Resurgent Tuberculosis Across London." *Social Science & Medicine* 93: 229–237.

Trompenaars, F., and C. Hampden-Turner (1993) *Riding the Waves of Culture: Understanding Cultural Diversity in Business.* London: Nicholas Brealey Publishing.

Tushman, M., and C. O'Reilly (1996) "Ambidextrous Organizations: Managing Evolutionary and Revolutionary Change." *California Management Review* 38: 8–30.

University of Tokyo, Faculty of Law Library (2004) *Tokyo Daigaku Keizai Gakubu Toshokan Syozou Tokubetsu Shiryou: Kokutetsu Saiken Kanri Iinkai Siryou Mokuroku* (in Japanese). Tokyo: University of Tokyo, Faculty of Law Library Special Materials: Catalogue of Materials from the Committee for Supervision on Restructure of JNR.

Unyusho (Ministry of Transport) (1986) *Unyu Hakusyo (in Japanese). White Paper of the Ministry of Transport, Tokyo).*

Urzúa, C. (2019a) "El asunto del Plan Nacional de Desarrollo (I)." *El Universal,* 22 July.

Urzúa, C. (2019b) "El asunto del Plan Nacional de Desarrollo (II)." *El Universal,* 29 July.

Useem, M. (1984) *The Inner Circle.* New York: Oxford University Press.

Van de Pijl, K., and H. Sminia (2004) "Strategic Management of Public Interest Organizations." *Voluntas* 15 (2): 137–155.

Van de Ven, A. (2007) *Engaged Scholarship: A Guide for Organizational and Social Research.* Oxford: Oxford University Press.

Van de Ven, A., D. Polley, R. Garud, and S. Venkatamaran (1999) *The Innovation Journey.* Oxford: Oxford University Press.

Van Dooren, W., G. Bouckaert, and J. Hallighan (2010) *Performance Management in the Public Sector.* Abingdon: Routledge.

Van Dooren, W., and S. Van de Walle (2011) *Performance Information in the Public Sector. How It Is Used.* Basingstoke: Palgrave Macmillan.

Van Gestel, N., P. T. de Beer, and M. van der Meer (2009) *The Quagmire of Welfare State Reform. Changes in the Organization of Social Security.* Amsterdam: Amsterdam University Press (in Dutch).

Van Gestel, N., and B. Hillebrand (2011) "Explaining Stability and Change: The Rise and Fall of Logics in Pluralistic Fields." *Organizational Studies* 32: 231–251.

Van Thiel, S. (2013) *Research Methods in Public Administration and Public Management.* London: Routledge.

Van Wart, M. (1998) *Changing Public Sector Values*. New York: Garland Publishing.

Vangen, S., and C. Huxham (2010) "Introducing the Theory of Collaborative Advantage." In *The New Public Governance*, edited by S. Osborne, 163–184. London: Routledge.

Vecchi, I. V., and M. Hellowell (2018) "Public Private Partnerships: Recent Trends and the Central Role of Managerial Competences." In *The Palgrave Handbook of Public Administration and Management in Europe*, edited by E. Ongaro and S. van Thiel, 381–402. London: Palgrave Macmillan.

Velasco, E. (comp.) (2010) *Gestión estratégica*. México: Escuela de Administración Pública del Distrito Federal.

Verhoest, K., B. G. Peters, G. Bouckaert, and B. Verschuere (2004a) "The Study of Organisational Autonomy: A Conceptual Review." *Public Administration and Development* 24 (2): 101–118.

Verhoest, K., B. Verschuere, B. G. Peters, and G. Bouckaert (2004b) "Controlling Autonomous Public Agencies as an Indicator of New Public Management." *Management International* 9 (1): 25–35.

Verhoest, K., S. Van Thiel, P. Laegreid, and G. Bouckaert (eds) (2012) *Government Agencies. Practices and Lessons from 30 Countries*. Basingstoke: Palgrave Macmillan.

Vibert, F. (2007) *The Rise of the Unelected. Democracy and the New Separation of Powers*. Cambridge and New York: Cambridge University Press.

Vining, A. (2011) "Public Agency External Analysis Using a Modified 'Five Forces' Framework." *International Public Management Journal* 14 (1): 63–105.

Virtanen, T. (2013) "Context in the Context – Missing the Missing Links in the Field of Public Administration." In *Context in Public Policy and Management: The Missing Link?* edited by C. Pollitt. Cheltenham and Northampton, MA: Edward Elgar.

Vogel, R. (2014) "What Happened to the Public Organization? A Bibliometric Analysis of Public Administration in Organizational Studies." *American Review of Public Administration* 44 (4): 383–408.

Waldo, D. (1948) *The Administrative State: A Study of the Political Theory of American Public Administration* (1st ed.). New York: Ronald Press.

Waldo, D. (1952a) "Development of Theory of Public Administration." *American Political Science Review* 46: 81–103.

Waldo, D. (1952b) "Development of Theory of Public Administration: Replies and Comments." *American Political Science Review* 46: 500–503.

Waldo, D. (1984) *The Administrative State: A Study of the Political Theory of American Public Administration* (2nd ed.). New York: Holmer and Meier.

Walker, R. M. (2010) "Strategy: Which Strategic Stances Matter?" In *Public Management and Performance: Research Directions*, edited by R. M. Walker, G. A. Boyne, and G. A. Brewer, 227–252. Cambridge and New York: Cambridge University Press.

Walker, R. M., G. A. Boyne, and G. A. Brewer (eds) (2010) *Public Management and Performance: Research Directions*. Cambridge and New York: Cambridge University Press.

Walter, I., S. Nutley, J. Percy-Smith, D. McNeish, and S. Frost (2004) *Improving the Use of Research in Social Care Practice*. London: Social Care Institute for Excellence.

Waltman, L., N. J. van Eck, and E. C. M. Noyons (2010) "A Unified Approach to Mapping and Clustering of Bibliometric Networks." *Journal of Informetrics* 4 (4): 629–635.

Weber, M. (1946) "From Max Weber: Essays in Sociology." In *Bureaucracy* (translated H. H. Gerth and C. Wright Mills). New York: Oxford University Press.

Weick, K. (1976) "Educational Organizations as Loosely Coupled Systems." *Administrative Science Quarterly* 24 (4): 1019.

Weick, K. (1995) *Sensemaking in Organizations*. Thousand Oaks, CA: SAGE.

Weick, K. (2001) *Making Sense of the Organization*. Malden, MA: Blackwell.

Weick, K., and R. Quinn (1999) "Organizational Change and Development." *Annual Review of Psychology* 50: 361–386.

Weiss, C. (1979) "The Many Meanings of Research Utilization." *Public Administrative Review* 39 (5): 426–431.

Weiss, C. (1999) "The Interface between Evaluation and Public Policy." *Evaluation* 5 (4): 468–486.

Weiss, J. (2017) "Trust as a Key for Strategic Management? The Relevance of Council – Administration Relations for NPM-Related Reforms in German Local Governments." *Public Management Review* 19: 1399–1414. DOI: 10.1080/14719037.2016.1266023.

Welsh Water (2018) Welsh Water 2050. Accessed January 2, 2021. https://corporate.dwrcymru.com/en/about-us/our-plans/water-2050

Wernerfelt, B. (1984) "A Resource based Theory of the Firm." *Strategic Management Journal* 5 (2): 171–180.

Wilkins, A. G., and W. G. Ouchi (1983) "Efficient Cultures: Exploring the Relationship between Culture and Organizational Performance." *Administrative Science Quarterly* 28: 468–481.

Wilson, I. (1994) "Strategic Planning Isn't Dead – It Changed." *Long Range Planning* 27 (4): 12–24.

Wolmer, C. (2002) *Broken Rails: How Privatisation Wrecked Britain's Railways.* London: Aurum Press.

Wynen, J., K. Verhoest, E. Ongaro, and S. Van Thiel (2014) "Innovation-Oriented Culture in the Public Sector: Do Managerial Autonomy and Result Control Lead to Innovation?" *Public Management Review* 16 (1): 45–66.

Xu, H. (2010) *A Study of the Government Public Health Expenditure.* Beijing: China Press of Finance and Economy.

Yang, K., and J. Hseih (2007) "Managerial Effectiveness of Government Performance Measurement." *Public Administration Review* 67 (5): 861–879.

Yesilkagit, K., and S. van Thiel (2008) "Political Influence and Bureaucratic Autonomy." *Public Organization Review* 8: 137–153.

Yin, R. K. (2009) *Case Study Research: Design and Methods* (4th ed.). London: SAGE.

Young, D. (2001) "Non Profit Organizations: Strategic and Structural Implications." *Non Profit Management and Leadership* 12 (2): 139–157.

Zahra, S. (1990) "Increasing the Board's Involvement in Strategy." *Long Range Planning* 25 (6): 109–117.

Zahra, S., and G. George (2002) "Absorptive Capacity: A Review, Reconceptualisation and Extension." *Academy of Management Review* 27: 185–203.

Zangrandi, A. (1994) *Autonomia ed Economicità.* Milan: EGEA.

Ziller, J. (2003) "The Continental System of Administrative Legality." In *Handbook of Public Administration,* edited by G. Peters and J. Pierre, 260–268. London: SAGE.

Zucker, L. (1987) "Institutional Theories of Decision Making." *Annual Review of Sociology* 13: 443–464.

Zupic, I., and T. Čater (2015) "Bibliometric Methods in Management and Organization." *Organizational Research Methods* 18 (3): 429–472.

Index

Note: Page numbers in *italics* indicate a figure and page numbers in **bold** indicate a table on the corresponding page.

personnel 5, 45–48, 56, 61, 65, 92, 150, 172, 190, 212, 214–215, 244, **245–247**, 265–266, 269; elite 265–266; military 54; reallocation of 242, *243*; senior 156; *see also* personnel management

personnel management 91, 172, 175

perturbation 277–278n2

PESTEL (Politics, Economics, Sociological factors, Technology, Environment, Law) 30–31, 34, 36, 40, 230

PESTELI (Politics, Economics, Sociological factors, Technology, Environment, Law, Industry) 31

Peters, Guy 61, 172, 176–180, 183, 256

Pettigrew, Andrew 28, **29**, 56, 68, 77, 80, 82, 122, 133, 147, 149–156, 159, 164–165, 196

Pettigrew brand 164

Pettigrew triangle 154

phenomenology 272–273; idealist 272; realist 272–273

philanthropy 136–138; 'philanthrocapitalism' 136, 138; 'venture philanthropy' 136

physics 277–278n2; Einstein-based model 161; meta- 273; Newtonian-based model 161

Planning, Programming and Budgeting System (PPBS) 34

pluralism 4, 94, 156, 162, 166, 176; bounded 166; methodological 4

plurality 1, 51, 128, 201, 256, 264, 271, 276

policy documents 163

policy network 10, 111, 117, 124, 202

policy sector 37, 39, 170, 178, 188, 203, 230, 233, **246–247**, 256, 260

policy space 91, 228

political clientelism 176

political corruption 213

political economy 4, 6, 8, 79, 87, 94, 115, 149, 151, 165, 167, 188

political ideology 165

political institutions 111, 178, 182, 252, 256

political parties 103, 111, 164, 213, 256

political rule: personalized and charismatic 5

political science 3, 96, 111, 144, 172, 255, 257–258; strategic management as 255–258

political-societal expectations 171, 208, 215–216

political system 97, 179, 182–183, 241, **245, 248**, 255–256, 267; consensual 111, 116, 182–183; majoritarian/adversarial 182–183

politicians 5, 8, 48, 54, 97–99, 166, 183, 202, 211–213, 250–251, 256, 259, 266–267, 275–276; elected 8–9, 98–99, 159, 166, 250; executive 176, 182

politico-administrative 'Houses' 169–217

polities 31, 111, 171, 175–176, 179, 189, 195, 209, 244; 'compound' 176; supranational 176

Pollitt, C. 112, 152, 172–175, 189, 191, 194–196, 217n1; *see also* Pollitt and Bouckaert model

Pollitt and Bouckaert model 172, 175–183

Popper, Karl 270

Porter, Michael 13, 41–44, 50, 72, 98, 108, 230; *see also* Porterian models; Porterian school

Porterian models 41, 44, 99

Porterian school 4

Portugal 177, 196

positioning school 13, 201, 227, 230, 233; *see also* strategic positioning school

positivism 150, 174, 253, 271–273

post-Fordism 115–120, 126

postmodernism 271

power 8–9, **29**, 40, 55–57, 62, 83, 93, 104, 111–112, 115–117, 134–135, 141, 145, 148–149, 162–163, 165, 167–168, 179, 195, 202, 224, 263, 266; Asymmetric Power model 111; balance of 148–149, 168; bargaining 41–42; base 58, 149, 162; buyer 42, 141; causal 174; causal 174; central 111; coercive 231; decision 61, **246**; definition 67; devolution of 117; devolved 111, 144; diffusion of 111; direct 158; directive 89; explanatory 8, 16, 66, 229, 264, 268; 'hoarding' 111; inequalities 143; investor 82; legislative 39; market 41; organizational 48, 58, 163; policy-making 111; political 266; shared 121; societal 166; super- 60; traditional 93, 155; voting 138; *see also* power relations; power school

power distribution sector 192

power relations 5, **29**, 67, 70, 89, 150–151, 165; informal 5; pluralist 40, 103

power school 212

practices: analysis of 240–249; co-creating 14, 249; excellent 249; good 240, 252; revolutionary 238; smart 239–240; transformative 238; *see also* best practices

practitioners 14, 36, 77, 89, 110, 120, 153–154, 190, 235, 238, 249, 252, 257, 274–275

pragmatism 180–181

precedent 180

principal-agent model 103–104

principal-agent theory 9, 145

principals 9, 44, 80, 216

private firms 1, 9, 28, 31, 35, 43, 70–71, 75, 79–80, 111, 113–115, 117, 127, 129, 135, 141–142, 144, 154, 168–169, 190, 231, 233

private sector 1, 58–59, 65, 69, 71, 75, 78–79, 81–82, 84, 86, 96–98, 108, 115–116, 122,

public sector agencies 10, 31, 35, 75, 165
public servant 180, 196, 213, 244; senior 176, 182, 213
public services agencies 11, 30, 156; *see also* public services organizations
public services field 277; process study in 155–158
public services organizations 1–2, 7, 11–14, 16, 26, 28, **29**, 41, 50, 55, 57, 59, 63, 68, 70, 71–72, 76, 78–79, 82, 86–87, 89–90, 96–97, 122–123, 129, 147, 149, 157, 159, 167, 169–171, 173, 175, 180–181, 183, 185, 188–189, 194, 196, 200, 202, 207, 209, 211, 214–217, 218–219, 223, 225–229, 233–234, 235, 237, 252, 254–255, 257–258, 268, 270, 274, 277; autonomy of 12, 171, 181, 214–215; legitimacy of 180–181; obligations and accountability bases of 171; political-societal expectations towards 171; strategic management of/for 1, 14, 41, 79, 87, 173, 188, 217, 219, 252, 254; strategic management models for 1–2; 'strategic space' of 14, 79, 171, 182, 194, 202, 207–216, 277; strategy making in 171, 181; *see also* public services organizations, management of
public services organizations, management of 169–217; absence of strategy 216; accountability bases of 215–216; administrative traditions approach 175–183; complexity of context 173–175; context and strategy 169–175; context vs environment 170–171; context, autonomy, strategic space, and strategic management 207–216; and culture 183–188; governance and networks 200–202; neo-Weberian state 194–196; NPM cluster and doctrines 189–194; organizational autonomy 208–210, 214–215; outcome-based management 197–199; political-societal expectations 215–216; politico-administrative context 172; Pollitt and Bouckaert model 172, 175–183; Royal Marsden NHS Foundation Trust 192; 'schools of strategy' approach 216–217; theoretical frames for analysis 175–189; transformative effects of administrative reforms and strategic management 189–207
public spending 119
public sphere 143
public value *21*, 59, 97–99, 120, 123, 135, 146, 225, 231–232, 275–276; model 127; strategic triangle 142
public value approach/model 96–99, 127
public value perspective 97–98, 135, 143, 193, 276

Public Value school 13, **29**, 44, 59, 71, 96–99, 191, 196, 199, 201, 225, 231–232, 275
punctuated equilibrium models 164, 167
purchaser-provider split 204

QinetiQ 75, 192–193
quality circles 62
quantitative methods 15, 271–272
quantum mechanics 277–278n2
quasi autonomous non-governmental organizations (QUANGOs) 83
quasi firms 190
quasi markets 6, 11, **29**, 50, 126, 147, 190, 194–195
Quebec 99, 105–108; Clair Commission 105; Health and Social Services Centres (HSSC) 105–107; local community service centres (CLSCs) 108; Ministry of Health and Social Services (MSSS) 105, 108; regional health authorities (RHAs) 105, 107–108, 163–164

radical right 8, 75, 94, 147, 155, 159, 163
Rainey, Hal 222–223, 277
Reagan, Ronald 8, 116
realist tradition 271–273
Receptive and Non Receptive Contexts for Change model 155, 166
receptivity factors 159
reciprocity 10, 158
Red Cross 141
re-election constraint 8
reforms: administrative 11, **29**, 54, 172–173, 177, 182, 189–207, 211, 213–214, 266; centralizing 163; civil service 38; contextual factors 183; contractarian 80; corporate governance 82, 84, 190; decentralization 5; doctrines of 2, 10, 37, 80, 165, 189; *good-enough* management 63; governance 201–202; governmental 218; institutional 50; local government 64; managerial 175, 194, 214; managerialist 68; narratives 10–11, 153, 167, 185, 189, 201–202, 208, 215–216; NG 110, 126, 153; NPM 10, **29**, 68, 83, 87, 96, 108, 111–112, 129, 149, 151, 153, 159, 169–170, 189–190, 193, 219; political 5, 211; public governance 200; public policy 8, 98, 164; in public sector 2, 8, 167, 277; public services 167; of public management 2, 4–11, 36, 87, 112, 153, 172, 175–176, 188–189, 194, 207–208, 277; strategic 105; structural 79, 104, 163, 204; top-down 68
regulation 4, 31, 55–57, 59, 91–92, 120, 172, 192, 194, 214–216, 260–263, 267; de- 31, 165, 211; external 86; self- 55, 124
reinstitutionalization 163

Printed in the United States
by Baker & Taylor Publisher Services